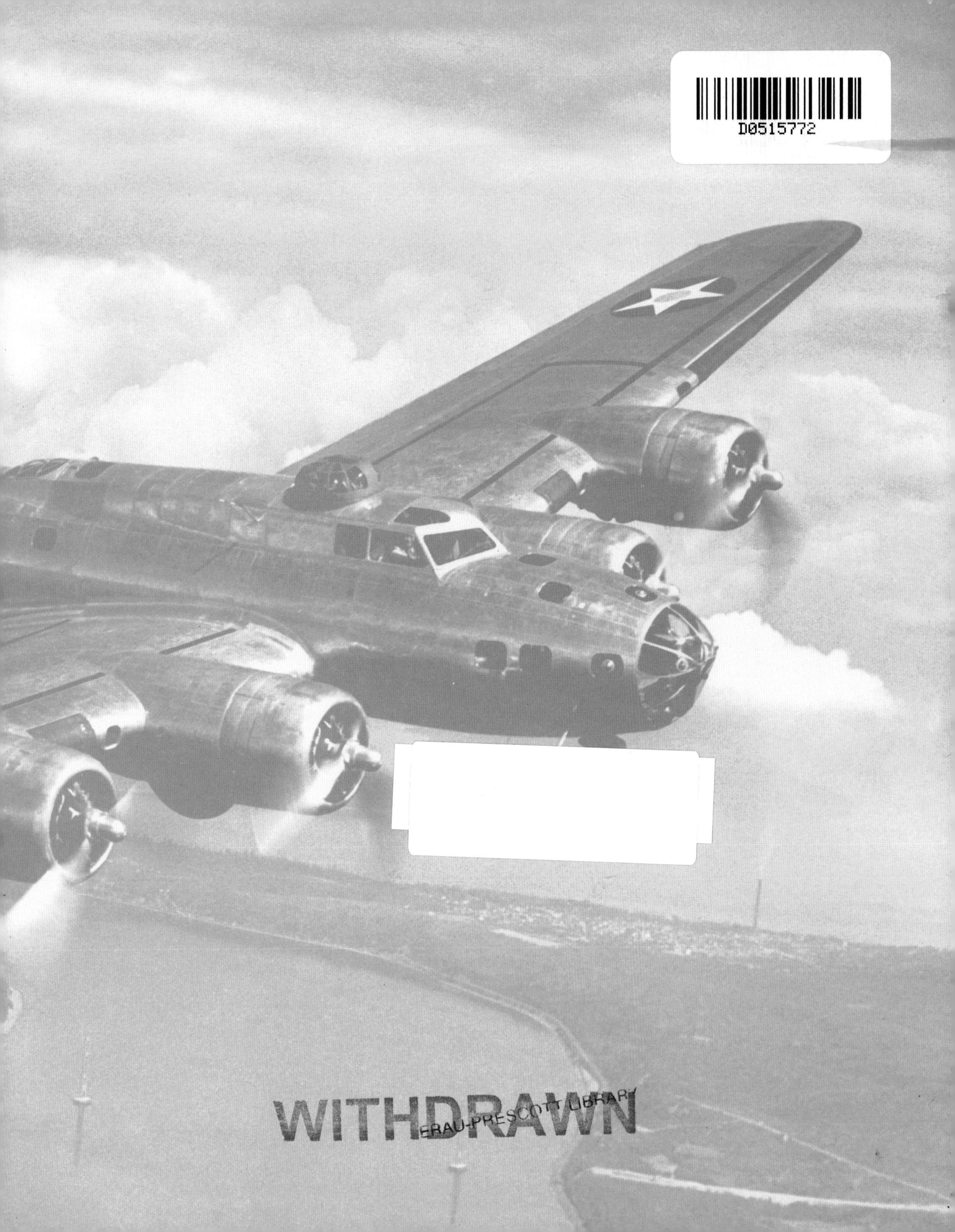

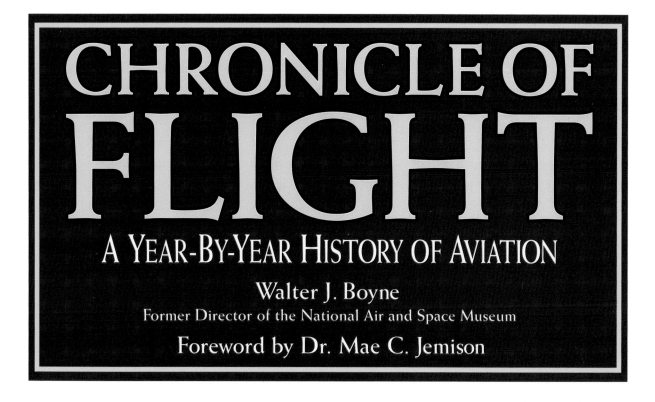

CHRONICLE OF FLIGHT

A YEAR-BY-YEAR HISTORY OF AVIATION

Walter J. Boyne

Former Director of the National Air and Space Museum

Foreword by Dr. Mae C. Jemison

Publications International, Ltd.

Writer: **Walter J. Boyne** is a retired colonel in the United States Air Force and a prominent military and aviation consultant and author. Mr. Boyne is a former director of the National Air and Space Museum and the author of *The Smithsonian Book of Flight, The Leading Edge,* and *Classic Airplanes,* as well as a host of other military and aviation titles.

Louis Weber, CEO
Publications International, Ltd.
7373 North Cicero Avenue
Lincolnwood, Illinois 60712

Permission is never granted for commercial purposes.

Manufactured in China.

8 7 6 5 4 3 2 1

ISBN: 0-7853-7246-6

Library of Congress Control Number: 2003101564

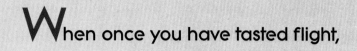

When once you have tasted flight,

you will forever walk the earth with your eyes turned skyward,

for there you have been, and there you will always long to return.

—Leonardo da Vinci

Contents

Foreword

By Mae C. Jemison

For thousands of years, humans around the world, in every culture, society, and nation, have looked skyward and attempted to imagine what could be found up there.

When I was born, in the middle of the twentieth century, I entered a world where everything seemed possible. My generation grew up during an era when the limits to human travel—speed, distance, and location—were broken daily. Our potential was seemingly limitless. And being a child who possessed, as all children do, great enthusiasm and faith, I assumed I would be a part of this incredible journey of human spirit and imagination.

I was also close to the beginnings of the space revolution, which broke the shackles holding human movement to the ground, allowing us to soar past the atmosphere and leave our planet behind. I was vividly aware of the travails and triumphs of the past. Trials and challenges not only of physics, mechanisms, and funding, but at times of imagination. What should we do with this wonderful advancement in human flight? Who should participate?

Mae C. Jemison

When I thought of flying, no single person or event colored my visions. I learned about, daydreamed of, and stumbled across myriad contributions to the world of aviation. Filling my mind were drawings and models of working gliders from Egyptian tombs; Chinese kites carrying humans, fireworks and rockets; colorful hot-air balloons; dirigibles and the *Hindenburg* disaster; World War I dogfights,

World War II bombing raids and primitive rocket attacks; Pan Am commercial airliners; sonic booms over Chicago heralding travel at Mach speeds; Gemini rendezvous missions in space and the slow ascent of the Saturn Five from the launch pad on its way to the moon; the fictitious flying saucers of *War of the Worlds* and *The Day the Earth Stood Still* contrasted against the surprising style of the USS Enterprise on *Star Trek*. And people of all kinds! Icarus and Daedelus, Bessie Coleman, the Wright brothers, Charles Lindbergh, Yuri Gagarin, the Tuskegee Airmen, Werner von Braun, engineers who designed the SR-71 using slide rules, Valentina Tereshkova, even the wide-eyed child attempting to fold the perfect paper airplane. All formed my vicarious appreciation for aviation.

My career in aviation is somewhat analogous to the history of human flight—a long drought nurtured only by imagination and hopefulness, followed by an accelerating deluge of activities and milestones. I am not a pilot and never sought to be one; my fascination with flight is about where it can take us.

My first up close and personal experience with flight and airplanes took place in 1966 at a large rural park in Illinois when I was nine years old. A pilot with a small single-engine airplane was offering plane rides for twelve dollars. Before the plane took off with my older sister, I got to look at the gauges and just be close to it! I waved at her in the sky, and as the plane landed on the grassy field, I smiled as broadly as if I had been up there myself. Later, I accompanied my parents to O'Hare Airport as friends and relatives boarded Eastern Airlines "whisper jets." Still, not me . . . yet. But at sixteen, a few weeks before graduating from high school, I accompanied my biology teacher to O'Hare Airport. I had a Bell Labs scholarship, and we were on our way to visit the labs in New Jersey. My first airplane trip!

Thereafter, the flights came more frequently and traversed longer distances. I saw the 1964 World's

Fairground Exposition Park from the air. I flew to New York to visit my sister for the summer. I boarded a jet for San Francisco and Stanford University to start college. (Ironically, it was in a chemical engineering fluid dynamics class that I finally learned to write equations to describe how planes fly, while in a graduate level astronautical and aeronautical engineering class I learned about biomedical fluid mechanics). In medical school I first traveled across the Atlantic Ocean and the Sahara Desert in an airplane. I flew with the Flying Doctors of Kenya to deliver health care to Turkana villagers and in the cargo plane of the Flying Tigers to work in a refugee camp in Thailand.

Each step, each year, increased my comfort not only with traveling in aircraft but also understanding their operations, utility, and versatility. As an Area Peace Corps Medical Officer in Sierra Leone, I called for a military aircraft to evacuate a critically ill volunteer. As the doctor attending the patient, I, in a sense, became part of the crew. I picked up and evacuated people in helicopters and small planes where the only navigational aids were topographical maps, compasses, and visually following dirt roads.

It was at NASA that I fully joined the world of aviation. As a mission specialist astronaut I was not expected to fly aircraft—take off and land—but to do everything in between. Our standard aircraft were T-38 Air Force supersonic trainers. Learning to operate the Space Shuttle and its instruments fulfilled my childhood fantasy. At Mach 25, I had the privilege of belonging to a group of the very few people ever to leave the earth, the few people who touched the face of our future.

Past experiences and our imagination assure us that flight offers endless possibilities. What we will do with these incredible opportunities is truly up to us. We can look forward to advances in aviation providing new vantage points from which to view the earth and ourselves. For example, remote sensing allows us to assess our crops, mineral resources, weather patterns, atmosphere pollution, or military capa-

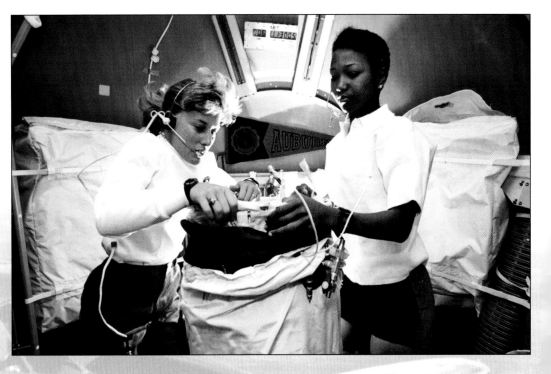

Jan Davis and Mae Jemison (right)

bilities. Travel will change as suborbital commercial passenger planes ferry us from New York to Tokyo or Johannesburg in three hours. Personal planes take off from parking lots—the George Jetson vehicle made manifest. Recreational parasailing and hang gliding flourish. And interplanetary space travel remains at the forefront of our minds.

Aviation is not just about how airplanes fly or how spacecraft launch or the operations required to keep them aloft; as vessels change and evolve, these tasks will change. Aviation is about the extension of human reach and vision, both figuratively and literally.

This wonderful book, *Chronicle of Flight*, takes us on the incredible journey from the days we stared up at the sky and imagined the possibilities to the first time a woman traveled into space. The past 100 years of flight have been quite an adventure. Imagine what the coming 100 years have in store!

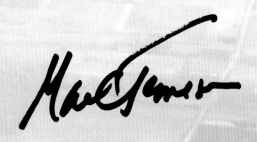

Higher, Faster, and Farther

The twentieth century is unquestionably the century of flight; the last 100 years have been shaped by aviation in a way no other time period has ever been affected by any invention. As remarkable as the automobile, the railroad, and even the steam engine were, their effects were more protracted than those of the aircraft and stimulated far fewer additional inventions. And though the complete impact of the computer is still untold, those effects derive indirectly from aviation, which did more to spur the use and growth of the computer than any other industry. Aviation's constant need for faster and more powerful computers laid the groundwork for the journey into space.

It was fortuitous that aviation's beginnings in 1903 coincided with an explosion in the growth of both still and motion pictures. Progress in these areas enabled an unprecedented documentation of the birth and growth of aviation. From the very beginning of piloted, powered flight, aviation has been regarded as a great adventure. Even today, as passenger miles are accumulated in the billions, crowds still gather near the runways of airports simply to watch these marvelous vehicles of the sky. For the same reason, air shows are one of the most popular outdoor events in the world, second only to soccer as a draw for the masses.

In *Chronicle of Flight*, the history of aviation is illustrated through hundreds of photographs, each one recording a moment in time when the people involved—designers, manufacturers, pilots—were convinced they had done their absolute best with the time and materials available to them. It is safe to say that none of the millions of aircraft built, nor the thousands of spacecraft, have ever been intended as second best. A purity of purpose and a fanatical attention to detail characterize the aerospace industry in its manufacture of both aircraft and spacecraft; this effort is illustrated in the marvelous pictorial record created over the twentieth century.

The quest for perfection and the attention to detail is necessitated by the danger inherent in flying. Although danger is no doubt part of the appeal of flying, it is ever present and must be acknowledged by participants. Fortunately, as aircraft have become intrinsically more dangerous because they are flying higher, faster, farther, and more often, safety records have improved remarkably. Such advancement is hard earned and expensive, but the benefits are well worth the effort.

As safety and performance have improved, aviation has become more fun. The earliest aircraft were extremely difficult to fly; the pilots had to literally wrestle them about the sky, using muscle to overcome problems of trim and stability. Over time, aircraft were made easier to fly, and laborsaving devices such as trim-tabs, autopilots, and improved instrumentation were installed. Aviators began using aircraft for entertainment purposes: racing, flying cross-country, aerobatics, or simply lazing about the sky on a pretty afternoon. Although aircraft never became as inexpensive as the automobile, the cost of flying has been held somewhat in check by the availability of good used aircraft and of home-built aircraft for those skilled and perservering enough to create them.

Wright Brothers' first flight

Douglas DC-3

While enjoyment in personal aircraft has increased, the concept of having fun on an airliner has been largely eroded by the conversion of airline travel to a mass-transit system. The advent of terrorism and the security precautions necessary to combat it have further diminished the pleasure of airline travel. Nonetheless, no other form of transportation compares when it comes to time and money saved.

In the course of the twentieth century, military aircraft led the aerodynamic way. Well funded by government expenditures, the manufacturers of military aircraft were able to push the performance envelope farther and faster. In that same period of time, the procurement of military aircraft declined in direct relation to their growth in cost. This phenomenon gave rise to Augustine's Law, which posits that if the trend continues, an air force will be able to afford only one aircraft for all its needs. It has not quite reached that level yet, but while the United States built hundreds of thousands of military aircraft during World War II, it is now buying them at the rate of a few dozen per year. Other nations face the same problems, and aircraft are now considered a platform to carry newly developed weapons rather than as weapon systems in themselves.

This new concept of aircraft simply being a place to put new weapons has kept some types, such as the Boeing B-52 and KC-135, in service for more than 50 years. This is important in terms of economy—if you amortize a $6 million B-52 over 50 years, it is an amazingly inexpensive weapon. But perhaps more important than reasons of economy

or anything else, at the end of almost a solid century of warfare, the aircraft and its new generation of precision-guided munitions have assumed a vastly greater role than ever before. For the first time since 1945, an alternative method of obtaining decisive results from the air is now available with the efforts of stealth aircraft, cruise missiles, airborne command and control systems, and the use of massive satellite systems for intelligence, communication, navigation, and meteorology. These are artfully combined in combat to create incredibly accurate bombing systems that may prove to be the way out of the nuclear dilemma, for they can achieve decisive results without having to resort to dropping thermonuclear bombs. There is some irony in this, of course, because it was the airplane that enabled the use of atomic weapons in the first place.

The path from the tracks scratched in the sands of Kitty Hawk by the Wright Flyer to the footprints on the moon to the probes that have ventured out of the solar system has been long, swift, and exciting. You'll see this history etched in the images that follow.

Walter J Boyne

wboyne@cqi.com

F-35 Joint Strike Fighter

CHAPTER ONE

Ancient Times to 1913:

From Dreams to Reality

Humans dreamed of flying thousands of years before any individual ever imagined it would be possible. Dreams of flying occurred in all civilizations and eras, to people of both genders and all ages. There is something in the human soul that longs to free oneself from gravity, to leap into the air, and speed along with the ease of the wind. Dreams of flying may be intoxicating...or terrifying. Just like flying itself.

The mere thought of people flying probably took hold in prehistoric societies. Surely hunters wished to soar above the earth to spot their prey. And primitive warriors, about to engage in tribal warfare, must have wanted wings to see whatever lay on the other side of the next hill.

Wright Flyer (1903)

Wright Military Flyer (1908)

It is amazing that human flight was delayed until 1783 for lighter-than-air and 1903 for heavier-than-air flight. The materials with which to make balloons had been available for thousands of years. Simple gliding flight might have been possible for an equally long period, had there been someone with the insight to adapt the basic model provided by soaring birds into wood and fabric.

Perhaps more surprising than the delay in achieving balloon flight was the 120-year interval between the Montgolfier brothers' efforts in 1783 and the success of the Wright brothers in 1903. During that 12-decade period, there were numerous advances in science, and many brilliant individuals put their minds to accomplishing powered flight. It would seem, in retrospect, that with a concentrated effort to build on the ideas of Sir George Cayley and others, flight might have been achieved. Octave Chanute, a nineteenth century patron of flight, hoped to be the driving force behind such a group effort. He saw himself as a central clearing-house for ideas on flight and hoped that some magic combination of personalities, brains, and ideas would solve the problem of heavier-than-air flight.

Chanute was in fact correct—it was a magic combination of personalities, brains, and ideas that solved the problem of flight, but in the persons of Orville and Wilbur Wright. Instead of the collective effort that Chanute envisaged in which his own ideas might be combined with those of Otto Lilienthal, Clement Ader, John Montgomery, the Wrights, Augustus Herring, and Samuel Pierpont-Langley to create—at last—a flying machine, it was the synergistic effort of the two quiet, reserved, and very businesslike brothers from Ohio that solved the mystery of flight.

If the 120-year interval between balloon flight and powered flight is remarkable for its length, the four years in which the Wright brothers worked to create a successful aircraft is even more remarkable for its brevity. In that time, they went from inquisitive inventors seeking information about the experiments of others to the forefront of aviation, completely outstripping all competition. At the time of their great success at Kitty Hawk on December 17, 1903, the Wrights were at least a decade ahead of their most advanced competitors and light-years ahead of the others.

The Wright brothers obtained this lead in part by virtue of their systematic, scientific approach, but the real advantage they possessed—the one that no other experimenter had even begun to achieve—was their insight into the basic problems of flying an airplane. They were able to calculate very precisely what would be needed in terms of lift, power, and most important, control. Unlike every other experimenter of the time, the Wrights understood that an aircraft would have to be flown in three dimensions. It was not going to simply be steered with an oar like a rowboat or chauffeured about the sky with the turn of a steering wheel. They also knew they would have to learn to fly, and they became proficient at piloting their gliders before they ever attempted powered flight.

Unfortunately for the Wrights, and fortunately for the horde of soon-to-be competitors, their basic understanding of flight would be partially revealed to anyone who watched them fly. It was obvious to the knowledgeable that the Wrights were controlling their aircraft in three dimensions, about the three axes of flight, and that their piloting was expert. All that remained for would-be competitors was to adopt the general Wright design and either copy their control system directly or cobble together one that derived from it but appeared different enough that it could be defended in court.

As brilliant as the Wright brothers were as engineers, scientists, and pilots, they were hopelessly naive when it came to business and law. The Wrights patented their control system and presumed that those who used their patented system in other aircraft designs would pay a reasonable royalty. Nothing could have been further from the truth. The Wrights became embroiled in legal battles that sapped their collective strength and led to stagnation in their design process. In the meantime, hundreds of others took their basic ideas and, in many instances, improved upon them. The ten-year lead they had possessed in 1903 had dwindled to perhaps three or four years by 1908 and had disappeared entirely by 1912, the year of Wilbur's death. By that time, the basic Wright design to which they had clung was not only obsolete, but it had also gained a reputation as a pilot killer because of a long string of fatal accidents. The Wrights as inventors were passé, but all of Europe and some of America was ablaze with competitors, who daily coaxed their craft to new records in height, speed, altitude, and distance. New manufacturers, such as Glenn Curtiss, Louis Blériot, A. V. Roe, and many more, appeared with new designs and new approaches.

The Wrights had set the century of flight on fire in 1903, altering the course of world history. Orville would live until 1948: He had the opportunity to witness the introduction of jet aircraft, supersonic flight, and huge passenger planes. On a more personal level, he, unlike Wilbur, would live to see their true achievement—an invention that changed the course of history—recognized all over the world.

Curtiss Golden Flyer

DAEDALUS AND ICARUS Flight has always evoked feelings of both adventure and danger, as illustrated by the poignant story of Daedalus and Icarus. According to Greek mythology, Daedalus fell out of favor with King Minos of Crete and was imprisoned. Determined to escape, he made wings out of feathers and wax for himself and his son, Icarus. The wings worked well, and Daedalus escaped to Crete. Unfortunately, Icarus flew too close to the sun, melting the wax. He fell into the sea and drowned.

MONTGOLFIER BALLOON Given that the materials necessary for a balloon ascent—closely woven cloth, rope, and hot air—had been available for centuries, it is amazing that the first flight of a full-scale balloon did not take place until the Montgolfier brothers' experiments in 1783. Even then, balloons were expensive to build, and it was fortunate that the Montgolfiers came from a wealthy family.

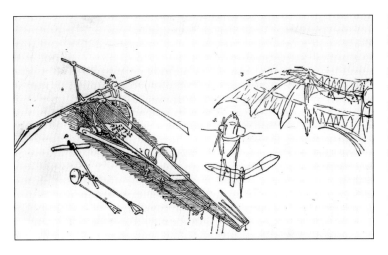

DA VINCI FLYING MACHINE

Leonardo da Vinci (1452–1519) was not the first to dream of making a flying machine, but he was the first to begin to reduce the problem of flight to practical considerations. Recognizing that humans would not have the strength to fly using only their arms, he sought to harness both arm and leg movement to cause wings to flap. True human-powered flight was still four centuries away.

BATTLE OF FLEURUS On June 26, 1794, a balloon was used in war for the first time at the Battle of Fleurus. The reports gained by observers in the balloon were communicated to the French commander, Count Jean-Baptiste Jourdan, and were reportedly important in deciding the favorable outcome for the French revolutionary forces. Ironically, Jourdan had refused the use of a balloon the previous year, saying that he would prefer a battalion to a balloon.

OTTO LILIENTHAL One of the greatest early pioneers of flight, Otto Lilienthal made his first successful flight in 1891. He flew hang gliders from a specially built hill, controlling them by shifting his weight. While he had some success, his method of control was an inherent limitation on the size of the aircraft. Lilienthal was killed in a crash in 1896 after some 2,000 gliding flights. His data was later used by the Wright brothers for some of their computations.

FLIGHT TIMELINE

400 B.C. Egyptian model glider is made (found in 1898).

circa 400 B.C. Mo Tzu invents the kite in China.

circa 400 B.C. Archytas builds a small wooden bird that is suspended from an arm and propelled by either steam or compressed air.

A.D. 62 Hero's "Aeolipile" steam-driven sphere illustrates reactive propulsion.

400 The Chinese rotary-wing top is flown; it is the first human-made object of any kind flown under power.

600 The Chinese use kites as part of a semaphore signaling device.

850 The Chinese invent gunpowder.

1250 Roger Bacon predicts the creation of an ornithopter and a lighter-than-air craft.

1306 Parachute jumps are made in China during the coronation of Fo-kin.

1483 Leonardo da Vinci produces his "Helix," the design sketch of a helicopter.

1670 Francesco de Lana-Terzi designs a lighter-than-air machine using thin-wall copper tubes evacuated of air.

1687 Sir Isaac Newton formulates the Laws of Motion, which include the third law "for every action there is an equal and opposite reaction."

SAMUEL PIERPONT LANGLEY
The third secretary of the Smithsonian Institution, Samuel Pierpont Langley spent many years studying the problems of heavier-than-air flight. His greatest success came in the form of powered free-flight models, which he called Aerodromes. His greatest failure came when he scaled up the models to build a full-size, human-carrying Aerodrome. Attempts to fly the full-size Aerodrome were made on two occasions; both attempts ended in abrupt crashes caused by structural failure.

COUNT FERDINAND VON ZEPPELIN The dirigibles designed by Count Ferdinand von Zeppelin captured the imagination of the German people. Even when his airships met with disaster, the public stood by him, and he became the leading name in the huge dirigibles that Germany planned to use for military and commercial purposes. Unfortunately, the hydrogen-filled airships were fragile and vulnerable to violent weather. They were too expensive to use as a weapon and too dangerous to use to carry passengers.

OCTAVE CHANUTE GLIDER After a highly successful career in business, American Octave Chanute took up the challenge of flight, creating a number of hang gliders with two or more sets of wings. Chanute was generous with both his knowledge and his finances and encouraged many others to experiment with flying machines, including the Wright brothers. In many ways, he acted as an information clearinghouse.

THE WRIGHT BROTHERS Orville and Wilbur Wright worked together as an intuitive team, striving to become the first to fly a heavier-than-air machine. They succeeded, going in four short years from inquiries and a simple kite to the first successful aircraft. Of all the experimenters of the time, they alone saw that an aircraft had to be controlled about its three axes of flight—and that the pilot had to learn to fly it.

FLIGHT TIMELINE

1709 Bartholomeu Lourenço de Gusmão demonstrates a hot-air balloon model in Lisbon. Some say he may also have demonstrated a glider.

1781 Karl Friedrich Meerwein designs, builds, and purportedly flies a glider-ornithopter.

1782 The Montgolfiers fly a model balloon.

April 25, 1783 The Montgolfiers fly a full-scale balloon without passengers.

August 27, 1783 Professor Jacques Charles releases an unpiloted hydrogren balloon and begins an era of Charliers.

September 19, 1783 The Montgolfier brothers launch a balloon carrying a sheep, a cock, and a duck at Versailles.

October 15, 1783 Francois Pilâtre de Rozier ascends in a tethered hot-air balloon to become the first aeronaut.

November 21, 1783 Francois Pilâtre de Rozier and the Marquis d'Arlandes make the first free flight in a balloon.

December 1, 1783 Professor Jacques Charles and M. Robert make the first hydrogen balloon free flight.

January 7, 1785 Jean-Pierre Blanchard and Dr. John Jeffries cross the English Channel in a hydrogen balloon.

WRIGHT GLIDER The Wright glider of 1901 had been a disappointment, but the 1902 glider fulfilled all of the Wright brothers' expectations. In it, they made glide after glide at Kitty Hawk, North Carolina, learning to fly, and realizing that they had at last solved the problem of control. There remained only the challenge of installing an engine, which they would do in the 1903 Wright Flyer.

WRIGHT FLYER At 10:35 A.M. on December 17, 1903, Orville Wright made a 120-foot flight into history. Wilbur is seen at the right, watching in awe. The photo was taken by a box camera that the Wrights had positioned on a tripod. One of their helpers, John Daniels, snapped the shutter at exactly the right time to record the event. At this moment, the Wrights were ten years ahead of all competitors.

WRIGHT FLYER In 1904, the Wrights moved their flying operations to Huffman Prairie, outside of Dayton, Ohio. Their 1904 machine proved to be a disappointment to them. They are seen here, near the building that housed the Flyer, discussing the problem. As always, they are dressed neatly, with collar and tie. It was not until 1905 that the Wrights created the first practical airplane, having solved the problems encountered the previous year.

ERNEST ARCHDEACON GLIDER

France had been first in balloon flight, and Ernest Archdeacon felt that France was destined to be first in heavier-than-air flight as well. He devoted both his time and his money to bring that about. Archdeacon was at first inspired by the Wright brothers' success; he made a crude copy of the Wright design as a glider. Later he slandered their capabilities and their veracity.

MONTGOMERY GLIDER Professor John J. Montgomery was an early experimenter with models and gliders. In 1905, he created a fragile tandem-wing glider that was lifted into the air by a balloon and released to glide to the ground. Only one successful glide was made; two other attempts resulted in near crashes and a third in the death of exhibition parachutist Dan Maloney. Montgomery died in the crash of an "improved" version of his glider in 1911.

ALBERTO SANTOS-DUMONT

The Wrights had many rivals in Europe, and none were more colorful or capable than Alberto Santos-Dumont, shown here in his derby hat in front of the diminutive Demoiselle aircraft that he designed and flew. Santos-Dumont, a wealthy Brazilian, was an expert pilot of small dirigibles. He made the first flight of an aircraft in Europe on October 23, 1906—a 197-foot hop in his 14-*bis*.

FLIGHT TIMELINE

June 15, 1785 Francois Pilâtre de Rozier and Jules Romain are killed while trying to cross the English Channel in a combination hot-air/hydrogen balloon.

January 9, 1793 Jean-Pierre Blanchard makes the first balloon ascent in America.

June 26, 1794 A balloon is used in warfare for the first time at the Battle of Fleurus.

October 22, 1797 Andre Garnerin successfully parachutes from 3,000 feet.

1799 Sir George Cayley produces an airplane design with fixed wings and a cruciform tail.

1804 Sir George Cayley constructs a model glider.

October 8, 1808 Congreve rockets are used to attack the French in a harbor at Boulogne.

1814 The British use Congreve rockets against Fort McHenry in Baltimore, inspiring the words to "The Star-Spangled Banner."

July 6, 1819 Madame Marie Blanchard becomes the first woman to die in an aero accident when her hydrogen balloon catches fire.

November 7–8, 1836 Charles Green and two passengers fly a hot-air balloon from London to Germany, 480 miles, in 18 hours.

1840 William Hale invents spin-stabilized rockets.

ROBERT ESNAULT-PELTERIE Like Ernest Archdeacon, Robert Esnault-Pelterie attempted to copy the Wrights and "improve" on their design in the process. Unfortunately, he claimed in a well-publicized lecture that his "exact" copy of the Wright glider had not performed well because the wing-warping used by the Wrights was inherently flawed. The French engineer persisted, however, and eventually manufactured aircraft of his own design.

COLONEL CODY American-born Samuel Franklin Cody capitalized on the fact that his name was the same as the famous Wild West showman, Buffalo Bill Cody, and adopted the title of colonel. He experimented successfully with human-lifting kites and then built the British Army Aeroplane No. 1, a large aircraft clearly derived from the Wright Flyer. Cody made the first successful flight in Great Britain on October 16, 1908. In 1909, he became a naturalized British citizen.

ALEXANDER GRAHAM BELL The inventor of the telephone, Alexander Graham Bell (at far right), had long been fascinated with flight. He believed the solution to a successful powered, piloted flying machine would be found in an inherently stable kite. His experiments led him to create tetrahedral kites made of many triangular cells. They flew very well as kites, but their inherent drag ruled them out as a competitor of the ordinary aircraft.

SANTOS-DUMONT 14-BIS Alberto Santos-Dumont was a wealthy Brazilian who mesmerized Paris with his sensational exploits with airships of his own design. In 1906, he created the unorthodox 14-*bis* in which he made the first flight of an aircraft in Europe on October 23, 1906, followed by a longer flight on November 12. The 1 4-*bis* was an aeronautical dead end, but Santos-Dumont's next effort, the Demoiselle, would be a hit.

NULLI SECUNDIS Great Britain commanded the seas but did not fund aviation to the same degree as did the French and German governments. The first British airship, the *Nulli Secundis (Second to None)* was brought to completion by American Samuel F. Cody. Equipped with an Antoinette V-8 engine, the airship flew successfully on three occasions, once achieving a speed of 20 miles per hour. It was eventually rebuilt as a semirigid airship and then dismantled.

FLIGHT TIMELINE

1843 William Henson patents the Aerial Steam Carriage, a proposal for a practical flying machine.

1849 Sir George Cayley tests the first glider to carry a person.

August 22, 1849 Austria uses hot-air balloons to bomb Venice.

June 1853 Sir George Cayley has his coachman make a free fight in a glider.

1858 Gaspard-Félix Tournachon (Nadar) takes the first aerial photograph from a balloon.

1859 John Wise and two others fly from St. Louis to Henderson, New York, in a hydrogen balloon.

1860 Jean Joseph Etienne Lenoir invents the internal combustion engine, which will prove necessary for heavier-than-air flight.

1861 Thaddeus Lowe makes the first aerial telegraphic transmission from a balloon.

August 3, 1861 *Fanny*, a steam tug used by John La Mountain, becomes the first aircraft carrier.

October 1, 1861 The Army Balloon Corps is formed.

November 1861 The *George Washington Parke Custis*, a coal barge, is converted into army service as a balloon boat, a craft for inflating and launching balloons.

1862 G. P. D'Amecourt of France builds the first steam-powered model helicopter.

VOISIN-FARMAN NO. 1 BIPLANE Two of the greatest names in French aviation joined hands to build this record-breaking Voisin-Farman No. 1 biplane. Gabriel Voisin (a bitter critic of the Wright brothers) and the English-born Henri Farman would both become aircraft manufacturers. Their collaboration, the Voisin-Farman No. 1 biplane, flew a circular flight covering one kilometer on January 13, 1908, winning the 50,000-Franc Grand Prix d'Aviation Deutsch-Archdeacon. The aircraft had virtually no roll control.

GLENN HAMMOND CURTISS The Wrights had rivals in the United States as well, and the most competitive of them was Glenn Curtiss. Like the Wrights, Curtiss had experience in bicycles, but he went on to become a motorcycle racer who built powerful, light-weight engines. Alexander Graham Bell prevailed upon him to join the Aerial Experiment Association (A.E.A.), and there Curtiss designed his first airplane. Sadly, the Wright brothers and Curtiss became locked in a bitter patent war.

CORNU HELICOPTER Vertical flight has always fascinated engineers, for it seemed to be the way to make flight immediately practical. Unfortunately, vertical flight was far more demanding than conventional flight, as would be discovered over the years. Progress was made, bit by bit, however, thanks to pioneers like Paul Cornu, who made a free flight of 20 seconds at an altitude of about one foot on November 13, 1907, at Lisieux, France.

THE AERIAL EXPERIMENT ASSOCIATION

The great inventor, Alexander Graham Bell, formed the A.E.A. with the express purpose of "getting in the air." From the left, the key members are: Frederick W. "Casey" Baldwin (often confused with balloonist Thomas Baldwin); Lieutenant Thomas E. Selfridge, who would later become the first man to die in a heavier-than-air craft accident; Glenn Curtiss; Alexander Graham Bell; and J.A.D. McCurdy, who would make the first flight in Canada. The identity of the last man is unknown.

SEPTEMBER 17, 1908, CRASH Orville Wright and Lieutenant Thomas Selfridge had leveled off at about 100 feet when Orville heard a tapping sound. He immediately cut power and turned back to make a landing, but there were two thumping noises and a severe vibration. The airplane skidded to the right, then dropped straight down to the ground. At the last moment, Orville's efforts to control the airplane brought the nose up—but not enough. The plane hit the ground at full speed, and Selfridge became the first man to die in a powered heavier-than-air craft accident. Orville was severely injured but was able to return the following year and complete the military trials.

FLIGHT TIMELINE

1862 Thaddeus Lowe uses the balloon *Intrepid* for observation in the Battle of Fair Oaks.

1865 Charles de Louvrie of France designs the first jet-engine plane.

1865 Jules Verne's book *From the Earth to the Moon* forecasts future space travel.

1867 The design for the delta wing is patented in England.

1870 During the Franco/Prussian War, balloons are used to carry mail, government papers, and important public officials to safety from the besieged city of Paris.

1870–1871 Alphonse Penaud flies model helicopters using rubber-band motors.

October 8, 1883 Albert Tissandier flies an electric-powered dirigibile.

August 9, 1884 The French army airship *La France* makes a closed-circuit flight on electric power.

1889 Otto Lilienthal publishes *Bird Flight as the Basis of the Flying Art.*

October 9, 1890 Clement Ader of France makes a hop from level ground in a steam-powered plane.

May 6, 1896 Samuel Pierpont Langley makes a successful flight of a steam-powered model Aerodrome.

FIRST U.S. ARMY AIRSHIP This is the first U.S. Army Airship, the "Signal Corps No. 1," designed by Captain Thomas Baldwin. An orphan who made good, Baldwin was a real Horatio Alger character. He succeeded as a balloonist before designing this airship. He became a good friend of Glenn Curtiss, installing Curtiss engines in his designs. Baldwin and Curtiss successfully demonstrated this airship at Fort Myer, Virginia, in the late summer of 1908.

LE MANS, FRANCE, 1908 At Le Mans, France, in 1908, Wilbur Wright shocked the world with the masterful way he flew, making sharp turns that astounded the crowds. Many Europeans, particularly the French, believed that the Wrights were liars who only claimed to have flown. Wilbur's brilliant exhibition proved to them that the Wrights had succeeded where everyone else had failed. From that point on, the Europeans treated the Wrights as rock stars are treated today.

LEON DELAGRANGE One of the earliest French aviation pioneers, Leon Delagrange endeared himself to American hearts when, upon seeing Wilbur Wright fly at Hunaudieres (five miles south of Le Mans, France), he shouted, "Well, we are beaten. We just don't exist." Delagrange took the first woman, Thérèse Peltier, to fly on July 8, 1908. He was well liked, and the aviation world was saddened on January 24, 1910, when he became the first of many to be killed flying a Blériot.

WILBUR WRIGHT AT LE MANS The Europeans were astounded by the size of the Wright Flyer and by how well it was built. They were also amazed at the meticulous way that Wilbur checked every fitting of the aircraft before every flight. What they did not know was that on the first flight in France in 1908, the airplane Wilbur was about to fly had never before been flown. It was not only a demonstration but also a test flight.

LE MANS, 1908 The demonstrations by the Wright brothers in Europe soon became gigantic social events, and fashionable women came out to spend hours waiting until the weather was just right so that it was safe to fly. Here three well-dressed women examine an, as yet, unassembled Flyer.

FLIGHT TIMELINE

August 10, 1896 After more than 2,000 successful flights, Otto Lilienthal dies of injuries sustained in a glider crash.

July 11, 1897 The ill-fated Salomon August Andrée expedition attempts to fly a balloon over the North Pole; three people vanish.

1899 Orville and Wilbur Wright experiment with a model biplane kite to test the key idea of wing warping.

1900 The Wright brothers produce their first glider.

July 2, 1900 Count Ferdinand von Zeppelin successfully flies his first dirigible, the LZ 1.

1901 The second Wright glider is tested at Kitty Hawk.

June 1901 Samuel Pierpont Langley makes ¼-scale model Aerodrome and flies it successfully with an internal combustion steam engine.

August 14, 1901 Gustave Whitehead claims powered flight.

October 1901 Austrian Wilhelm Kress attempts to fly a powered heavier-than-air craft from water but fails. His is the first aeroplane with a gasoline-powered engine.

October 19, 1901 Alberto Santos-Dumont flies a dirigible around the Eiffel Tower.

FORT MYER, 1908 The simplicity of the construction of the Wright Flyers is evident here. The Wright brothers were careful to minimize weight and maximize strength, and their artisanship was elegant. Of all of the elements of the Flyer's design, the least obvious but most important were the highly efficient propellers the Wrights designed and carved. They also designed and built their own engines, which had many advanced features for that time period.

FORT MYER The familiar buildings of Fort Myer, Virginia, still in use today, form the backdrop for one of Orville's 1908 flights. The Wrights typically flew quite low, often no more than 20 feet off the ground, during the demonstration flights. The forward elevator surfaces would be called a "canard surface" today and were an inadvertent safety feature, for they tended to prevent an abrupt stall. Instead, the Flyer would simply "mush" flatly to the ground.

BRITISH ARMY AEROPLANE NO. 1 The Wrights had set the pattern, as is evident in this British Army Aeroplane No. 1. On October 16, 1908, Samuel Franklin Cody made the first officially recognized flight in Great Britain, flying 1,390 feet at Farnborough, where the great international air shows are still held every other year. Cody was killed in a crash in 1913, and his son Frank was killed in air battle during World War I.

JUNE BUG Glenn Curtiss was to become the Wright brothers' greatest rival. Here is Aerodrome #3, *June Bug,* the third plane to be flown by Alexander Graham Bell's A.E.A. and by far the most successful. Its first flight took place on June 21, 1908; it won the *Scientific American* Trophy on July 4, 1908.

FARMAN BIPLANE At the time of the Wrights' first flight in 1903, they were ten years ahead of all competitors. By 1909, after their demonstrations in the United States and Europe, competitors began to catch up, using ideas clearly derived from the Wrights' design. The Flyer-like Farman biplane, flown here at Blackpool, England, by the popular Louis Paulhan, shows a vast improvement over the original Farman designs.

FLIGHT TIMELINE

September–October 1902 The Wright brothers test their first successful glider and ultimately make nearly 1,000 flights.

1903 Konstantin E. Tsiolkovsky advocates the use of liquid propellants for spaceships.

October 7, 1903 Samuel Pierpont Langley's full-size Aerodrome crashes on its first test flight.

December 8, 1903 Samuel Pierpont Langley's Aerodrome crashes on its second flight attempt.

December 17, 1903 The Wright brothers achieve powered, controlled flight at Kitty Hawk.

1904 Robert Esnault-Pelterie flies a glider with ailerons.

May 26, 1904 The Wrights start flying the Flyer II and ultimately make 105 flights.

September 20, 1904 Wilbur Wright makes a successful closed-circuit flight.

November 9, 1904 Wilbur Wright flies for more than five minutes.

June 6, 1905 Gabriel Voisin lifts off from a river in a "boxkite" glider towed by a motorboat.

June 23, 1905 The Wrights fly the Flyer III, the world's first practical airplane.

September 12, 1906 Jakob Ellehammer makes a sustained tethered flight.

GNOME ROTARY ENGINE The impact of the Gnome rotary engine in 1909 was incredible. Designed by brothers Louis and Laurent Seguin, the idea was not unique to them but the execution was. Their little Gnome rotary had a fixed crankshaft about which the cylinders rotated; the propeller was attached to the cylinders. The first Gnome believed to have flown was installed in a Voisin owned by Louis Paulhan. It generated 50 horsepower at 1,200 RPM.

1909 MILITARY FLYER Here, Orville Wright is shown discussing a technical detail with his good friend Lieutenant Frank Lahm at the 1909 military trials at Fort Myer. Lahm, a 1901 graduate of West Point, was himself a pilot, having won the first James Gordon Bennett Cup in 1906. Lahm was the first U.S. Army officer to fly as a passenger, and he was one of the first two officers Wilbur Wright taught to fly.

BLÉRIOT MODEL XI Louis Blériot created a long series of aircraft, but it was his Model XI that propelled him into history with his remarkable July 25, 1909, flight across the English Channel. Blériot had been present at Wilbur Wright's aerial demonstration in France and unhesitatingly adopted the wing-warping technique for his monoplane. Examples of the Model XI, modified with more powerful engines and carrying two people, served as observation planes early in World War I.

BLÉRIOT'S CROSS-CHANNEL FLIGHT Competition was keen to be the first across the English Channel, and Louis Blériot made sure that he was up before his arch-rival Hubert Latham on the morning of his flight. Blériot's leg had been burned, he was very uncomfortable, and his Anzani engine began losing power en route, but he persisted and made a spectacular landing at Northfall Meadow near Dover Castle. The 36½-minute flight changed England's status as an island forever.

FLIGHT TIMELINE

September 30, 1906 Lieutenant Frank Lahm wins the Gordon Bennett Cup.

October 23, 1906 Alberto Santos-Dumont makes a short flight in his 14-*bis.*

November 12, 1906 Alberto Santos-Dumont makes the first officially recognized flight of a heavier-than-air plane in Europe.

1907 Horatio Phillips achieves flight in a 22-horsepower Multiplane, but the flight is never officially recognized.

July 11, 1907 Louis Blériot flies his Type VI, the *Libellule,* the first plane with cantilever wings.

August 1, 1907 The Aeronautical Division of the U.S. Army Signal Corps is formed.

October 26, 1907 Henri Farman sets a European distance record of 2,530 feet.

November 13, 1907 Paul Cornu makes a short free flight in an experimental helicopter.

Late November 1907 Louis Blériot flies the Type VII, the first aircraft with a tractor engine, enclosed fuselage, a rear-mounted tail, and a two-wheel main undercarriage with tailwheel.

November 30, 1907 Curtiss Motor Vehicle Company, the first U.S. airplane company, is formed.

REIMS AVIATION MEET There are motion-picture films of the air meet at Reims, France, but they do not reveal the lush, romantic beauty of that time nearly as well as this illustration by W. H. Foster, based on a color sketch made on the spot by Charles Hoffbauer. The illustration captures both the variety and the intimacy of the event, with an Antoinette flying serenely by a Wright Flyer, with other aircraft in the background.

REIMS AVIATION MEET Either a composite photo or an air traffic controller's nightmare, this image reveals Europe's sudden fascination with aviation, as illustrated by the crowds at the magnificent *La Grande Semaine d'Aviation de la Champagne,* the seminal air show at Reims, France, in August 1909. The week ended with the Gordon Bennett Race. Thirty-eight aircraft were entered, and twenty-three actually flew, with nine types represented. Glenn Curtiss was the fastest, at 47 miles per hour, in his Curtiss pusher. Suddenly, the Wrights had rivals!

GLENN CURTISS AT REIMS Glenn Curtiss was an engine man, and he powered his Curtiss-Herring No. 1, the *Reims Racer,* with a 60-horsepower V-8 engine of his own design and manufacture. With it he won the Gordon Bennett Cup at the world's first international air show at Reims, France, setting a world speed record of 47 miles per hour around a closed course—just beating out Louis Blériot. The Wrights had declined to participate, and the victory made Curtiss world famous.

FLIGHT TIMELINE

January 13, 1908 Henri Farman makes the first one-kilometer circuit flight in Europe, flying around a pylon 500 meters away and winning 50,000 francs.

March 12, 1908 The A.E.A. develops the *Red Wing.*

May 14, 1908 Charles Furnas becomes the first ever air passenger when he flies with Wilbur Wright.

May 19, 1908 Thomas Selfridge solos in an A.E.A. plane, the *White Wing.*

July 4, 1908 Glenn Curtiss wins the *Scientific American* Trophy in *June Bug.*

July 8, 1908 Thérèse Peltier becomes the first female air passenger.

August 8, 1908 Wilbur Wright flies at Le Mans, France.

September 3, 1908 Flight trials of the Wright military plane begin.

September 6, 1908 Leon Delagrange flies for ½ hour in Europe.

September 17, 1908 Lieutenant Thomas Selfridge is killed in the crash of a Wright aircraft.

October 16, 1908 American Samuel Franklin Cody makes the first airplane flight in England.

1909 The first Gnome rotary aircraft engine appears.

1909 Robert Goddard concludes that liquid oxygen and liquid hydrogen would be an excellent propellant.

LOUIS BLÉRIOT AT REIMS
Already the toast of Europe after his pioneering flight across the English Channel on July 25, 1909, Louis Blériot was heavily favored to win the Gordon Bennett Cup at Reims. Monoplanes had less wind resistance and were favored over biplanes for speed. Bléroit almost succeeded, coming in just six seconds behind Glenn Curtiss' gold-tinted biplane.

LEFEBVRE AT REIMS The Wright brothers, for reasons of business or of class, refused invitations to participate in contests such as the Reims meeting. However, three of their Wright Flyer biplanes were entered, one of them flown by Eugène Lefebvre. The Wright Flyer had some unforgiving characteristics, and Lefebvre became the first pilot to die in a powered heavier-than-air craft when he crashed on September 7, 1909.

ESNAULT-PELTERIE Robert Esnault-Pelterie persisted in his engineering efforts and developed a succession of interesting monoplanes. Some had quite unusual features, such as the single main-wheel undercarriage of the REP.2 monoplane of 1908. Pelterie also designed and built his own REP engines. His aircraft were fast for the time but noted for their instability. This made them more maneuverable in the hands of an accomplished pilot but more difficult for a beginner to fly.

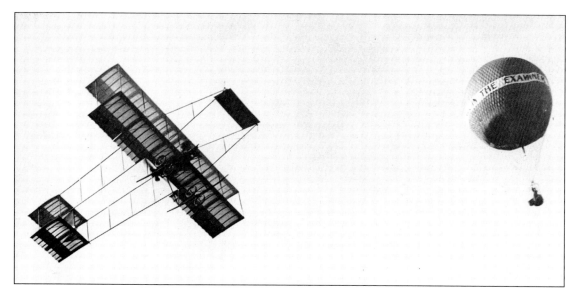

PAULHAN AT LOS ANGELES AVIATION MEET It was a glorious—and dangerous—time to be an aviator. Aeroplanes, as they were being called, were so new that almost every flight could break a record. Here the very popular Louis Paulhan is seen setting a new altitude record of 4,165 feet at Dominguez Field, Los Angeles, in January 1910. Paulhan died in 1963 at the age of 80—most unusual for a pioneer flyer.

FABRE HYDROPLANE Aviators immediately perceived that there were many different bodies of water—lakes, rivers, and oceans—that would make excellent fields from which seaborne aircraft could land and take off. Among the earliest experimenters was Henri Fabre, whose canard (elevator-in-front) surfaced pusher monoplane made the first flight from water at Martigues, near Marseilles, France, on March 28, 1910. Pilot Jean Becu is shown here. Fabre produced a more advanced seaplane in 1911.

FLIGHT TIMELINE

1909 The king of Spain flies in the first Spanish airship, the *España*.

February 23, 1909 J.A.D. McCurdy makes the first flight in Canada in the A.E.A.'s *Silver Dart*.

April 24, 1909 The first motion pictures are taken from an airplane piloted by Wilbur Wright in Italy.

July 13, 1909 Pioneer manufacturer A. V. Roe becomes the first Briton to fly an all-British craft in England.

July 25, 1909 Louis Blériot flies across the English Channel from Calais, France, to Dover, England.

August 27, 1909 Henri Farman becomes the first to fly a distance of 100 miles.

August 29, 1909 Glenn Curtiss wins the Gordon Bennett Cup with a speed of 47 miles per hour.

September 7, 1909 Eugène Lefebvre is the first pilot to be killed in a crash.

October 16, 1909 Count Ferdinand von Zeppelin founds Delag, the world's first commercial airline.

January 10, 1910 The first U.S. airplane meet is held at Dominguez Field, south of Los Angeles.

January 19, 1910 Army Lieutenant Paul Beck drops dummy bombs from an airplane piloted by Louis Paulhan.

BARONESS RAYMONDE DE LAROCHE Elise Deroche (better known by her assumed title of Baroness Raymonde de Laroche) was a friend of Gabriel Voisin and was taught to fly by Voisin's chief instructor. In October 1909, she made a solo flight of some 300 yards; she earned her pilot's license in March 1910, becoming the first woman to do so. The stylish and brave de Laroche died in a crash in 1919.

LEON DELAGRANGE Shown here in a Voisin aircraft in which he had collaborated, Leon Delagrange was at the forefront of aviation in France from 1907 forward. It is almost certain that he, like Henri Farman, Gabriel Voisin, and Louis Blériot, would have established an aircraft manufacturing company bearing his name, had his life not been cut short in a crash. This was all too often the fate of early aviators, a fact of which they were very conscious.

DAILY MAIL RACE Early photographs of aircraft in flight are relatively rare, but they are often very beautiful because most flights were made early in the morning or late in the evening, when the air was still. This striking image shows Louis Paulhan flying his Farman biplane in the *Daily Mail* London-to-Manchester race on April 28, 1910. Paulhan won the race—and its £10,000 prize.

LOUIS PAULHAN The *Daily Mail* promoted aviation with prizes, because aviation promoted sales. Nothing could have been more exciting than a race between an Englishman, Claude Grahame-White, and a Frenchman, Louis Paulhan. Both men flew similar Farman aircraft to cover the 185 miles from London to Manchester in less than 24 hours, with no more than two stops. Even though the more experienced pilot, Paulhan, won, *Daily Mail* sales still went up.

CLAUDE GRAHAME-WHITE Aviator Claude Grahame-White is shown inspecting the "kite-windlass" used by Colonel Samuel Cody to experiment with carrying people. Grahame-White was one of Great Britain's most popular aviators, possessing great skill, the looks of a film star, and an ingratiating personality. Reportedly as skillful a race car driver as an aviator, he owned his own automobile agency in London. Unlike most of his contemporaries, Grahame-White lived to be 80 years old.

FLIGHT TIMELINE

March 8, 1910 Baroness Raymonde de Laroche becomes the first licensed female pilot.

March 28, 1910 Henri Fabre's seaplane makes the first flight from water.

June 2, 1910 Charles Rolls of Rolls-Royce makes a round-trip crossing of the English Channel.

June 13, 1910 Charles Hamilton wins $10,000 for completing a flight from New York to Philadelphia.

July 9, 1910 Walter Brookins flies his Wright biplane to above one mile.

July 12, 1910 Charles Rolls is killed when he crashes in his Wright Flyer.

July 31, 1910 The Bristol Boxkite flies for the first time.

August 27, 1910 J.A.D. McCurdy transmits and receives radio messages from a Curtiss biplane.

September 2, 1910 Blanche Scott is the first American woman to fly solo.

September 8, 1910 The first mid-air collision occurs in Austria.

September 23, 1910 Peruvian Georges Chavez makes the first flight over the Alps but is killed on landing.

October 14, 1910 Ralph Johnstone sets a world altitude record of 9,714 feet in a Wright biplane.

WRIGHT CRASH The Wright Flyer was not just an unforgiving aircraft, it had an inherent aerodynamic flaw that killed many of its pilots. Charles Stewart Rolls, cofounder of Rolls-Royce, was vastly interested in aviation. Unfortunately, he was killed on July 12, 1910, in this crash of a British-built Wright Flyer in which he was practicing spot landings. In his honor, the radiator badge of Rolls-Royce motorcars, which previously had been painted red, were painted black in mourning.

GEORGES CHAVEZ In the summer of 1910, a prize of 70,000 lire ($14,000) was offered to the first pilot to fly the Alps between Brig, Switzerland, and Domodossola, Italy. A 23-year-old Peruvian, Jorge Chavez Dartnell (Georges Chavez) succeeded in doing so on September 23. But just 44 feet above his landing spot, the wings of his Blériot XI folded up and he crashed, dying four days later. Such crashes severely tarnished the Blériot reputation.

NIEUPORT MONOPLANE, 1910 Not everyone borrowed inspiration from the Wrights; a host of designers borrowed from Blériot. Edouard Nieuport was one of the most successful of them, designing small, fast aircraft that set a speed record of 82.73 miles per hour and a distance record of 460 miles. The Nieuport machines had an elegance that was retained in the long series of Nieuport fighters during World War I.

LIEUTENANT THEODORE G. ELLYSON All over the world, young military men saw in the aeroplane a new weapon that they could use in defense of their country. Lieutenant Theodore G. Ellyson, Naval Aviator No. 1, was among them. He conducted experiments with the catapult launch systems that became standard equipment on board U.S. Navy ships.

LIEUTENANT MYRON CRISSY AND PHILIP PARMALEE Lieutenant Myron S. Crissy and Philip O. Parmalee dropped the first live bombs from a Wright Type B biplane on January 15, 1911. Crissy Field in San Francisco was later named after the former. Parmalee was a part of the Wright exhibition team and had carried the first air freight (several bolts of silk) the previous November.

FLIGHT TIMELINE

October 16, 1910 Walter Wellman fails in an attempt to fly the dirigible *America* across the Atlantic.

October 28, 1910 Maurice Tabuteau sets a closed circuit record of 289 miles.

November 14, 1910 Eugene Ely is the first pilot to take off from a ship, the USS *Birmingham*.

January 15, 1911 Lieutenant Myron Crissy and Philip Parmalee drop the first live bomb from an aircraft.

January 18, 1911 Eugene Ely makes the first landing on a ship, the deck of the USS *Pennsylvania*.

January 26, 1911 Glenn Curtiss operates his hydro-aeroplane in San Diego.

February 22, 1911 Airmail service starts between Allahabad and Naini Junction in India.

February 25, 1911 Glenn Curtiss taxies his amphibious airplane (with retractable landing gear) from its hangar to the water. He takes off and flies a few circuits around the bay, then extends the landing gear and lands on a beach at Coronado.

March 1911 The United States Navy establishes a naval aviation branch.

March 24, 1911 Roger Sommers carries 13 passengers in his single-engine pusher biplane for ½ mile.

April 11, 1911 The College Park U.S. Army Flying School is formed in College Park, Maryland.

CAL RODGERS IN *VIN FIZ* Looking every inch the daring aviator, Calbraith Perry Rodgers is shown at the controls of the Wright biplane in which he made the first coast-to-coast flight in 1911. The flight began on September 17, 1911, and included 15 accidents, many broken bones, and a brain concussion. It ended on November 5, 1911. Rodgers crashed to his death in April 1912 when he dove through a flock of seagulls and one jammed his rudder.

FIRST AIRMAIL FLIGHT Postmaster General Frank Hitchcock hands aviator Earle E. Ovington, a former assistant to Thomas Edison, a sack of mail to carry on the first official airmail flight in the United States. Ovington flew in a Queen monoplane, which was essentially a Blériot built on Long Island. The flight, which took place on September 23, 1911, was from Garden City to Mineola, New York, a distance of about three miles.

ELY LANDS ON THE USS *PENNSYLVANIA* Eugene Ely was hired by the Curtiss Exhibition Company as a pilot. He became the first pilot ever to take off from a ship on November 14, 1910, when he flew a Curtiss pusher from the USS *Birmingham*. On January 18, 1911, he became the first ever to land on a ship, this time the USS *Pennsylvania* (shown here). Ely lost his life in October of the same year during an exhibition in Georgia.

ROLAND GARROS Roland Garros was one of France's greatest aviators in peace and in war. Shown here in a tiny Santos-Dumont Demoiselle, Garros was the first pilot to fly the Mediterranean Sea, doing so in a Morane-Saulnier monoplane on September 23, 1913. It was in a Morane-Saulnier Model L that Garros would become the first man to use a machine gun shooting forward through the propeller to gain an aerial victory.

ANDRE BEAUMONT WINS To avoid difficulties with their superiors, military officers sometimes had to adopt a different name to compete. Such was the case with Jean Conneau, a French navy lieutenant who flew under the nom de plume of Andre Beaumont in the grueling 1911 "Circuit of Europe" race. An expert navigator, Conneau beat both Roland Garros and the tough competitor Jules Vedrines to win the equivalent of $50,000.

FLIGHT TIMELINE

May 21–26, 1911 Jules Vedrines wins a difficult European race of 842 miles in a Morane-Saulnier Monoplane.

July 1, 1911 The first U.S. Navy plane, the *Triad*, is flown.

July 22–26, 1911 The *Daily Mail*'s £10,000 "Round Britain" race takes place.

August 2, 1911 Harriet Quimby becomes the first female American pilot.

September 5, 1911 Roland Garros sets a world altitude record of 13,945 feet in a Bléroit.

September 9, 1911 The first aerial postal service is inaugurated in England.

September 11, 1911 The first British dirigible, the *Mayfly*, fails to lift off on its first flight attempt.

September 17, 1911 Cal Rodgers embarks on a flight from New York to California.

September 23, 1911 Earle Ovington makes the first U.S. airmail flight.

September 24, 1911 The *Mayfly* breaks up during a second flight attempt.

November 1, 1911 Italian pilot Giulio Cavotti drops bombs on Turkish troops in Libya. It is the first wartime bombing.

November 5, 1911 Cal Rodgers completes his transcontinental flight, becoming the first person to cross the United States by airplane.

JULES VEDRINES This unusual photograph catches Jules Vedrines with a fairly pleasant look on his face, a rarely seen phenomenon. Vedrines was noted for his vicious temper and his ability to insult anyone, regardless of their rank or position in life. Here, his Deperdussin monoplane is fitted with a Gnome rotary engine. In the rotary engine, the cylinders rotated with the propeller around the fixed crankshaft.

HARRIET QUIMBY A journalist by trade, the attractive and vivacious Harriet Quimby was the United States' first licensed female pilot. She learned to fly in 1911 at the age of 36 and toured with the Moisant International Aviators exhibition team. Quimby was the first woman to fly the English Channel, doing so on April 16, 1912, in a Blériot XI. Sadly, she was killed on July 1, 1912, when she was thrown out of her Blériot over Boston Harbor.

MAYFLY The British government placed an order with the shipbuilding firm of Vickers for a Zeppelin-type airship, formally designated Naval Airship No. 1 but called the *Mayfly*. Some 512 feet long and filled with 663,518 cubic feet of hydrogen, the *Mayfly* could not lift off on its first flight attempt, which took place on September 11, 1911. Its weight was cut by three tons, and the *Mayfly* was towed out for a second attempt on September 24, 1911, but promptly broke in half.

CURTISS HYDROPLANE

Glenn H. Curtiss' greatest contributions to aviation were the seaplane and the flying boat. Here his triplane-hydro of mid-1911 is being serviced prior to flight. The third wing generated an extra 200 pounds of lift but was not used in subsequent Curtiss hydroplanes.

The Wrights also experimented with flying boats and float planes but never achieved anywhere near the success of Curtiss. His seaplanes and flying boats became the heart of the Navy's aviation effort, and his Model F-5L combined British expertise with his own designs. The twin-engine Model H series (developments of the Wellman's *America*) were invaluable for anti-U-boat warfare.

AVRO G A. V. Roe was originally preoccupied by triplanes but soon developed both monoplanes and biplanes as well. One of these was this Avro G, which featured an enclosed cabin. Intended for the British Army Trials of 1912, the G had a 60-horsepower Green engine and a maximum speed of 62 miles per hour. Underpowered, no production ensued. But just one year later, the immortal Avro 504 would appear.

HENDON AIR REVIEW By 1912, England, France, Germany, and Russia were convinced that aircraft would have some utility in case of war, and each nation began holding events where various designs were compared and evaluated. Monoplanes dominated in this 1912 event at Hendon, but they would soon be banished from the British inventory because of concerns about structural strength. Hendon, just north of London, is now the home of the Royal Air Force Museum.

CURTISS PUSHER Although he too borrowed heavily from the Wrights, Glenn Curtiss was an innovator, and this aircraft, almost certainly a Model A-1, was just a step away from the world's first successful amphibian, the Curtiss Triad. At the controls is Lieutenant John Towers, the third Naval officer qualified to fly. He went on to become known as "the architect of naval aviation."

NIEUPORT SEAPLANE AT SCHNEIDER TROPHY RACE Two of the sleek Nieuport seaplanes were entered in the 1913 Schneider Trophy race at Monaco. Both were powered by 100-horsepower Gnome rotary engines. The first was flown by Gabriel Espanet and was forced to retire on lap eight. The second was flown by Charles Weyman, who completed 24 laps. The winner was Maurice Prévost in a Deperdussin, which averaged 46 miles per hour, powered by a 160-horsepower Gnome rotary engine.

DEPERDUSSIN The most advanced aircraft of its time, the Deperdussin was powered by a 100-horsepower Gnome rotary engine. Designed by Louis Bechereeau and Andre Herbemont, the Deperdussin racers set speed records, one being a sensational 126.67 miles per hour. They also won races, including the Gordon Bennett Cup and the Schneider Trophy. Unfortunately, the firm's founder, Armand Deperdussin, was an embezzler who was sent to jail in 1913.

FLIGHT TIMELINE

November 12, 1912 Navy Lieutenant Theodore G. Ellyson is catapult-launched from an anchored barge.

1913 The U.S. Army establishes its first permanent aviation school at North Island in San Diego.

February 6, 1913 Frank T. Coffyn affixes aluminum floats to a Wright Model B for the first hydro flight in a Wright Flyer.

March 5, 1913 The first U.S. Aero Squadron is formed.

April 16, 1913 The 1913 Monaco Hydroaeroplane main event, the first Schneider Trophy race, is held. It is an individual time trials event in which pilots attempt to fly 174 miles in the shortest time. Maurice Prévost wins in a Deperdussin.

April 17, 1913 Gustav Hamel flies nonstop from Dover, England, to Cologne, Germany.

May 10, 1913 Didier Mason, a French-born American mercenary, bombs Mexican gunships.

May 13, 1913 Igor Sikorsky flies *Le Grand*, the first four-engine aircraft.

June 1913 Glenn L. Martin delivers his first aeroplane—a Model TT—to the U.S. Army.

August 27, 1913 Peter Nesterov performs the first aerial loop.

September 18, 1913 The immortal Avro 504 flies for the first time.

MORANE-SAULNIER The dainty Morane-Saulnier L was a formidable war plane, used by the French, British, and Russian air forces. Flown by Flight Sub-Lieutenant Reginald A. J. Warneford, it became the first aircraft to destroy a Zeppelin, dropping bombs on a LZ 37 over Belgium on June 7, 1915. Warneford received the Victoria Cross for his exploit. Roland Garros also used the Morane-Saulnier L to revolutionize air warfare. Both men later died for their countries.

LOUGHEAD (LOCKHEED) MODEL G

Allan and Malcolm Loughead (pronounced Lockheed) built their first aircraft in a garage at the corner of Polk and Pacific streets in San Francisco. They called it the Model G so it would not sound like their first attempt. The Model G took to the air on June 15, 1913, and was, at the time, the largest seaplane ever built in the United States. With a top speed of 63 miles per hour, the Model G took paying passengers for a ride around the Bay.

Malcolm went on to make a fortune in the automobile industry with his patented Lockheed hydraulic brake system. A third brother, Victor, wrote some excellent books on early aviation.

SOPWITH TABLOID Called the "Tabloid" because of its diminutive size, this 1913 Sopwith biplane led to a dynasty of fighters during World War I, including the Pup, Camel, Dolphin, and Snipe. Equipped with floats, the Tabloid won the 1914 Schneider Trophy race.

FLIGHT TIMELINE

September 21, 1913 Adolphe Pégoud makes the first sustained inverted flight.

September 23, 1913 Roland Garros crosses the Mediterranean in a Morane-Saulnier monoplane, traveling 588 miles in 7 hours, 53 minutes.

September 29, 1913 Maurice Prévost, flying a Deperdussin "monocoque," wins the Gordon Bennett Cup with a speed of 126.67 miles per hour.

November 18, 1913 Lincoln Beachey executes the first loop-the-loop ever accomplished in the United States.

December 28, 1913 Georges Legagneux achieves an altitude of 20,079 feet, logging the first altitude record above 20,000 feet.

ADOLPHE PÉGOUD Displaying all the dash and élan that made him such a formidable aerobatic pilot, Adolphe Pégoud is shown in his specially strengthened Blériot. Pégoud gained fame by performing the first inside aerial loop near Buc, France. He and the amazed crowd were unaware that Peter Nesterov had performed the same feat in Russia a month earlier. Pégoud was shot down and killed during World War I.

DUNNE BIPLANE It can truly be said that almost every new and revolutionary advance in aviation has been seen many years before. Such is the case with swept wings, which became essential after World War II but could be found as early as 1913 in the radical—but very stable—Dunne series of aircraft. It also foreshadowed the flying wing. Developed by John William Dunne, the tailless swept-wing concept would reappear throughout aviation history.

CHAPTER TWO

1914 to 1923:

Tempered in the Fire of War

After witnessing the flight of the Montgolfier balloon in Paris in 1783, Benjamin Franklin instantly remarked about the possible use of balloons in war. The Wright brothers knew from the start that their invention would have military uses, and they hoped that the flying machine might make war impossible by removing the element of surprise.

Fokker D VII

By 1913, aircraft had been used combat in Mexico, North Africa, and the Balkans. Although they scarcely removed all elements of surprise, they did give patriotic young men the chance to vent their wrath upon the enemy by dropping bombs and firing pistols.

When World War I began on August 1, 1914, every major nation—except the United States—had significant aerial components in their military forces. By 1914, Germany and France had each expended the equivalent of $26 million on their respective air services (measured in 1914 dollars). Russia had spent $12 million; Great Britain is estimated to have spent $9 million. The United States had spent only $400,000. U.S. spending exceeded only Austria-Hungary, which had expended just over $318,000.

France began the war with some 140 aircraft for 21 squadrons. Great Britain's Royal Flying Corps (RFC) had roughly 180 aircraft, about half of which were unfit for service. The Royal Naval Air Service (RNAS) had 50 aircraft and fewer pilots. Germany went to aerial war with its characteristic efficiency. It could put 250 first-line aircraft in the field, with a pilot for each, along with no less than 9 dirigibles. Its Austro-Hungarian ally could field just under 50 aircraft. Imperial Russia had 250 ill-maintained aircraft and 14 dirigibles spread widely across the country.

Curtiss NC-4

These wood and fabric aircraft were derived from civil models, though some had been purchased to primitive military specifications in regard to equipment. They were almost evenly divided between monoplanes and biplanes, with approximately the same performance characteristics—a top speed of 60 or 70 miles per hour, a stall speed of 50 to 60 miles per hour, an endurance of an hour or two, and the capability to carry a pilot and an observer but little or no armament. They were fragile, cranky, unreliable, difficult to fly, and subject to structural failure if pressed too hard.

Despite this, within the first six months of the war, these aircraft, and their slightly more sophisticated descendants, demonstrated virtually every type of modern aerial combat, including strategic bombing, tactical bombing, close air support, reconnaissance, aerial photography, map-making, artillery spotting, aerial combat, clandestine spy missions, and the dropping of supplies to troops. More importantly, within the first two months of the war, reconnaissance reports from aerial observers resulted in decisive battles that directly affected the outcome of the war. In the East, it was the Battle of Tannenberg, which was possible only because German aerial reconnaissance teams detected the movement of the Russian Army. In the West, it was the Battle of the Marne, which came about only because both British and French aerial observers detected the right-wheel movement of the German Army. In both instances, perhaps the most remarkable thing was that the respective high commands believed the aerial reports and took action on them.

By January 1915, two facts emerged. The first was that loss of aircraft and human life was high—new industries were needed in the homelands to supply sufficient planes and crews. The second was that while aerial warfare could not be decisive in breaking the stalemate on the western front, it was nonetheless essential to the conduct of war. Having airpower did not necessarily mean that you would win the war, but *not* having it certainly meant you would lose it.

What followed was a race to create specialized aircraft and develop tactics for their use. By 1918, after four years of vicious fighting, there were fighters

Vickers Vimy

capable of 130 miles per hour while carrying two machine guns, bombers able to carry a ton of bombs over a distance of several hundred miles, and reconnaissance planes that could fly at altitudes above 20,000 feet. Where 1914 aircraft had been relatively fragile, fighters could now pull high-G loads in dogfights, dive at high speeds, and take a surprising amount of damage. The Germans had fielded giant bombers with huge 138-foot wingspans, and the British were preparing an aircraft to bomb Berlin.

As impressive as the improvements were, they paled in comparison to the speed at which the aircraft industry grew. More than 225,000 aircraft were produced during the war. In Great Britain, the total production for the first ten months of 1918 was 26,685 aircraft and 29,561 engines. The RFC had grown from 140 aircraft into the mighty Royal Air Force, with more than 22,000 planes in service around the world. Even Germany, hard-pressed by the long war and the Allied blockade, ended the war with an air force of more than 11,000 planes.

The four years of warfare spurred a revolution in quality as well. Before the war, planes were hand-made, one or two at a time. By the middle of the war, aircraft and engines were produced using mass production. Aircraft engineering went from intuition to very sophisticated systems of design that developed whole families of aircraft. The more advanced aircraft required up-to-date systems of radio communication, bombsights, oxygen, heated flying clothes, synchronized guns, and more.

To support the advances, the entire industrial infrastructure of the major nations had to be revised. In the United States, for example, there was a mass recruitment of foresters to provide sufficient spruce from the Pacific Northwest. Acres of castor beans were planted to provide the essential castor oil for lubricating rotary engines. New industries were created to manufacture instruments, flying wires, radiators, and other essentials that thousands of aircraft demanded. These industries required a precision that exceeded any previous mass-manufactured object, and this in turn required new machinery and new techniques.

World War I was both the hammer and the anvil by which aviation was changed into a tempered tool that promised to revolutionize warfare and civilian life. The war advanced aviation at an amazing rate, achieving performance gains in 4 years that might have taken 20 in peacetime. When the war ended, there were dozens of new designs on the drawing boards in every country, with the exception of Russia, which was still racked by the Bolshevik revolution. There were thousands of pilots available to fly either surplus aircraft from the war or the few new aircraft that were being manufactured. And there were speed, altitude, distance, and duration records to be set; airline routes to be pioneered; new areas of the globe to be explored; and a new sector of the economy—aviation—to be exploited.

In the five years following the end of the war, aviation would be pushed to limits never dreamed of, and the aviator would become a mythic figure in the popular imagination.

PENSACOLA Not surprisingly, it was the young men of the Navy who took to aviation, while their seniors adopted a wait-and-see attitude toward the new invention. Eager young flyers flocked to Pensacola, Florida, for their initial flight training, and the naval air station there became the premier naval flight training station in the world. Shown here is a 1914 lineup of early Curtiss flying boats, including the Model F (nearest) and the AH-13 (second from the bottom).

IL'YA MUROMETS The first four-engine aircraft in the world was the Sikorsky S-21, called "The Great Baltic" or, more commonly, "The Grand." First flown on March 2, 1913, it launched a series of four-engine Sikorsky aircraft including the famous S-22A Il'ya Muromets, shown here flying at Korpusnoi Aerodrome near Moscow in February 1914. Very advanced, with an enclosed cabin and room for 16 passengers, the S-22A led in turn to a series of capable four-engine bombers.

1914 CURTISS AMERICA The continuing success Glenn Curtiss experienced with his flying boats led to the ambitious Model H *America,* with which wealthy Rodman Wanamaker sought to win *The Daily Mail's* £10,000 prize for the first aerial crossing of the Atlantic Ocean. The flight attempt was to be made on August 5, 1914, but was canceled when war broke out. The design led to a long line of Navy flying boats.

1914 AIRBOAT LINE On January 1, 1914, Thomas Benoist, an aircraft manufacturer from St. Louis, signed a contract with the city of St. Petersburg, Florida, to begin the first passenger airline in the world. The airline's first passenger was former Florida Mayor A. C. Phiel. He paid $400 for the 23-minute flight on the Type XIV flying boat, which was piloted by Tony Jannus.

SOPWITH SCHNEIDER CUP WINNER The tiny Sopwith Tabloid was fitted with a 100-horsepower Gnome rotary engine and twin floats. In it, Harold Pixton won the 1914 Schneider Cup at a speed of 86.75 miles per hour, then set a record of 92 miles per hour for seaplanes. The Tabloid was the direct predecessor of the famous series of Sopwith fighters in World War I.

FLIGHT TIMELINE

1914 The Chinese Army Air Arm is formed.

January 1914 The Naval Aeronautical Center is established at NAS Pensacola, Florida.

January 1914 The Il'ya Muromets bomber is flown for the first time.

January 1, 1914 Tony Jannus flies a Benoist flying boat between Tampa and St. Petersburg, Florida, to inaugurate the first regularly scheduled passenger airline.

February 23, 1914 A prototype of the Bristol Scout flies.

April 1914 The Fokker M.5, a prototype of the Eindecker, appears.

April 25, 1914 Navy Lieutenant P.N.L. Bellinger makes the first U.S. combat flight off Vera Cruz, Mexico, to scout for sea mines.

May 6, 1914 Navy Lieutenant P.N.L Bellinger's aeroplane is hit by rifle fire. This is the first recorded U.S. aerial combat damage.

July 7, 1914 Robert Goddard secures a patent for his two-stage solid fuel rocket.

August 1, 1914 Germany declares war on Russia. In subsequent days, it becomes a true world war, with Allies versus the Central Powers.

August 22, 1914 The British RFC takes a reconnaissance of German lines.

August 26, 1914 Russian staff Captain Peter Nesterov rams an Austrian plane; both pilots are killed.

ZEPPELIN Z IV It is difficult to imagine the tremendous grip that the dirigible had upon the public's imagination, especially in Germany, where Count Ferdinand von Zeppelin's creations were regarded with enormous pride. Here, the Army Zeppelin Z IV demonstrates a water landing. Germany's belief in the Zeppelin was so strong that both its Army and Navy developed their own programs of Zeppelins for bombing and reconnaissance.

ROYAL AIRCRAFT FACTORY B.E.2c

His Majesty's Balloon Factory at Farnborough, England, became the Royal Aircraft Factory in 1910. In 1911, the young Geoffrey de Havilland designed the Blériot Experimental (B.E.) 1. This was developed into the B.E.2 series with the B.E.2c becoming one of the Royal Flying Corps principal aircraft, serving for reconnaissance, artillery spotting, and bombing. It was no match for German fighters when they appeared, and many a British crew was lost in an unequal battle.

De Havilland went on to a brilliant career developing both military and civil planes that led the aviation world and included the D.H.4, the Tiger Moth, the Mosquito, the Comet, and a series of jet fighters.

AVRO 504 The Avro 504 is usually remembered as a trainer, but it was a combat aircraft in the early days of World War I and made some sensationally successful strategic bombing flights to attack German Zeppelin sheds. This one was forced down and flown in German markings.

CAPRONI TRIMOTOR The Italians had a penchant for trimotor aircraft in both World War I and World War II and for the same reason—a shortage of powerful engines that would have permitted twin-engine designs. This Caproni Ca 32 typified the many variations of the design, which was used with great success against the Austrians during World War I.

FLIGHT TIMELINE

August 27, 1914 The first RFC squadrons arrive in France.

August 30, 1914 German Army Lieutenant Ferdinand von Hiddessen bombs Paris from his Taube; a woman is killed.

October 5, 1914 Corporal Louis Quénault and Sergeant Joseph Frantz of the French Air Force shoot down a German Aviatik. It's the first victory in aerial combat.

November 21, 1914 Three Avro 504s bomb Zeppelin sheds at Friedrichshafen, Germany.

December 21, 1914 A German airplane drops bombs on Dover; it's the first attack on England.

December 25, 1914 Seven British hydroaeroplanes are launched from Royal Navy carriers. They succeed in bombing German facilities in Cuxhaven.

January 19, 1915 The first Zeppelin raids begin in England.

February 17, 1915 HMS *Ark Royal*, the first ship converted to aircraft duty, launches a seaplane to reconnoiter Turks at Gallipoli, Turkey.

March 3, 1915 The United States forms the National Advisory Committee for Aeronautics (NACA), which will become the National Aeronautics and Space Administration (NASA) in 1958.

CURTISS AB-3 FLYING BOAT
Navy Lieutenant P.N.L. Bellinger flew the first U.S. aerial military operations in a Curtiss AB-3 flying boat, searching for sea mines in Vera Cruz, Mexico, on April 25, 1914. On May 6, Bellinger's aircraft was the first to be hit by enemy fire while on active service. Twenty-seven years later, Bellinger was at Pearl Harbor, pleading for extensive aerial reconnaissance to warn of a Japanese attack. Unfortunately, his pleas were ignored.

1914 ALBATROS B I This early Albatros B I has yet to acquire the large triangular tail surfaces that would later identify the Albatros line. It was soon succeeded by the much cleaner B II, which, powered by a 100-horsepower Mercedes engine, could reach top speeds of 66 miles per hour. Later, when more powerful engines became available, the Albatros C series emerged. These became some of the most successful observation planes of World War I.

AVRO 504S AT BELFORT On November 21, 1914, four Avro 504 aircraft, led by Squadron Commander E. F. Briggs, took off from Belfort, France, to bomb the Zeppelin sheds at Friedrichshafen, Germany—125 miles away. One 504 failed to take off, but the other three snaked their way across Lake Constance at ten feet above the water. They climbed and dropped nine bombs that heavily damaged the target. Briggs' aircraft was shot down, but the other two returned safely.

LINCOLN BEACHEY The adage about not asking for something because you might get it proved only too apt for the legendary stunt pilot Lincoln Beachey. After captivating audiences in Curtiss pusher aircraft, especially his clipped wing "Little Looper," Beachey contracted for a clipped-wing monoplane. Unfortunately, it was not adequately stressed, and it broke up while Beachey was doing aerobatics over San Francisco on March 14, 1915. Beachey drowned in the wreckage.

DE HAVILLAND D.H.2 The inability to fire a machine gun through a whirling propeller led to pusher designs like this de Havilland D.H.2, powered by a 100-horsepower Gnome rotary engine and capable of 93 miles per hour. Very rugged and aerobatic, the D.H.2 was popular with British pilots and was an adequate antidote to the German Fokker Eindecker.

FLIGHT TIMELINE

April 1, 1915 Roland Garros uses a machine gun fired through a propeller (unsynchronized) to shoot down a German plane.

May 31, 1915 The first Zeppelin raid on London kills seven civilians.

June 1, 1915 The prototype de Havilland D.H.2 makes its first flight.

June 5, 1915 Flight Sub-Lieutenant R.A.J. Warneford is awarded the Victoria Cross for dropping a bomb on an LZ 37. He is killed 12 days later.

July 1915 Fokker E 1 monoplanes ("E" standing for *eindecker*, or monoplane) arrive at the front, the first to have a synchronized gun firing through the propeller.

July 15, 1915 Lieutenant Kurt Wintgens scores a victory with an Eindecker fitted with a synchronized gun.

July 25, 1915 Captain Lanoe Hawker of the RFC earns the first Victoria Cross for air-to-air combat.

Fall 1915 The "Fokker Scourge" begins as Fokker Eindeckers reign supreme on the western front.

December 12, 1915 Hugo Junkers' J 1 "Tin Donkey," the first all-metal monoplane, makes its inaugural flight in Germany.

January 1916 *Kampfgeschwader Nr. 1*, the German elite bombing unit, receives Gotha IV bombers.

ZEPPELIN-STAAKEN V.G.O. I
While the United States was still absorbed in exhibition flying, giving little thought to military aircraft, European nations were progressing rapidly. This huge Zeppelin-Staaken V.G.O. I made its first flight on April 11, 1915. With three 240-horsepower Maybach engines and a wingspan of 138 feet, 5 inches, the V.G.O. I had a top speed of about 70 miles per hour. Later versions had five engines and a top speed of 81 miles per hour.

HANDLEY PAGE O/400 The prototype Handley Page O/100 made its first flight on December 17, 1915, from Hendon Airdrome near London. After much development, production O/100s went into combat. The O/400 shown here was similar to the O/100 except for a larger 360-horsepower Rolls-Royce Eagle engine, a revised fuel system, and greater structural strength and bomb load. The top speed of the O/400 was 97 miles per hour, and more than 400 were delivered before the war ended in 1918.

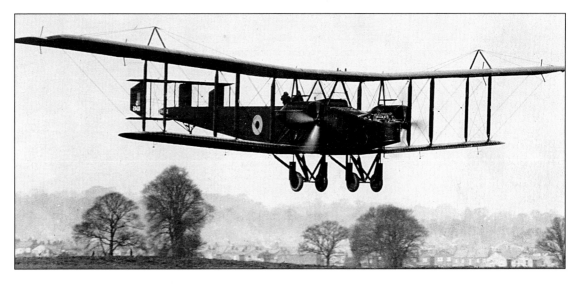

ZEPPELIN L 9 The Zeppelin numbering system was confusing to the layperson. The builder applied an LZ number, which the Army used, but the Navy changed this to an L number. Thus the L 9 was actually the LZ 36 to the Zeppelin company that built it. This beautiful aircraft made a total of 148 flights, of which four were air raids and 74 were reconnaissance. It was destroyed when a sister ship caught fire in an adjacent shed on September 16, 1916.

ROLAND GARROS A pioneer aviator in France, Roland Garros also proved to be an innovative fighter pilot. Working with the Morane-Saulnier company, Garros experimented with steel wedges on the propeller to deflect machine-gun bullets fired through the propeller arc. Fitting the device to a parasol wing Morane-Saulnier L, he shot down three German aircraft before being shot down himself. After escaping from Germany, he returned to flying, only to be shot down and killed on October 5, 1918.

SHORT TYPE 184 The Short Type 184 seaplane, with its huge wings and disproportionately sized ailerons, may not look like a deadly combat machine, but it was. On August 17, 1915, a Short 184 operating from the seaplane carrier HMS *Ben-My-Chree* sank an enemy Turkish ship with an 810-pound air-launched torpedo—the first such sinking in history. Some 900 Model 184s were built, and they were used in almost every theater of war. The aircraft's top speed was 68 miles per hour.

FLIGHT TIMELINE

January 1916 The first aero squadron to serve outside the United States, 1st Company, 2nd Aero Squadron, sails from San Francisco to the Philippines.

January 12, 1916 German fighter aces Oswald Boelcke and Max Immelmann receive the *Pour le Mérite* (Blue Max) medal.

January 13, 1916 Curtiss Aeroplane & Motor Company Incorporated is formed in Buffalo, New York.

January 21, 1916 The Navy begins experimenting with aircraft radio at Pensacola.

February 9, 1916 Captain A. D. Smith flies a Martin S (Hall Scott engine) to set a world hydroaeroplane record of 8 hours, 42 minutes.

February 12, 1916 The U.S. Post Office seeks bids for carrying the mail by air in Massachusetts and Alaska.

March 16, 1916 The 1st Aero Squadron, commanded by Captain B. D. Foulois, becomes the first U.S. tactical air unit in the field.

March 29, 1916 Lieutenant R. C. Saufley sets an American altitude record of 16,010 feet for hydroaeroplanes at Pensacola.

April 1916 The French use air-to-air rockets for the first time, firing Le Prieur rockets from a Nieuport fighter.

April 7, 1916 Captain B. D. Foulois and Lieutenant Dargue are fired on by Mexican troops at Chihauahua City.

ADOLPHE PÉGOUD Famous for "looping the loop," the popular Adolphe Pégoud (left) had also made the first parachute jump from an airplane in France. An excellent pilot, he had six confirmed victories before he was killed in combat with an enemy photo-reconnaissance plane on August 31, 1915. Ironically enough, the man who killed him was a former student Pégoud had taught to fly, Unteroffizier Kandulski. His motoring companion here is M. Montemier.

CAPTAIN OSWALD BOELCKE
Captain Oswald Boelcke was one of the most important German aviators in history. At the time of his death, he was Germany's leading ace, with 40 victories, and was also a great organizer and tactician. Awarded the *Pour le Mérite* after his eighth victory, Boelcke went on to organize *Jagdstaffel 2,* selecting his own pilots, including Baron Manfred von Richthofen. He was only 25 when he was killed in a midair collision with a member of his own unit, Erwin Böhme, on October 28, 1916. Boelcke's manual of air tactics is still highly regarded.

NIEUPORT 11 The Nieuport heritage may be seen in this lovely Nieuport 11 of 1915. Called the *Bébé* for its tiny size, it was a fast, maneuverable aircraft flawed only by its sesquiwing structure. In a high-speed dive, the V strut sometimes put a twisting movement on the lower wing, causing it to separate from the aircraft. Despite this, the *Bébé* helped put an end to the Fokker Eindecker's reign of terror.

CURTISS JN-3 While European skies were filled with first-rate fighters and bombers, the best the American Army could provide its flyers was the Curtiss JN-2, shown here upgraded to JN-3 status. The pipe-smoking officer is none other than Captain Bennie Foulois, who would someday head the U.S. Air Corps. The airplane led to the famous JN-4 Jenny, one of the classic trainers in history.

LAFAYETTE ESCADRILLE No one thought anything about smoking next to oil-soaked fabric-covered airplanes in 1916 when this photo of Lafayette Escadrille members was taken. Pictured, from the left, are Sergent Elliot Christopher Cowdin, Lieutenant Alfred de Laage deMeux, Captiaine Georges Thenault, and Sous-Lieutenant William Thaw. Cowdin and Thaw were founding members of what was first called the Escadrille Americaine. Both survived the war but died young: Cowdin at 46, Thaw at 40.

FLIGHT TIMELINE

April 20, 1916 American pilots form Escadrille Americaine to fight in France. The name is changed to Lafayette Escadrille in November after German protest (they did not want Americans to come into the war on the side of France).

May 18, 1916 Kiffin Rockwell scores the first victory for Escadrille Americaine.

May 22, 1916 Albert Ball scores his first two victories.

May 28, 1916 The Sopwith Triplane makes its first flight.

June 9, 1916 Lieutenant R. C. Saufley sets an endurance record of 8 hours, 51 minutes, then crashes to his death.

June 18, 1916 German ace Max Immelmann is killed.

June 18, 1916 H. Clyde Balsley of Escadrille Americaine is the first American to be shot down; he survives.

June 23, 1916 Victor Chapman of Escadrille Americaine is the first American killed.

June 29, 1916 The first Boeing aircraft, the Boeing B & W, flies.

August 1916 A prototype D.H.4 flies.

August 6, 1916 René Fonck gains his first victory; he will become the leading French ace of the war.

August 7, 1916 The Wright-Martin Aircraft Company is formed after the first of many mergers in the aviation industry.

BARON MANFRED VON RICHTHOFEN Few enemies have captured the imagination of Americans so much as Baron Manfred von Richthofen, the leading German ace of World War I, with 80 victories. He was not yet 25 when he won the *Pour le Mérite*—the "Blue Max." Ironically, much of his latter-day fame came via his mention in the popular Charles Schulz comic strip, "Peanuts." Called "The Red Baron" because he painted his aircraft that color, Richthofen was a dedicated patriot and an excellent leader.

SPAD VII Designed by Louis Bechereau, the SPAD VII was first flown in April 1916. It was an immediate success, offsetting the new Albatros fighters being introduced by the Germans. More than 6,500 were built, and with a 180-horsepower Hispano Suiza engine, the SPAD VII reached 118 miles per hour. It was very sturdy and could out-dive German fighters. It was used by all the Allied air forces and was preferred by the top French aces.

S.E.5A Many of the aircraft from the British Royal Aircraft Factory were not considered to be first-rate. The S.E.5a was an exception. Designed by H. P. Folland, it proved to be a sturdy airplane and a good gun platform. When powered by a 200-horsepower V-8 Hispano Suiza engine, the S.E.5a had a top speed of 135 miles per hour. Less maneuverable than the Sopwith Camel, it was far safer for new pilots to fly.

BREGUET 14 The utilitarian Breguet AV Type 14 was a high-performance aircraft when it debuted on November 21, 1916. With a top speed of 114 miles per hour, it was faster than most German fighters of the time. A rugged steel, aluminum, and wood construction enabled it to take a lot of battle damage. It was used as a bomber and a reconnaissance plane. American pilots preferred the Breguet 14 to the de Havilland DH-4.

ALBATROS D I Few fighter aircraft possess qualities that make them immediately dominant. However, the sleek Albatros D I, which debuted in 1916, quickly wrested air superiority from the de Havilland D.H.2 and Nieuport 11. With a top speed of 109 miles per hour and twin forward-firing machine guns, the Albatros was especially effective against enemy reconnaissance aircraft. The D I's wooden fuselage was strong and easy to manufacture.

FLIGHT TIMELINE

September 1916 The French SPAD VII enters service.

September 2, 1916 The first plane-to-plane radio contact is established over North Island, California, when telegraph messages are exchanged between two aircraft two miles apart.

September 2, 1916 The first German Zeppelin is shot down over England.

September 5, 1916 Leefe Robinson is awarded the Victoria Cross for destroying a German dirigible.

September 12, 1916 Sperry Company and P. C. Hewitt demonstrate guided missile equipment.

September 17, 1916 Baron Manfred von Richthofen gains the first of his 80 victories.

September 23, 1916 Eleven Zeppelins raid England.

October 7, 1916 H. E. Honeywell wins the National Balloon Race with a flight from Muskogee, Oklahoma, to Cascade, Iowa—a distance of 866 kilometers.

October 12, 1916 Tony Jannus, the famous test pilot who piloted the first airliner, is killed demonstrating Benoist planes in Russia.

October 28, 1916 Leading German ace Oswald Boelcke is killed in a midair collision with Erwin Böhme, a member of his own unit.

GOTHA G IV BOMBER The German Gotha bomber proved to be an effective warplane, able to bomb England from bases on the Belgian coast. With its two 260-horsepower Mercedes pusher engines, it could reach a top speed of 87.5 miles per hour and a maximum altitude of 21,000 feet. The bomb load varied from 600 to 1,000 pounds. It was used on daylight raids at first, but once the British created an air defense system, the Gotha became a night bomber.

SOPWITH TRIPLANE The Sopwith Triplane was perhaps more famous for the planes that imitated it than it was in its own right. The intent of Tom Sopwith was to provide a better rate of climb and an improved view by spreading the wing area over three narrow-chord wings. Only about 150 "Tripehounds," as they were called, were built, but they made a deep impression on the Germans and resulted in Anthony Fokker building his more famous Dr I triplane.

BRISTOL F2B Designed by Frank Barnwell and first flown on September 9, 1916, the Bristol F2B became known as the Bristol Fighter. It had an unfortunate combat debut, losing four out of six aircraft on its first combat sortie. However, the aircraft was strong, fast (123 miles per hour), maneuverable, and—in the hands of a capable crew—able to meet any German aircraft on more than equal terms. It was used for many years after the war.

SPAD XIII The French SPAD XIII became the great workhorse of Allied air forces during late 1917 and 1918. It was strong, fast, and able to dive at great speeds. Unfortunately, its 235-horsepower Hispano Suiza geared engine was unreliable. Reports indicate that as many as 66 percent of SPAD XIIIs were out of commission on any given day. These are U.S. Army Air Service SPADs in their postwar markings.

FLIGHT TIMELINE

November 18, 1916 Seven JN-4s, originating in New York City, complete the first cross-country National Guard flight.

November 20, 1916 Ruth Law sets a world record for female pilots by flying from Chicago to New York in 8 hours, 55 minutes, 35 seconds.

November 21, 1916 The Breguet 14 makes its first flight.

January 5, 1917 The Smithsonian Institution gives Robert Goddard a $5,000 grant for rocket work.

January 16, 1917 Baron Manfred von Richthofen is awarded the *Pour le Mérite* (Blue Max) medal.

January 19, 1917 The Gallaudet Aircraft Company (a direct ancestor of today's General Dynamics) is formed.

February 11–12, 1917 A German D.F.W. shoots down two enemy bombers in the first successful night fighting between aircraft.

February 13, 1917 The Aircraft Manufacturers Association is formed to permit cross-licensing of patents for the war effort.

March 6, 1917 The first Airco (de Havilland) D.H.4s arrive in France.

March 25, 1917 Billy Bishop gets his first victory (he will go on to become the leading surviving British ace with 72 victories).

SOPWITH CAMEL This is the Sopwith Camel today, as seen in U.S. colors at the Old Rhinebeck Aerodrome, Cole Palen's legacy to the history of flight. The Royal Air Force's Captain Roy Brown was flying a Camel when he fired the shots that killed Baron Manfred von Richthofen on April 21, 1918. Others dispute this claim, preferring to believe that the "Bloody Baron" was downed by a chance rifle shot. Richthofen's death greatly demoralized the German air force.

LIEUTENANT COLONEL WILLIAM AVERY BISHOP Billy Bishop became a symbol of the loyalty of the British Empire as the personable Canadian pilot ran his score of victories to 72—the second highest in the Royal Air Force. He was awarded the Victoria Cross for a daring attack on a German airdrome. Unfortunately, historians, who in recent years have analyzed German reports, question many—if not most—of Bishop's victories.

L.W.F. MODEL F The otherwise undistinguished L.W.F. Model F takes flight on August 21, 1917, powered by a Liberty engine, marking the very first time a Liberty engine flew. This was a history-making event, as the Liberty engine was to become the primary U.S. contribution to World War I airpower. L.W.F. initially stood for Lowe, Willard, and Fowler; later, when the company changed hands, it stood for "Laminated Wooden Fuselage," a company trademark.

FLIGHT TIMELINE

April 1917 "Bloody April": 150 RFC aircraft are destroyed, primarily by Albatros D III fighters.

April 5, 1917 The potent Bristol F2B "Brisfit" fighter moves into combat on the western front with the RFC.

April 6, 1917 The United States declares war on Germany. Rated 14th of world air powers, the United States has only 83 pilots and 109 obsolete aeroplanes in service.

April 9, 1917 Dayton-Wright Aircraft Company is formed to manufacture Liberty-powered DH-4 biplanes.

April 12, 1917 The Breguet 14, a famous French bomber, arrives at the front.

May 1917 French squadrons begin to receive the SPAD XIII, a famous fighter.

May 6, 1917 Albert Ball, the top British ace of the time, scores his 44th victory; he is killed the next day.

May 18, 1917 The U.S. Navy experiments with self-sealing fuel tanks, using double-walled tanks with layers of felt, gum rubber, and Ivory-soap paste.

May 20, 1917 The Curtiss-designed "Large America" flying boat is the first airplane to sink a German submarine (U-36).

May 25, 1917 Twenty-one Gothas raid England in the first mass bombing; 95 people are killed.

June 1917 The first of the German "Giant" bombers, a Staaken R VI, is delivered.

GOTHA G V BOMBER Some aircraft look the part, some aircraft sound the part—the Gotha bomber did both. The name Gotha became generic for German multiengine bomber, and it replaced the Zeppelin as an image of fear and destruction in Great Britain. The Gotha G V had two 260-horsepower Mercedes engines and a top speed of 88 miles per hour. The Gotha had a disastrous impact on British morale in its initial daylight raids over England in the summer of 1917.

ALBERT BALL Great Britain tried not to glorify its pilot aces (unlike other countries), but eventually morale fell so low that heroes were needed. Captain Albert Ball was a perfect British hero—young, brave, and mildly eccentric. One of his idiosyncrasies was harmless enough—he played the violin while walking around the campfire. Ball led the famous No. 56 Squadron into action, scoring more than 40 victories before being shot down and killed on May 7, 1917, at the age of 20.

LOTHAR VON RICHTHOFEN Germany made no bones about celebrating its aces, and when Lothar von Richthofen began to score victories in his brother's unit, the authorities were delighted. One facet of German propaganda was to use images of the aces on postcards, candy boxes, cigarette packages, and even advertisements. Lothar scored 40 victories and survived the war, only to be killed in a postwar flying accident.

DE HAVILLAND DH-4 The de Havilland D.H.4 was originally designed by young Geoffrey de Havilland and was used successfully by the RAF. The de Havilland DH-4 (different designation) shown here was built in the United States and was the only type of American-built warplane to reach the front. Used for both reconnaissance and bombing, the DH-4 was so vulnerable to enemy fire that it was called the "flaming coffin" by its crews.

GROUND CREWS LOAD BOMBS In every air force, in every war, the fliers depend upon the ground crews for support. Without them, the war wouldn't last a day. Here, German enlisted personnel load bombs onto a Gotha G V, for later release over London. The German bombing raids caused such a furor that several badly needed RFC squadrons were withdrawn from the western front—just as the Germans had hoped.

SOPWITH PUP This photo captures the initiation of aviation carrier history, with Squadron Commander E. H. Dunning landing a Sopwith Pup on the converted light cruiser HMS *Furious* while it was underway on August 2, 1917. Sadly, only five days later, Dunning's triumph turned to tragedy; he was killed when his aircraft stalled and went over the side of the cruiser as he made a second landing attempt. It is interesting to note that the aircraft and the *Furious* traveled at nearly the same speed.

FLIGHT TIMELINE

June 13, 1917 Fourteen Gothas raid London, killing 162 civilians and injuring 432. The populace demands a home defense system.

July 1917 Sopwith Camel fighters, the most successful planes based on number of kills (1,294), go into action.

July 21, 1917 Congress approves a gigantic $640 million for S.C. Aviation Service. This amount is eight times more than all U.S. aviation allocations since 1898.

July 26, 1917 The Richthofen Flying Circus, a group of elite pilots, forms.

August 2, 1917 Squadron Commander E. H. Dunning lands a Sopwith Pup on the deck of the HMS *Furious*, becoming the first pilot to land on a moving ship. He is killed five days later trying to repeat this effort.

August 11, 1917 Billy Bishop earns the Victoria Cross for his role in an attack on an enemy airfield.

August 21, 1917 The first two Fokker triplanes arrive at Baron Manfred von Richthofen's base.

August 21, 1917 The first Liberty engine is flown in a L.W.F. Model F plane.

August 30, 1917 German ace Werner Voss flies a Fokker Dr I triplane into combat for the first time, scoring three aerial victories.

September 1917 A prototype of the Handley Page O/400—the best British bomber of the war—flies for the first time.

FOKKER DR I The Fokker Dr I triplane is usually associated with Baron Manfred von Richthofen, even though he scored most of his victories in Albatros fighters. The triplane was slow but had a remarkable rate of climb and was extremely maneuverable. Like many Fokker products of the time, it suffered quality control problems that limited its production to less than 300 aircraft. Many Dr Is were painted like this one, but von Richthofen's was mostly red.

PFALZ D III The sleek Pfalz D III was one of the most attractive looking but least publicized aircraft of World War I. Germany was a relatively new nation, and Bavaria had retained nominal control of its own armed forces and tried to equip its air force with products of Bavarian factories. The fuselage band of this handsome aircraft contains the Bavarian blue and white diamond pattern.

GEORGES GUYNEMER AND SHOT DOWN SPAD

The beloved French ace Captain Georges Guynemer is shown here by his SPAD, which was reportedly shot down by friendly French antiaircraft fire on September 24, 1916. Guynemer had a total of 53 victories when he was shot down once again on September 11, 1917, this time by Lieutenant Kurt Weissmann. His body was lost in an artillery barrage that covered the crash site. Guynemer flew a special cannon-armed SPAD XII for many of his victories. His death was a shock to the French, and French school children were taught that he had simply flown into a cloud and disappeared—the truth was too unbearable for old and young alike.

FLIGHT TIMELINE

September 11, 1917 French ace Georges Guynemer is shot down and killed.

September 17, 1917 Zeppelin-Staaken R planes, capable of carrying one-ton bombs, raid England.

September 23, 1917 Werner Voss is killed in a heroic, epic dogfight with the British No. 56 Squadron.

October 11, 1917 The RFC forms the 41st Wing, dedicated to strategic bombing.

October 29, 1917 The first American-made DH-4 flies with the #4 Liberty engine.

November 7, 1917 The Russian revolution begins.

November 18, 1917 The U.S. Navy begins combat operations with Tellier flying boats in France.

November 20, 1917 The Battle of Cambrai takes place. Low-level attacks on both sides set a future pattern for air-to-ground warfare.

November 21, 1917 The U.S. Navy demonstrates a radio-controlled flying bomb.

November 27, 1917 Benny Foulois takes over as the Chief of Air Service, American Expeditionary Force (AEF).

December 1917 Katherine Stinson sets an American cross-country duration record with a flight of nine hours and ten minutes, from San Diego to San Francisco.

JUNKERS J 1 Zeppelins were not the only aircraft with nomenclature problems. Junkers called this advanced armored attack plane the Junkers J 4, but it was designated the Junkers J 1 by German air force authorities. Although slow and difficult to maneuver, the J 1 was immensely strong, enabling it to operate in close cooperation with the troops on the front line. Some 277 J 1s were built, and they were often used to drop ammunition and rations to cut-off outposts.

SALMSON 2A.2 The Salmson 2A.2 was one of the most underrated observation planes of the war—but not by American crews. It was much more highly regarded than the de Havilland DH-4s that came later in the war. The Salmson was powered by an unusual Salmson water-cooled radial engine, which was very reliable.

CAPTURED HANDLEY PAGE The folding wings of the Handley Page bomber enabled it to be stowed in conventional hangars where its 100-foot wingspan would not have fit. This captured example is being inspected by German ground crews. They have already changed the insignia in preparation for flight tests. Testing enemy aircraft was practiced by both sides in both World Wars.

ZEPPELIN-STAAKEN R VI The Zeppelin-Staaken R VI was perhaps the best of the German "R" (*Riesenflugzeug*) planes. Its wingspan of slightly more than 138 feet was larger than any German bomber of World War II. It had a top speed of 84 miles per hour and was capable of carrying 4,400 pounds of bombs over short distances. The four 245-horsepower Maybach engines were mounted in tandem, and there were ten wheels to the undercarriage.

FLIGHT TIMELINE

January 1918 The Fokker D VII wins a fighter competition in Berlin.

January 19, 1918 The U.S. School of Aviation Medicine is founded.

January 23, 1918 The first U.S. Army balloon ascends in France.

February 1918 The first U.S. squadrons form in France.

February 16, 1918 A plant opens at Romorantin, France, to assemble American planes.

February 18, 1918 The 95th Aero Squadron, the first "all-American" unit, arrives in France.

March 21, 1918 A gigantic German offensive begins.

April 1918 Fokker D VIIs, the best fighters of the war, become operational.

April 1, 1918 Britain establishes the Royal Air Force (RAF) out of the Royal Flying Corps (RFC) and the Royal Naval Air Service (RNAS).

April 12, 1918 Zeppelins raid England. It is the last raid of the war to cause casualties.

April 13, 1918 An Argentine pilot, in a Morane-Saulnier Parasol, is the first to cross the Andes Mountains.

April 14, 1918 Lieutenants Douglas Campbell and Alan Winslow score the first U.S. air victories when they shoot down Pfalz and Albatros aircraft over their airdrome.

AIRMAIL SERVICE BEGINS The Curtiss JN-4H was used to inaugurate the first continuously scheduled airmail service between Washington, D.C., and New York City on May 15, 1918. The JN-4H was powered by a 150-horsepower Wright-Hispano engine and had a better performance than earlier Jennies. President and Mrs. Woodrow Wilson attended the takeoff ceremonies. Unfortunately, the New York–bound pilot got lost immediately after takeoff.

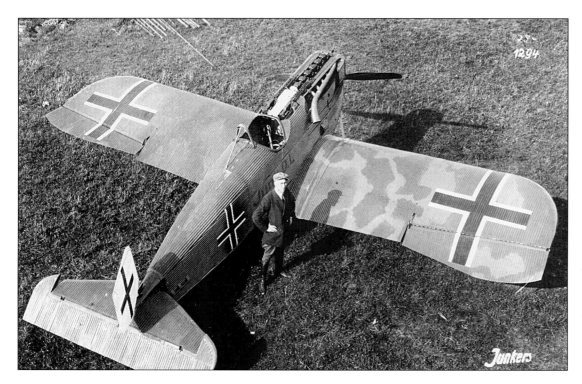

JUNKERS D 1 One of the most advanced aircraft of World War I was the German Junkers D 1 (called the J 9 by Junkers). The sleek cantilever-wing fighter was ordered into production, but only a few test aircraft got to the front. With a 185-horsepower B.M.W. engine, it was capable of 119 miles per hour. The all-metal construction was invaluable given the weather conditions on the western front.

LIEUTENANT DOUGLAS CAMPBELL The first American to become an ace flying with an American unit was Lieutenant Douglas Campbell, who had also scored the second American victory of the war. Campbell flew with Eddie Rickenbacker and others in the 94th Aero Squadron, which used the famous Hat in the Ring insignia.

BREGUET 14 Crews of the American 96th Observation Squadron received the Breguet 14 with enthusiasm. This sharp picture reveals the details of the ring-mounting, used for the rear defense, and the unusual automatic flaps of the Breguet. The engine was a 300-horsepower Renault. The Breguet 14 A.2 was an observation aircraft, while the 14 B.2 was a bomber.

DE HAVILLAND DH-4 After the war, the de Havilland DH-4 became the workhorse of the U.S. Army service. It was modified to place the pilot and observer closer together to improve teamwork, and many were rebuilt with steel tube fuselages. Powered by the 12-cylinder Liberty engine, many DH-4s were adapted to carry the mail.

FLIGHT TIMELINE

April 21, 1918 Baron Manfred von Richthofen is shot down and killed.

May 11, 1918 The first American-built DH-4 arrives in France.

May 15, 1918 The Packard LePere fighter flies.

May 15, 1918 The Army establishes airmail service between New York and Washington, D.C.

May 29, 1918 General John Pershing makes nonflyer Mason Patrick the Chief of Air Service, AEF.

June 5, 1918 Hugh Trenchard heads the "Independent Air Force" to attack the German homeland.

June 12, 1918 The first AEF bomber squadron, the 96th Aero Squadron, forms. Members fly French aircraft.

June 19, 1918 Francesco Baracca, the leading Italian ace with 34 victories, is killed.

July 9, 1918 Major James McCudden, one of Britain's top aces, is killed when his aircraft crashes on takeoff.

July 26, 1918 One-eyed pilot Mick Mannock, a British ace with 73 victories, is shot down in flames.

August 1918 Fokker D VII fighters score 565 kills in one month.

August 2, 1918 The first combat flight of an American DH-4 is a fiasco.

FOKKER E V The Fokker E V (later the D VIII) attained a top speed of 128 miles per hour on a 110-horsepower Oberursel rotary engine. It was clearly a design of the future, with its clean cantilever parasol wing, but the E V ran into the familiar Fokker quality control problems, and there were several crashes from wing failure. When the problem was remedied, the E V returned to battle as the D VIII. By then, the war was virtually over.

EDDIE RICKENBACKER Captain Eddie Rickenbacker got into flying the hard way, by giving up a lucrative career as a top auto racer (equivalent to $1 million earnings today) to become an enlisted chauffeur for the top brass. He then schemed to get into flying school and eventually talked his way into combat. He proved to be not only a great ace, with 26 official victories, but also a great leader, commanding the famous 94th Aero Squadron.

NIEUPORT 28 The Nieuport 28 obtained its top speed of 121 miles per hour from a 160-horsepower Gnome rotary engine. The aircraft was very maneuverable but had some inherent structural faults. The leading edge of the top would collapse in a dive, and the fuel lines would break from vibration and cause catastrophic fires. Despite this, American pilots, like this one in the 95th Aero Squadron, were glad to have them—they were better than no planes at all.

FOKKER D VII Considered by many historians to be the best fighter of World War I, the Fokker D VII was said to make good pilots of bad pilots and aces of good pilots. After winning a fighter competition in January 1918, the D VII began reaching combat units by March, and there were 700 in service by November 1918. The near-cantilever wings and the steel tube fuselage pointed to the future of fighter construction.

MARTIN BOMBER The United States was busily trying to create an aircraft industry with American-made designs that could enter combat if the war lasted through 1919. One of these was the Martin MB-1. Its performance with two 400-horsepower Liberty engines was superior to that of the Gotha, for it had a top speed of 100 miles per hour, a range of 560 miles, and a bomb load of up to 1,800 pounds.

FLIGHT TIMELINE

August 17, 1918 The Martin GMB, the first American-made bomber, makes its first flight.

August 21, 1918 The Nieuport 29, one of most important fighters of the 1920s, flies for the first time.

September 12–15, 1918 The Battle of St. Mihiel marks the largest deployment of aircraft in a single operation to date. Billy Mitchell commands 1,480 aircraft (including those in the service of French, British, U.S., and Italian air forces).

September 18, 1918 Major Rudolph Schroeder sets a world altitude record of 28,890 feet at McCook Field.

September 25, 1918 Eddie Rickenbacker earns the Medal of Honor for success in combat.

September 26, 1918 Leading French ace, Captain René Fonck, shoots down six German planes in one day, including four Fokker D VIIs.

September 28, 1918 Renegade Frank Luke is killed after shooting down 3 balloons to bring his total score to 21. As the second-ranking American ace, he receives a posthumous Medal of Honor.

October 2, 1918 The Kettering Bug, an early guided missile, makes its first flight.

October 24, 1918 The Fokker D VIII arrives at the front.

CAPTAIN WILLIAM G. BARKER
Canadian Captain William G. Barker scored 53 victories, the last of them in one of the epic dogfights of World War I. He entered the war in 1915 as a machine gunner but transferred to the Royal Flying Corps. Most of his victories were scored in Italy. His last three kills came in a heroic battle against 15 Fokker D VIIs on October 27, 1918. Badly wounded, he shot down three and was awarded the Victoria Cross.

BOEING AND AIRMAIL The first Boeing aircraft was the prototype of this handsome floatplane, the B & W Model C. It was designed by Navy Commander Conrad Westervelt and was test-flown by William E. Boeing himself. Two more were built, and then Boeing received an order for 50 Navy seaplane trainers. A replica of the B & W was built in 1966.

REGULAR FLIGHTS BETWEEN LONDON AND PARIS After the war, both France and Britain were eager to have airline service connect their capitals. Here, on February 8, 1919, a Farman Goliath of the *Compagnie des Grande Express Aériene,* piloted by Lucien Boussoutrot, is boarded by 15 passengers for the 150-minute flight from Le Bourget to London. About 360 of the Goliaths were built in 17 versions. The aircraft's top speed was 87 miles per hour; power was supplied by two reliable Salmson radial engines.

THOMAS-MORSE MB-3 Military procurement after World War I was very competitive. The Thomas-Morse Company of Ithaca, New York, won a competition with its SPAD-like MB-3 fighter. In the bidding to produce the aircraft, however, Boeing won and entered the fighter business with the MB-3A. Thomas-Morse never had another substantial contract, and Boeing went on to become a giant in the industry. In the 1929 Oscar-winning film *Wings,* MB-3As masqueraded as SPADs and Albatros D IIIs.

NC-4 FLYING BOAT The Curtiss Aeroplane and Engine Company became the largest manufacturer of aircraft in the United States during World War I, thanks to contracts for the Curtiss JN-4 Jenny trainer and a wide variety of naval flying boats. The largest and best of the flying boats was the NC-series, intended to fly across the ocean to war. Instead, on May 31, 1919, the NC-4 became the first aircraft to fly across the Atlantic.

FLIGHT TIMELINE

October 27, 1918 Major William Barker engages in an epic dogfight with 15 Fokker D VIIs. He scores three victories before he is shot down and wounded; he is awarded the Victoria Cross.

November 6–7, 1918 Robert Goddard demonstrates rockets before the military.

November 11, 1918 The armistice ends World War I.

December 4–22, 1918 Four JN-4s fly coast-to-coast.

1919 Many military aircraft are modified for civil use as transports, mail planes, and personal craft.

1919 The first Lawson airliner is designed.

February 5, 1919 The first sustained airline service starts with Deutsche Luft-Reederei between Berlin and Weimar, Germany.

March 1919 International air service opens between Vienna and Padua, Italy.

March 22, 1919 The first regular international passenger service begins between Paris and Brussels by Lignes Aeriennes Farman.

May 26, 1919 Robert H. Goddard's report on "A Method of Reaching Extreme Altitudes" is published by the Smithsonian Institution.

May 31, 1919 A Curtiss NC-4 completes the first transatlantic crossing.

NIEUPORT 29 Nieuport fighters were always good looking, but the most beautiful of them first flew on August 21, 1918. The Nieuport-Delage NiD 29 was too late for combat in World War I, but it became one of the most important fighters of the 1920s and was used by France, Spain, Belgium, Italy, Sweden, Argentina, and Japan. Specialized versions were used to set world speed records.

VICKERS VIMY One of the most important record setters in history, the Vickers Vimy was intended to bomb Germany when it first flew on November 21, 1917. None of the planes saw operational service, but John Alcock and Arthur Whitten Brown used the Vimy to cross the Atlantic nonstop for the first time; Ross and Keith Smith used a Vimy to fly from England to Australia.

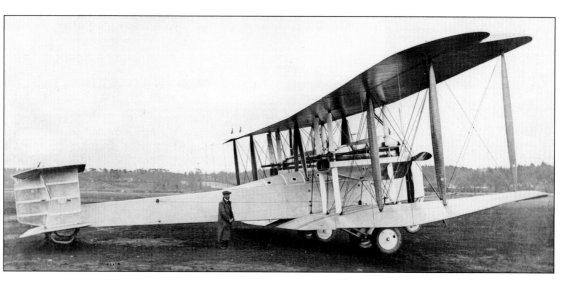

R-34 AIRSHIP The year 1919 was seminal for aviation, and the competition between heavier-than-air craft and lighter-than-air craft was intensified by the success of the Royal Air Forces R-34. Between July 2 and July 13, 1919, the R-34 made a successful round-trip crossing of the Atlantic.

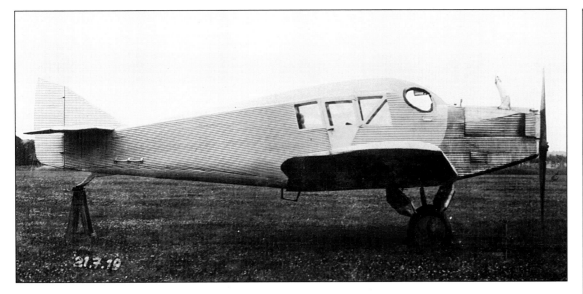

JUNKERS F 13 Little known today, the Junkers F 13 was a milestone in the development of air transports. First flown on June 26, 1919, it spawned a historic dynasty of transports that included the famous Junkers Ju-52/3m of World War II fame. Over time, 320 F 13s were built in many variants, but the importance of the design was the impetus it gave all-metal construction.

1919 TRANSCONTINENTAL RELIABILITY RACE Brigadier General Billy Mitchell made it his responsibility to gather public backing for the Air Service, and one of his first attempts was to hold the 1919 Transcontinental Reliability Race. Seventy-four planes entered; eight planes completed the race; and five men died in the process. Lieutenant Belvin W. Maynard, called "The Flying Parson," won in his modified DH-4, completing the round-trip on October 31, 1919, in 9 days, 4 hours, and 25 minutes.

FLIGHT TIMELINE

June 14–15, 1919 John Alcock and Arthur Whitten Brown make the first non-stop transatlantic flight in a Vickers Vimy.

July 2–13, 1919 The British Army R-34 airship makes a transatlantic round-trip flight.

October 24, 1919 Aeromarine opens an airline between Key West, Florida, and Cuba with three flying boats.

December 10, 1919 Ross and Keith Smith fly a Vickers Vimy from England to Australia.

1920 Zeppelin-Staaken's 18-passenger, 4-engine all-metal airliner is ready to test.

January 1920 Raymond Orteig offers a $25,000 prize to the first pilot who can make a nonstop flight from New York to Paris.

February 7, 1920 Joseph Sadi-Lecointe sets a world speed record of 171 miles per hour in a Nieuport 29.

February 27, 1920 Major R. W. Schroeder sets an altitude record of 33,113 feet in a Liberty-powered LePere.

May 1, 1920 The U.S. Navy begins experimental work with all-metal structures.

May 26, 1920 The Boeing G.A.-X twin-engine attack triplane is tested.

May 31, 1920 Italian pilots Arturo Ferrarin and Guido Masiero fly from Rome to Tokyo in SVA.9 biplanes.

BOEING MODEL B-1 Seattle was a natural place to think of building flying boats, and Boeing accepted the challenge with its Model B-1, which was used to fly the mail between Seattle and Victoria, Canada. The design heavily drew on the Curtiss HS-2Ls (of which Boeing built 50 for the Navy), but the Model B-1 was much smaller, so it was easier and more economical to operate. With a 200-horsepower Hall-Scott engine, it had a top speed of 90 miles per hour.

FOKKER F II PROTOTYPE Tony Fokker moved out of Germany at the close of World War I and quickly set up shop in his native Holland. He used the same design methods and manufacturing techniques to create a long line of successful transport aircraft beginning with this prototype of the Fokker F II five-passenger transport. About 30 were built, followed by a series of larger aircraft built to the same formula.

FLIGHT TIMELINE

June 4, 1920 The U.S. Army Air Service is created with 1,516 officers and 16,000 men authorized.

June 8, 1920 Lieutenant John E. Wilson makes a record parachute jump of 19,801 feet.

June 21, 1920 The Navy arranges to have J. V. Martin retractable gear installed on a Vought VE-7 airplane.

July 15–August 24, 1920 Four Air Service aircraft fly from New York to Nome, Alaska, and back.

August 2, 1920 Famous stunt pilot Omer Locklear is killed in a night flight in Los Angeles.

August 15, 1920 Laura Bromwell breaks the world loop-the-loop record for women with 87 consecutive loops.

September 8, 1920 A transcontinental mail route from New York to Chicago to San Francisco via plane/train is completed.

September 18, 1920 Rudolph Schroeder sets a record of 34,508 feet in a LePere.

September 30, 1920 Forty-seven Army Air Service aircraft crews report 832 forest fires.

October 1920 Donald W. Douglas organizes the David-Douglas Company to build the Cloudster.

DOUGLAS CLOUDSTER This carefully posed photo is truly history in the making, for it shows the building of the very first Douglas aircraft, the Cloudster. The Cloudster proved to be an instant success and led to a long line of commercial and military aircraft. Piloted by test pilot Eric Springer, the Cloudster first flew on February 24, 1921, and was the first aircraft ever able to lift a useful load exceeding its own weight.

VERVILLE VCP-R Some engineers are blessed by fate; some are cursed. The talented Alfred Verville fell into the latter group. He designed some of the greatest airplanes of the 1920s but never became a nationally known figure. This is his Verville VCP-R, which won the 1920 Pulitzer Trophy race at approximately 156.5 miles per hour, piloted by Lieutenant Corliss C. Moseley, standing here. A Junkers F 13 is visible in the background.

DAYTON-WRIGHT Perhaps the most advanced racing machine of the 1920s was the Dayton-Wright RB-1, the initials standing for Howard Rinehart and Milton C. Baumann, the principal designers. With its retractable landing gear and variable camber wings that used flaps on both leading and trailing edges, there was literally nothing like it. Unfortunately, it was plagued by technical problems and never achieved its full potential.

NIEUPORT 29 France's standard Nieuport fighter in the postwar years was often modified for racing, as was the case with this Nieuport 29V (for *vitesse*, or speed). In it, one of the all-time-champion racing pilots, Joseph Sadi-Lecointe, won the 1920 Gordon Bennett Cup race. This aircraft had its wings clipped so it would be faster yet retain its marvelous maneuverability. In it, Sadi-Lecointe became the first pilot to exceed 300 kilometers (171 miles) per hour.

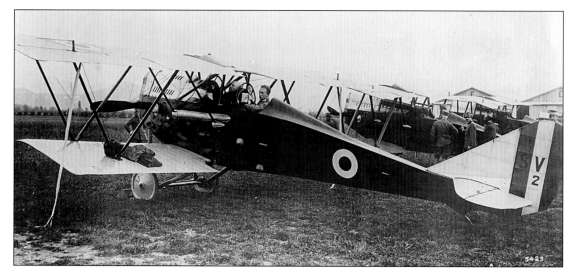

ANSALDO The Italian Air Force, like the U.S. Air Force, had used many foreign designs during World War I and wished to have Italy produce its own aircraft. The Ansaldo S.V.A.5 was one of the best of these, and it was developed into a two-seater, shown nearest here, as the S.V.A.9 and S.V.A.10. The S.V.A.5 fighter version, with a 265-horsepower S.P.A. engine, had a top speed of 140 miles per hour.

SAVOIA The 1920 Schneider Trophy went to this Savoia S.12*bis,* powered by a 480-horsepower Ansaldo San Giorgio engine. Flown by Commandante Luigi Bologna, the flying boat had lap speeds of about 106 miles per hour. Eight other contestants withdrew, so it was an easy win. The era of the flying boat racer would not last much longer since faster seaplanes were about to emerge.

CIERVA C.6 The concept of vertical flight has always haunted aeronautical engineers. One approach, not as difficult to manufacture as a helicopter, was the autogiro. The autogiro rotor was not powered, as is a helicopter rotor, and rotates from the forward motion of the autogiro. Juan de la Cierva discovered that flexible rotors could be articulated to offset the imbalance between advancing and retreating blades. The Cierva C.6 is shown here.

FLIGHT TIMELINE

November 1, 1920 Regular U.S. international passenger service begins between Key West, Florida, and Havana, Cuba, with Aeromarine-West Indies Airways.

November 1, 1920 The Sperry Messenger is tested.

November 4, 1920 The U.S. Navy continues a series of bombing tests against the obsolete battleship USS *Indiana.*

November 24, 1920 The prototype Dornier Delphin (Dolphin), antecedent of the famous Wal (Whale), flies.

November 25, 1920 Lieutenant Corliss C. Moseley wins the first Pulitzer Trophy in a Verville VCP-R Racer at 156.5 miles per hour.

December 14, 1920 The first fatal accident in scheduled air service occurs when a Handley Page O/400 crashes at Cricklewood, England.

1921 George de Bothezat, a Russian-born engineer working for the U.S. Air Service, builds a large, complex helicopter that is moderately successful.

1921 The Soviets establish a laboratory for research on solid-propellant rockets.

1921 Soviets begin initial airline service with a demilitarized Il'ya Muromets-type aircraft.

January 10, 1921 A "W" style, 700-horsepower, 18-cylinder engine is tested at McCook Field.

STAAKEN E 4/20 The most advanced airliner in the world in 1920, the all-metal, cantilever-wing Staaken E 4/20 was designed by Albert Rohrbach. Four 245-horsepower Maybach engines powered the Staaken, which carried a crew of 2 and 18 passengers. The Allied Control Commission deemed it dangerous as a possible warplane and forced it to be scrapped, a great loss to aviation. It might have been seen as too great a commercial threat as well.

LIEUTENANT WILLIAM D. CONEY Lieutenant William Coney was tasked to fly from coast-to-coast in a DH-4 in less than 24 hours. He did so on February 24, 1921, flying from San Diego to Jacksonville, Florida, in 22 hours, 27 minutes. On March 25, 1921, he began the return trip, leaving from Jacksonville, Florida. His engine gave him trouble, and, lost in a fog, he crashed into a tree. He was injured so severely that he died five days later. Accident rates were incredibly high for the first 60 years of flight.

JACK KNIGHT Known as "the hero of the airmail," James H. "Jack" Knight was as tough as he looks, for it took guts to successfully fly the mail at night and in adverse weather. He is shown here in a much-modified de Havilland DH-4, equipped with a "one-man" sending and receiving radio set. The five-tube transmitter and the seven-tube receiver were the most advanced electronics in the air at the time.

FOKKER F III Name recognition was important in merchandising aircraft in the 1920s, just as it is today. The great flyer Bert Acosta lent his name to the Acosta Aircraft Corporation, which boasted of this Fokker F III passenger plane. Note that the cockpit is still open, with instruments mounted on the wing root over the pilot's head.

FLIGHT TIMELINE

January 26, 1921 The U.S. Post Office reports daily flights over 3,460 miles of routes.

February 18, 1921 C. C. Eversole makes a freestyle parachute escape from a U.S. DH-4.

February 22–23, 1921 Jack Frye and others complete the first coast-to-coast airmail flight in 33 hours, 20 minutes.

February 24, 1921 Lieutenant William D. Coney completes a solo transcontinental flight from Rockwell Field, San Diego, to Jacksonville, Florida, in 22 hours, 27 minutes. On March 25, 1921, he is mortally injured in a crash on the return flight.

February 24, 1921 The Douglas Cloudster, the first in a long line of Douglas aircraft, flies.

March 23, 1921 Lieutenant Arthur Hamilton makes a 23,700-foot parachute drop at Chanute Field, Illinois.

April 14, 1921 KLM introduces the Fokker F III five-passenger airliner. This begins a period of Fokker airline dominance.

May 1921 The McCook Field–designed, Boeing-built G.A.-X flies for the first time. The armored, twin-engine triplane attack bomber, with eight machine guns and a cannon, is a failure.

June 9, 1921 The National Advisory Committee for Aeronautics (NACA) authorizes the construction of a wind tunnel at Langley Aeronautical Laboratory.

MARTIN MB-2 This is the very first of the production Martin MB-2 bombers that were Brigadier General Billy Mitchell's pride and joy. Martin built 20, and another 85 were built by competitors. They made history by sinking the ex-German battleship *Ostfriesland* in the July 1921 bombing trials off the Virginia Cape. Powered by two 420-horsepower Liberty engines, the MB-2s had a top speed of 99 miles per hour and a range of 558 miles.

BOEING G.A.-X In the 1920s, the Air Service's engineering division sometimes created designs and hired companies to build them. Such was the case with the Boeing G.A.-X, an armored triplane intended for ground attack. Test pilot Harold R. Harris used to roar with laughter when he told of the incredible noise made by the two Liberty engines rattling the armor plate. The aircraft was overweight and slow and did not get much use.

VICKERS VERNON The relatively sleek Vickers Vimy was developed into the portly Vickers Vernon transport, which served in the Middle East to help enforce Great Britain's "air control" policy during the 1920s. Although ungainly looking and decidedly slow at a maximum speed of 103 miles per hour, the Vernons did good work as transports, air ambulances, and cargo planes.

R-38 British engineers designed and built the R-38 based on information gathered from examining crashed Zeppelins. They then altered the information to suit their own ideas. This resulted in a loss of structural integrity. The United States' offer to buy the R-38 was quickly accepted, and an American crew began training to fly it. On August 24, 1921, on its fourth flight, the R-38 broke up in the air. Forty-two people were killed; only two survived.

DOUGLAS CLOUDSTER Curiously enough, the very first Douglas aircraft, the Cloudster, had the characteristic look of most Douglas aircraft to come in that it was obviously sturdy, neatly but not radically streamlined, and extremely functional in appearance. The success of the Cloudster led to orders for Navy torpedo planes and ultimately to orders for the Douglas World Cruiser, the first aircraft to fly around the world.

FLIGHT TIMELINE

July 12–21, 1921 Brigadier General Billy Mitchell's Martin MB-2 bombers sink the battleship *Ostfriesland* in a demonstration attack.

July 29, 1921 Brigadier General Billy Mitchell leads 17 bombers in an exhibition "raid" on New York City.

August 1, 1921 Preliminary tests begin on what will become the Norden bomb-sight.

August 4, 1921 Lieutenant John Macready, USAS, flies the first crop duster, using a Curtiss JN-4D conversion.

August 11, 1921 Simulated deck landing tests begin in anticipation of the first U.S. aircraft carrier, the USS *Langley*, becoming operational.

August 24, 1921 An American-owned British dirigible R-38 breaks up in the air; 42 people die.

September 23, 1921 The United States Air Service continues bomb tests, sinking the USS *Alabama*.

September 28, 1921 John Macready sets a world altitude record of 34,509 feet in a LePere LUSAC-11.

October 15, 1921 Compania Espanola de Trafico Aeroeo, predecessor of Iberia airlines, begins operations.

November 5, 1921 Bert Acosta wins the Pulitzer Trophy race in a Curtiss Racer at 176.7 miles per hour.

REFUELING The world has grown accustomed to the magic of aerial refueling, with giant Boeing tankers off-loading fuel to fighters and bombers all over the world. It all began here, on November 12, 1921, with a heroic Wesley May climbing from Frank Hawk's Lincoln Standard to Earl Daugherty's Curtiss Canuck, carrying a five-gallon container of gas for the world's first aerial refueling. The two men were giants in those days!

BERT ACOSTA WINS PULITZER Bert Acosta was one of the most glamorous of the early aviators. He is shown here in front of the Curtiss factory with the Pulitzer Trophy he won at Omaha, Nebraska, in November 1921. He was not flying this aircraft but a similar Curtiss CR-2. He won the Pulitzer averaging about 177 miles per hour. The Curtiss racers were the beginning of a dynasty that would dominate the industry for the next decade.

November 12, 1921 The first air-to-air refueling: Wesley May steps from the wing of a Lincoln Standard to the wing of a Curtiss Canuck with a five-gallon can of fuel strapped to his back.

November 15, 1921 The airship ROMA flies for the first time at Langley Field, Virginia.

December 1, 1921 Helium is used for the first time in an airship, the nonrigid Navy C-7.

December 29, 1921 A world endurance record of 26 hours, 18 minutes, 35 seconds is set in a Junkers-Larson BMW (Junkers 13).

January 16, 1922 The Navy issues parachutes for use in heavier-than-air craft.

February 7, 1922 The Lawrance J-1 radial engine completes a 50-hour test. This will lead to a revolution in engines.

March 13–June 16, 1922 Portuguese pilots fly from Lisbon to Brazil in Fairey III aircraft.

March 20, 1922 The U.S. Navy commissions its first aircraft carrier, the USS *Langley*.

March 23, 1922 A NACA report shows that the jet engine would consume four times more fuel than a piston engine at 250 miles per hour but would be more efficient at altitude.

CAPRONI TRIPLANE FLYING BOAT Even great firms like Caproni sometimes have engineering lapses. This was the case with the far too ambitious Caproni Ca 60 Triple Hydro-Triplane, which was intended to carry 100 passengers and serve as a prototype for an even larger version. It made an initial flight of about one mile, but a second attempt resulted in a crash.

BREGUET 19 Derived from the Breguet 14, the model 19 was as successful in peace as the 14 had been in war, with some 2,000 being built between 1923 and 1927. The Breguet 19 was widely exported and was used by both sides in the Spanish Civil War. While its performance was moderate—a top speed of 133 miles per hour and a range of 500 miles—it was rugged and easy to repair in the field.

USS LANGLEY The birth of American sea-borne airpower occurred with the commissioning of the USS *Langley*, a collier converted to an aircraft carrier. It served as a training ship and perished during World War II while it was ferrying Curtiss P-40s to the Far East. Seen landing is the rare Martin MO-1 observation plane.

FOKKER D XIII The classic Fokker D VII lines remain in the much cleaner and more powerful Fokker D XIII, which, with its English Napier Lion engine of 570 horsepower, could reach a top speed of 168 miles per hour. The D XIII is historically important because it was used by the clandestine predecessor of the Luftwaffe to train pilots at Lipetsk, Russia, during the 1930s.

BERLINER HELICOPTER Emil Berliner (the inventor of the Victor phonograph) had begun experimentation with vertical flight in 1908. Working with his son Henry, his 1922 attempt included rotors mounted on wings and driven by an engine mounted on the fuselage nose. A third rotor, mounted in the rear, was used to increase or decrease lift. The rotors proved to be too small, and the wings interfered with the air flow, so the aircraft was abandoned.

SUPERMARINE SEA LION Considered by some to be a great aviation proponent and by many others an annoyance, Noel Pemberton-Billing founded the Supermarine Aircraft Company, which specialized in seaplanes. Flown by Henry Biard, the Sea Lion won the 1922 Schneider Cup at 145.7 miles per hour. The plane could hit 160 miles per hour on the straightaway. Its configuration presaged the later utilitarian Supermarine Sea Walrus (affectionately known as the "Shagbat"), which saved so many RAF pilots' lives during World War II.

DOOLITTLE IN DH-4 Lieutenant Jimmy Doolittle used a de Havilland DH-4 to make the first coast-to-coast flight in less than 24 hours. Flying from Florida to California on September 4, 1922, Doolittle did the trip in 21 hours and 19 minutes, with one stop for fuel, shown here, at Kelly Field in Texas. Doolittle was not only a great pilot but a real intellect, earning his masters and doctorate from M.I.T. between October 1923 and June 1925.

FLIGHT TIMELINE

April 1922 Germany and the Soviet Union set up a secret training and manufacturing base in the Soviet Union for Germany's use.

April 7, 1922 The first midair collision between passenger airliners takes place in France when a D.H.18 and a Farman-Goliath collide. All of the crew members are killed, along with seven passengers.

April 25, 1922 Eddie Stinson completes a successful test of the Stout ST-1, the Navy's first all-metal airplane.

May 1922 The Breguet 19 bomber prototype flies; it will become the most widely used military aircraft between the wars.

June 10, 1922 Guglielmo Marconi states that radar could be used in fog or thick weather to identify passing ships.

June 12, 1922 Captain A. W. Stephens (later a famous balloonist) makes a parachute jump from a supercharged Martin MB-2 at 24,206 feet.

June 16, 1922 Henry Berliner demonstrates a helicopter at College Park, Maryland; on July 16, it hovers at 12 feet.

August 12, 1922 Henry Biard pilots a Supermarine Sea Lion to win the Schneider Cup at 145.7 miles per hour.

September 4, 1922 The Curtiss R-6 is flown for the first time at Curtiss Field, New York.

NIEUPORT-DELAGE Engineers designing racing planes could often come up with very streamlined wings, fuselages, and tail surfaces, but in the early days, they still had to contend with high-drag radiators, struts, and landing gears. The barrel-shaped objects in the landing gear of the Nieuport-Delage racer are the (relatively) low-drag Lamblin radiators. Georges Kirsch won the 60,000-franc 1921 Coupe Deutsch race in this sleek sesquiplane aircraft at 173 miles per hour.

DE HAVILLAND D.H.9A While racers grew sleeker, the workhorse aircraft stayed pretty much the same, as this drag-laden de Havilland D.H.9A clearly shows. Flown in the hot temperatures of the Middle East and India, the broad wings of the de Havilland still generated enough lift to fly well. These aircraft were used in British "air control" tactics, which maintained peace among the warring tribes from the air—at considerably less expense than using ground forces.

CURTISS R-6 The Curtiss racers were designed to intrigue the U.S. military with their performance and the promise of their conversion to a fighter aircraft. The CR series, designed by Mike Thurston and Henry Routh, were very clean biplanes, which used the Curtiss CD-12 engine. The CR series inspired the Curtiss R-6, which won the 1922 Pulitzer Trophy. This aircraft, flown by Lieutenant Lester J. Maitland, placed second at 198.8 miles per hour.

VOUGHT VE-7 One of the least famous but most valuable early airplanes to the U.S. Navy was the Vought VE-7, shown here taking off from the United States' first aircraft carrier, the USS *Langley*. The Vought VE-7 was also used by the Army Air Service. The hooks on the landing-gear spreader bar were used to engage wires on the *Langley*'s deck upon landing. The VE-7 led to a long line of scouting aircraft and, ultimately, to the Corsair.

FLIGHT TIMELINE

September 4, 1922 Jimmy Doolittle flies a de Havilland DH-4B from Florida to California in 21 hours, 19 minutes.

September 14, 1922 The L.W.F. Owl, the largest plane yet built for air service, makes its first flight.

September 20, 1922 Joseph Sadi-Lecointe, in a Nieuport-Delange 29, is the first to set a world air speed record exceeding 200 miles per hour. He averages 212.01 miles per hour.

September 27, 1922 Radar is demonstrated at the Naval Aircraft Radio Lab.

September 27, 1922 The Navy has its first mass torpedo practice against live targets by Torpedo One; 8 hits out of 17 launches.

October 6, 1922 Oakley Kelly and John Macready make a duration flight of 35 hours, 18 minutes, 30 seconds in a Fokker T-2.

October 14, 1922 Curtiss R-6 racers finish first and second in the Pulitzer Trophy race.

October 17, 1922 Lieutenant V. C. Griffin makes the first takeoff from an American aircraft carrier, the USS *Langley*, in a Vought VE-7.

October 18, 1922 Brigadier General Billy Mitchell sets the world air speed record at 222.97 miles per hour in a Curtiss R-6.

U.S.D. 9A The Engineering Division at McCook Field designed the U.S.D. 9A as an improved version of the de Havilland DH-4. The U.S.D. 9A was a fine airplane, especially useful in experiments as with this very early version of a controllable pitch propeller. Tests like these often inspired civilian manufacturers to come up with their own version of what was obviously a needed product. Army aircraft of the period were always beautifully maintained, as this gleaming example shows.

AEROMARINE AND USS LANGLEY This is a beautiful shot of an Aeromarine 39-B about to land on the USS *Langley*. Of interest are the arresting wires stretched across the deck and the funnel exhausting at the side of the *Langley*, which had been converted from a collier and named after Samuel Pierpont Langley. The Aeromarine's big wings provided plenty of lift, and its landing speed was not much greater than the *Langley*'s forward speed, but it was still a hazardous operation.

DORNIER WAL This is the twin-engine Dornier Wal (Whale), which was used on many distance, rescue, and exploration flights and became the most influential flying boat of its time. First flown on November 6, 1922, the Wal was built in Italy first, followed by Japan, Spain, the Netherlands, and Switzerland before at last being produced in Germany. With its rugged structure, it could operate in relatively rough seas and also withstand catapult operation from mid-ocean refueling ships.

VICKERS VIRGINIA The prototype of a long series of successful aircraft, this is the number one Vickers Virginia, first flown on November 24, 1922. Note the machine gun positions in the upper wings, which provided both great defensive power and a lot of drag. They were removed in later aircraft. The Virginia served as the RAF's primary heavy bomber from 1924 until the mid 1930s. Its top speed was 108 miles per hour, and the range was 985 miles.

DE BOTHEZAT HELICOPTER On December 18, 1922, the impressive-looking de Bothezat helicopter was flown successfully at McCook Field, Ohio, by Colonel Thurman Bane for 1 minute, 42 seconds at an altitude of six feet. Designed by Dr. George de Bothezat, a Russian émigré and mathematician, the helicopter flew twice more, once lifting five people. It demonstrated a high degree of inherent stability and might well have been developed further.

LIEUTENANT RUSSELL MAUGHAN AND CURTISS R-6 The sleek series of Curtiss racers served both the Army and the Navy well and fostered a long line of biplane fighters. Lieutenant Russell Maughan won the 1922 Pulitzer Trophy in an R-6 at 205.8 miles per hour; in second place was Lieutenant Lester J. Maitland (also in an R-6) at 198.8 miles per hour. Four days later, Brigadier General Billy Mitchell set a world speed record of 222.97 miles per hour in an R-6.

FLIGHT TIMELINE

October 20, 1922 Harold R. Harris makes the first emergency parachute jump, leaping from a Loening M-8 after a collision with a Fokker monoplane.

October 23, 1922 The American Propeller Company demonstrates a reversible pitch propeller.

October 26, 1922 Lieutenant Godfrey DeChevalier makes the first landing on the USS *Langley* in an Aeromarine 39-B.

November 2, 1922 Qantas starts scheduled service.

November 6, 1922 The prototype Dornier J Wal makes its first flight. It will become one of the most important flying boats of the era.

November 11, 1922 Etienne Oehmichen sets a record in his helicopter for straight-line, flying 1,181 feet; on November 17, he flies 1,722 feet.

December 18, 1922 Colonel Thurman Bane flies a de Bothezat helicopter for 1 minute, 42 seconds at McCook Field.

December 27, 1922 Japan commissions its first aircraft carrier, *Hosho*. It is one of only a few Japanese ships to survive World War II.

January 5, 1923 Cloud seeding is accomplished over McCook Field.

January 9, 1923 Juan de la Cierva makes an officially observed flight in a C-4 autogiro.

AIRMAIL SERVICE This photograph depicts two stalwarts of the time, the modified de Havilland DH-4 mail plane and the Ford Model T mail truck. This scene was repeated many times at the tiny airports that serviced the airmail routes, with the heavy sacks of mail being stowed in the forward mail compartment. With few instruments, fewer navigation aids, and frequently bad weather, flying the mail was a hazardous occupation. Icing was a particular hazard in the wire-braced biplanes.

BOEING PW-9 After its success with the MB-3A, Boeing wanted to stay in the fighter game and developed a series of its own designs, beginning with the Model 15, the XPW-9. This is the second prototype, showing its clean nose entry, unequal span wings, and "N" strut bracing. Less visible was the very streamlined tunnel radiator. Both the Army and the Navy bought production versions, starting the long fighter competition with Curtiss. Its top speed was 160 miles per hour.

FOKKER T-2 The Fokker T-2 was flown by Lieutenants Oakley G. Kelly and John A. Macready across the United States on May 2–3, 1923, posting world records for distance (2,516.55 miles), endurance (26 hours, 50 minutes), and for speeds over 1,500, 2,000, 2,500, 3,500, and 4,000 kilometers. The pilot sat right next to the Liberty engine. An auxiliary pilot's position in the fuselage enabled them to trade off flying duties.

SISKIN III Like the United States, Great Britain used to parcel out its production orders carefully to keep as many manufacturers in business as possible. When Armstrong-Whitworth won a fighter competition with its Siskin, it was not long before Bristol, Gloster, Vickers, and Blackburn were building them under contract. Redesigned with an all-metal structure as the Siskin III, the aircraft served as a first-line fighter until 1932. Its top speed of 156 miles per hour was typical for the period.

FLIGHT TIMELINE

February 7, 1923 Lieutenant Russell Meredith wins the Distinguished Flying Cross by flying a doctor to a dying man on Meredith Island, across frozen Lake Michigan.

February 21, 1923 The de Bothezat helicopter achieves sustained flight for 2 minutes and 45 seconds at an altitude of 15 feet.

March 5, 1923 Igor Sikorsky starts his firm, Sikorsky Aero Engineering Corporation, in the United States.

March 5, 1923 An auxiliary jettisonable gas tank is fitted to a Thomas-Morse MB-3A fighter. This extends the aircraft's range to 400 miles.

March 29, 1923 Lieutenant Lester Maitland sets a speed record of 239.92 miles per hour in a Curtiss R-6.

March 29, 1923 Lieutenants Harold R. Harris and Ralph Lockwood set a world speed record for 1,000 kilometers at 127.24 miles per hour in a specially modified DH-4L.

April 17, 1923 Lieutenant Harold R. Harris sets two speed records in a DH-4L: 114.35 miles per hour (1,500 kilometers) and 114.22 miles per hour (2,000 kilometers).

April 17, 1923 USN Lieutenant Rutledge Irvine sets a world altitude record with a 1,000-kilogram load: 11,609 feet in a Douglas DT over McCook Field.

CURTISS PW-8 Curtiss put its racing experience into its fighter designs, as is evident in this beautiful prototype of the Curtiss PW-8. One innovation for fighters was the use of wing surface radiators (the dark sections on the upper wing) instead of a higher-drag conventional radiator. It added greatly to speed but was a maintenance nightmare and would have been impractical in combat. It was replaced on production aircraft with the tunnel radiator developed by Boeing.

BARLING BOMBER The Air Service was always fascinated by big airplanes. The Engineering Division/Witteman Lewis/Barling Bomber was big in name, wingspan (120 feet), weight (42,569 pounds), and number of engines (six)—but it was short on performance. Designed by Walter Barling, the aircraft set some weight-to-altitude records, but its inability to carry bombs over any distance condemned it to failure.

AERIAL REFUELING The desirability of aerial refueling was evident to all, and successive experiments were made to develop the technique. Here 1st Lieutenants Lowell H. Smith and John P. Richter are refueling in a DH-4B from another DH-4. In late August 1923, they set an endurance record of 37 hours, 15 minutes, after refueling from two alternate refuelers. Smith kept the Liberty engine running by banging on the Lunkenheimer fuel valve every few minutes with a hammer.

USS *SHENANDOAH* The U.S. Navy saw the dirigible as a sensible means of reconnaissance, particularly when filled with safe helium as a lifting agent. The USS *Shenandoah* flew for the first time on September 4, 1923, and was sent around the country showing the Navy's flag. The *Shenandoah* broke up in a storm over Ava, Ohio, on September 3, 1925; 14 members of the 43-person crew were killed.

FLIGHT TIMELINE

May 2–3, 1923 U.S. Army Lieutenants Oakley Kelly and John Macready make the first nonstop coast-to-coast flight in 26 hours, 50 minutes in the Fokker T-2.

May 14, 1923 A prototype Curtiss PW-8 fighter is received by the USAS, the beginning of a long line of Curtiss biplane fighters.

May 26, 1923 Lieutenant H. G. Crocker completes a nonstop, transcontinental, south to north flight in a DH-4B, flying from Houston, Texas, to Gordon, Ontario, in 11 hours, 55 minutes.

June 6–7, 1923 The Navy sets 15 records for Class C seaplanes.

June 20, 1923 The all-metal Gallaudet CO-1 flies for the first time.

June 26, 1923 Lieutenants Lowell H. Smith and John P. Richter achieve the world's first complete midair hose refueling.

August 21, 1923 Navigation beacon lights between Chicago and Cheyenne are completed.

August 22, 1923 The giant Barling Bomber makes its first flight.

September 4, 1923 The Navy dirigible USS *Shenandoah* makes its first flight.

September 5, 1923 Air Service planes sink the decommissioned USS *Virginia* and *New Jersey*.

SPERRY MESSENGER Lawrence Sperry was the son of Elmer Sperry, who pioneered the use of the gyroscope in instruments. Lawrence built the Sperry Messenger, which had been designed by the Engineering Division. The Messenger was a small biplane intended for the same kind of liaison work done by the Piper Cub in World War II. Sperry was lost in a flight over the English Channel on December 13, 1923. The plane was recovered, but Sperry was never found.

CURTISS R2C-1 The Curtiss line was developed into the R2C-1 series of racers, which were slightly larger and carried a 507-horsepower Curtiss D-12A engine. Lieutenant Alford Williams won the 1923 Pulitzer Trophy race at 243.68 miles per hour and later raised the world speed record to 266.6 miles per hour in a sister ship.

CURTISS CR-3 SCHNEIDER CUP WINNER Lieutenant David Rittenhouse flew the beautiful little Curtiss CR-3 racer to victory in the 1923 Schneider Trophy race, winning at an average speed of 181 miles per hour. Second place went to Lieutenant Rutledge Irvine, also in a CR-3, and running at 173.347 miles per hour. Floatplanes could be faster than landplanes, despite the drag of the floats, because water provided a longer takeoff and landing run. The aircraft was powered by a 485-horsepower Curtiss D-12 engine.

GLOSTER GREBE The Gloster Grebe was typical of British fighters of the period and served from 1923 to 1928. Differing little in concept from World War I fighters, the Grebe was an open-cockpit biplane with fixed gear and a fixed-pitch propeller. The armament was the standard two .303 Vickers machine guns. It was a delightful aircraft to fly and excelled in formation maneuvers. Top speed with a 400-horsepower Jaguar radial engine was 151 miles per hour.

DIXMUDE One of the great mysteries of aviation was the sudden disappearance of the French airship *Dixmude,* formerly the German L 72. The Germans had built L 72 as a lightweight high-altitude bomber; the French intended to employ it as a low-level test vehicle for airship routes between France's African colonies. On December 18, 1923, the *Dixmude* departed on another trip—and disappeared. Charred wreckage found later indicated it might have been struck by lightning.

FLIGHT TIMELINE

September 28, 1923 Lieutenant David Rittenhouse wins the Schneider Trophy for the United States in a Navy Curtiss CR-3 racer at 181 miles per hour.

October 1–6, 1923 The National Air races take place in St. Louis.

October 6, 1923 The Navy's Lieutenant Alford Williams wins the Pulitzer Trophy in a Curtiss R2C-1 racer at 243.68 miles per hour.

October 10, 1923 The *Shenandoah,* the first dirigible to use helium, is christened.

November 1, 1923 Robert Goddard's first small liquid-fuel rocket is tested.

November 4, 1923 USN Lieutenant Alford Williams sets a world speed record of 266.6 miles per hour in a Curtiss R2C-1.

November 6, 1923 USN Lieutenant Alford Williams sets a time-to-climb record: 5,000 feet in one minute in a Curtiss R2C-1.

December 13, 1923 Lawrence Sperry crashes his Messenger in the English Channel. The plane is recovered, but Sperry's body is never found.

CHAPTER THREE

1924 to 1933:

The Heart of the Golden Age of Flight

Aviation matured during this decade, going from the reckless youth of global war through a rebellious adolescence that paralleled the ribald excesses of the Jazz Age and finally emerging ruefully adult and sobered by the depression that wracked the world. Some of the most famous aviation manufacturers would begin business; some of the most beautiful aircraft in history would be created; and some of the most famous flyers would blaze their way across the horizon. Civilian aviation would first catch up with and then surpass military aviation in performance and technology. Aircraft would be used in wars around the world. Although small in scale compared to World War I, these conflicts illustrated an ongoing need for the air weapon—even in minor battles.

Ryan *Spirit of St. Louis*

Like the rest of the business world, the business of aviation would see a boom and bust during this decade. Military spending was at a standstill despite the desire—even the need—for improved military aircraft. Most nations adopted the policy of fostering the survival of aircraft companies by sharing out very small contracts as widely as possible so each management team and its engineers could be maintained intact, along with a small skilled workforce.

The military also adopted the very sound practice of using its aircraft and pilots to set records that grasped the public's attention. Thus, in 1924, the United States sent its four Douglas World Cruisers on the first successful aerial circumnavigation of the world. Great Britain, Italy, and the United States battled it out for the honor of winning the Schneider Trophy, and Great Britain succeeded with its remarkable Supermarine seaplanes. Germany, still recovering from the violent economic aftermath of losing the war, contributed with the magnificent *Graf Zeppelin*, by far the most successful of all the great airships. For its part, France set dozens of speed and distance records, making the names of flyers like Joseph Sadi-Lecointe, Dieudonne Costes, and Maurice Bellonte famous around the world.

It was also in 1924 that aviation contributed one of the most important innovations in its history, the introduction of crop dusting by the Huff-Daland Dusters. This was the start of what is now known as "agricultural aviation." The Dusters were originally used to spray insecticides on crops, but the aircraft were soon used for disease control, planting crops, stocking fish, fighting forest fires, and a hundred other compassionate uses that saved tens of millions of lives and trillions of dollars in commerce.

While the government sustained (barely) the military manufacturers, the civilian industry depended on investments to build its factories and sales to sustain them. The 1920s saw three factors that helped the civilian industry greatly. The first was the gradual disappearance of war surplus aircraft due to crashes and wear and tear. It was possible to buy a Curtiss Jenny for as little as $150 in 1920, but it was more difficult to do so in 1926. The second was the unprecedented boom in the stock market, which, in the United States in particular, made the initial offering of stock sales from virtually unknown and completely unproven companies both easy and profitable. The third was by far the most important and that was the flight of Charles Lindbergh from New York to Paris in his Ryan monoplane on May 20–21, 1927. The aviation bonfire was burning when Lindbergh took off, but his flight had the effect of throwing a bucket of gasoline on the fire.

There were a number of explanations for Lindbergh's effect upon the popular imagination. The contest for the Orteig Prize was dramatic; it was a challenging flight that had already incurred several fatalities by the time Lindbergh arrived in New York to begin his attempt. The competition was severe. The well-liked and well-organized Richard Byrd was standing by in his formidable Fokker trimotor, while the disorganized and disliked Charles Levine was casting about for a pilot for his proven Bellanca. Lindbergh was an underdog, and the public likes an underdog. Ten days before Lindbergh took off, two famous French flyers, the great ace Charles Nungesser and Francois Coli, were lost in their own transatlantic attempt. The odds seemed stacked against Lindbergh when he made his now-famous bumpy early-morning takeoff from Roosevelt Field.

Lindbergh succeeded where all others had failed. Even more important, he turned out to be a handsome, well-spoken, intelligent individual who, with

Supermarine S.6B

Lockheed Vega

becoming modesty, perfectly fulfilled the role of hero not only for America but for the world.

Lindbergh made aviation come alive, giving it a spark that sent it soaring to new heights with the advent of a series of innovations, including the reliable Wright Whirlwind engine that had powered the *Spirit of St. Louis*.

The new and powerful sentiment for aviation was reflected in the popular culture of the time. Aviation films, including the first film ever to win an Oscar, *Wings*, were extremely well received. For the wealthy, it became as socially progressive to own an aircraft as to own a yacht, and the fine old magazine *The Sportsman Pilot* lovingly recorded the comings and goings of the rich and famous all over the country. Aircraft were used by businesses for practical tasks such as flying along pipelines, making swift delivery of photographs for newspapers, and, to a very limited degree, serving as executive aircraft.

But records and racing caught the public imagination, and heroes emerged to follow in Lindbergh's mighty footsteps. Among them was Amelia Earhart, who resembled Lindbergh so much in physical appearance and in her mannerisms that she was inevitably called "the Lady Lindy." Jimmy Doolittle, who had earned his doctorate in aeronautical engineering at M.I.T., flew a series of record flights and performed the first outside loop.

After leaving the service, he became America's premier racing pilot in the Granville brothers' hot Gee Bee racer. He had a host of colleagues, including Wiley Post, Frank Hawks, Roscoe Turner, Clarence Chamberlin, and others, all of whom had a devoted following in press and public.

The American aviation experience was replicated around the world. Great Britain honored its great flyers, including Sir Charles Kingsford Smith, Jimmy and Amy Mollison, Flight Lieutenants John Boothman and George Stainforth, and many more.

As hotly contested as the races were, so was the technology of transports. Boeing created the first modern transport in 1933 with its twin-engine Model 247, beginning a dynasty of Boeing transports. Douglas countered the same year with its remarkable DC-1, the sire of the famous DC line. These would lead to a revolution in the air transport industry, since the Douglas series of aircraft would for the first time make flying passengers profitable without a subsidy.

The stock market crash of 1929 and the subsequent depression put a damper on the aviation firestorm Lindbergh had created, but it did not extinguish it. Aviation was still a young and vital industry with the capacity to draw from its own resources all that was necessary not only to survive but to progress.

HUFF-DALAND DUSTERS Here Huff-Daland Dusters lay down a spread of insecticide. Huff-Daland had limited success selling the Army and Navy a few aircraft before it ultimately was acquired by Keystone Aircraft. One of its great contributions, however, was the creation of a professional agricultural aircraft, starting an industry that quite literally saved cotton farming in the United States. The original crop-dusting firm, Huff-Daland Dusters, ultimately became Delta Airlines.

DOUGLAS WORLD CRUISER The Douglas Aircraft Company was boosted into the big time with the successful round-the-world flight of its Douglas World Cruisers in 1924. Four big biplanes, powered by specially modified Liberty engines, left Seattle on April 6. Two of the planes completed the journey on September 28. It was as much a triumph of logistics as it was good piloting, but it showed the world what the U.S. Air Service could do.

FOKKER C V One can see the influence of the Fokker D VII design in this postwar Fokker C V. The aircraft first flew in May 1924 and became one of the most successful military aircraft of the time. A two-seat multipurpose plane with a top speed of 135 miles per hour, the Fokker C V was sold to many countries. Germany captured several during the early days of World War II, later employing them on the eastern front in night operations.

FOCKE-WULF FW A 16B A far cry from the later Kurt Tank designs for Focke-Wulf, this A 16b resembles the Messerschmitt M 17 in its stark simplicity. The A 16 was designed as a three- or four-passenger transport, with the pilot seated up front and out in the open. It was succeeded by the very similar A 17 of which ten were sold to Lufthansa. This, the *Borkum,* was used by Berliner Lokal Anzeiger for newspaper transport.

FLIGHT TIMELINE

February 21, 1924 The first airmail in Alaska is flown by Carl Eielson in a DH-4H.

April 6, 1924 Four Douglas World Cruisers depart Seattle to attempt the first round-the-world flight.

April 16–May 19, 1924 Stanley Goble and Ivor McIntyre circumnavigate Australia in 90 hours.

May 1924 The Fokker C V makes its first flight.

May 19, 1924 Lieutenant John Macready sets a new American altitude record in a LePere LUSAC-11 at 35,239 feet.

June 23, 1924 Lieutenant Russell Maughan completes a "Dawn to Dusk" flight in a Curtiss PW-8. He makes five stops en route and covers 2,670 miles in 21 hours, 48 minutes, and 30 seconds.

June 23, 1924 The first Focke-Wulf, the A 16 four-passenger monoplane, flies.

July 1, 1924 TAT, in cooperation with the Pennsylvania railroad, begins transcontinental travel—air by day, train by night.

August 1924 The Savoia-Marchetti S.55 flies for the first time.

August 24, 1924 The dirigible ZR-3 is completed in Germany for war reparations. Delivery to the United States is scheduled for October.

September 28, 1924 Two Douglas World Cruisers land in Seattle to complete the first flight around the world.

CURTISS PW-8 "DAWN TO DUSK" This beautiful Curtiss PW-8 was flown by Lieutenant Russell Maughan in his "Dawn to Dusk" flight of June 23, 1924. With five stops en route, he flew from New York to San Francisco. The aircraft was repainted to appear pristine for this publicity photograph. The PW (Pursuit Water-cooled)-8 was powered by a 440-horsepower Curtiss D-12 engine, had a top speed of 171 miles per hour, and led to a long series of Curtiss fighters.

FIAT C.R.1 The beginning of a famous line of Fiat fighters designed by Celestino Rossatelli, the C.R.1 shows the famous Warren truss "W" style wing bracing that would characterize his biplane fighters over the years. The C.R.1 had a top speed of 169 miles per hour and set the pattern for future *Regia Aeronautica* fighters with its maneuverability.

U.S. ARMY TC-7 The U.S. Army experimented cautiously with nonrigid airships over the years until finally abandoning all efforts in 1937. The U.S. Navy continued development through World War II and in the postwar years, finding "blimps," as they were called, excellent for antisubmarine work. Here one of the most famous of the Army airships, the TC-7, is shown with a Sperry Messenger hooked on, forecasting later Navy work with the *Akron* and the *Macon* dirigibles.

FOKKER F VII Streamlining was not always given top priority during the early 1920s. Despite its blunt angularity, this Fokker F VII prototype was relatively clean, and it became the sire of one of the most successful series of transports in history. The basic design was easily adapted for trimotor power, and, as the F VIIA/3m, it became the preferred transport for many European airlines. Its top speed was 115 miles per hour.

SAVOIA-MARCHETTI S.55 First flown in August 1924, the Savoia-Marchetti S.55 became one of the most successful transports of the period and was perhaps the most unique. With its twin catamaran-type flying boat hulls, sleek cantilever wings, and tandem engines, the S.55 was unlike anything in the sky. It was the forerunner of a successful line of flying boats, including those used in mass flights under the leadership of Air Marshal Italo Balbo.

FLIGHT TIMELINE

October 15, 1924 The LZ 126, from Friedrichshafen, Germany, arrives in the United States after an 81-hour flight. It becomes the the USS *Los Angeles* (ZR-3).

December 15, 1924 A Sperry Messenger successfully makes an aerial hookup onto the trapeze of the U.S. Army Airship TC-3.

December 25, 1924 Mrs. Calvin Coolidge christens the USS *Los Angeles* (ZR-3).

1925 The French Potez 25, a general-purpose biplane, makes its first flight.

January 3, 1925 The Fairey Fox flies for the first time, revolutionizing RAF thinking on engines and aircraft.

January 24–25, 1925 Scientists in 25 aircraft fly above the clouds to view a total eclipse of the sun. The new USS *Los Angeles* (ZR-3) carries Naval Observatory scientists.

February 2, 1925 President Calvin Coolidge signs the Kelly Bill, authorizing contract air transportation of airmail.

February 22, 1925 The de Havilland D.H.60 Moth flies for the first time.

March 12, 1925 The Fokker F VII flies for the first time.

April 8, 1925 The first night carrier landings are made on the USS *Langley*.

April 13, 1925 Henry Ford starts an airplane freight line to operate between Detroit and Chicago.

LOS ANGELES **LZ 126** On October 15, 1924, this airship arrived from Friedrichshafen, Germany, as the LZ 126, one of a long line of illustrious German Zeppelin airships. On December 25, 1924, Mrs. Calvin Coolidge christened it the *Los Angeles,* a United States Navy airship. The *Los Angeles* was the longest lived and most successful of all U.S. dirigibles, and it remained in service until 1932, when it had accumulated 4,320 flying hours.

POTEZ 25 In an era when an aircraft was considered a wild success if it sold more than 20 examples, the French Potez 25 stood head and shoulders above most. More than 4,000 of the type were sold over a ten-year period to air forces around the world. The Potez 25 served equally well as a reconnaissance aircraft, light bomber, and, if the opposition was right, even as a fighter.

FAIREY FOX The elegant Fairey Fox first flew on January 3, 1925, using the same Curtiss engine that powered the CR-3 Schneider Trophy racers. In Great Britain, home of Rolls-Royce, Napier, Bristol, and other great engine manufacturers, using an American engine was worse than heresy—it was treason. But the Fox was faster than contemporary fighters, and it was ordered for production—using a Rolls-Royce engine!

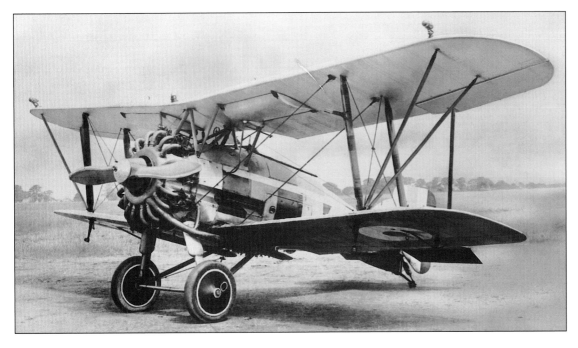

GLOSTER GAMECOCK In the years between wars, most nations attempted to keep as many aircraft companies alive as possible by sharing out the production orders. Gloster succeeded with its tiny (less than 30-foot wingspan) Gamecock, of which almost 100 were acquired by the Royal Air Force. Superbly maneuverable and fast for the time at 155 miles per hour, the Gamecock led to the more famous Gauntlet and Gladiator fighters.

DE HAVILLAND D.H.60 MOTH Although it's difficult to tell from this photograph, the de Havilland D.H.60 Moth was a clean biplane that would lead to the Tiger Moth, one of the most famous and beloved trainers of all time. The prototype, powered by a de Havilland Gypsy engine of 60 horsepower, was first flown on February 22, 1925. It is shown here being towed through a street in London en route to the flying field.

FLIGHT TIMELINE

July 7, 1925 The first Boeing 40A flies, establishing Boeing in the airmail business.

August 31–September 10, 1925 Commander John Rogers attempts to fly from San Francisco to Hawaii in a PN-9 patrol plane. Forced down at sea, he travels 450 miles by sail for ten days until he is picked up.

September 3, 1925 The USS *Shenandoah* is torn apart by a line squall when ordered to fly into a stormy area by official flight orders.

September 4, 1925 The tri-motor Fokker F VIIa/3m flies. It will become important all over the world.

October 12, 1925 Lieutenant Cy Bettis, in an Army Curtiss R3C-1 landplane racer, wins the Pulitzer Trophy race. He sets two unofficial speed records.

October 27, 1925 Lieutenant Jimmy Doolittle sets an official world speed record for seaplanes in a Curtiss R3C-2 at 242.166 miles per hour.

November 24, 1925 The prototype ANT-4 (Tupelov TB-1) bomber flies.

December 17, 1925 Billy Mitchell is found guilty by court martial of discrediting the U.S. Army.

January 6, 1926 Deutsche Lufthansa is formed.

January 22–February 10, 1926 Commandante Ramón Franco makes the first east-west crossing of the South Atlantic in a Dornier Wal.

RYAN AIR LINES DAVIS-DOUGLAS CLOUDSTER Donald Douglas and his partner, David R. Davis, built the Davis-Douglas Cloudster in 1921 for a nonstop transcontinental flight that was not completed due to engine failure. The aircraft was purchased in 1925 by T. Claude Ryan, who used it in his Los Angeles–San Diego Airline. Ryan eventually had Douglas modify it to carry ten passengers, five on each side of a narrow aisle.

SUPERMARINE SOUTHAMPTON It is difficult to believe that the many-strutted Southampton flying boat came from the same man who designed the beautiful Supermarine Spitfire, but that is the case. The Southampton, first flown on March 25, 1925, was actually R. J. Mitchell's first great success. Almost 70 of the flying boats, which had 75-foot wingspans and were capable of 108 miles per hour, were built for patrol duty. The Southampton Mk II aircraft had weight-saving aluminum hulls.

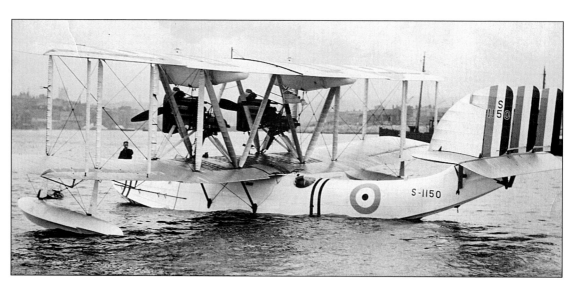

(FORD) STOUT 2-AT William Stout was one of the great engineers of the 1920s. The 2-AT of 1924 resembled the Fokker airliners of the period but was executed in metal and was powered by the ubiquitous 400-horsepower Liberty engine. Three 2-ATs flew with Florida Airways during its brief history, and they also served with Henry Ford's private air express service. The design led directly to the famous Ford Tri-Motor. This is *Maiden Dearborn IV*.

BOEING MODEL 40 Only one Boeing Model 40 was built, to meet the requirements of a Post Office competition for a Liberty-powered aircraft to replace the de Havilland DH-4. First flown on July 7, 1925, the Model 40 had much better performance than the DH-4, with a top speed of 135 miles per hour and a range of 700 miles. With a major redesign, it became the Model 40A, one of the more important aircraft of the era.

FOKKER F VIIA Tony Fokker was well aware of the importance of the Fokker name; he kept his airplanes prominently marked with it so there could be no doubt. This is the Fokker F VII, which performed so well in the 1925 Ford Reliability Tour that it inspired Henry Ford to come up with an all-metal competitor. Fokker transports were particularly favored by the Dutch on their long-distance routes to the East Indies.

FLIGHT TIMELINE

January 29, 1926 Lieutenant John Macready sets a U.S. altitude record of 38,704 feet in an XCO-5A.

February 6, 1926 Pratt & Whitney produces the first Wasp engine.

March 16, 1926 Robert Goddard launches the world's first liquid-fueled rocket, which flies 184 feet to become the "Kitty Hawk" of rocketry.

April 16, 1926 The Department of Agriculture purchases its first crop duster.

May 9, 1926 Richard E. Byrd and Floyd Bennett fly over the North Pole in a Fokker "Josephine Ford."

May 14, 1926 Roald Amundsen and Lincoln Ellsworth fly over the North Pole in the dirigible *Norge*, landing in Teller, Alaska, after a 70-hour flight from Norway.

May 20, 1926 President Calvin Coolidge signs the Air Commerce Act, regulating civil aeronautics.

May 23, 1926 Western Air Express begins operations between Salt Lake City and Los Angeles.

June 11, 1926 The prototype Ford Tri-Motor flies for the first time.

July 2, 1926 The U.S. Army Air Corps is created.

November 3, 1926 The Boeing F2B-1 single-seat fighter flies, beginning a long line of Navy and Army biplane fighters.

CURTISS R3C-2 Here, the inimitable Jimmy Doolittle stands on a sister ship of the Curtiss R3C-2 in which he won the 1925 Schneider Trophy. Doolittle was a skilled boxer and gymnast before learning to fly in the U.S. Army. He then became a top aerobatic and racing pilot and the only individual to win the Schneider, Bendix, and Thompson trophies. A scientist with a doctorate from M.I.T., Doolittle had a brilliant combat career in World War II.

FRANCO'S DORNIER WAL The Dornier Do J Wal (Whale) was used for many exploratory flights. This, the *Valencia,* was used by Commandante Ramón Franco. An Italian by birth, Franco was called "the Columbus of the Air" by his fellow Spaniards. On January 22, 1926, he, along with three crew members, took off from Melilla, Spain, in another Wal, the *Plus Ultra,* crossing the South Atlantic to land in Buenos Aires, Argentina, on February 10.

VARNEY AIRLINE FLIGHT Walter T. Varney was a legendary airline pioneer, and this photo records the April 6, 1926, inaugural flight of a Swallow biplane powered by a Curtiss C-6 water-cooled engine. The mountainous route from Elko, Nevada, to Pasco, Washington, required more power, and Wright J4 engines were installed. This was a time of transition, and the air-cooled radial engine would soon dominate passenger aircraft design.

FOKKER "JOSEPHINE FORD" Here we see Richard Byrd's Fokker F VIIa decked out with signs proclaiming that the Josephine Ford is a Fokker product powered by Wright Whirlwind engines. Byrd used this aircraft, which was piloted by Floyd Bennett, to fly over the North Pole on May 9, 1926. The validity of Byrd's claim was later questioned based on the elapsed time of flight.

NORGE The *Norge (Norway)* was a semirigid Italian airship created by Colonel Umberto Nobile. First flown in 1925 as the N-1, it was purchased by Roald Amundsen and Lincoln Ellsworth to fly to the North Pole, with Nobile as its pilot. After long preparation, they flew from Spitsbergen, Norway, to Teller, Alaska, in 70 hours, landing on May 14, 1926. The trans-Arctic flight covered 2,485 miles.

FLIGHT TIMELINE

December 21, 1926 Five Loening COA-1 amphibians depart Kelly Field, Texas, on a Pan American Goodwill flight.

1927 The Curtiss XB-2 Condor bomber, ordered in 1926, flies for the first time.

January 15, 1927 Boeing Aircraft begins Boeing Air Transport, predecessor of United Air Lines.

March 9, 1927 The Navy buys its first transport plane, a Ford Tri-Motor, XJR-1.

March 9, 1927 Captain H. C. Gray ascends to 28,910 feet in a free balloon for an American record.

March 14, 1927 Pan American Airways is formed.

April 4, 1927 Colonial Air Lines initiates regular passenger service between Boston and New York.

April 12, 1927 Clarence Chamberlin and Bert Acosta set an American flight duration record of 51 hours, 11 minutes, and 25 seconds.

April 28, 1927 The Ryan NYP *Spirit of St. Louis*, Charles Lindbergh's airplane, is flown for the first time.

May 2, 1927 The Pan American Goodwill flight of 22,065 miles ends at Bolling Field, Washington, D.C. Two of the ten pilots were killed en route when two COA-1s collided over Buenos Aires.

May 4, 1927 Captain H. C. Gray reaches 42,470 feet in a free balloon.

FORD TRI-MOTOR PROTOTYPE
Henry Ford bought the Stout Metal Plane Company in 1925, beginning a seven-year participation in the aviation industry. This is the Ford 4 AT-1, the first of the line, distinguished by its open cockpit. Later models had more familiar lines, with the cockpit enclosed. The word Tri-Motor was used as a trademark, to distinguish Fords from trimotor Fokkers. A total of 199 Tri-Motors were built, and they became famous as airliners.

MARTIN T3M-2 Just as Curtiss underbid Martin to build Martin MB-2 bombers, Martin underbid Curtiss to get a contract to build T2M and T3M torpedo planes for the Navy. It was a dog-eat-dog world in aviation those days, and price-cutting was a standard tactic. Martin ultimately delivered 360 of the type, a large quantity for the period. The big Martins (53-foot span, 8,000 pounds) were rugged and had a top speed of 114 miles per hour.

DE HAVILLAND D.H.66 HERCULES Although tiny by today's standards, the de Havilland company was amazingly versatile in its ability to create aircraft both large and small. The D.H.66 Hercules first flew on June 30, 1926, powered by three 420-horsepower Bristol Jupiter radial engines. Eleven of the aircraft were built, each named for a famous city. With a crew of three and seven passengers, the Hercules was used primarily by Imperial Airways.

CURTISS P-1B HAWK The first of the Curtiss Hawk series was the sleek PW-8, which shared some of the features of the earlier Hawk racers. This P-1B was ordered in August 1926, just one month after the Army Air Service became the Army Air Corps. This was an all-Curtiss product, with a Curtiss D-12 engine and a Curtiss steel propeller. Top speed was about 155 miles per hour, with a rarely reached service ceiling of 23,000 feet.

BOEING F2B-1 The first XF2B-1 flew on November 3, 1926; its performance pleased the Navy, which ordered an initial batch of 32 F2B-1s. The sharp-looking little Boeing fighter became nationally famous as it performed with "The Three Sea Hawks," the first Navy aerobatic team and the forerunner of the Blue Angels. The F2B-1 was very fast for the time, with a top speed of 158 miles per hour.

FLIGHT TIMELINE

May 5, 1927 Lieutenant C. C. Champion flies a Wright Apache seaplane to 33,455 feet, setting a new altitude record for seaplanes.

May 8, 1927 Lieutenant Charles Nungesser and Captain Francois Coli disappear in an attempted Paris–New York flight.

May 17, 1927 The Bristol Bulldog fighter flies for the first time.

May 20–21, 1927 Charles Lindbergh flies solo nonstop from New York to Paris.

May 25, 1927 Jimmy Doolittle does the first outside loop.

June 4–6, 1927 Clarence Chamberlin and backer Charles A. Levine fly nonstop from New York to Germany in 43 hours, 49 minutes.

June 28–29, 1927 In a Fokker (Atlantic) trimotor named *Bird of Paradise*, Lieutenants Albert F. Hegenberger and Lester J. Maitland fly from Oakland, California, to Honolulu, Hawaii (2,407 miles), the longest distance ever completed over open sea.

June 29, 1927 Admiral Richard Byrd makes an unsuccessful transoceanic attempt in a Fokker F VIIIa/3m *America*.

July 5, 1927 Germans form the Society for Space Travel.

July 25, 1927 Lieutenant C. C. Champion sets a world altitude landplane record of 38,418 feet in a Wright Apache.

SHORT SINGAPORE I

The all-metal twin-engine Short Singapore I flying boat was first flown on August 17, 1926. No production orders ensued, but it paved the way for follow-up orders of four-engine versions of the aircraft. The original Singapore had a top speed of 128 miles per hour and conclusively proved the advantage of metal construction for British flying boats.

Great Britain, with its far-flung empire, had the greatest need for flying boats, and though flying boats were slow compared to landplanes, they were five times as fast as the ships that plied the seas between the United Kingdom and India or Singapore.

CHARLES A. LINDBERGH

Charles Lindbergh inspired the world with his solo New York to Paris flight on May 20–21, 1927. He won the $25,000 Orteig Prize and became famous overnight. Fortunately, his personality was able to handle the fame, and he became a pioneering advocate of air transport. With his wife Ann acting as navigator, radio operator, and copilot, he pioneered many of the air routes used today.

WALTER BEECH One of the truly great names in aircraft manufacturing, Walter Beech sits to the right of Art Goebel, who flew the Travel Air *Woolaroc* to first place in the tragedy-laden Oakland-to-Hawaii Dole air race of 1927. Beech later left Travel Air to found the Beech Aircraft Company, whose first aircraft was the beautiful Model 17 Staggerwing.

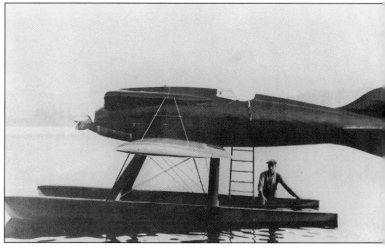

MACCHI M.39 The famous Italian designer Mario Castoldi created the Macchi M.39 for the 1926 Schneider Trophy race. Flown by Major Mario de Bernardi, the M.39 won at an average speed of 246.496 miles per hour. The M.39 was powered by an 800-horsepower Fiat 12-cylinder engine driving a fixed-pitch wooden propeller. In just a few years, innovations such as flaps, controllable pitch propellers, better brakes, and retractable landing gear would make seaplane racers obsolete.

WESTLAND WAPITI Designed to a specification that required (for economy) the use of the available components of the de Havilland D.H.9A aircraft of World War I (primarily the two-bay biplane wings), the Westland Wapiti was handicapped from the start. Nonetheless, it became a workhorse of the RAF; 517 were built, and some were still in service in 1939. The Wapitis were effective in the RAF's "air control" method, used for maintaining peace in the Middle East.

KEYSTONE PATHFINDER CRASH The Orteig Prize for the first flight across the Atlantic between New York and Paris lured many flyers to compete. One of the best prepared teams was that of Lieutenant Commander Noel Davis and his navigator Stanton H. Wooster. They had a special Keystone trimotor, the *American Legion,* built for the attempt. Unfortunately, Davis crashed on a practice heavyweight takeoff on April 26, 1927, and both men were killed.

August 1927 The first Huff-Daland bombers are delivered to the Air Corps.

August 17, 1927 Art Goebel and William Davis win the $25,000 Dole air race.

September 1, 1927 American Railway Express and major U.S. airlines begin air express operations.

October 12, 1927 Wright Field is dedicated; it becomes the primary research and development site for the Air Corps.

October 14–15, 1927 Dieudonné Costes and Joseph Le Brix make the first nonstop crossing of the South Atlantic in a Breguet 19.

October 28, 1927 Pan Am establishes an international air station at Key West, Florida.

November 16, 1927 The USS *Saratoga,* an aircraft carrier, is commissioned.

December 14, 1927 The USS *Lexington,* an aircraft carrier, is commissioned.

1928 The NACA develops a cowling for radial engines.

January 7, 1928 The Polikarpov U-2 (later Po-2) makes its first flight.

February 7–22, 1928 Bert Hinkler flies solo from England to Australia.

February 28, 1928 The Navy contracts with Consolidated for the XPY-1, the first U.S. monoplane flying boat.

WHITE BIRD Charles Lindbergh's historic flight came on the heels of a series of disastrous attempts to fly the Atlantic. Even while Lindbergh was flying to New York from St. Louis to begin his attempt, Captain Francis Coli and the great French ace Lieutenant Charles Nungesser had taken off in the *Oiseau Blanc (White Bird)* to fly from Paris to New York. They disappeared on May 8, 1927, and no trace of them was ever found.

BRISTOL BULLDOG PROTOTYPE Competition for production contracts was fierce in Great Britain, and the Bristol Bulldog had to face stiff competition from the date of its first flight on May 17, 1927. An aerobatic marvel, it dazzled the crowds at the annual display at Hendon in July. The RAF bought 320 Bulldogs, and many more were sold to foreign buyers. Cleaned up and with a 480-horsepower Bristol Mercury engine, it was capable of a top speed of 190 miles per hour.

SPIRIT OF ST. LOUIS A modification of a basic Ryan design, the *Spirit of St. Louis* was tailored to Charles Lindbergh's specific needs. For reasons of weight and balance—and because Lindbergh did not wish to be sandwiched between the fuel tank and engine in the event of a crash—the forward section of the fuselage contained the main fuel tank, and there were no windscreens for a view ahead.

CLARENCE CHAMBERLIN AND CHARLES LEVINE Pictured here are Charles Levine (center left) and Clarence Chamberlin (center right). Chamberlin and Levine flew from New York to land within 110 miles of Berlin on June 6, 1927—a distance of 3,911 miles. Their aircraft, the Wright Bellanca *Columbia* had been Lindbergh's first choice for his New York to Paris flight on May 20–21, 1927.

FLIGHT TIMELINE

March 30, 1928 Flying a Macchi M.52, Major Mario de Bernardi attains a record speed of 318.623 miles per hour over a three-kilometer course.

April 12–14, 1928 The Junkers W 33 *Bremen* makes the first east-west crossing of the Atlantic.

April 15–21, 1928 Captain George Hubert Wilkins and pilot Carl Ben Eielson fly a Lockheed Vega over a 2,200-mile polar route, Alaska to Norway, in 20 hours, 20 minutes.

May 16, 1928 Transcontinental Air Transport (TAT), the predecessor of TWA, is formed.

May 23, 1928 The tragic flight of Italian airship *Italia* begins.

May 31–June 9, 1928 Charles Kingsford Smith and Charles Ulm fly from San Francisco to Australia.

June 1928 A prototype Hawker Hart two-seater flies.

June 11, 1928 Fritz Stammer makes the first piloted rocket-powered flight in the *Ente (Duck)*.

June 20, 1928 Braniff Airways is formed.

June 25, 1928 The Boeing 100 prototype for the P-12 and F4B makes its first flight.

July 3–5, 1928 Italians Arturo Ferrarin and Carlo del Prete set a straight-line distance record: 4,466 miles in a Savoia-Marchetti S.64.

BIRD OF PARADISE FLIGHT FROM OAKLAND TO HAWAII
Two Air Corps Lieutenants, Lester J. Maitland and Albert F. Hegenberger, became the first to fly from California to Hawaii, landing at Wheeler Field, Oahu, on June 29, 1927. The 2,407-mile flight in the Fokker (Atlantic) trimotor *Bird of Paradise* took 25 hours and 40 minutes.

HUFF–DALAND LB-1 The United States has always liked big bombers, from this Huff-Daland LB-1 to the Boeing B-52. The LB-1 was an attempt to have it all in one package—the streamlining afforded by one Packard 2A-2540 engine rated at 800 horsepower and the wing area to carry a big bomb load. The top speed of 120 miles per hour was good, but the engine was simply unreliable. Huff-Daland was eventually taken over by Keystone.

USS LEXINGTON The beautiful USS *Lexington* (CV-2) was one of the United States' first large aircraft carriers. Like the *Saratoga* (CV-3), it was built from a hull originally intended for a battle cruiser. With a maximum length of 888 feet and a displacement of 38,500 tons, the *"Lady Lex"* and its 80 airplanes could steam at 33 knots. It fought bravely through the early days of World War II but was lost during the Battle of the Coral Sea in May 1942.

CESSNA DESIGN NO. 1 Sometimes a simple idea is enough for success. Clyde Cessna believed in clean lines, cantilever wings, and high speeds. This aircraft, completed on August 10, 1927, was Cessna Design No. 1 and was powered by a 90-horsepower Anzani engine. It led to a line of Cessna high-wing cantilever monoplanes and helped establish Cessna as a brand name. Cessna aircraft were prominent in racing during the golden age of flight.

FLIGHT TIMELINE

September 18, 1928 The *Graf Zeppelin*, the world's most successful dirigible, is launched.

September 19, 1928 The Packard Diesel, the first diesel engine to power a heavier-than-air craft, flies.

November 14, 1928 The Fairey Long-Range Monoplane flies. It will set many records.

December 19, 1928 The first American autogiro, the Pitcairn, is flown.

December 20, 1928 Captain George Hubert Wilkins and Carl Ben Eielson fly their Lockheed Vega over Antarctica.

January 1929 A Soviet TB-1 aircraft bomber flies from Moscow to New York.

January 1929 The first Link Trainer is sold.

January 1–7, 1929 Major Carl Spaatz, Captain Ira Eaker, First Lieutenant Harry Halverson, Second Lieutenant Elwood Quesada, and Staff Sergeant Roy Hooe conduct an endurance flight in the Fokker C-2A *Question Mark*, setting a world record of 150 hours, 40 minutes, and 15 seconds.

January 2, 1929 Bobbie Trout sets a female endurance record of 12 hours, 11 minutes in a Golden Eagle monoplane.

January 30, 1929 Elinor Smith sets a new female endurance record in a Brunner-Winkle Bird, flying 13 hours, 16 minutes.

MARINE CORPS DH-4S For many years, the Marine Corps received semiobsolete aircraft such as modified de Havilland DH-4s. They used them with vigor and élan, however, and developed close-air support tactics with them in combat in Nicaragua. Boeing rebuilt these aircraft with metal fuselages as 02B-1s and delivered 30 of them to the First Aviation Group of the Marine Corps in early 1925.

TRAVEL AIR WOOLAROC The Travel Air *Woolaroc,* piloted by Art Goebel with navigator Lieutenant William Davis, won the ill-fated Dole air race to Hawaii on August 17, 1927, making the flight in 26 hours, 17 minutes, and 33 seconds. Goebel and Davis, along with the crew of the second-place aircraft, the Breese *Aloha,* survived; two other planes went missing en route, and a third aircraft crashed searching for them.

LOCKHEED VEGA One of the most important aircraft of its decade, the prototype Lockheed Vega made its first flight on July 4, 1927. It flew in the Dole air race as the *Golden Eagle* but was lost at sea. The tragedy did not inhibit sales, however, and the Vega was soon setting records all over the world. The Vega epitomized designer Jack Northrop's insistence on clean design and innovative structures.

WINGS FOKKER D VII CRASH A movie stunt pilot crashed this genuine World War I Fokker D VII for the Oscar-winning film *Wings* in 1927. Note the triangular shape at the rear of the fuselage—a camera for in-flight footage. Two D VIIs and two SPAD VIIs were crashed for the film.

POLIKARPOV PO-2 Designer Nikolai Polikarpov would never have believed that this comely biplane, the Po-2, would become the most produced aircraft in history, with more than 33,000—and perhaps as many as 40,000—built. The simple primary trainer was used in many arenas, including combat in World War II and Korea. Its 100-horsepower radial engine provided a top speed of 97 miles per hour, but it was more comfortable at a cruise of 70 miles per hour.

FLIGHT TIMELINE

February 1929 Boeing, United Air Lines, Pratt & Whitney, and Standard Steel Propeller merge into United Aircraft and Transport Company.

February 4–5, 1929 Frank Hawks and Oscar Grubb set a nonstop transcontinental record in a Lockheed Air Express: 18 hours and 22 minutes.

February 12, 1929 Anne Morrow and Charles Lindbergh get engaged.

March 9, 1929 Charles Lindbergh inaugurates airline flight to Mexico City.

March 16–17, 1929 Louise Thaden sets a female endurance record of 22 hours, 3 minutes, 12 seconds.

April 23–24, 1929 Elinor Smith establishes a female endurance record of 26 hours, 21 minutes in a Bellanca.

April 24–26, 1929 RAF pilots fly a Fairey Long-Range Monoplane nonstop from England to India—4,130 miles.

May 8, 1929 Lieutenant Apollo Soucek sets a world altitude record of 39,140 feet in a Wright Apache landplane.

May 28, 1929 Marvel Crosson sets a female altitude record of 24,000 feet.

June 4, 1929 Lieutenant Apollo Soucek sets a world altitude record (38,650 feet) for seaplanes in a float-equipped Wright Apache.

MACCHI M.52 The Schneider Trophy race had become the most prestigious international aviation event in history, and Italian dictator Benito Mussolini supplied lavish funds to his Schneider teams, demanding that they win for the honor of Italy. In 1929, a 1,000-horsepower Fiat engine and 94-octane gasoline drove the M.52R to second place at 284.20 miles per hour. Flown by Warrant Officer Dal Molin, the M.52R was substituting for the more advanced M.67, which had crashed.

KOHL, FITZMAURICE, AND VON HUNEFELD It was an unlikely quartet that flew the Junkers W 33 *Bremen* on the first successful east-to-west crossing of the North Atlantic by airplane. The crew, consisting of German pilots Carl Spinder and Hermann Kohl; a passenger, Baron von Hunefeld; and an Irish navigator, Major James Fitzmaurice, took off from Ireland on April 12, 1928, and landed in Labrador on April 14. Here Kohl, Fitzmaurice, and Von Hunefeld are greeted as heroes upon their return to Munich.

FOKKER SOUTHERN CROSS
One of the longest and most daring flights of the Roaring Twenties was the May 31–June 9, 1928, trip from San Francisco to Brisbane, Australia. Charles Kingsford Smith and Charles Ulm piloted the plane, with Harry Lyon and James Warner serving as navigator and radio operator respectively. The Fokker F VIIb/3m *Southern Cross,* with three reliable Wright Whirlwind engines, carried them safely through violent storms to become the first to fly across the Pacific.

BOEING P-12E Boeing was a serious competitor in the fighter business, eager to match everything Curtiss did with something just a little bit better. The biplane, open cockpit, and fixed gear layout was conventional as was the wooden wing and bolted aluminum tube fuselage structure. Called the F4B by the Navy, the stubby little fighter was popular with both services. The P-12E model had a top speed of 189 miles per hour.

GEORGE HUBERT WILKINS AND CARL BEN EIELSON

The fourth Lockheed Vega built was purchased by Captain George Hubert Wilkins for an expedition sponsored by the *Detroit Daily News*. Carl Ben Eielson was the pilot on the flight from Point Barrow, Alaska, across the Arctic to Spitzbergen, Norway, starting on April 15, 1928. The trip was interrupted by a forced landing and two dangerous takeoffs from the snow. (There were two because on the first one, Wilkins was outside the aircraft pushing and could not clamber back on board in time.) Wilkins was knighted as Sir Hubert for the flight, and Eielson won the Harmon Trophy.

FLIGHT TIMELINE

July 2–12, 1929 Loren Mendell and R. B. Reinhart set a new endurance record of 246 hours, 44 minutes in a Wright-powered Buhl biplane.

July 7, 1929 Transcontinental Air Transport (TAT) sets up combined air-rail service, going coast-to-coast in 48 hours.

July 9, 1929 Roger Q. Williams and Lewis Yancey fly nonstop from the United States to Spain (3,400 miles) in a Bellanca.

July 10, 1929 The *Spokane Sun God*, a Buhl CA-6, completes a nonstop round-trip from Spokane, Washington, to New York in 115 hours, 45 minutes, with aerial fueling.

July 13–30, 1929 Dale Jackson and Forest O'Brien set a refueling duration record of 420 hours, 17 minutes in a Curtiss Robin.

July 25, 1929 The Dornier Do X makes its first flight.

August 1929 The Junkers 33 seaplane makes its first rocket-assisted takeoff.

September 24, 1929 Jimmy Doolittle demonstrates blind flying.

September 27–29, 1929 Dieudonné Costes and Maurice Bellonte fly from Paris to Manchuria, China, for a world distance record of 4,912 miles in *Point d'Interrogation*.

September 30, 1929 The Opel Sander Rak. 1, a glider powered by rockets, makes a 75-second flight.

SAVOIA-MARCHETTI S.64 The Savoia-Marchetti S.64 was specifically designed for long-distance flights. Between July 3 and July 5, 1928, it set a straight-line distance record of 4,466 miles from Rome to Natal, Brazil. The pilots, Captain Arturo Ferrarin and Major Carlo del Prete, had originally intended to fly to Rio de Janeiro but decided to land at Natal for safety reasons. Despite a profusion of struts and booms, Savoia-Marchettis were always very handsome aircraft.

JUAN TRIPPE One of the great airline visionaries, Juan Trippe foresaw the need for ocean-spanning aircraft decades before anyone else and went on to found Pan American Airways. Trippe's business methods did not always endear him to his competitors, but he was willing to take risks that others were not. With Boeing's William Allen, Trippe took the biggest gamble of all when he ordered the revolutionary Boeing 747. Like most of his gambles, this one paid off handsomely.

PITCAIRN AUTOGIRO The autogiro seemed to be capable of assuming the role the helicopter eventually filled. Unlike the helicopter, the rotor of the autogiro is not powered and depends upon the forward speed of the aircraft for lift. This is a Pitcairn PCA-2, one of two purchased. This aircraft, with its 975-horsepower Wright engine, landed on the USS *Langley*. Note the Consolidated NT-1 in the background.

GRAF ZEPPELIN The *Graf Zeppelin* was by far the most successful airship in history, from its christening on July 8, 1928, to its final days in storage in Germany. The *Graf Zeppelin* flew farther, longer, and with less trouble than any other airship. It served as a polar explorer and made a record-shattering round-the-world flight in 1929 that seemed to signal the arrival of a new era in air transport.

GLOSTER GAUNTLET Created by the same man who designed the famous S.E.5 of World War I, H. P. Folland, the Gloster Gauntlet went into series production in 1934 and eventually equipped 14 RAF squadrons. A delightful aircraft to fly, the Gauntlet was an obsolete open-cockpit, fixed-undercarriage biplane with only two forward-firing guns. The engineering leap from this aircraft to the Hawker Hurricane in 1935 was truly spectacular.

FLIGHT TIMELINE

November 22, 1929 Amelia Earhart sets a speed record for women: 184.17 miles per hour in a Lockheed Vega.

November 28–29, 1929 Richard Byrd and Bernt Balchen fly over the South Pole.

November 29, 1929 Curtiss completes the first Prestone-cooled pursuit aircraft.

January 25, 1930 American Airways (now American Airlines) is formed.

May 1, 1930 The prototype Polikarpov I-5 single-seater biplane flies.

May 5–24, 1930 Amy Johnson becomes the first woman to fly solo from England to Australia.

May 6, 1930 The Boeing Monomail flies.

May 15, 1930 Ellen Church becomes the first flight attendant for Boeing Air Transport, on a Boeing 80A.

May 18, 1930 The *Graf Zeppelin* crosses the South Atlantic for the first time.

May 27, 1930 Roscoe Turner sets an east-west record of 18 hours, 43 minutes, 34 seconds in a Vega.

June 4, 1930 Lieutenant Apollo Soucek sets a world altitude record in a Wright Apache landplane at 43,155 feet.

June 12, 1930 The last RAF biplane bomber, the Handley Page Heyford, flies for the first time.

FAIREY LONG-RANGE MONOPLANE The RAF purchased two examples of the Fairey Long-Range Monoplane, the first of which crashed on a record attempt in 1929. The second aircraft was much more successful, setting several long-distance records, including a 5,309-mile flight from England to South Africa in February 1933. The Fairey relied on thick, long cantilever wings of 82-foot span for lift and a 570-horsepower Napier Lion engine for power.

VOUGHT VO-1 The Germans and the British had experimented with the concept of an aerial aircraft carrier during World War I. In the postwar years, it seemed to be particularly desirable to the U.S. Navy, which created the dirigibles *Akron* and *Macon* for that role. Much preliminary testing was done with the *Los Angeles,* however, shown here with a Vought VO-1 observation plane hooked on. Ultimately, the fragility of airships made the idea impractical.

REFUELING THE QUESTION MARK Four top USAAF World War II leaders were on the Atlantic (Fokker) C-2A *Question Mark* during its remarkable 150-hour, 40-minute, 15-second flight, which ended on January 7, 1929. They included Major Carl Spaatz, Captain Ira Eaker, First Lieutenant Harry Halverson, and Second Lieutenant Elwood Quesada. Also on board was Staff Sergeant Roy Hooe. Douglas C-1 tanker planes provided the fuel. Aerial refueling would become critically important after World War II.

FLIGHT TIMELINE

June 20, 1930 Randolph Field, the "West Point of the Air," is dedicated.

July 21, 1930 Forest O'Brien and Dale Jackson set a 647-hour, 28-minute endurance record.

July 23, 1930 Pioneer aviator Glenn Curtiss dies.

July 25, 1930 Aircraft designer Chance Vought dies.

July 29, 1930 The British dirigible R-100 flies from England to Canada in 78 hours.

August 5, 1930 Pancho Barnes sets a women's speed record of 196.1 miles per hour in a Travel Air.

August 6, 1930 Frank Hawks sets an east-west solo record in a Travel Air "Mystery Ship": 14 hours, 50 minutes, 43 seconds.

August 13, 1930 Frank Hawks sets a west-east solo record: 12 hours, 15 minutes, 3 seconds.

September 1, 1930 Speed Holman wins the first Thompson Trophy in a Laird "Solution" at 201.9 miles per hour.

September 1–3, 1930 Dieudonné Costes and Maurice Bellonte make the first east-west crossing from Paris to New York in 37 hours, 18 minutes.

October 1930 The Polish PZL P-7 fighter appears; the Polish Air Force becomes the first in the world with an all-metal monoplane fighter squadron.

CAPTAIN FRANK HAWKS One of the most prominent aviators of the Golden Age, Captain Frank Hawks set many of his records in Lockheed aircraft like this beautiful Air Express. The aircraft was extremely important because it mounted one of the first NACA cowlings, used to reduce drag and improve cooling—a major contribution to aviation. Hawks set a transcontinental record, with Oscar Grubb, of 18 hours and 22 minutes in this aircraft on February 4–5, 1929.

TRANSCONTINENTAL AIR TRANSPORT Beginning on July 7, 1929, Transcontinental Air Transport (TAT) operated the "Lindbergh Line," a 48-hour service from New York to Los Angeles. Passengers combined the use of a Ford 5-AT Tri-Motor with the trains of the Pennsylvania and Santa Fe railroads.

BREGUET 19 The Breguet 19 made its first flight in 1922 and went on to a long and glorious career, making many record flights and serving the armed forces of many countries. This is the Breguet 19 Super Bidon, named the *Point d'Interrogation (Question Mark)*. The crew, pilot Dieudonné Costes and navigator Maurice Bellonte, flew it from Paris to New York on September 1–3, 1930, in 37 hours and 18 minutes.

BUHL SPOKANE SUN GOD On July 10, 1929, the *Spokane Sun God* completed a memorable 7,200-mile flight from Spokane, Washington, to New York and back in 115 hours and 45 minutes, with 11 refueling contacts, always using Texaco fuel. Nick B. Mamer piloted; Art Walker acted as copilot and refueler. A sesquiwing cabin biplane, the *Spokane Sun God* was a standard Buhl CA-6 fitted with extra tanks.

HEINKEL HE 12 Ernst Heinkel designed both the catapult and the He 12 aircraft shown in this photo. The aircraft was catapulted from the liner *Bremen* from a position 248 feet off New York on July 22, 1929. Upon arrival, the He 12 was christened the *New York* by the mayor of that city. Germany was fascinated with the concept of using catapult ships to expedite the transfer of mail—and also with their military potential.

October 5, 1930 The British dirigible R-101 crashes en route from England to India.

October 13, 1930 The prototype Junkers Ju 52, one of the most famous transports in history, flies.

October 19, 1930 Gottlob Espenlaub flies a glider powered by Sander rockets.

November 1930 The Handley Page H.P.42 airliner flies for the first time.

November 9, 1930 Roy Ammel flies a Lockheed Sirius from New York to Canal Zone, 2,700 miles in 24 hours, 35 minutes.

November 24, 1930 Ruth Nichols sets a new east-west female transcontinental record of 16 hours, 59 minutes.

November 25, 1930 The Fairey Hendon, the first British metal monoplane bomber, flies.

December 2, 1930 Ruth Nichols makes a west-east transcontinental flight in 13 hours, 22 minutes.

December 22, 1930 The Tupelov TB-3, a standard Soviet four-engine bomber, flies for the first time. It is the largest airplane in the world at the time.

December 30, 1930 Robert Goddard fires a liquid-fueled rocket to 2,000 feet at 500 miles per hour.

January 4, 1931 William Swan flies over New Jersey in a glider powered by ten small rockets.

DORNIER DO X With a 157-foot wingspan and a gross weight of 123,200 pounds, the Dornier Do X was the biggest aircraft in the world at the time of its first flight on July 25, 1929. On October 21, it lifted 169 people (including 9 stowaways). Italy bought two of the aircraft, but unfortunately the Do X was underpowered, even with 12 engines, and was not a commercial success.

CONSOLIDATED NY-2 Late in his life, Jimmy Doolittle often remarked that his greatest contribution to aviation was the introduction of "blind flying," as instrument flight used to be called. On September 24, 1929, with Ben Kelsey on board as a safety pilot in the Consolidated NY-2, Doolittle made a takeoff and landing entirely by instruments—the first in history. The culmination of ten months of hard work, the flight revolutionized aviation.

SUPERMARINE S-6A The Supermarine S-6A, flown by Flight Officer H.R.D. Waghorn, won the 1929 Schneider Trophy race at Calshot, England. The race was distinguished by very potent competitors, including French and Italian entries, but almost all suffered technical problems. Waghorn's average of 328.6 miles per hour broke all records and was the second straight victory for Great Britain. It needed only one more win to retire the Schneider Trophy for all time.

JUNKERS G 38 The huge 144-foot wingspan Junkers G 38 was a preliminary step toward a flying-wing aircraft. The first of these four-engine aircraft flew on November 26, 1929, and only two were built in Germany. Japan built six as the Mitsubishi Ki-20 Type 92 heavy bomber. The G 38b could carry a maximum of 34 passengers and a crew of 7, cruising at 127 miles per hour.

FLIGHT TIMELINE

January 4–9, 1931 Bobbie Trout and Edna Cooper set a female refueling duration record of 123 hours in a Curtiss Robin.

January 6, 1931 General Italo Balboa leads 12 Savoia-Marchetti S.55 flying boats in a formation flight across the South Atlantic.

January 7, 1931 Beryl Hart and Lieutenant Bill Mac-Claren are lost in a transatlantic attempt.

February 26–March 1, 1931 Lucien Bossoutrot and Maurice Rossi set a new closed-circuit record of 5,481 miles in a Blériot 110.

February 28, 1931 Imperial Airways begins service from England to Central Africa.

March 3, 1931 The Fairey Gordon makes its first flight.

March 6, 1931 Ruth Nichols sets a female altitude record of 28,743 feet in a Lockheed Vega.

March 25, 1931 The first production model of the Hawker Fury flies.

March 26, 1931 Swissair is formed. The airline will push the pace of European transport lines.

March 31, 1931 Knute Rockne is killed in the crash of a Fokker transport, sealing the fate of wooden transport aircraft in America.

April 1931 The German counterpart to the DC-3, the Junkers Ju 52/3m, makes its first flight.

FORD BYRD ANTARCTIC EXPEDITION Richard Byrd used a Ford AT-4 for his flight over the South Pole, naming it Floyd Bennett for the pilot who flew him over the North Pole. The aircraft was equipped with a 525-horsepower Wright Cyclone center engine using a three-blade propeller. The two outer engines were the standard 220-horsepower Wright Whirlwinds. Bernt Balchen was the pilot for the historic flight on November 28–29, 1929, with Harold June and Ashley McKinley as crew members.

TRAVEL AIR "MYSTERY SHIP" The larger-than-life Pancho Barnes set a women's speed record of 196.1 miles per hour on August 5, 1930, at Los Angeles in a Travel Air "Mystery Ship." She purchased the aircraft, with its Wright J-6 Whirlwind engine, for $12,500. Other great pilots who flew "Mystery Ships" included Jimmy Doolittle, Frank Hawks, Jimmy Haizlip, and Doug Davis. A bit of trivia: The sound of Barnes's engine was recorded for use in the Howard Hughes' film *Hell's Angels*.

TAYLOR CUB E-2 C. Gilbert Taylor designed the Taylor Cub E-2 to be powered by a number of engines, including the Continental A40, Aeromarine AR3-40, and Szekely SR3-35. Despite the Depression, the charming Cubs sold fairly well until a fire destroyed the factory. William Piper acquired the design rights and, being a much better marketer than Taylor (or anyone else in the lightplane business!), set new sales records with the bright yellow Piper Cub.

HANDLEY PAGE H.P.42 Drag reduction was not the first consideration of the Handley Page designers—they built the big H.P.42 airliners to be safe and comfortable. The first real flight of the aircraft took place in November 1930; and eight of the aircraft entered service with Imperial Airways in 1931. The H.P.42 had a 120-foot wingspan and could accommodate a crew of 4 and 18 to 24 passengers. Its top speed was 120 miles per hour.

FLIGHT TIMELINE

April 2, 1931 Leroy Grumman's new firm, an offshoot of his relationship with Grover Loening, gets a contract for the immortal Fifi, the FF-1 two-seat, retractable gear, biplane fighter. It's the start of a fighter dynasty.

April 8, 1931 Amelia Earhart establishes the autogiro altitude record of 18,415 feet in her Pitcairn autogiro.

April 13, 1931 Ruth Nichols sets a female speed record of 210.6 miles per hour in a Lockheed Vega.

April 13, 1931 The Boeing XB-901 (later known as the YB-9 "Death Angel") flies for the first time. It will ultimately lead to the Boeing B-17.

May 26, 1931 The Consolidated P2Y makes its first flight.

May 27, 1931 Professor Auguste Piccard and Paul Kipfer reach 51,775 feet in a balloon.

May 28, 1931 Lieutenant W. Lees and Fred Brossy fly 84 hours, 33 minutes, unrefueled, in a diesel-powered Bellanca.

May 31, 1931 The first drone plane is flown by radio control from another plane.

June 4, 1931 The Dornier Do X arrives in New York.

June 23–July 1, 1931 Wiley Post and Harold Gatty fly the Lockheed Vega *Winnie Mae* around the world in 8 days, 15 hours, 51 minutes.

FRANK WHITTLE Air Commodore Frank (later Sir Frank) Whittle invented the jet engine. Initially, his invention was ignored as being impractical. Then, when it appeared not only practical but essential, development was taken out of his hands and given to others. Finally, after jet engines were ubiquitous, the British government made a partial settlement that did little to compensate him for his great idea.

LATÉCOÈRE 28 The slab-sided Latécoère 28 began life as a passenger plane, powered by a Renault 12Jb engine of 500 horsepower. Eight passengers and a crew of three (two pilots and an engineer) could be carried at a maximum speed of 139 miles per hour. Equipped with floats, a mail-carrying version of the aircraft was flown on April 11–12, 1930, by Jean Mermoz to a closed-circuit distance record for seaplanes of 2,677 miles.

BOEING MONOMAIL Boeing was unusual in that it could be both revolutionary and evolutionary. The Boeing Monomail was an all-metal, cantilever-wing aircraft with retractable landing gear and a top speed of 158 miles per hour. Later, it was converted to this configuration, carrying passengers for United Air Lines's Cheyenne–Chicago route. The basic structural design was used for both the Boeing Y1B-9 and the Model 247, and this experience led in turn to the B-17.

GLENN CURTISS AND CURTISS CONDOR Glenn Curtiss is shown here in the cockpit of a Curtiss Condor transport on May 30, 1930. In it, he retraced the record flight he'd made 20 years earlier from New York to Albany in his Curtiss pusher. The Condor transport was designed by George Page and was a development of the Curtiss B-2 bomber. Sadly, Glenn Curtiss would die from a pulmonary embolism on July 23 of the same year, at the age of 52.

FLIGHT TIMELINE

July 1, 1931 United Air Lines is formed from Boeing Air Transport, National Air Transport, Pacific Air Transport, and Varney Air Lines.

July 24–31, 1931 The *Graf Zeppelin* carries 12 scientists on an Arctic flight.

July 28–30, 1931 Russ Boardman and Johnnie Polando fly their Bellanca from New York to Istanbul, setting a world record of 5,011 miles in 49 hours, 20 minutes.

July 28–August 6, 1931 Amy Johnson flies from England to Tokyo in nine days in a de Havilland Puss Moth.

August 11, 1931 A Polish PZL P-11 prototype flies.

September 3, 1931 Lowell Bayles wins the Thompson Trophy in a Gee Bee Z at 236.23 miles per hour.

September 4, 1931 Jimmy Doolittle sets a transcontinental record of 11 hours, 16 minutes to win the Bendix Race.

September 13, 1931 Flight Lieutenant John Boothman wins permanent possession of the Schneider Trophy for England in an uncontested event.

September 23, 1931 The *Akron* flies for the first time.

September 29, 1931 Flight Lieutenant George Stainforth flies a Supermarine S.6B at 407.5 miles per hour to establish a new world speed record. It's the first flight of more than 400 miles per hour.

PUBLICITY SHOT FROM *HELL'S ANGELS* In his film *Hell's Angels,* Howard Hughes showcases some of the greatest aviation photography in history, thanks to his desire for accuracy and disregard for safety. He assembled a reported 87 aircraft for the film, including four genuine Fokker D VIIs and three genuine S.E.5as. Several crashes and three deaths occurred during filming. Outtakes from *Hell's Angels,* particularly the big dogfight scene, were used in dozens of other films.

WRIGHT APACHE The Wright Aeronautical Corporation was highly successful with engines but unsuccessful with aircraft, building only a few over time. The XF3W Apache distinguished itself as a record setter. Flown by the brilliant young officer Lieutenant Apollo Soucek, the Apache established a world altitude record of 39,140 feet on May 8, 1929. Then, Soucek used a 450-horsepower Pratt & Whitney engine to set a new record of 43,155 feet on June 4, 1930.

HAWKER FURY Considered by many to be the most beautiful biplane fighter ever built, the Hawker Fury clearly shows the stamp of designer Sydney Camm's hand. The first RAF airplane capable of more than 200 miles per hour, the first production model of the Fury flew on March 25, 1931. A standard RAF Fury was powered by a 525-horsepower Rolls-Royce Kestrel engine and carried the standard two .303 Vickers machine-gun armament.

R-100 The British government wished to have a fleet of dirigibles to link its far-flung empire. Two were built: the R-101 by the government and the R-100 by a subsidiary of the Vickers company. The R-100 made a successful round-trip flight across the Atlantic in the summer of 1930; the R-101 crashed on October 5, 1930, on an attempt to fly to India. This ended British interest in rigid airship development.

JUNKERS JU 52/3M One of the great transports of all time, the Junkers Ju 52/3m first flew in April 1931. It was used extensively by Deutsch Lufthansa and many other airlines and became the standard Luftwaffe transport during World War II, the counterpart of the U.S. C-47. With three 725-horsepower BMW engines, the "Tante Ju" (Auntie Ju) had a top speed of only 170 miles per hour, but it was extremely rugged and reliable.

BOEING Y1B-9 AND XP-26 In 1931, the Boeing company produced the Army Air Corps' most advanced bomber, the Y1B-9 "Death Angel," and the most advanced fighter, the P-26A "Peashooter." Both aircraft combined modern and obsolete features. The Y1B-9 had an all-metal fuselage, cantilever wing, and retractable landing gear but retained the open cockpit. The P-26 was all metal but retained wire-braced wings and a fixed (if neatly streamlined) landing gear.

HAROLD GATTY AND WILEY POST Between June 23 and July 1, 1931, Wiley Post (right) and Harold Gatty, his navigator, blazed a 15,474-mile trail around the world in their white Lockheed Vega, the *Winnie Mae,* named for the daughter of the flight's sponsor, F. C. Hall. Post had lost an eye in an oil-field accident but flew very well nonetheless. The oil stains show that the Pratt & Whitney Wasp engine has been working hard.

LAIRD SOLUTION Flown by the redoubtable Jimmy Doolittle, the beautiful little Laird Super Solution biplane won the 1931 Bendix Race on September 4, 1931, at an average speed of 223.038 miles per hour. Doolittle went on to Newark to set a transcontinental record of 11 hours and 16 minutes.

SCHNEIDER TROPHY TEAM In 1931, Great Britain gained permanent possession of the Schneider Trophy by winning its third race in a row. Here we see the team of three Supermarine racers, from left an S.6B, an S.6A, and an S.6B. The last won the September 13, 1931, race, flown by Flight Lieutenant John Boothman at 340.08 miles per hour. Great Britain was the only country to enter the Schneider race that year. U.S., Italian, and French designers failed to have aircraft ready in time.

AKRON The United States was determined to build superior airships for its Navy, and the first of these, the beautiful helium-filled *Akron*, made its debut flight on September 23, 1931. The 785-foot-long *Akron* was powered by eight 560-horsepower Maybach engines and had a top speed of 79 miles per hour. The *Akron* was lost in a storm over the Atlantic on April 4, 1933; only 3 of the 76 crew members survived.

FLIGHT TIMELINE

March 23–26, 1932 The French continue long-distance record-breaking with a 6,587-mile closed-circuit flight. The aircraft, a Blériot 110 called *Joseph Le Brix*, is flown by Lucien Bossoutrot and Maurice Rossi.

March 24–28, 1932 Jimmy Mollison flies a Puss Moth from England to Capetown, South Africa, in 4 days, 17 hours, 30 minutes.

April 19–28, 1932 C. W. A. Scott flies from England to Darwin, Australia, in a Gypsy Moth, in 8 days, 20 hours, and 47 minutes.

May 20–21, 1932 In a Lockheed Vega, Amelia Earhart becomes the first woman to fly solo across the Atlantic.

June 19, 1932 The Dewoitine D.500 makes its first flight.

June 30, 1932 The *Los Angeles* is decommissioned after more than 4,000 hours in the air.

July 21, 1932 Von Gronau and the crew of his Dornier Wal complete a round-the-world flight in 111 days—the first in a flying boat.

August 13, 1932 The Granville brothers' Gee Bee R-1 Super-Sportster makes its first flight.

August 14–21, 1932 Louise Thaden and Frances Marsalis establish a women's world endurance record of eight days, four hours, five minutes in a Curtiss Thrush.

SUPERMARINE S.6B Flown by Flight Lieutenant George Stainforth, this Supermarine S.6B set a world speed record of 407.5 miles per hour on September 29, 1931. The airframe was designed by Reginald J. Mitchell and led indirectly to the Supermarine Spitfire. The 2,300-horsepower engine was influential in the development of the Rolls-Royce Merlin. Seaplanes were used to set speed records, despite the drag of the pontoons, because they had long stretches of water from which to take off and land.

PANGBORN AND HERNDON Clyde Pangborn and Hugh Herndon, Jr., stand by their Bellanca Skyrocket *Miss Veedol* on October 5, 1931. Two days earlier they had left Sabishiro Beach in Japan for the first nonstop flight from Japan to the United States. They flew 41 hours and 13 minutes to cover the 4,465 miles to Wenatchee, Washington. The landing gear on the Bellanca had been rigged to drop off (to reduce drag), so they had to make a belly landing.

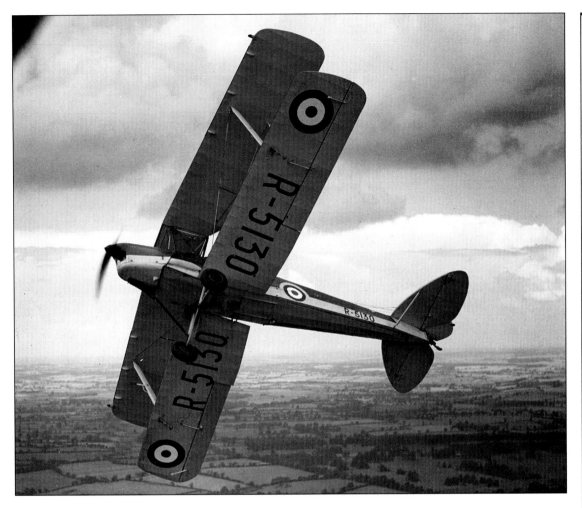

DE HAVILLAND D.H.82A TIGER MOTH One of the most popular training aircraft of all time, the Tiger Moth first flew on October 26, 1931, and many are still flying. The Tiger Moth was not replaced as a trainer in Great Britain until 1955 but continued in service with the Royal Navy until 1960. Many have been used in films, masquerading as both Allied and German World War I aircraft.

SIKORSKY S-40 Pan American Airways purchased three Sikorsky S-40 flying boats for use on its expanding routes. These were the first Clipper Ships, named the *American Clipper, Caribbean Clipper,* and *Southern Clipper.* With a 38-passenger capacity and a cruise speed of 115 miles per hour, the S-40s were powered by four Pratt & Whitney Hornet engines of 575 horsepower. Charles Lindbergh piloted the first passenger flight in an S-40 on November 19, 1931.

FLIGHT TIMELINE

August 18, 1932 Auguste Piccard sets a new balloon altitude record of 53,153 feet.

August 18–19, 1932 Jimmy Mollison makes the first east-west solo flight across the North Atlantic in 31 hours, 20 minutes.

August 25, 1932 Amelia Earhart becomes the first woman to make a nonstop transcontinental flight.

August 29, 1932 Jimmy Haizlip wins the Bendix, setting a transcontinental record of 10 hours, 19 minutes in a Wedell-Williams racer.

September 3, 1932 Jimmy Doolittle ends his racing career, winning the Thompson Trophy at 252.6 miles per hour, then setting a world speed record for landplanes of 296.287 miles per hour.

September 5, 1932 Mae Haizlip flies a Wedell-Williams racer to set a women's speed record of 252.5 miles per hour.

September 7, 1932 Thomas Settle and Wilfred Bushnell set a balloon world-distance record of 963.12 miles.

September 16, 1932 Cyril Uwins flies a Vickers Vespa to set a world altitude record of 43,976 feet.

September 25, 1932 Lewis Yancey flies a Pitcairn PCA-2 to set an autogiro altitude record of 21,500 feet.

November 4, 1932 The Beech Model 17 Staggerwing makes its first flight.

DEWOITINE D.501 PROTOTYPE First flown on June 19, 1932 (just three months after the Boeing P-26's first flight), the Dewoitine was a clean, attractive monoplane powered by a 660-horsepower Hispano Suiza engine. This aircraft is the D.501 fighter, converted for testing by the *Aeronavale*. A later version, the D.510, was in widespread use at the outbreak of World War II.

GEE BEE RACER The Granville brothers of Springfield, Massachusetts, had gone from obscurity to fame with the success of their original Gee Bee Model Z of 1931. In 1932, they created two Gee Bees, the R-1 for the Thompson Trophy race and the R-2 for the Bendix Race. Jimmy Doolittle became the pilot for the R-2, winning the Thompson handily at 252.6 miles per hour, then setting a world land speed record of 296.287 miles per hour on September 3.

FLIGHT TIMELINE

JIMMY MOLLISON AND PUSS MOTH Jimmy Mollison was one of Great Britain's favorite sons because he made a practice of flying small airplanes over long distances. The de Haviland D.H.80A was a favorite of his, and he flew "The Hearts Content," on several long-distance flights. Fitted with an additional 160-gallon tank, the Puss Moth had a 3,600-mile range. In it, Mollison made the first solo east-west Atlantic crossing on August 18–19, 1932, in just 31 hours and 20 minutes.

BEECH 17 Walter H. Beech's career in industry was enhanced by his close association with other greats, including Clyde Cessna and Lloyd Stearman. Despite doing very well with Travel Air, Beech, like so many of his era, was determined to launch his own company and build the finest private planes in the world. He did so in the depth of the Great Depression, flying this aircraft, the very first Beech Model 17, on November 4, 1932.

November 14–18, 1932 Amy Johnson (now married to Jimmy Mollison) flies solo from England to South Africa, in a Puss Moth in 4 days, 6 hours, 54 minutes, to set a new record.

December 11–18, 1932 Amy Johnson makes a record-setting return journey from South Africa in seven days, seven hours, five minutes.

January 26, 1933 The Institute of Aeronautical Sciences is founded.

February 6–8, 1933 A Fairey Long-Range Monoplane sets a world distance record of 5,309.24 miles.

February 6–9, 1933 Jimmy Mollison flies from England to Brazil. He is the first to achieve solo flights across both the North and South Atlantic and the first to fly solo from England to South America.

February 8, 1933 The Boeing Model 247 transport, a development of the Monomail and the YB-9, makes its first flight.

April 4, 1933 The dirigible *Akron* crashes into the sea off the New Jersey coast. Seventy-three people die.

April 21, 1933 The *Macon* makes its first flight.

June 22, 1933 The Tupolev RD (Distance Record) aircraft makes its first flight.

July 1933 Amelia Earhart breaks her own transcontinental record, making the flight in 17 hours, 17 minutes, 30 seconds.

GEORGE PUTNAM, PAUL MANTZ, AND AMELIA EARHART George Putnam and Amelia Earhart had an unusual marriage for the time; in retrospect he appeared to be more her manager and promoter than her husband. Paul Mantz was one of the great flyer-businesspeople of his time, making a good living working with Hollywood on films and catering to the aviation needs of celebrities. The engine is a reliable Pratt & Whitney Wasp, about to be installed in Earhart's Lockheed Vega.

DORNIER DO 23 Germany was anxious to get back into the war-plane business after World War I, and one of its first major efforts was the Dornier Do 11, which had a high accident rate. Modified into the Do 23, it was still never entirely successful and was phased out of bombing duty to serve as a training plane or as an aerial mine detector. With two BMW V-12 engines it had a top speed of 161 miles per hour.

CARL B. SQUIER AND LOCKHEED ORION Considered at the time to be the best airplane salesperson in the world, the personable Carl Squier's motto was "make a friend, sell a plane." He did just that for Lockheed. During a time of grave financial crisis, Squier sold five of the beautiful Orions, like the one shown. He is patting his personal pride, his Packard.

P-26 The Boeing Model 248 was tested by the Army as the XP-936, but it was designated the P-26A in service. The prototype first flew on March 20, 1931, and attained a maximum speed of 222 miles per hour. The Army bought 111 as P-26As, followed by an additional 25 as P-26Bs and P-26Cs. Somewhat tricky to land, the P-26s were popular with their pilots and saw action with the Philippine Air Force in World War II.

FLIGHT TIMELINE

July 1, 1933 Because United Air Lines tied up rights to all Boeing 247 production, TWA asks Douglas aircraft to develop a competitive aircraft. Douglas's response, the DC-1, makes its first flight on this date.

July 1, 1933 Roscoe Turner sets a westbound transcontinental record of 11 hours, 30 minutes, in a Wedell-Williams racer.

July 1–15, 1933 Italo Balbo brings 23 Savoia-Marchetti S.55 flying boats from Rome to Chicago, via New York. This is the first formation flight across the North Atlantic.

July 9–December 19, 1933 Charles and Anne Lindbergh make a 29,000-mile survey flight in their Lockheed Sirius.

July 15–17, 1933 Steponas Darius and Stasys Girenas fly from New York to Soldin, Germany, but are killed in a crash on arrival.

July 15–22, 1933 Wiley Post flies the Lockheed Vega *Winnie Mae* around the world solo in 7 days, 18 hours, 49 minutes. He had a new radio compass and new autopilot.

July 22–24, 1933 Jim and Amy Mollison become the first husband-wife team to fly east-west across the Atlantic.

August 5–7, 1933 Flying from New York to Syria, French pilots Maurice Rossi and Paul Codes set a world distance record of 5,657 miles.

BOEING MODEL 247 The Boeing Model 247 was the first truly modern airliner. All metal, with cantilever wing and retractable landing gear, the 247 could carry ten passengers in relative comfort at 180 miles per hour. This is the first 247 to be delivered to United, which was part of the Boeing industrial complex. All other transports—Fords, Fokkers, Curtisses—were obsolete from the moment this Boeing flew. The Model 247 also led to the Boeing B-17.

MACON The *Macon* made its first flight on April 21, 1933, just 17 days after its sister ship, the *Akron*, crashed. Both airships had been designed as aerial aircraft carriers, and the *Macon* gained considerable experience in launching and recovering the pretty Curtiss F9C Sparrowhawk fighters. On February 12, 1935, a gust of wind damaged the *Macon*'s control surfaces, and it crashed into the sea off the California coast; 81 were saved and only 2 died.

WINNIE MAE AND WILEY POST Perhaps the most famous of all the Lockheed Vegas, the globe-girdling *Winnie Mae* can still be seen in the National Air and Space Museum. Wiley Post flew the aircraft around the world with navigator Harold Gatty in 8 days, 15 hours, and 51 minutes, landing on July 1, 1931. On July 22, 1933, he landed in New York after flying solo around the world in 7 days, 18 hours, and 49 minutes.

DOUGLAS DC-1 TWA needed to replace its wood-wing Fokker airliners and couldn't buy Boeing 247s, so they asked the industry for a comparable aircraft. Douglas responded with the remarkable DC-1, the first of a Douglas dynasty of airliners. The first and only DC-1 made its initial flight on July 1, 1933, and quickly led to the even more advanced DC-2. The DC-1 went to Spain during the Spanish Civil War. It crashed at Malaga and was abandoned.

POLIKARPOV I-16 Perhaps the most advanced fighter in the world at the time of its first flight on December 31, 1933, the powerful little Polikarpov I-16 would prove itself in combat in Spain, Finland, Manchuria, and over Mother Russia. Known as the "Mosca" (Fly) by the Spanish Republican air arm, the I-16 proved itself superior to the Nationalist Heinkel He 51 and Fiat C.R. 32 biplanes. Obsolete by 1941, it still fought valiantly against the invading Germans.

FLIGHT TIMELINE

September 1933 The famous Portuguese flyer General Francesco de Pinedo is killed in a Bellanca on takeoff from Floyd Bennett Field.

September 1933 Jimmy Wedell wins the Thompson Trophy in a Wedell-Williams Special, then sets a world speed record for landplanes of 305.33 miles per hour.

September 7–8, 1933 Six Consolidated P2Y-1 flying boats set a formation distance record, flying nonstop from Norfolk, Virginia, to Coco Solo, Canal Zone.

September 25, 1933 Roscoe Turner sets a west-east transcontinental record of 10 hours, 4 minutes, 55 seconds.

September 28, 1933 Gustave Lemoine sets a new world altitude record of 44,820 feet in a Potez 50.

October 4–11, 1933 Sir Charles Kingsford Smith flies from England to Australia solo in a Percival Gull in 7 days, 4 hours, 44 minutes.

October 12, 1933 The *Macon* flies from Lakehurst to Sunnyvale in 70 hours.

December 31, 1933 A prototype of the Polikarpov I-16 makes its first flight; it will be the first monoplane fighter with retractable landing gear and an enclosed cockpit to go into squadron service.

CHAPTER FOUR

1934 to 1943:

From the Depths of the Depression to the Cauldron of War

In 1934, aviation began to emerge from the dark recesses of the depression, shaking off the exuberance of the past and becoming far more professional. All over the world, new designs were on the drawing boards of both military and commercial manufacturers. These aircraft would dictate both the pace of civil aviation progress and the military prowess of nations, particularly those aggressor countries who were determined to go to war.

Boeing B-17E

But there were tragic losses as well, highlighted by the dramatic explosion of the dirigible *Hindenburg* over Lakehurst, New Jersey, on May 6, 1937. This was followed soon after by the disappearance of the revered Amelia Earhart on her second attempt at a round-the-world flight in 1937. There were military losses, too, as the smaller wars in China, Spain, Ethiopia, and South America were superseded in 1939 by World War II.

One fascinating aspect of this decade was the proliferation of new military types. Within the space of three years, 1934 to 1936, there occurred the debut of the Messerschmitt Bf 109, Hawker Hurricane, Supermarine Spitfire, Boeing B-17, Heinkel He 111, Curtiss P-36, Mitsubishi G3M, Morane-Saulnier MS.406, and many others that would see action in World War II. Quite remarkably, given the disparity in the resources of each country involved, these new aircraft had comparable performance parameters, which speaks to the genius of their designers.

Curtiss P-40E   In commerce, there would be a flowering of excellent types, beginning with the Douglas DC-3 but extending across frontiers to the British Empire series flying boats, the German Focke-Wulf Fw 200 Condor, and the French Dewoitine D.332 and Italian Savoia-Marchetti S.M.75 trimotors. Business aircraft had a similar burst of international brilliance that included the Beech Model 17 Staggerwing, de Havilland D.H.88 Comet, Messerschmitt Bf 108 Taifun, and Caudron Simoun. And for the private individual, there were the Piper Cub, the de Havilland Puss Moth, and Henri Mignet's amusing but dangerous *Pou de Ciel (Flying Flea)*.

Around the world, there were gains in the number of aircraft in service, the number of passenger miles flown, the acres of crops sprayed, and the return on investment from aviation companies. There were gains in performance, too, as the official land speed record rose to 469.22 miles per hour in the Messerschmitt Bf 109R (Me 209 VI) and the altitude record to 56,046 feet in a Caproni-161*bis* biplane. Howard Hughes, having designed and built his own Hughes H-1 racer with which he set both a land speed record and a U.S. transcontinental record, chose a Lockheed Model 14 to make the swiftest trip around the world, taking only 3 days, 19 hours, and 8 minutes.

In the years after World War I, philosophies of airpower appeared. Some were authored by well-known leaders such as the RAF's Hugh Trenchard, Italy's Giulio Douhet, and the United States' Brigadier General Billy Mitchell. Although there were many differences in their respective approaches, all agreed that command of the air was essential: The way to win a war was to attack the "vital centers" of the enemy—before they attacked yours. While their ideas were sound, they were not backed financially by any of the democratic nations, which allowed their armed forces to fall into complete disarray in the years between the wars. This was in sharp contrast to the totalitarian countries, including Germany, Japan, and the Soviet Union, where the military budget funded strong air forces.

Germany and Japan were thus endowed with a tremendous advantage at the beginning of World War II. By choosing to determine the date the war would start, they timed the introduction of new technology to their air forces so they could be at maximum strength when war began. Thus, for Germany on September 1, 1939, and for Japan on December 7, 1941, their respective air forces were at the peak of their form. Both had the latest and best aircraft, both had extensive combat experience (Germany's gained in Spain, Japan's in China and in border conflicts with the Soviet Union), and both would use them to overwhelm initially weaker enemies.

Air power allowed Germany to defeat Poland, Denmark, Norway, Holland, Belgium, and Luxembourg in swift campaigns that were relatively inexpensive. Air power in fact seduced Japan, allowing it to make the colossal mistake of becoming involved in a World War against China, the United States, and Great Britain. But it also allowed Japan to make a series of sweeping victories in late 1941 and for the first five months of 1942.

As expert as both Germany and Japan were in the application of air power against weaker opponents, neither nation had any concept of the scale of air power that was required to fight a global war. Both believed that air forces of 3,000 to 5,000 front-line planes, flown by expert crews, were adequate. Both were wrong by a factor of 15 or more.

Of all the nations involved in the war, only the United States and the Soviet Union understood just how large an effective air force would have to be. They also had the industrial capacity to create such a force. Great Britain understood that a large air force was needed but despite its best efforts could not create one of the necessary size, because it devoted far too many resources to its Bomber Command.

Germany began the war against the Soviet Union with fewer first-line aircraft available than it had at the time of the fall of France. In the first few months of the war, the Luftwaffe was able to decimate the Soviet Air Force—but it could not reach either the Soviet aircraft factories or training bases. Japan began the war with clearly superior aircraft and crews but had such a small industrial base and an even smaller crew training system that it could not replace the losses incurred in the Battles of the Coral Sea and Midway.

By 1943, the tide was shifting swiftly away from the once victorious Axis powers to the Allies and to the Soviet Union. In the United States, new aircraft were coming off the factory lines in ever increasing numbers, and pilots and crews were flowing at an inexhaustible rate. The Soviet Union was also beginning to feel its new strength, with more and better aircraft racing off production lines. While Germany and Japan made enormous efforts to catch up, both timing and technology were now firmly on the side of the Allies.

Airpower through 1943 had been important in many instances, decisive in a few but always influential. However, the groundwork in airpower, training, and armament had been laid so that the Allies could forge ahead in the next two years of the war and utterly defeat the countries that had started the war. In the process, they would build the technical foundation for a revolution in civil and military aviation in the postwar period.

Focke-Wulf Condor Fw 200C

CONSOLIDATED P2Y-2 RANGER Isaac M. "Mac" Laddon, who gained his greatest fame with the Consolidated PBY-Catalina and, later, the B-36 Peacemaker, joined Consolidated in 1927. He designed the successful Commodore twin-engine flying boats, from which the P2Y-2 patrol planes were derived. The Ranger made several notable long-range flights, including a nonstop formation flight from San Francisco to Honolulu on January 10–11, 1934. At a cruise speed of 117 miles per hour, the aircraft was capable of flying 1,180 miles with a 2,000-pound bomb load.

FLYING THE MAIL February 18, 1934, marked the start of an ill-starred adventure: the Army flying the mail. Pictured here is Pilot Lieutenant Herman A. Schmid at the Municipal Airport in Chicago. He carried the first load of mail in a Curtiss Shrike attack plane. Most Army aircraft did not have adequate instrumentation, a shortcoming that led to 57 crashes and many lost lives carrying the mail. In addition, few of the pilots had instrument training because of budget restrictions.

SIKORSKY S-42 Igor Sikorsky's small firm on Long Island built one good design after another, creating in the Sikorsky S-42 one of the most beautiful flying boats of the era. Ten were built, and each could carry almost twice as many passengers twice as far—and almost as fast—as a Douglas DC-3. The *Brazilian Clipper* was the first to fly, leaving the water on March 30, 1934. The S-42s pioneered Pan American's Pacific route.

FAIREY SWORDFISH Officially called the Swordfish but affectionately referred to as "the Stringbag" for its many wires, the prototype of this noble warplane made its first flight on April 17, 1934. It became one of the great aircrafts of World War II by virtue of its daring raid on Taranto, Italy, on November 11, 1940, and its key torpedo attack on the *Bismarck* in 1941. With a maximum speed of 139 miles per hour, the "Stringbag" was slow but rugged.

DOUGLAS DC-1 The Douglas DC-1 was TWA's answer to United's Boeing 247. Powered by two Pratt & Whitney Hornet engines of 700 horsepower each, the DC-1 used Jack Northrop's multicellular wing structure. The aircraft almost crashed during its first flight on July 1, 1933, but went on to prove itself as the most modern airliner in the sky. On May 13, 1934, Jack Frye set a coast-to-coast record of 11 hours and 31 minutes in the DC-1. Only one was built, since larger DC-2s then DC-3s soon filled the production line.

FLIGHT TIMELINE

January 10–11, 1934 Six Consolidated P2Y-1 flying boats make a nonstop formation flight from San Francisco to Honolulu.

January 18, 1934 Qantas is established as an airline in Australia.

February 18–19, 1934 Eddie Rickenbacker and Jack Frye set a passenger transport record in the DC-1, flying from Los Angeles to New York in 13 hours and 2 minutes, to protest President Franklin Roosevelt's cancellation of airmail contracts.

February 19, 1934 President Franklin Roosevelt cancels airline airmail contracts; the U.S. Army Air Corps will fly the mail.

February 28–April 25, 1934 Laura Ingalls completes a solo tour of South America in a Lockheed Air Express.

April 11, 1934 Commander Renato Donati flies a Caproni 113 to a world altitude record of 47,352 feet.

April 16, 1934 Northwest Airways becomes Northwest Orient Airlines.

April 17, 1934 Eastern Air Transport becomes Eastern Airlines.

April 17, 1934 The de Havilland D.H.89 Dragon Rapide makes its first flight.

April 17, 1934 The Fairey Swordfish, the immortal "Stringbag," prototype makes its first flight.

MARTIN B-10 An all-metal cantilever monoplane with cowled engines, enclosed cockpits, and retractable gear, the Martin B-10 was a truly revolutionary aircraft when it appeared at Wright Field in October 1932. When combined with the new and secret Norden bombsight, the B-10B established bombing as the principal Air Corps mission and set the stage for USAAF operations in World War II. Models exported to the Netherlands East Indies saw combat against the Japanese.

GLOSTER GLADIATOR PROTOTYPE The last operational biplane fighter of the RAF, this prototype Gloster Gladiator was first flown on September 12, 1934. It still had the open cockpit, fixed gear, and wooden propeller of its predecessor, the S.E.5a of World War I. Both planes had been designed by H. P. Folland. Some 480 were built, and they gave gallant service in Norway, Greece, Malta, and the Middle East. Production Gladiators had a cockpit canopy and hit 257 miles per hour.

Macchi MC.72 Seaplane The ultimate racing floatplane, the Macchi MC.72 was designed to win the 1931 Schneider Trophy race to prevent the British from taking permanent possession of the trophy. The MC.72 was powered by two Fiat AS.5 engines placed in tandem on a common crankcase and generating 2,850 horsepower. Unable to compete in the race for technical reasons, Warrant Officer Francesco Agello set a world speed record of 440.68 miles per hour on October 23, 1934—a floatplane record that still stands.

De Havilland Comet One of the most beautiful aircraft of its era, the de Havilland D.H.88 Comet was designed for the MacRobertson race from Mildenhall, England, to Melbourne, Australia, sponsored by Sir MacPherson Robertson. Powered by de Havilland Gypsy engines of 230 horsepower each, this aircraft, called the *Grosvenor House,* was painted a rich scarlet with white trim and won the October 1934 race in 70 hours, 54 minutes, and 18 seconds. The Comet's design inspired the famous Mosquito of World War II.

FLIGHT TIMELINE

May 8–23, 1934 Jean Batten beats Amy Johnson's England–Australia solo record by flying the same distance in 14 days, 22 hours, and 30 minutes.

May 13, 1934 Jack Frye sets a coast-to-coast record of 11 hours, 31 minutes in a DC-1.

May 13, 1934 American Airways becomes American Airlines.

June 1, 1934 The Air Corps ceases to deliver airmail.

June 5, 1934 William G. Swan, piloting a glider powered by 12 rockets, attains an altitude of 200 feet in Atlantic City, New Jersey.

June 18, 1934 Engineers begin designing the Boeing Model 299X, which will eventually become the B-17 Flying Fortress.

July 9, 1934 "Sleeper service" is inaugurated on Curtiss Wright Condors on the Chicago–New York route.

July 19, 1934 Curtiss Sparrowhawks, without landing gear, fly from the USS *Macon* on scouting expeditions.

July 19–August 20, 1934 Lieutenant Colonel H. H. Arnold leads ten Martin B-10s from Bolling Field to Fairbanks, Alaska, on a photographic survey.

July 28, 1934 Major W. E. Kepner and Captains A. W. Stevens and O. A. Anderson reach 60,613 feet in a balloon; the balloon collapses, and the men bail out.

BOEING P-26A The "Peashooter," as it was called, was well liked by pilots; young officers avidly sought duty in Hawaii flying this sweet airplane. The P-26A was not without its problems, however, for even with the flaps that were retrofitted to lower its landing speed, it was still quite a handful to land. The tall headrest was necessary to protect the pilot in case the plane turned over on its back.

ROSCOE TURNER One of the most glamorous figures of the golden age of flight, Roscoe Turner was a superb pilot with magnificent style. Whether he was flying cross-country with Gilmore, his lion cub, or posing in the dashing uniform he designed for himself, Turner was always "on." He won the Thompson Trophy three times before retiring from racing. He then established a successful flight school and fixed-base operation.

HELEN RICHEY On December 31, 1934, Helen Richey became the first woman to pilot a commercial airliner when she flew the Washington, D.C., to Detroit route for Central Airlines. She had soloed in April 1930, then went on to become a stunt and racing pilot. Later, Richey set class records for speed and altitude in her Aeronca C-2. She flew as Amelia Earhart's copilot in the 1936 Bendix Race; they finished fifth.

MESSERSCHMITT "BF 109R" Nazi Germany was well aware of the prestige that accrued from speed records, and the Messerschmitt firm designed the Me 209 (called Bf 109R for propaganda purposes) specifically to beat the speed record set by the Macchi MC.72 on October 23, 1934. Powered by a 2,770-horsepower Daimler-Benz engine, the Me 209 was extremely tricky to fly, but on April 26, 1939, Fritz Wendel set a speed record of 469.22 miles per hour.

HEINKEL HE 111 Designed to be both a bomber and a commercial transport, the Heinkel He 111 made its first test flight on February 24, 1935. The He 111 was a very advanced aircraft for the time but was obsolete on the western front by 1942 and on the eastern front by 1943. Short of replacements, the Germans were forced to use it in one role or another until the last day of World War II.

CONSOLIDATED PBY This nostalgic shot shows the new overtaking the old as a Consolidated XP3Y-1 (later the PBY Catalina) passes a formation of Martin PM-1 flying boats, signaling that the monoplane era had arrived. First flown on March 28, 1935, the beloved Catalina (said to "take off, cruise, and land at 120 miles per hour") became the most produced and most versatile flying boat of World War II, serving in torpedo, antisubmarine, bombing, attack, air-sea rescue, and patrol roles.

BRISTOL BLENHEIM The prototype of the Bristol Blenheim series was first flown on April 12, 1935. Called *Britain First,* it was an attempt by Lord Rothermere, owner of the *Daily Mail* newspaper, to spur modernization of RAF bombers. This is a restoration of a later model Blenheim, flown in 1987. The Blenheim led to a long series of successful Bristol warplanes, including the Bolingbroke, Beaufort, and Beaufighter; the latter was one of the most versatile aircraft of World War II.

Douglas XTBD-1 Devastator Pictured on its April 15, 1935, first flight, the prototype Douglas XTBD-1 Devastator marked the transition of the United States Navy from biplane to monoplane torpedo bombers. Its 800-horsepower Pratt & Whitney engine provided a top speed of 202 miles per hour. A 1,000-pound torpedo could be carried externally. The aircraft was too slow for modern warfare, and Devastator squadrons were so severely mauled at the Battle of Midway that the type was withdrawn from operations.

Grumman XF3F-1 Grumman's great success with its first aircraft, the XFF-1, led to Navy orders for smaller single-seaters, including the F2F and F3F series. This is the barrel-shaped XF3F-1, of which 54 were ordered for fleet duty. The XF3F-1 had troubles in test flights. Test pilot Jimmy Collins eerily predicted his death in a 9-G dive test, and two more prototypes crashed before Bill McAvoy successfully gave the XF3F-1 a thumbs-up on June 20, 1935.

LAURA INGALLS Laura Ingalls could not hear reporters after her July 11, 1935, record-breaking flight from Floyd Bennett Field, New York, to Burbank, California, in just 18 hours, 19 minutes, and 30 seconds. She was temporarily deafened by engine noise from her specially built Lockheed Orion 9D, the *Auto-da-Fé*. On September 12, 1935, she set a record in the opposite direction, flying from Burbank to Floyd Bennett Field in 13 hours, 34 minutes, and 5 seconds.

BOEING B-17F The prototype of the B-17 made its first flight on July 28, 1935. Although production was slow at first, eventually 12,731 were built, and they distinguished themselves in every theater of war. The B-17F had received many improvements and engaged in many of the major air battles of 1943, including the Schweinfurt and Regensburg raids. The rugged construction of the B-17 allowed it to endure heavy battle damage.

MORANE-SAULNIER MS.405 Externally similar to the more familiar MS.406, the MS.405 made its first flight on August 8, 1935, a little more than two months after its chief rival, the Messerschmitt Bf 109, which flew on May 28. France's aviation industry was in chaos, and only 572 model 406s had been delivered by the time war broke out. The MS.406, which had a top speed of 302 miles per hour, fought valiantly but to no avail.

WILL ROGERS AND WILEY POST Will Rogers was the Jay Leno/Dave Barry/Jerry Seinfeld of his time, mesmerizing audiences with homespun humor in theaters, radio, films, and the press. Rogers loved flying, and Wiley Post (right) proposed an easygoing flight around the world in a hybrid aircraft, a mixture of Lockheed Explorer and Orion parts, with floats not designed for it. The aircraft was nose-heavy, and Post crashed on takeoff at Point Barrow, Alaska, killing them both, on August 15, 1935.

FLIGHT TIMELINE

April 16–23, 1935 Pan Am flies a Clipper from Oakland to Hawaii. This marks the start of Pacific route building.

May 8, 1935 Amelia Earhart becomes the first person to fly nonstop from Mexico City, Mexico, to Newark, New Jersey, in 14 hours, 18 minutes, 30 seconds.

May 9, 1935 The Navy dispatches 46 Consolidated P2Y flying boats to Midway Island on a secret mission.

May 18, 1935 The worst air disaster to date occurs over Moscow when a hotshot fighter pilot shows off and flies into the ANT-20 *Maxim Gorkii*, the largest aircraft in the world. Fifty-six people die.

May 28, 1935 The Messerschmitt Bf 109 flies for the first time. It will become the most produced fighter in Germany, with more than 33,000 built.

July 11, 1935 Laura Ingalls establishes an east-west transcontinental speed record for women, flying from Floyd Bennett Field, New York, to Burbank, California in 18 hours, 19 minutes, 30 seconds.

July 23, 1935 The first report on what becomes known as radar is made to the Air Defense Research Committee.

July 28, 1935 The Boeing B-17 prototype (actually Model 299X) makes its first flight.

JUNKERS JU 87 STUKA First flown on September 17, 1935, the Junkers Ju 87 Stuka was without question the most sinister aircraft of World War II. It looked and sounded evil, but the Ju 87 was simply an efficient aircraft for its dive-bombing task. It could only operate when the Germans had aerial superiority. When they did not (for example over England during the Battle of Britain), the slow and vulnerable Ju 87s were shot out of the sky.

HOWARD HUGHES A solemn-faced Howard Hughes stands beside his record-breaking H-1 racer. In it, he set the absolute landplane speed record of 352.38 miles per hour on September 13, 1935, and a transcontinental record of 327.5 miles per hour on February 19, 1937. Jim Wright flew a replica of the aircraft on July 2, 2002, and is currently exhibiting it at air shows.

GODDARD AND ROCKET It is rare when you can hold the future in your hands, but that's exactly what Charles Lindbergh, Robert Goddard, and Harry F. Guggenheim, with their two assistants at the left, are doing on September 25, 1935. Lindbergh aided Goddard's experiments with liquid rockets, finding financial backing for him. This one was planned to reach the stratosphere at 700 miles per hour. Goddard's experiments powered the way to space.

HAWKER HURRICANE After designing beautiful open-cockpit, fixed-gear, two-machine gun biplanes for years, Sydney Camm created the enclosed cockpit, retractable gear, eight-machine gun, cantilever monoplane Hurricane, shown here on its first flight on November 6, 1935. Powered by a Rolls-Royce Merlin engine, the Hurricane became the most important British fighter in the Battle of Britain, though it was overshadowed in the press by the Supermarine Spitfire. As the "Hurribomber," it became a very successful close-air support aircraft.

FLIGHT TIMELINE

August 8, 1935 The Morane-Saulnier MS.405 flies for the first time.

August 15, 1935 Wiley Post and Will Rogers are killed in a plane crash at Point Barrow, Alaska.

September 1935 Harold Neumann wins the Thompson Trophy in a Howard DGA-6 Special, *Mister Mulligan*.

September 12, 1935 Laura Ingalls sets a west-east transcontinental record for women: 13 hours, 34 minutes, 5 seconds.

September 13, 1935 Howard Hughes sets a landplane speed record of 352.38 miles per hour in a plane designed to his specifications.

September 15, 1935 Alexander de Seversky sets an amphibian speed record: 230.413 miles per hour.

September 17, 1935 The infamous Junkers Ju 87 Stuka flies for the first time.

October 30, 1935 The Boeing B-17 prototype crashes and burns at Wright Field while taking off with its innovative control lock in the locked position.

November 6, 1935 The Hawker Hurricane prototype flies.

November 11, 1935 Albert Stevens and Orvil Anderson set a balloon altitude record of 72,395 feet in the *Explorer II*.

MARTIN M-130 CHINA CLIPPER At the time of this photo, November 22, 1935, the Martin M-130 *China Clipper* was the most efficient flying boat in the world. Shown here, it is departing San Francisco Bay for Manila, via Honolulu, Wake, and Guam Islands, as Pan American Airways inaugurates transpacific airmail service. A fast, comfortable aircraft for the time, the *China Clipper* corresponded to today's Concorde in terms of prestige and luxury. None of the three Martin M-130s built survive today.

DOUGLAS DC-3 First flown as the Douglas Sleeper Transport on December 17, 1935, complete with 16 sleeping berths, the sleek new airliner became the most important piston-engine airliner in history. As the DC-3, it carried 14 to 28 passengers and was eagerly purchased by airlines around the world. More than 13,000 of the type were built, including 10,692 as C-47s. The C-47 served in every theater of war.

HINDENBURG The first flight of the *Hindenburg* took place on March 4, 1936. It is shown here on its first flight to New York, passing the Empire State Building (which had been designed to allow dirigibles to dock at its summit) en route to its normal U.S. landing destination, Lakehurst, New Jersey. This beautiful sight does not even hint at the airship's tragic future.

AMELIA EARHART Amelia Earhart was determined to see women gain a place in aviation, and she devoted herself to the task. She is shown here in an uncharacteristically glamorous pose, in front of the specially modified Lockheed Electra 10E in which she would attempt a round-the-world flight that would keep as close to the equator as possible. In July 1937, Earhart disappeared near Howland Island in the Pacific.

FLIGHT TIMELINE

November 13, 1935 New Zealand pilot Jean Batten completes a record flight from Lympne, England, to Natal, Brazil, in 2 days, 13 hours, and 15 minutes.

November 22, 1935 Pan Am inaugurates transpacific airmail service in the *China Clipper*. A round-trip flight takes 122 hours, 42 minutes.

November 29, 1935 A propeller deicer is announced by the Bureau of Air Commerce.

December 17, 1935 The Douglas Sleeper Transport, DC-3 prototype, flies.

January 13–14, 1936 Howard Hughes, flying a Northrop Gamma, sets a west-east nonstop transcontinental record of 9 hours, 26 minutes, 10 seconds.

February 9, 1936 It is announced that 40,000 people are at work on $35 million worth of WPA aviation projects.

February 10, 1936 Rocket research begins at the Guggenheim Aeronautical Laboratory of the California Institute of Technology (GALCIT). The project will eventually lead to Jet Assisted Take-Off (JATO).

February 17, 1936 Aviation pioneer and inventor Hiram Maxim dies at age 66.

February 19, 1936 Billy Mitchell dies in New York at age 58.

March 4, 1936 The LZ 129 *Hindenburg*, the world's largest airship, flies for the first time.

SUPERMARINE SPITFIRE
Designed by Reginald J. Mitchell, the Supermarine Spitfire was one of the most beautiful fighters of World War II. Although Mitchell was quite ill at the time, he lived to see the first flight on March 5, 1936. He died without knowing that the Spitfire would be Great Britain's most important fighter of World War II; more than 22,000 would be built. Fast, maneuverable, and a delight to fly, the Spitfire's only failing was its limited range.

FAIREY BATTLE The prototype of the Fairey Battle was first flown on March 10, 1936. The RAF, which believed in the light bomber concept, purchased 2,200 of the type. Capable of only 210 miles per hour at sea level, the aircraft were too slow and too lightly armed for combat. The Germans shot them down in droves during the Battle of France, and the aircraft were withdrawn from combat.

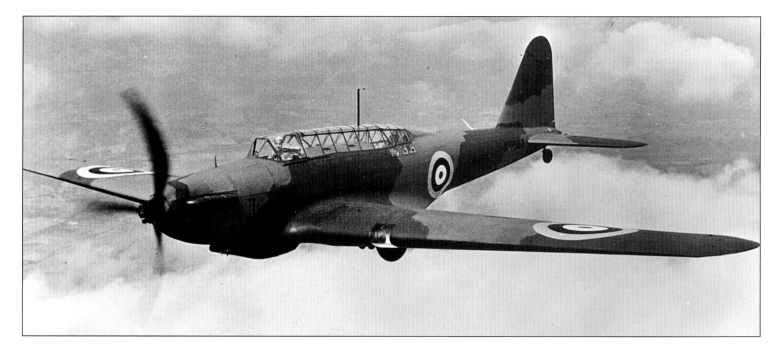

WESTLAND LYSANDER A great test pilot and a wonderful author, Harald Penrose was in the cockpit on this first flight of the Westland Lysander on June 15, 1936. Intended for Army Cooperation work, the "Lizzie," as it was called, found its niche operating as a clandestine aircraft, taking spies into and out of occupied Europe. Lysanders also operated as air-sea rescue aircraft and target tugs. The top speed was 219 miles per hour, but landings could be made at very low speeds.

VICKERS WELLINGTON Known to the British public as the "Wimpey," the Vickers Wellington was the backbone of Bomber Command through late 1942, when it was supplemented by four-engine bombers. First flown on June 15, 1936, the Wellington featured Barnes Wallis' geodetic latticework construction, which was able to absorb a great deal of punishment. Some 11,461 Wellingtons were built. It served as a first-line bomber until March 13, 1945, operating extensively with Coastal Command.

FLIGHT TIMELINE

March 5, 1936 The Supermarine Spitfire prototype flies for the first time.

March 10, 1936 The Fairey Battle, a total failure of a light bomber, makes its first flight.

March 17, 1936 The Armstrong Whitworth Whitley, which will become one of the RAF's three main bombers in the early days of World War II (the others: Wellington, Hampden), flies for the first time.

April 1936 A rocket engine is flight tested in a modified Heinkel He 112.

April 1936 Rocket scientist Wernher von Braun moves into a new center at Peenemünde, Germany.

April 1936 The Fieseler Storch, a true short takeoff and landing (STOL) aircraft, flies for the first time.

April 4, 1936 The *Yorktown*, the first American aircraft carrier designed for that task, is launched.

April 15, 1936 Hans Pabst von Ohain begins work on his jet engine at Heinkel.

May 5, 1936 Italian forces conquer Ethiopia.

May 6–14, 1936 The *Hindenburg* flies from Friedrichshafen, Germany, to Lakehurst, New Jersey, in 61 hours, 50 minutes. The return flight takes 49 hours, 3 minutes.

May 12, 1936 The Messerschmitt Bf 110 prototype flies.

JUNKERS JU 52/3M The photo angle imparts a gliderlike aspect ratio to the wing of the stout Junkers Ju 52/3m. This is a still from "The Battle of Britain" and purports to be the Junkers Ju 52/3m that carried Feldmarschall Erhard Milch on an inspection tour. The Ju 52 was the Luftwaffe's equivalent of the U.S. Douglas C-47; it fought throughout the war in every theater and was subsequently used in several countries as a transport.

MICHEL DETROYAT WINS THOMPSON TROPHY

A smiling Michel Detroyat, winner of the $20,000 September 3, 1936, Thompson Trophy race, stands next to the propeller of his 380-horsepower Renault engine in his Caudron C-460. American racing pilots were a rather rough-hewn crew, and they protested bitterly, saying Detroyat had been subsidized by the French government, while they had to pay for their own entries. Detroyat placed ahead of Earl Ortman in a 780-horsepower Rider R-3.

BERYL MARKHAM The official caption for this photo reads, "Mrs. Beryl Markham, young British matron, is flying the Atlantic." She did indeed make a daring transatlantic flight from Abingdon, England, to Nova Scotia, crash-landing her Percival Vega Gull in a swamp on September 5, 1936. The first woman to fly solo east to west across the Atlantic, she gained fame later with her memoirs of a swinging life in Africa and probably would not have described herself as "matronly."

JEAN BATTEN On November 13, 1935, 23-year-old New Zealand pilot Jean Batten completed a record flight from Lympne, England, to Natal, Brazil, in 2 days, 13 hours, and 15 minutes. Then, on October 18, 1937, she completed a record 5-day, 18-hour, and 15-minute crossing from Darwin, Australia, to Lympne, England, again in her Percival Gull.

LOUISE THADEN Louise Thaden was one of the most competent female pilots of the golden age of flight but never received her fair share of publicity. At 23, she already held many endurance, speed, and altitude records and had placed first in the 1929 Woman's Air Derby. Her greatest achievement was winning the 1936 Bendix Trophy race, with Blanche Noyes as copilot. She flew her Beech Model C17-R Staggerwing at only 65 percent power to average 165.6 miles per hour.

FLIGHT TIMELINE

May 19, 1936 The Consolidated XPBY-1 prototype flies for the first time.

May 22, 1936 The Herrick Vertiplane, a combination aircraft/autogiro, is tested.

June 6, 1936 The first production of 100 octane gasoline is initiated.

June 7, 1936 Ira Eaker completes the first transcontinental blind flight.

June 15, 1936 The Vickers Wellington, which uses Barnes Wallis' geodetic construction, flies for the first time.

June 15, 1936 The Westland Lysander makes its first flight.

June 25, 1936 The bomber version of the Bristol 142, the Blenheim, flies for the first time.

June 26, 1936 The Focke-Wulf Fw 61 twin-rotor helicopter makes its first flight.

July 18, 1936 The first battle of the Spanish Civil War takes place.

July 20, 1936 German Ju 52/3m transports airlift Nationalist troops from Spanish Morocco to Spain. It is the first large-scale airlift in the world.

July 23, 1936 The Short Canopus, the first of the four-engine Empire flying boats, makes its first flight.

August 7, 1936 The first six Heinkel He 51 fighters arrive in Spain in packing crates marked "furniture."

LIORÉ ET OLIVIER LÉO 451
First flown on January 16, 1937, the Lioré et Olivier LéO 451 was the best bomber France possessed in World War II, with a top speed of 300 miles per hour and a range of 1,040 miles. Unfortunately, only five were ready when war broke out in September 1939; by the time France fell in June 1940, about 450 had been produced, but not many were combat-worthy because of the failure of the French aviation industry.

VICKERS WELLESLEY The Vickers Wellesley featured Barnes Wallis' strong, lightweight, and damage-resistant geodetic structure. The first production Wellesley appeared on January 30, 1937, and was considered a "medium bomber" with a top speed of 264 miles per hour and a bomb load of 2,000 pounds. The aircraft was used to set a distance record of 7,157 miles in 1938 and served well in the Italian East African campaign.

BLACKBURN SKUA The Blackburn Skua was a radical advance over all previous Royal Navy aircraft when it appeared. It was the first all-metal aircraft with retractable landing gear and flaps to be used on British carriers. This is the prototype aircraft, first flown on February 9, 1937. Later aircraft were more refined and had some successes in the Norwegian campaign in 1940. Too slow at 225 miles per hour, the Skua was soon relegated to target tow-duty.

ESPAÑA Billy Mitchell's prophecies seemed to be fulfilled for the first time in combat on April 30, 1937, when the Nationalist battleship *España* was reportedly sunk by Loyalist aircraft. Later reports, however, indicate that the sinking was actually caused by a mine.

FLIGHT TIMELINE

August 14, 1936 French pilot M. Detre flies a Potez 50 to 48,698 feet, a new record.

August 22, 1936 Charles Ward Hall, founder of Hall Aluminum Aircraft, is killed in the crash of an aircraft of his own design, the "Monoped."

September 3, 1936 Michel Detroyat wins the Thompson Trophy for France in his Caudron C-460 at 264.26 miles per hour.

September 4, 1936 Louise Thaden wins the Bendix Trophy race in a Beech Model C17-R Staggerwing at 165.6 miles per hour.

September 4, 1936 Ben O. Howard and his wife, Maxine, are seriously injured in the crash of their racer, *Mr. Mulligan.*

September 4–5, 1936 Beryl Markham makes the first east-west solo transatlantic crossing by a female pilot.

September 28, 1936 Britain regains the altitude record with a flight to 49,967 feet in a Bristol Type 138A.

October 13, 1936 Soviet I-15 fighters, the first of 1,400 Soviet aircraft, arrive in Spain.

October 15, 1936 The Nakajima Ki-27 prototype flies.

October 21, 1936 Pan Am begins weekly passenger service from San Francisco to Manila.

HINDENBURG EXPLOSION The aggressive politics of Nazi Germany prevented the United States from selling helium for use in the *Hindenburg*. Far more dangerous, hydrogen was used instead, and being lighter, its use allowed an increase in passenger capacity from 50 to 70. After one successful season, the *Hindenburg* caught fire and exploded at Lakehurst, New Jersey, on May 6, 1937. Thirty-six people were killed in the accident, which brought an end to dirigible passenger service.

LOCKHEED XC-35 Lockheed Project Engineer Ferris Smith designed a circular cross-section fuselage for the basic Lockheed Model 10 so that it could be used for high-altitude experiments with a pressure cabin. The aircraft was quite successful, winning the 1937 Collier Trophy, and, on one occasion, averaging 350 miles per hour (with a tailwind!) on a flight from Chicago to Washington.

POLAR SHIP Americans were fascinated by the Cyrillic writing on the Tupolev ANT-25. They were also fascinated by the three great Soviet aviators, Valeri P. Chkalov, Georgi F. Baidukov, and Alexander V. Belyakov, who flew from Moscow on June 18, 1937, landing in Vancouver, Washington, 63 hours and 25 minutes later, having covered almost 5,500 miles. The ANT-25 had a wingspan of 111 feet and a top speed of 153 miles per hour.

JAPANESE TROOPS The Japanese government built separate Army and Navy air forces to the same philosophy: small numbers of high-quality aircraft flown by superbly trained crews. The formula worked against ill-equipped nations, such as China, but failed against the Soviet Union. Oddly enough, Japan did not learn from this and persisted in the same philosophy, which proved disastrous in World War II when high-quality U.S. aircraft flown by excellent crews appeared in vast numbers.

October 29–30, 1936 Jimmy Mollison, in a Bellanca, sets a west-east solo record of 13 hours, 17 minutes, for a transatlantic flight.

December 9, 1936 Juan de la Cierva is killed in the crash of a KLM airliner.

December 21, 1936 The prototype Junkers Ju 88, the most versatile of the German bombers, makes its first flight.

December 27, 1936 The ANT-42 prototype, the first modern Soviet four-engine bomber, flies for the first time.

January 13, 1937 Martin Johnson, a famous flying explorer, dies in the crash of a Western Air Express plane near Los Angeles.

January 16, 1937 The Lioré et Oliver LéO 451 flies.

January 28–29, 1937 Twelve Consolidated PBY-1 flying boats fly from San Diego to Honolulu in 21 hours, 43 minutes, a record.

January 30, 1937 The Hall XPTBH-2 twin-float torpedo plane is delivered to the Navy.

February 9, 1937 The first British dive-bomber, the Blackburn Skua, flies for the first time.

February 19, 1937 Howard Hughes sets a transcontinental record in his H-1 racer: 7 hours, 28 minutes, 25 seconds at an average speed of 327.5 miles per hour.

MOSCOW TO CALIFORNIA FLIGHT OF ANT-25 Aviators in the Soviet Union had watched the French gather many distance records, and Andrei Tupolev decided that he could build an airplane that could do the same. The result was the handsome ANT-25, shown here after M. M. Gromov, A. B. Yumashyev, and S. A. Danilin flew from Moscow on July 12, 1937, to San Jacinto, California, covering 6,900 miles in 62 hours and 17 minutes. Twenty more ANT-25s were built as research aircraft.

AMELIA EARHART Amelia Earhart had set many records and decided that she would make one more grand attempt, flying around the world in a twin-engine Lockheed Electra that she called her "Flying Laboratory." That wasn't strictly true, for the Electra carried no scientific equipment but was instead stuffed with fuel tanks for the long flight. Earhart, with navigator Fred Noonan, disappeared on July 2, 1937, near Howland Island in the South Pacific.

BOULTON PAUL DEFIANT During the 1930s, many countries experimented with the basically flawed concept of the heavily armed two-seat fighter. The Boulton Paul Defiant was among the best of these. Shown here on its first flight date of August 11, 1937, the Defiant was no match for enemy single-seat fighters but proved to be a good night-fighter when equipped with airborne radar. The fighter had a top speed of 303 miles per hour.

LOCKHEED SUPER ELECTRA The success of the Douglas DC-2 impelled Lockheed to create a smaller but faster airliner to compete. The result was the Lockheed 14 Super Electra, designed by Hall Hibbard and Clarence "Kelly" Johnson, with huge Fowler flaps masterminded by Willis Hawkins. First flown on July 29, 1937, the Super Electra had only modest commercial success but was the basis for the highly successful Hudson, Lodestar, and Ventura/Harpoon designs. The 14N was the fastest model at 260 miles per hour.

FLIGHT TIMELINE

March 1, 1937 The first operational YB-17 is delivered to General Headquarters Air Force, in Langley Field, Virginia.

March 5, 1937 Allegheny Airlines is formed (it will later become USAir).

March 17, 1937 Amelia Earhart blows a tire when she tries to take off from Hawaii for her proposed world flight. She has to reschedule.

April 12, 1937 Frank Whittle tests his gas-turbine engine.

April 26, 1937 Germany bombs Guernica, Spain.

April 30, 1937 The Nationalist battleship *España* is reportedly sunk by the Republican air force.

May 6, 1937 The *Hindenburg* explodes at Lakehurst, New Jersey, while attempting to land.

May 7, 1937 The Lockheed XC-35, the first pressure cabin plane, flies.

May 8, 1937 Lieutenant Colonel Pezzi flies a Caproni 161 biplane to 51,362 feet for a new altitude record.

May 29, 1937 Louise Thaden sets a female national speed record in a Beech Staggerwing: 100 kilometers at 197.958 miles per hour.

June 11, 1937 Reginald J. Mitchell, designer of the Spitfire, dies at age 42.

BOEING XB-15 The Boeing XB-15 was gigantic at the time of its first flight on November 11, 1937, with its 149-foot wingspan and a maximum takeoff weight of 92,000 pounds. Intended as a true strategic bomber, the XB-15 was underpowered, but it taught Boeing much. Its wing was adapted for use on the Boeing Model 314 flying boat. The XB-15 was adapted for cargo use as the XC-105 and served its country well.

MACCHI CASTOLDI C.200 Italy, the nation holding the world absolute speed record with its 1934 Macchi Castoldi MC.72 seaplane, could not build adequate engines for its fighter force. This Macchi C.200 Saetta (Arrow), a delightful aircraft to fly, was first flown on December 24, 1937. Production versions had a top speed of 310 miles per hour and, while just adequate to handle a Hurricane, were totally at the mercy of Spitfires. Most were flown with the cockpit canopy removed.

CURTISS YIP-36 The venerable Curtiss company hired an engineer from Northrop, Donavan Berlin, to create its next fighter. Berlin, a big, charming man, designed the radial-engine, 290 miles-per-hour Model 75 Hawk for a 1935 competition. Called the P-36 by the Air Corps, it was used by both the French and the British and proved effective against the Messerschmitt Bf 109E. Modified with an Allison in-line engine, it became an even greater success as the P-40.

DORNIER DO 18 The Dornier company aggressively improved its designs over the years but always retained certain signature characteristics, such as the stub wing (sponsons) and the tandem-mounted engines. Dornier aircraft were noted for their good water-handling and stability in flight. On March 27–29, 1938, a catapult-launched Dornier Do 18 flew 5,215 miles from Devon, England, to Caravellas, Brazil—a world record. Dornier flying boats were used throughout World War II.

FLIGHT TIMELINE

June 18–20, 1937 A Soviet crew flies the ANT-25 from Moscow over the North Pole to the United States.

June 30, 1937 A Bristol Type 138A recaptures the altitude record with a flight to 53,937 feet.

July 1, 1937 Varney Air Transport becomes Continental Airlines.

July 2, 1937 Amelia Earhart disappears on her round-the-world flight.

July 7, 1937 Japan begins a full-scale invasion of China.

July 12–14, 1937 The ANT-25 (with a different Soviet crew) flies from Moscow over the North Pole to San Jacinto, California, a distance of 6,900 miles.

July 15, 1937 The Blohm und Voss Bv 138, a three-engine flying boat, makes its first flight. It will become a workhorse during World War II.

July 26, 1937 Jacqueline Cochran, flying a Stagger-wing Beech, sets a national speed record for women: 100 kilometers at 203.895 miles per hour.

July 27, 1937 The Focke-Wulf Fw 200 Condor makes its first flight.

July 29, 1937 The Lockheed Model 14 Super Electra makes its first flight.

August 11, 1937 The Boulton Paul Defiant, a two-seat fighter with power-operated turret, makes its first flight.

BELL XP-39 FIGHTER Bell's radical XP-39 fighter was first flown in April 1938. The aircraft featured a tricycle landing gear, an engine mounted behind the pilot, a propeller driven via a shaft, and the promise of a 37-mm cannon firing through the prop hub. Bell was a new entry and claimed speeds of 400 miles per hour, which the public loved. Production aircraft performance was mediocre and about half of the 9,558 built went to the Soviet Union.

EDWARD VERNON RICKEN-BACKER Captain Eddie had come a long way since being the American Ace of Aces in World War I. He had manufactured an automobile (the Rickenbacker), and he purchased Eastern Airlines on April 22, 1938, which he ran at a profit with a combination of energy, tough love, profanity, and attention to detail. A tough bird, he survived a crash in an Eastern Airline DC-3 and an ordeal floating on a raft in the Pacific after his B-17 went down.

HOWARD HUGHES AND LOCKHEED MODEL 14 After setting a transcontinental speed record and an absolute landplane speed record in an aircraft of his own design, Howard Hughes sought to break the record for a flight around the world. He picked the Lockheed Model 14 for the task and completed a 14,791-mile journey around the world in 3 days, 19 hours, and 8 minutes. Landing in New York on July 14, 1938, Hughes and his crew were given a heroes' welcome.

DOUGLAS CORRIGAN Douglas Corrigan had worked on Lindbergh's *Spirit of St. Louis* and was determined to fly the Atlantic in his ancient $325 Curtiss Robin. The authorities refused, so Corrigan said he was going to fly to California instead. He took off from New York on July 17, 1938, and landed near Dublin, Ireland, claiming that he had misread his compass. Dubbed "Wrong-Way Corrigan," he became an instant folk hero.

ALEXANDER P. DE SEVERSKY AND JACQUELINE COCHRAN

Flying this Seversky AP-7, Jacqueline Cochran won the 1938 Bendix Trophy race on September 3. The aircraft was similar—but not identical—to the Seversky P-35s being purchased by the Air Corps. Alexander P. de Seversky was glad to have Cochran fly the airplane, because it proved it was "easy to fly." Not a good businessperson, Seversky was ousted from his company but went on to become a famous air-power proponent. Cochran became the foremost female pilot in the world.

FLIGHT TIMELINE

August 23, 1937 The first completely automatic landing of a heavier-than-air craft is made at Wright Field.

August 24, 1937 A Junkers Ju 52/3m flies from Kabul to China.

October 16, 1937 The Short Sunderland prototype flies for the first time.

November 1, 1937 The first Civil Air Regulations go into effect.

November, 11, 1937 The Boeing XB-15 makes its first flight. It is the first of the very large modern bombers in the United States.

November 13, 1937 Jean Batten completes a record 5-day, 18-hour, and 15-minute crossing from Darwin, Australia, to Lympne, England.

December 3, 1937 Alexander de Seversky flies from New York to Havana in 5 hours, 2 minutes, 51 seconds, setting a record.

December 24, 1937 The Macchi C.200 Saetta prototype flies for the first time. It will be the first monoplane fighter with canopy and retractable gear in the Italian Air Force.

December 29, 1937 Service between New Zealand and the United States is inaugurated by Pan Am using a Sikorsky S-42 *Clipper.*

1938 The U.S. Army buys seven Kellet Y6-1B Autogiros for liaison use.

LOCKHEED ELECTRA Prime Minister Neville Chamberlain hated flying, but he smiles the politician's smile as he deplanes from a Lockheed Electra (G-AEPR) on September 16, 1938, after meeting with Adolf Hitler. Two weeks later he would fly to Munich in a Lockheed Super Electra, returning with a scrap of paper that dismembered Czechoslovakia, but in his words promised "Peace in our time."

DEWOITINE D.520 The D.520 was the best French fighter of World War II. This is the prototype, equipped with test instrumentation on its right wing. The D.520 was powered by an 835-horsepower Hispano-Suiza engine and had a top speed of 332 miles per hour. The first flight took place on October 2, 1938, but only 700 had been delivered by the time of France's surrender in 1940. Captured D.520s were used by Germany's allies.

CURTISS XP-40 The Curtiss company knew that it had to improve on the performance of its Model 75 (P-36) if it was to remain competitive. In a manner that reflected company style, it created the new Model 81 by grafting an Allison engine to a Model 75 airframe. The result was the XP-40, which first flew on October 14, 1938, and became the Air Corps' most important fighter for the next several years.

DOUGLAS 7B PROTOTYPE The Douglas 7B was intended as an attack plane with a range of 1,200 miles and a bomb load of 1,200 pounds—a tough requirement for 1937. First flown at Mines Field on October 26, 1938, the 7B interested foreign buyers. On January 23, 1939, it crashed with a French observer on board. The aircraft was redesigned as the DB-7 and became famous as the A-20 Havoc, a tough, fast bomber.

ROSCOE TURNER AND HIS TURNER-LAIRD L-RT-14 SPECIAL Roscoe Turner was one of the most flamboyant aviators of the golden age of flight, but he was also a shrewd businessperson who knew how to market himself. A superb flyer, he was the only pilot ever to win the Thompson Trophy three times, twice in this aircraft. When the aircraft was designed, a retractable gear was suggested, but Turner said too much could go wrong.

FLIGHT TIMELINE

January 9, 1938 The Aichi D3A "Val" dive-bomber makes its first flight.

January 11, 1938 The Pan Am Sikorsky S-42B *Samoan Clipper* is destroyed in a mysterious fire, which claims the life of Edwin C. Musick and six crew members.

January 29, 1938 Designer Gerard (Gerry) Vultee and his wife are killed in a plane crash.

February 6, 1938 A composite flying boat arrangement is tested with the separation of the upper seaplane *Mercury* from the lower "parent" flying boat *Maia*.

February 10, 1938 A Hawker Hurricane flies cross-country (with a big tailwind) at an average of 408 miles per hour.

February 17, 1938 Six B-17s leave on a goodwill flight to South America.

April 22, 1938 Captain Eddie Rickenbacker buys Eastern Airlines for $3.5 million.

April 28, 1938 The Brewster Buffalo undergoes full-scale wind-tunnel tests at Langley Field, Virginia, in drag-cleanup efforts that improve speed by 31 miles per hour.

June 9, 1938 British Purchasing Commission buys hundreds of Lockheed Hudsons and North American Harvards, waking up U.S. industry.

June 23, 1938 The Civil Aeronautics Authority is created by the Civil Aeronautics Act.

SHORT S.20 MAIA FLYING BOAT AND SHORT S.21 MERCURY COMPOSITE AIRCRAFT It was difficult to get sufficient range for transatlantic crossings in the 1930s and still carry a reasonable cargo. Many solutions were sought, including in-flight refueling, but one of the most unusual was the composite arrangement of the Short S.20 *Maia* and S.21 *Mercury* aircraft. Both aircraft used full power for takeoff. On July 21, 1938, the *Mercury* separated from the *Maia* and flew to Montreal, a distance of 2,930 miles, with a 600-pound payload.

LOCKHEED P-38 The radical Lockheed P-38 was the brainchild of Hall Hibbard and Kelly Johnson, two of aviation's greatest engineers. The layout of twin engines placed in booms with a central pilot's nacelle came after extensive comparison with other designs. Also new was the tricycle landing gear. As advanced and sleek as the P-38 was, it would undergo many modifications before becoming suitable for combat.

MITSUBISHI A6M ZERO The Mitsubishi A6M Zero, designed by Jiro Horikoshi, was the most famous Japanese fighter of World War II. Horikoshi's task was to provide a maneuverable, well-armed fighter plane with exceptional range. To do so, he had to design a very clean, very lightweight airframe. The Zero dominated air combat for the first few months of World War II but could not compete with the later American fighters.

BOEING MODEL 314 Considered by many to be the most beautiful and best performing flying boat in history, the Boeing Model 314 commenced transatlantic passenger service with Pan American on June 28, 1939. Passengers paid $675 for a round trip—about $8,000 by today's standards. Twelve of the aircraft were built, and they served magnificently during the war. The 314 cruised at about 180 miles per hour, and service was very luxurious. This is the *Yankee Clipper*, photographed on March 3, 1939.

FLIGHT TIMELINE

July 10–14, 1938 Howard Hughes makes a record round-the-world flight, in 3 days, 19 hours, 8 minutes.

July 11–August 10, 1938 Intense air fighting takes place between the Soviets and Japanese in Manchuria.

July 17–18, 1938 Douglas "Wrong-Way" Corrigan flies from New York to Ireland in 28 hours, 13 minutes in a 9-year-old Curtiss Robin.

July 21–22, 1938 *Mercury*, the upper component of the Short-Mayo composite, makes the first commercial crossing of the North Atlantic by a heavier-than-air craft.

July 28, 1938 Pan American's *Hawaiian Clipper* disappears.

August 10–11, 1938 The Focke-Wulf Fw 200 prototype is flown nonstop from Berlin to New York.

August 22, 1938 The Civil Aeronautics Authority becomes effective.

August 23, 1938 Frank Hawks and a passenger are burned to death in the crash of the Gwinn Aircar.

August 29, 1938 Alexander de Seversky sets an east-west speed record of 10 hours, 2 minutes, 57 seconds.

September 3, 1938 Jacqueline Cochran wins the Bendix Trophy race in a Seversky AP-7 at ten hours, three minutes.

CONSOLIDATED **XB-24** The Air Corps wanted Consolidated to build Boeing B-17s, but Reuben Fleet said no. A contract was signed for a new bomber on March 30, 1939, and the XB-24 made its first flight on December 29 of the same year—an amazing success. Designed with the Davis wing for long range, the B-24 became a workhorse. Approximately 18,000 were made—more than any other U.S. warplane.

WILLY MESSERSCHMITT CONGRATULATING FRITZ WENDEL Fritz Wendel accepts Willy Messerschmitt's congratulations after setting the world speed record of 469.22 miles per hour in the souped-up and deadly Messerschmitt Me 209 on April 26, 1939. The aircraft was designed to fly only for brief periods before it overheated. There was a later Me 209 fighter design, but it was not successful. Wendel's record stood for many years before Darryl Greenamyer beat it on August 16, 1969, flying 483 miles per hour in a modified Grumman Bearcat.

VICKERS WELLINGTON The Vickers Wellington, first flown on June 15, 1936, was Great Britain's most important heavy bomber at the start of the war. This No. 214 Squadron Wellington is participating in the August 1939 Annual Air Defense Exercise; the white crosses indicate "friendly force." On December 18, 1939, 24 Wellingtons were sent on a daylight raid to bomb naval targets at Wilhelmshaven, Germany. Twelve were lost, and Britain turned to night bombing.

MITSUBISHI G4M BOMBERS The Mitsubishi G4M was perhaps the best known of the Japanese bombers. First flown on October 23, 1939, the G4M was fast at 292 miles per hour and had a very long range, some 2,700 miles. As with the Mitsubishi Zero, however, this performance came at the expense of such things as an adequate armor plate, self-sealing tanks, and sufficient defensive machine guns. As a result, the *Betty,* as the United States called it, was quite vulnerable.

COLONEL ROSCOE TURNER
Here you have Roscoe Turner at his Clark Gable best: a winning smile, neatly waxed mustache, immaculate uniform, and a hot airplane—in this case one he helped design—the Laird Turner racer. In it, he won the Thompson Trophy twice (in 1938 and 1939), making him the only three-time winner (he won in 1934 flying a Wedell Williams racer).

FLIGHT TIMELINE

September 5, 1938 Roscoe Turner wins the Thompson Trophy at 283.41 miles per hour.

September 14, 1938 The *Graf Zeppelin II*, the last Zeppelin to be built, flies for the first time.

September 21, 1938 Chief of Air Corps Major General Oscar Westover crashes to his death in a Northrop A-17A.

September 29, 1938 The Munich Agreement guts Czechoslovakia.

October 2, 1938 The Dewoitine D.520, the best French fighter of World War II, flies for the first time.

October 6, 1938 The Short *Mercury* sets a long-distance record for seaplanes: 5,007 miles.

October 11, 1938 Harald Penrose makes the first flight of a Westland Whirlwind, the only twin-engine single-seat fighter to serve with the RAF in World War II.

October 14, 1938 The Curtiss XP-40 prototype flies for the first time.

October 22, 1938 Lieutenant Colonel Mario Pezzi regains the world altitude record for Italy, attaining 56,046 feet in a Caproni 161-*bis* biplane; this remains the world record for piston-engine aircraft.

October 26, 1938 The first Douglas Model 7B is flown. The aircraft will be developed into the A-20 Havoc series.

CONSOLIDATED C-87 When the Consolidated B-24 Liberator first flew on December 29, 1939, neither manufacturer Reuben Fleet nor designer Mac Laddon could have believed that more than 18,000 would be built, including 300 transports like this C-87 for the USAAF. The C-87 could carry a crew of 5 and 20 passengers or an enormous load of cargo. Many of the C-87s flew for Convair's Consairway Division, a contract carrier that operated in Pacific war zones.

HANDLEY PAGE HALIFAX Handley Page had long been Great Britain's principal supplier of heavy bombers. When the Halifax first flew on October 25, 1939, it seemed destined to fulfill the tradition. More than 6,100 Halifax bombers were built, and they served nobly in a number of roles, including mine-laying and maritime reconnaissance. It never became as popular as the Lancaster with either the RAF or the public, though its performance was closely comparable.

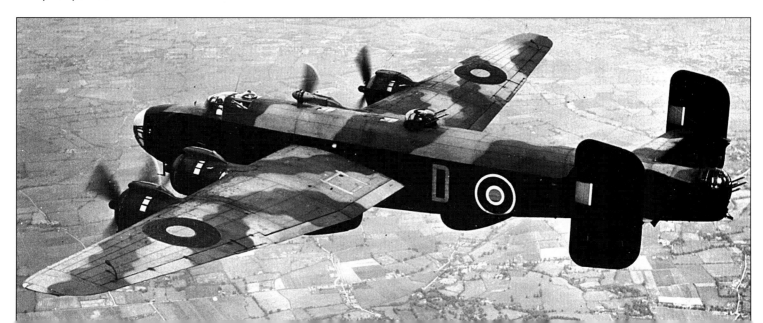

FOKKER D XXI Shown in Finnish markings, the Fokker D XXI was a radical departure from the traditional Fokker biplane practice but retained the usual Fokker construction techniques. The little monoplane made its first flight on February 27, 1936, and was soon the primary fighter for the Netherlands Air Force. The D XXI gave a good account of itself in Finland against the Soviet Union and against the Germans when they invaded Holland in May 1940.

GERMAN PARATROOPERS AND JUNKERS JU 52/3M TRANSPORTS The Germans had a highly trained force of paratroops that they used to good effect in the successful campaigns in the spring of 1940. The paratroops introduced an element of surprise that paralyzed Allied resistance. However, in 1941, a German paratroop invasion of the island of Crete was so costly that they were subsequently used only on a very limited basis.

FLIGHT TIMELINE

November 5–7, 1938 The RAF establishes a new distance record, using a Vickers Wellesley single-engine long-distance monoplane to fly from Egypt to Australia (7,157 miles), in 48 hours.

December 10, 1938 James Wyld develops a regeneratively cooled liquid-rocket motor, which becomes the basis for the JATO system.

December 16, 1938 The NACA high-speed motion picture camera is developed.

December 31, 1938 The Boeing 307, the first pressurized airliner, flies for the first time.

December 31, 1938 The Civil Aeronautics Authority (CAA) is reorganized into the Civil Aeronautics Board.

1939 The NACA continues development of laminar flow airfoil.

1939 The NACA combined-loads testing machine is developed.

January 27, 1939 The Lockheed XP-38 Lightning flies for the first time.

February 1939 The NACA begins reevaluating jet propulsion for aircraft.

April 1, 1939 The Mitsubishi A6M Zero prototype flies for the first time.

April 20, 1939 The first free-flight tunnel is placed into operation at Langley Field, Virginia.

CHANCE VOUGHT F4U CORSAIR The inspired design of a team led by Rex Beisel, the Chance Vought F4U was a great leap forward for the company, which had never previously attempted anything so sophisticated and so ambitious. After some teething troubles, the Corsair became immensely popular with both Navy and Marine pilots. The "bent wing bird" had a fabulous war record, with 2,140 victories against only 189 losses.

HAWKER HURRICANES The Royal Air Force took a beating in the Battle of France in the spring of 1940. Many of its aircraft were destroyed on the ground in the opening attacks on May 10, and more still had to be abandoned when the British Army retreated. Here beautiful Hawker Hurricanes are shown battered and abandoned. They would be sorely missed in the coming Battle of Britain.

GERMAN PARATROOPS Germany opened its May 10, 1940, invasion of France, Belgium, and the Netherlands with parachute troops attacking key installations—bridges, rail centers, and selected forts. The psychological effect of the German troops dropping out of the sky was enormous, destroying Allied morale. The drop aircraft is the sturdy Junkers Ju 52/3m *Tante Ju* workhorse.

SAVOIA-MARCHETTI S.M.79 BOMBERS Officially called the "Sparviero" (Sparrowhawk), the very efficient Savoia-Marchetti S.M.79 bomber had the unofficial nickname of "humpback"—for obvious reasons. The Italians were forced to use three engines on most of their bombers because they lacked sufficiently high-powered engines to use just two. The S.M.79 was particularly effective as a torpedo plane, and the Italian Air Force became extremely skillful in torpedo attacks. The aircraft's top speed was about 270 miles per hour.

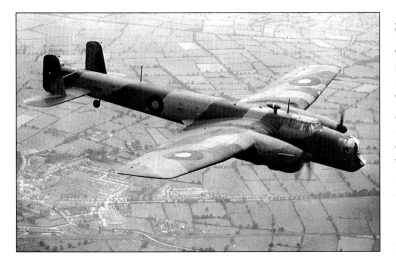

ARMSTRONG WHITWORTH WHITLEY The Armstrong Whitworth Whitley was one of Great Britain's primary bombers in 1940. First flown on March 17, 1936, the Whitley had an odd nose-down attitude in flight, thanks to the unusual angle of incidence at which the wing was mounted. The Whitley did leaflet bombings but soon switched to bombs, dropping them on Berlin on August 25, 1940. After 1942, the Whitley served primarily with Coastal Command.

April 26, 1939 Fritz Wendel pilots a Messerschmitt Me 109R (209 VI) to set a world speed record of 469.22 miles per hour.

May 9, 1939 Dale White and Chauncey Spencer seek to include African Americans in air-training programs.

May 27, 1939 The Petlyakov Pe-2 bomber flies for the first time.

June 20, 1939 A Heinkel He 176 is the first aircraft to fly with a liquid-propellant rocket.

June 28, 1939 Boeing 314 Clippers begin transatlantic service.

July 6, 1939 The first scheduled airmail service takes place with a rotary-wing aircraft, a Kellett KD-1B, in Eastern Airlines markings, between Philadelphia and Camden, New Jersey. The aircraft was flown by Captain John Miller.

July 7, 1939 Curtiss wins an order for 210 P-36As.

August 27, 1939 The Heinkel He 178, the world's first jet aircraft, flies for the first time.

September 1939 Igor Sikorsky flies the first successful helicopter.

September 1, 1939 Germany invades Poland; World War II begins.

December 29, 1939 The Consolidated XB-24 Liberator makes its first flight.

CAPRONI-CAMPINI The Caproni firm had a long relationship with Secondo Campini and cooperated to build the Caproni-Campini N.1, which made its first flight on August 28, 1940, thus becoming the second jet-powered aircraft to fly, following only the Heinkel He 178. The N.1 used a radial engine to drive a variable-pitch ducted fan compressor. Fuel could be introduced in the rear of the tailpipe to act as an afterburner. The aircraft's top speed was only 233 miles per hour.

SUPERMARINE SPITFIRE The Spitfire was an intricate design that took a great many hours to build, but the hard work paid off with high speed and superb maneuverability. It was an extremely adaptable aircraft, built in 37 variants and moving from a 900-horsepower Rolls-Royce Merlin engine to a 2,300-horsepower Griffon engine with no difficulty. German pilots treated the Spitfire with great respect. It served in every theater of World War II as well as in some postwar conflicts.

MESSERSCHMITT BF 109E The Spitfire's primary opponent during the early years of the war was the Messerschmitt Bf 109. This is the E model used in the Battle of Britain. The Spitfire and the Bf 109 were well matched, with the Spitfire having the advantage in a turn and the 109 in a dive. In most cases, the outcome of a one-on-one battle depended primarily on the quality of the pilots. More than 30,000 Messerschmitts were built.

DORNIER DO 17 The Dornier Do 17 set the aviation world on fire with its performance at a 1937 International Military Aircraft Competition in Zurich. The slim bomber was immediately dubbed "the Flying Pencil" by an appreciative press. The Luftwaffe began the war with 370 Do 17s on strength. It fought as a bomber and reconnaissance aircraft through 1942, when it was superseded by the larger and more capable but similar Do 217, shown here.

HEINKEL HE 111 The graceful elliptical wings of the Heinkel He 111 made it one of the most attractive aircraft of the Luftwaffe. Originally designed as a bomber and a commercial transport, the Heinkel He 111 was built in greater numbers than any other German bomber and was used in a wide variety of roles that included reconnaissance, minesweeping, glider tug, and cruise-missile launch. Slow and vulnerable by the end of the war, it suffered heavy losses.

HANDLEY PAGE HAMPDEN The Handley Page Hampden was one of the three main bombers of the RAF in 1939 (the others were the Armstrong Whitworth Whitley and the Vickers Wellington). At 254 miles per hour, the Hampden was the fastest of the trio, and it could carry up to 4,000 pounds of bombs. Unfortunately, the limited defensive armament of the Hampden made it vulnerable to attack, and it was soon relegated to mine-laying duties when larger bombers became available.

BLOHM UND VOSS BV 222 Originally intended as a transatlantic passenger transport for Deutsche Luft-Hansa, the six-engine Blohm und Voss Bv 222 Wiking made its first flight on September 7, 1940, long after the war had begun. With its 150-foot wing span and maximum overload weight of 108,026 pounds, the Wiking was underpowered even with its six Junkers Jumo 207 engines. The Wiking became a successful transport and reconnaissance aircraft, even though it was procured in very small numbers.

NORTH AMERICAN P-51 MUSTANG PROTOTYPE The British Purchasing Commission (BPC) came to North American Aviation with the request that they manufacture Curtiss P-40 fighters. On the advice of his engineers, North American President "Dutch" Kindelberger argued that his company could make a better fighter than the P-40 and do it in less than 120 days. Impressed, the BPC agreed to order 400 fighters, and the P-51, which many consider to be the best piston-engine fighter of World War II, was launched.

FLIGHT TIMELINE

June 1940 Heini Dittmar test-flies a rocket-powered DFS-194.

June 8, 1940 The carrier HMS *Glorious* is sunk by the *Scharnhorst*, a German battleship.

June 10, 1940 Italy declares war on Great Britain and France.

June 15–25, 1940 France surrenders.

August 17, 1940 Pilot Officer William M. L. Fiske becomes the first American to die in the service of the RAF.

August 24–25, 1940 Germany bombs London.

August 28, 1940 The Caproni-Campini N.1, an Italian jet, flies for the first time.

September 7, 1940 Luftwaffe night attacks on England begin.

September 7, 1940 The Blohm und Voss Bv 222 Wiking six-engine flying boat makes its first flight.

October 8, 1940 Formation of the Eagle Squadron with American pilots is announced.

October 26, 1940 The North American Mustang prototype makes its first flight.

November 11, 1940 The Italian Air Force makes its first and only attack on England.

November 11, 1940 England scores a great victory at Taranto, Italy, with the Fairey Swordfish.

DE HAVILLAND D.H.98 MOSQUITO

DE HAVILLAND D.H.98 MOSQUITO One of the great advantages of capitalism is the fact that individuals such as the late, great Geoffrey de Havilland are willing to invest their time, money, and talent for the good of the country. This was the case with the de Havilland Mosquito, which was not desired by the British Air Ministry but performed so well that it had to be purchased. The Mosquito became a fantastic bomber, fighter, and reconnaissance plane.

LOCKHEED HUDSON The Model 14 Super Electra had not been a commercial success for Lockheed, but good sales techniques and a bit of luck induced the British Purchasing Commission to place an initial order for 200 Hudsons in 1938. By the end of the war, almost 3,000 had been built, giving the British excellent service as antisubmarine warfare aircraft. A Hudson became the first American-built aircraft to score a victory in World War II.

CURTISS XSB2C-1 HELLDIVER The last of the long line of Curtiss Helldivers, the sleek-looking XSB2C-1 was a monoplane with an internal bomb bay, a 1,900-horsepower Wright R-2600 engine, and lots of development problems. This prototype flew on December 18, 1940, but crashed a few days later. The first production aircraft did not fly until June 1942. More than 7,000 were built, and they proved to be excellent aircraft from 1944 forward. The Helldiver's top speed was 295 miles per hour.

KAWANISHI H8K SEIKU (CLEAR SKY) Considered by many to be the very best flying boat of World War II, the Kawanishi H8K was powered by four Mitsubishi Kasei radial engines of 1,530 horsepower each. This provided a top speed of 290 miles per hour and a range of 4,445 statute miles. Called *Emily* in the Allied code system, the airplane had exceptionally strong defensive armament for a Japanese aircraft, carrying five 20-mm cannons and three 7.7-mm machine guns. Only 187 *Emilys* were built.

FLIGHT TIMELINE

November 25, 1940 The de Havilland D.H.98 Mosquito prototype makes its first flight.

November 25, 1940 The Martin B-26 Marauder flies for the first time.

December 18, 1940 The Curtiss XSB2C-1 Helldiver flies.

January 1941 The Kawanishi Navy H8K Seiku, one of the top flying boats of WW II, makes its first flight.

January 9, 1941 The Avro Lancaster prototype flies for the first time.

February 25, 1941 The Me 321 Gigant glider makes its first flight.

March 11, 1941 The Lend-Lease Act is authorized.

April 2, 1941 The Heinkel He 280 jet fighter makes its first flight.

April 18, 1941 The Me 262 makes its first flight under piston engine power.

April 23, 1941 Greece surrenders; German conquest of Balkans is complete.

May 6, 1941 The XP-47B prototype flies for the first time.

May 10–11, 1941 Rudolf Hess flies to England in a Messerschmitt Bf 110.

May 13–14, 1941 Twenty-one B-17s fly from Hamilton Army Air Field in Marin County, California, to Hawaii in the first mass deployment of U.S. Army bomber aircraft to the Pacific.

REPUBLIC XP-47 The man in the center is Alexander Kartveli, author of many of the great Republic aircraft designs. At his left is a Republic executive, C. Hart Miller, and on his right is Lieutenant Colonel Russell Keillor, a plant representative. The XP-47B prototype was first flown on May 6, 1941, by L. L. Brabham, and led to the long series of Thunderbolt fighters. Heavy but fast and rugged, the Thunderbolt was beloved by its pilots.

AVRO LANCASTER Unquestionably the best British bomber of World War II, the Avro Lancaster bore the brunt of the RAF Bomber Command's attacks on Germany during the later years of World War II. Powered by four Merlin engines of 1,640 horsepower, the Lancaster had a top speed of 287 miles per hour and could carry 14,000 pounds of smaller bombs or one 22,000-pound Grand Slam. Despite its great size, the Lancaster was fairly maneuverable, able to "corkscrew" away from German night-fighters.

GLOSTER E.28/39 This tiny jet can still be seen at the Science Museum in London. It was the third jet aircraft to fly, after the Heinkel He 178 and Caproni-Campini, and it was powered by Sir Frank Whittle's invention, the jet engine. P.E.G. Sayer made the first flight on May 15, 1941, starting a Gloster dynasty in jet fighters. With a top speed of 466 miles per hour, the aircraft was reportedly very pleasant to fly.

SOVIET AIRCRAFT The German onslaught on the Soviet Union began on June 22, 1941. Reichsmarschall Hermann Goering, commander of the Luftwaffe, was amazed at the number of Red Air Force aircraft destroyed. Here we see Polikarpov I-16s, a MiG-3, and a Tupolev SB-2 in the foreground. Reportedly, 1,800 Soviet aircraft were destroyed on the first day and thousands more within the first week of the attack. Most were obsolete, and a new generation of Red warplanes was coming.

FLIGHT TIMELINE

May 15, 1941 Britain's first jet, the Gloster E.28/39, flies for the first time.

May 20, 1941 Germans invade Crete in the largest Luftwaffe airborne assault of the war.

May 26, 1941 An RAF Catalina aircraft spots the *Bismarck*; it is attacked by Fairey Swordfish aircraft.

June 20, 1941 The U.S. Army Air Forces (USAAF) is formed; H. H. Arnold is Chief.

June 22, 1941 Germany invades the Soviet Union and destroys the Soviet Air Force on the ground.

August 1, 1941 The Soviet Union uses "parasite" dive-bombers for an attack on Romanian oil fields.

August 3, 1941 The first "Hurricat," a Sea Hurricane catafighter, scores a victory against a Focke-Wulf Fw 200 Condor.

August 7–8, 1941 The Soviet Union raids Berlin.

August 13, 1941 The Messerschmitt Me 163 prototype flies for the first time.

August 27, 1941 An RAF Hudson captures the U-570 in the North Atlantic.

September 20, 1941 A de Havilland Mosquito makes its first combat sortie over France.

September 23, 1941 First Lieutenant Hans-Ulrich Rudel sinks the Soviet battleship *Marat*.

GRUMMAN TBF AVENGER The very first attempt by Grumman to produce a torpedo bomber was an outstanding success, and the Avenger, which made its first flight on August 1, 1941, was soon ordered in large quantities. It was later built in large numbers by General Motor's Eastern Division as the TBM. A total of 9,839 Avengers were built; they served well as torpedo planes, dive-bombers, level bombers, and antisubmarine warfare aircraft.

CURTISS P-40 WARHAWKS
The very first good news that the United States experienced after the dismal start at Pearl Harbor was the superb performance of Claire L. Chennault's American Volunteer Group, the famous Flying Tigers. Flying well-worn Curtiss P-40s, the Flying Tigers dealt the Japanese a series of stunning blows using special tactics Chennault had devised. Heroes such as "Tex" Hill, "Pappy" Boyington, and Johnny Alison dove and zoomed their P-40s to defeat the more maneuverable enemy fighters.

MESSERSCHMITT ME 163 KOMET The radical rocket-powered Messerschmitt Me 163 was the product of genius Dr. Alexander Lippisch and the professionalism of the Messerschmitt design team. The tiny Komet set an unofficial speed record of 624 miles per hour on October 2, 1941, but the highly combustible liquid fuel propellants created maintenance and handling problems. The first Me 163s saw combat in July 1944, but their twin 30-mm cannons had such a low rate of fire that they were ineffective.

JUNKERS JU 87 Few aircraft have ever had a more sinister appearance, and fewer still had a more sinister reputation, than the Junkers Ju 87 Stuka. The Stukas acted as pinpoint artillery for German armored columns in the Polish and French campaigns but required the Luftwaffe to maintain air superiority to function. This became apparent during the Battle of Britain, where Stuka losses were so high that they were withdrawn from combat.

FLIGHT TIMELINE

October 2, 1941 The Messerschmitt Me 163 Komet rocket fighter reaches 624 miles per hour.

November 12, 1941 The British carrier *Ark Royal* is attacked by a German sub.

December 7, 1941 The Japanese Navy attacks Pearl Harbor. It's the first large-scale operation involving only carrier-based aircraft.

December 10, 1941 Land-based Japanese bombers sink the British battleship *Prince of Wales* and battle cruiser *Repulse*.

December 18, 1941 Buzz Wagner becomes the first U.S. ace of the war when he shoots down his fifth Japanese plane over the Philippines.

December 18, 1941 Reaction Motors, Inc., is formed to produce rocket engines. The company will ultimately produce engines used on the Bell X-1 and the North American X-15.

January 14, 1942 The Sikorsky XR-4 prototype, the first military helicopter, makes its first flight.

March 19, 1942 GALCIT Rocket Research Project becomes the Aerojet Corporation.

March 20, 1942 The first of three Mitsubishi J2M Raiden prototypes (code name *Jack*), makes its first flight.

April 2–9, 1942 The British suffer a naval disaster at the hands of Japanese airpower off the coast of Ceylon, off India.

PEARL HARBOR

The Japanese attack at Pearl Harbor on December 7, 1941, was an incomplete tactical success and the greatest strategic mistake in the history of the Japanese Empire. The Japanese felt that they were forced into war by the American embargo of oil and steel products and by the American demand that they give up their occupation of foreign lands in Asia. They did not believe they could win a long war but felt that the people of the United States and Great Britain were so decadent that a sharp blow—such as was delivered at Pearl Harbor—would drive the two democracies to make a peace settlement agreeable to Japan.

The exact reverse happened; the sneak attack galvanized the United States in a way that it had never been affected before. The mobilization of American industry was beyond the conception of both the Japanese and their German allies. The United States climbed from the depths of the Great Depression, becoming the most formidable military and industrial power in history, capable of producing in one year what Japan could produce throughout the four years of the war.

The Japanese also failed to make the most of their tactical success on December 7. Although they sank ships and destroyed airplanes in the first waves of the attack, their failure to return to destroy the oil storage facilities was a major error. In addition, their destruction of the U.S. battleship fleet forced the United States to rely on carriers, which turned out to be the decisive naval weapon of the war. In 1941, immediately after the attack, the United States had three carriers available for duty in the Pacific; the Japanese had ten. By 1945, the United States had 79 carriers and thousands of aircraft while the Japanese had two carriers—but lacked the planes and pilots to use them.

Mitsubishi dive-bombers prepare to attack Pearl Harbor.

Plane wreckage at Hickam airfield after the surprise attack on Pearl Harbor.

The battleships USS *West Virginia* and USS *Tennessee* after the Pearl Harbor attack.

Smoke pours from aircraft after an attack on a military airfield near Pearl Harbor.

LIEUTENANT COLONEL JIMMY DOOLITTLE Immediately after his April 18, 1942, raid on Tokyo, then Lieutenant Colonel Jimmy Doolittle was totally despondent. All of his aircraft had crashed, and he expected to be court-martialed upon his return to the United States. Instead, he was promoted to Brigadier General and awarded the Medal of Honor, which he accepted on the behalf of his fellow crew members. Doolittle was later given command of the Eighth Air Force, where he did outstanding work.

REPULSE SUNK BY JAPANESE Force Z, commanded by Admiral Thomas Phillips (known as Tom Thumb because of his small size) was to reinforce the British Far Eastern Fleet. Force Z included the battleship *Prince of Wales* and the battle cruiser *Repulse*. Phillips proceeded without air cover, believing that antiaircraft guns were adequate. The Japanese proved Phillips wrong by sinking both ships with land-based bombers and torpedo planes on December 10, 1941, shocking a world already stunned by Pearl Harbor.

KAWASAKI KI-61 HEIN The Kawasaki Ki-61 was the only Japanese production fighter to use a liquid-cooled engine, the Kawasaki Ha 40m, which was a version of the Daimler Benz DB 601 engine. Originally believed to be a German or Italian design, the aircraft was given the Allied code name *Tony*. The Ki-61 proved to be an able fighter but, like all Japanese aircraft, suffered from quality control problems in the field.

MITSUBISHI J2M RAIDEN The Japanese had previously stressed range and maneuverability in their fighters but demanded improved speed and rate of climb for the successor to the Zero. Jiro Hirokoshi responded with the Mitsubishi J2M Raiden (Thunderbolt), which first flew on March 20, 1942. The aircraft had a maximum speed of about 370 miles per hour and was much more ruggedly built than the Zero. Development difficulties and production problems kept total production low, but Japanese fighter pilots preferred the Raiden for attacks on the B-29.

MACCHI MC.205 Considered by many to be one of the best looking and best performing fighters of World War II, the Macchi MC.205 *Veltro* (Greyhound) was a development of the Macchi MC.202 *Folgore* (Thunderbolt), powered by a Fiat-built Daimler Benz DB 605 engine. The prototype made its first flight on April 19, 1942, but few production aircraft saw service before Italy's surrender in September 1943.

FLIGHT TIMELINE

August 17, 1942 USAAF bombers make the first raid on Europe, attacking railway yards in Rouen, France.

September 1942 A Japanese sub-based "Glen" drops four small bombs on Oregon.

September 2, 1942 The Hawker Tempest prototype makes its first flight.

October 1, 1942 The Bell XP-59, the first U.S. jet, makes its first flight.

October 3, 1942 The first successful A-4 (later becomes the V-2) rocket is launched at Peenemünde, Germany.

November 15, 1942 The Heinkel He 219, the best German night-fighter of the war, makes its first flight.

November 19, 1942 The Battle of Stalingrad begins.

January 9, 1943 The Lockheed C-69 Constellation makes its first flight.

January 27, 1943 USAAF bombers attack Germany.

January 30, 1943 De Havilland Mosquitos make the first daylight raid on Berlin.

February 13, 1943 The Chance Vought F4U-1 "Bent Wing Bird" goes into action.

March 2–4, 1943 Airpower wins the Battle of Bismarck Sea against the Japanese.

March 5, 1943 The Gloster Meteor prototype makes its first flight.

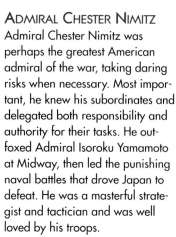

ADMIRAL CHESTER NIMITZ Admiral Chester Nimitz was perhaps the greatest American admiral of the war, taking daring risks when necessary. Most important, he knew his subordinates and delegated both responsibility and authority for their tasks. He outfoxed Admiral Isoroku Yamamoto at Midway, then led the punishing naval battles that drove Japan to defeat. He was a masterful strategist and tactician and was well loved by his troops.

NORTH AMERICAN B-25 MITCHELL The prototype of the Mitchell, the North American NA-40, first flew in January 1939, but crashed a few months later. An improved model was ordered into production and named after Brigadier General Billy Mitchell. The B-25 is perhaps most famous for the Doolittle raid on Tokyo on April 18, 1942, but the aircraft was very versatile and used all over the world. Here it is shown with a 75-mm cannon, an antiship weapon.

SHORT STIRLING BOMBERS The RAF requirement for a four-engine heavy bomber stipulated that the wingspan could not exceed 100 feet—so that it could fit within existing hangars. Short designer Arthur Gouge met the requirement with the Stirling, which first flew on May 14, 1939. Powered by four 1,650 Bristol Hercules engines, the Stirling was Great Britain's first four-engine bomber and served in a variety of roles. One of its most notable performances was in the first "thousand-bomber" raid on Cologne on May 30–31, 1942. More than 80 Stirlings participated with 598 Wellingtons, 131 Handley Page Halifaxes, 73 Lancasters, and 153 other bombers, in what was the precursor of the havoc about to be wreaked upon Germany.

KAGA The early Japanese carriers, such as the IJN *Kaga,* did not have the large island typical of American carriers. Capable of carrying 60 aircraft and making 27 knots, the *Kaga* participated in the war against China, sending its aircraft to bomb defenseless cities. The *Kaga's* greatest success came with its participation in the attack on Pearl Harbor. Just six months later, the *Kaga* was sunk in the Battle of Midway (June 3–4, 1942) by planes from the USS *Enterprise.*

YORKTOWN The *Yorktown,* badly damaged in the Battle of the Coral Sea (May 7–8, 1942), nonetheless returned to play a key role in the decisive victory of U.S. naval airpower over the Japanese fleet at the Battle of Midway. Unfortunately, the *Yorktown* was badly damaged at Midway, and then, under tow, was sunk by the Japanese submarine *I-168,* commanded by Captain Tanabe Yahachi. The tough old *Yorktown* finally sank on June 7, 1942.

FLIGHT TIMELINE

April 18, 1943 German troop transports are massacred off Cape Bon; 52 are shot down.

April 18, 1943 Admiral Isoroku Yamamoto is shot down and killed by P-38s.

May 16–17, 1943 The famous "Dam Busters" raid takes place.

June 15, 1943 The Arado Ar.234 Blitz, the world's first jet bomber, makes its first flight.

July 18, 1943 The U.S. Navy Airship K-74 is shot down by a German submarine. It's the only one lost in war to hostile action.

August 1, 1943 Junior Lieutenant Lydia Litvak, a female Soviet ace, is killed in action; she had 12 victories.

August 1, 1943 B-24s attack Ploesti, Romania; more than 50 of the 177 attacking aircraft are lost.

August 17, 1943 The Schweinfurt/Regensburg raids take place.

August 17, 1943 The RAF raids Peenemünde, Germany, killing 600 scientists.

August 17, 1943 A remote-control glide bomb, the Henschel Hs 293 A-1, is used for the first time.

August 31, 1943 The Grumman F6F Hellcat is used operationally for the first time. It becomes the highest scoring naval fighter of the war.

ADMIRAL ISOROKU YAMAMOTO Admiral Isoroku Yamamoto, though revered then and now, was actually a grievous liability for Japan. Unwilling to resign in protest to starting a war with the United States that he knew Japan would lose, he split his forces at the Battle of Midway, which took place between June 3 and 4, 1942. He failed to recognize that the U.S. intelligence knew of his plans. The result was a resounding defeat that changed the course of war, setting Japan on the road to a humiliating defeat.

AMERICAN PILOTS ENTER COMBAT American volunteers in the Eagle Squadron of the RAF engaged in combat on July 2, 1942. After the battle, Jim Daley (center) is questioned by Mike Duff, 121 squadron intelligence officer. From left to right, Wing Commander Peter Powell, R. F. Patterson (on wing), Squadron Leader Hugh Kennard, Leroy Skinner, and Clarence "Whitey" Martin prepare to give their accounts of the mission.

GRUMMAN XF6F-3 HELLCAT Although it resembled the F4F Wildcat, the Hellcat took advantage of Grumman's expanding knowledge of aerial warfare and had more armor and ammunition provided. The Hellcat first flew on June 26, 1942, and proved to be a formidable warplane, easily able to best the Zero and its successors. Credit must be given to the rugged, powerful, 2,000-horsepower Pratt & Whitney R-2800 engine, which powered it to a top speed of 380 miles per hour.

BELL XP-59A AIRACOMET The British gave the USAAF preliminary information on jet engines, which was incorporated into the design of the Bell XP-59A, America's first jet aircraft. Two General Electric Type 1-A turbojets powered the super-secret XP-59A, which made its first flight on October 1, 1942, flown by Robert M. Stanley. Flight performance was disappointing—at 413 miles per hour it was slower than standard piston fighters—but the Airacomet was a useful trainer.

GERMAN V-2 (A-4) ROCKET The desperate Germans turned to miracle weapons to help them somehow win the war. One of these was the first ballistic missile, the V-2, which had its first successful launch on October 3, 1942. The V-2 had a range of 200 miles and a 1,000-pound warhead and was impossible to intercept. Of the 3,200 successfully launched in combat, 1,400 landed in Britain. The V-2 led the way to the Intercontinental Ballistic Missile (ICBM) and then to space.

FLIGHT TIMELINE

September 9, 1943 The Italian battleship *Roma* is sunk by a German Fritz X guided missile.

September 12, 1943 Benito Mussolini is rescued by a Fieseler Storch aircraft.

September 20, 1943 The de Havilland Vampire makes its first flight.

October 14, 1943 A follow-up attack takes place on Schweinfurt, Germany; 60 planes are lost.

October 26, 1943 The Dornier Do 335 prototype flies for the first time.

December 13, 1943 The first long-range fighter escort flights take place.

MARTIN BALTIMORES: BATTLE OF EL ALAMEIN The RAF ultimately possessed 1,574 Martin Baltimores, using them with great effect in the Mediterranean. With two Wright R-2600 engines, the sometimes tricky Baltimore was fast at 308 miles per hour and was especially useful in North Africa during the October 23–24, 1942, Battle of El Alamein. The Baltimores suffered high losses at low altitude but came into their own on medium-altitude bombing missions. These Baltimores are shown flying over the Apenines in Italy.

BOEING XB-29 The biggest, most expensive gamble of the war was the Boeing B-29, which was riskier and more costly than the atomic bomb program. The XB-29 broke entirely new ground with new manufacturing techniques, new structure, a pressurized fuselage, new engines, new electric propellers, a central fire-control system, and many other innovations. The USAAF ordered 1,700 before the first one flew. After a troubled development program, the B-29 became the best bomber of World War II.

MESSERSCHMITT ME 262 The Germans might have had this radical jet fighter in operation over Europe in mid-1943 if their Luftwaffe chiefs had been clever enough to see the potential of the aircraft. Fortunately, they did not, neglecting the research necessary to developing the metals needed for the jet engines. As a result, the best fighter of World War II, the 540 miles-per-hour Messerschmitt Me 262, did not become operational until mid-1944, when it was far too late.

NORTHROP P-61 BLACK WIDOW The first U.S. night-fighter designed from scratch for the mission, the Northrop P-61 Black Widow was initially beset with development problems but by 1944 began to score successes in combat. A big aircraft, with a 66-foot wingspan and a gross takeoff weight of 36,200 pounds, the Black Widow was quite maneuverable and often surprised friendly Mustangs in a dogfight. The P-61 was a deadly adversary in both the European and Pacific theaters.

LOCKHEED CONSTELLATION Although the first flight of the Lockheed Constellation occurred on January 9, 1943, as a military C-69, the entire air-transport world was waiting for it to enter civilian service. Pan American World Airways inaugurated the first round-the-world commercial passenger service with this Constellation Clipper *America*. A group of publishers and editors was carried around the world in 13 days, with 101 hours of flying. Lockheed officials held sales talks at every stop.

BOEING B-17G When the Boeing Model 299 first rolled out in Seattle in 1935, a local journalist described it as a "Flying Fortress" because it had five machine guns. These were to prove inadequate in combat, and by the time the B-17G was being built, armament had grown to thirteen .50-caliber machine guns. Of the 12,726 B-17s that were built, 8,670 were G models.

CHANCE VOUGHT **F4U** CORSAIR This is the way to fly formation, stacked in close and tight, with each plane the same distance from the next. One of the United States' greatest advantages in World War II was its aircraft engine industry. The Pratt & Whitney R-2800 that powered the Corsair was one of the very best. The 2,000-horsepower engine endowed the fighter with a top speed of 417 miles per hour and a fast rate of climb.

GLOSTER METEOR PROTOTYPE A truly elegant aircraft, the Gloster Meteor went on to be developed in several versions for use by the RAF and many other countries. The prototype is shown here with (from the left) test pilots John Crosby Warren and Michael Daunt; Managing Director Frank McKenna; the inventor of the jet engine, Air Commodore Sir Frank Whittle; and the designer of the aircraft, W. George Carter.

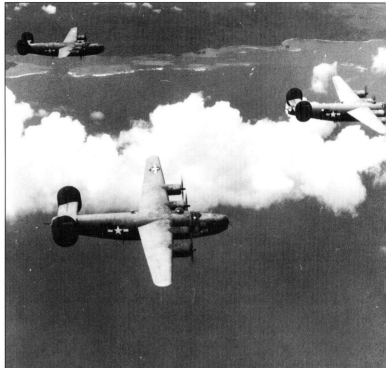

BOEING B-17ES IN FORMATION The Boeing B-17 had a generous 1,420-square foot wing area that endowed it with substantial lift and made it pleasant to fly. During the early part of the war, markings were under continuous revision, and the traditional red circle in the star would disappear because it could be mistaken for the Japanese insignia, a red circle representing the rising sun. There were a wide variety of camouflage patterns as well.

CONSOLIDATED B-24 LIBERATOR The Consolidated Aircraft Company was originally asked to build Boeing B-17s but declined, saying that it could build a better bomber of its own. The B-24 Liberator was the result, and it became the B-17s arch-competitor during the war. More than 18,000 Liberators were built, more than any other U.S. warplane. The Liberators' long, thin, Davis wing imparted a long range to the aircraft, making it especially suitable for antisubmarine work in the Atlantic.

LOCKHEED P-38G LIGHTNING The Lockheed P-38 Lightning was especially suited to the Pacific theater, where two engines were a comfort on long-range over-water missions. One of the most successful of these took place on April 18, 1943, when Army P-38s conducted a brilliant long-range raid, shooting down the Mitsubishi *Betty* carrying Admiral Isoroku Yamamoto, who planned the attack on Pearl Harbor. No other aircraft, Army or Navy, had the capability to execute such a raid.

GUY GIBSON HONORED On the night of May 16–17, 1943, Wing Commander Guy Gibson led the elite 617 Squadron of Lancaster in an attack on the German Möhne and Eder dams, using Barnes Wallis "bouncing bombs." Gibson coolly circled the dams while the bombing was going on and later received the Victoria Cross. Here General Henry H. Arnold hangs the Legion of Merit around Gibson's neck, with Air Marshal Sir William Welsh looking on.

CONSOLIDATED B-24 LIBERATOR Henry Ford did not want to engage in war work, but when the Ford Company finally got involved, it was in a big way, manufacturing B-24s by the thousands. The Liberator never had the public affection accorded the Boeing B-17, but it was well liked by its crews and flew in some of the roughest missions of the war, including the August 1, 1943, raid on the Ploesti oil center in Romania.

JACQUELINE COCHRAN

Jacqueline Cochran, shown here in the center of future women pilots, became director of the Women's Airforce Service Pilots (WASPs) on August 5, 1943. President Franklin Roosevelt ordered that the Women's Flying Training Detachment be combined with Nancy Love's Women's Auxiliary Ferrying Squadron (WAFS). The WASPs were treated like male cadets, receiving 220 hours of flight training. They ferried aircraft, towed targets, and tested repaired aircraft. Of the 1,074 who graduated, 38 died for their country.

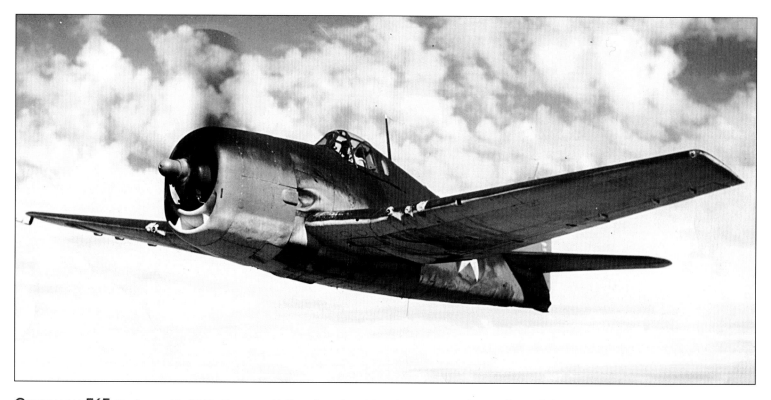

GRUMMAN F6F On August 31, 1943, Grumman Hellcats from the USS *Yorktown* engaged in combat with the Japanese, just two years and two months from the date they were first ordered by the Navy. Once in combat, the Hellcat proved to be a formidable foe, shooting down 4,947 enemy aircraft. Some 12,275 of the Hellcats were built, but they did not remain in operational service long after the war.

DORNIER DO 335 PFIEL (ARROW) After a very lengthy development program, the radical twin-engine Dornier Do 335 made its first flight on October 26, 1943, at a time when Germany desperately needed a high-speed interceptor. Despite its promise of a high speed of 478 miles per hour, the "push-pull" 335 never reached mass-manufacture. A shortage of critical equipment resulted in only about 45 being built. This is the second of ten preproduction aircraft undergoing evaluation in the United States at Patuxent River Naval Air Station.

YOKOSUKA D4Y SUISEI (COMET) Known to the Allies as *Judy,* the Yokosuka D4Y was powered by a 1,200-horsepower liquid-cooled Aichi engine. The *Judy* was the fastest dive-bomber of World War II, with a top speed of 360 miles per hour for the D4Y-2 shown here. With insufficient armor, the D4Y was very vulnerable. On August 15, 1945, the last Kamikaze attack of the war was made by a flight of eight *Suiseis,* under the command of Admiral Matome Ugaki.

CHAPTER FIVE

1944 to 1953:

From Sword to Plowshare to Sword Again

Both Great Britain and the United States began World War II convinced that a tight formation of heavily armed bombers could fight their way through enemy fighters and deposit bombs precisely on key enemy targets. They believed that if this was done often enough, the enemy would collapse from within, and no general engagement of armies would be required.

North American P-51 Mustang

The British learned their lesson by December 18, 1939, when 12 out of 21 Vickers Wellington bombers were shot down in a daylight raid on Wilhelmshaven, Germany. The RAF Bomber Command turned to night bombing, focusing on the Ruhr (a German industrial district), in an attempt to inflict severe damage on German industry. However, a 1941 analysis of RAF bombing revealed that only one of the ten attacking bombers got within five miles of targets in the Ruhr. All thoughts of precision bombing were abandoned, and the Royal Air Force turned to indiscriminate area bombing to attack Germany.

Despite the British experience, the United States believed it could send its Boeing B-17s and Consolidated B-24s in unescorted formations to targets deep in Germany to conduct precision daylight bombing. However, the battered and overextended Luftwaffe proved that it could not do so without unacceptable losses at Regensburg, Schweinfurt, and elsewhere.

The British never won their air battle against Germany, taking horrendous losses even through the 1944 Battle of Berlin. The United States found the answer to its problem in the North American P-51 Mustang, used as a long-range escort fighter. By February 1944, the USAAF had defeated the Luftwaffe in the air and on the ground, and U.S. bombers could range over Europe unimpeded except by the heavy antiaircraft artillery.

The defeat of the Luftwaffe allowed the United States to establish the complete air superiority necessary for the invasion on June 6, 1944, and for the subsequent defeat of the Nazi army. Air power was more than influential in the war in the Pacific. It was decisive.

In the Pacific, the overwhelming strength of the United States was applied with increasing ferocity in 1943. Dozens of new aircraft carriers filled with new fighters such as the Grumman F6F and Chance Vought F4U were dispatched. The Japanese were unable to match the United States in building ships or aircraft or in training pilots and were continually forced back. Ultimately, they were forced to rely on Kamikaze tactics in 1944 and 1945 as U.S. carriers drove the assault home.

The USAAF began bombing Japan with B-29s in 1944 and accelerated the pace in 1945, by which time it had achieved true air superiority. Its B-29s were able to range over Japan with little to fear from either Japanese fighters or antiaircraft. The B-29 low-level raid on Tokyo on March 9–10, 1945, was devastating, killing more than 70,000 people. The same punishment was meted out to other major Japanese cities, but the Japanese still would not surrender. It seemed probable that an invasion would be inevitable until August 6, 1945, when absolute aerial supremacy was demonstrated for the first time with the dropping of an atomic bomb on Hiroshima. Three days later, another atomic bomb fell on Nagasaki, and on August 15, the Japanese finally surrendered. Their decision to do so made an invasion unnecessary and undoubtedly saved tens of thousands of American lives. Ironically, it probably saved as many as six million Japanese lives. Perhaps two million would have been military casualties in an invasion, and another four million might have died of starvation, for Japan was gripped in famine.

Messerschmitt Me 262

91900

UNITED STATES AIR FORCE

Boeing B-47

No food imports were possible because its shipping had been destroyed, and its rice harvest was the worst in years. Another million people, from Korea to Formosa to the former Dutch East Indies, were starving under Japanese rule.

The "outbreak of peace" brought about the swiftest demobilization in history. On V-J day, August 15, 1945, the Army Air Forces had 2,253,000 personnel and 70,000 aircraft. Within two years, those numbers had plummeted to approximately 300,000 personnel, with 4,750 aircraft fit for combat. Military aircraft production in the United States, which had reached a peak rate of 100,000 per year in 1944, fell to about 700 in 1947. Companies that had employed as many as 100,000 workers were forced to cut back to a few thousand.

Despite this, new designs flourished. The jet age had arrived, along with new jet fighters such as the Lockheed P-80 and the North American P-86 and new bombers such as the North American B-45 and the Boeing B-47.

The war revolutionized flying. Airfields were built all over the world, and new means of navigation and communication made long-distance flying possible. New four-engine transports such as the Douglas DC-4 and Lockheed Constellation became available, and in Great Britain, de Havilland was working on a jet airliner unlike anything the world had ever seen.

There were also new political problems. The Soviet Union had not demobilized and instead brought East

Germany, Czechoslovakia, Romania, Bulgaria, Poland, and Hungary behind its "Iron Curtain." By 1948, a Cold War was going on, with the most obvious signal being the Soviet blockade of Berlin in April of that year. In a stunning application of air power, the United States elected to supply Berlin with all its necessary food and fuel by air with the Berlin Airlift. It was a tremendous diplomatic victory, for it succeeded admirably, and the Soviet Union was obliged to lift the blockade.

A pattern emerged that would persist for another four decades—the Soviet Union would use client states to extend its influence. The first of these was North Korea, which on June 25, 1950, invaded South Korea with the intention of unifying the two countries under Communist rule. The United States led the United Nations to intervene, and for three years, air power was the only means by which the badly outnumbered United Nations was able to contain the huge mass of North Korean and Communist Chinese forces.

The Korean War cast a pall on the economy, particularly on general aviation. Some 35,000 private planes were produced in 1946; by 1953, that number had fallen to 3,788. The bleak outlook was broken only by the brilliance of some of the new designs, which included the Beech Bonanza, Ryan Navion, Cessna 120, and the Globe Swift.

Unknown to all but a very few, a revolution was brewing. It would come on October 4, 1957, in the form of *Sputnik*, a simple Soviet satellite that signaled the dawn of a new era in flight.

LOCKHEED **XP-80** The Lockheed XP-80, the first American operational jet fighter, was also the first product of the famed Lockheed "Skunk Works," the design brain trust headed by Kelly Johnson. The aircraft made its first flight on January 8, 1944, and was capable of 594 miles per hour. The P-80 did not see service in World War II but was important in the Korean War. It also gave rise to many subsequent aircraft, including the T-33 and F-94.

BOEING **B-17G** The bomb bay of the Boeing B-17 was surprisingly small, given the aircraft's 103-foot, 9-inch wingspan and 65,500-pound gross weight. The aircraft could carry up to 17,600 pounds of bombs but only for short distances. On a long-distance raid, the bomb load would probably be 4,000 pounds. The turbo-superchargers are just visible on the underside of the engine compartment—they gave the Fortress its high-altitude capability.

BLOHM UND VOSS BV **238** Designed for long-range service and originally intended for transatlantic passenger service, the Blohm und Voss Bv 238 debuted on March 10, 1944, and was promptly overtaken by the war. It was the largest military flying boat built and flown during the war, with a 197-foot wingspan and 176,370 pounds of gross weight.

B-17 WITH GENERAL EISENHOWER The crew of the B-17 named *General Ike* lines up with pride to shake General Dwight D. Eisenhower's hand. The flying equipment by this time was extraordinary, with heated flying suits and excellent clothing—but it still got mighty cold at 25,000 feet.

FLIGHT TIMELINE

January 8, 1944 The Lockheed XP-80 makes its first flight.

February 16, 1944 The Curtiss XSC-1 Seahawk prototype debuts.

February 23, 1944 The German Wasserfall surface-to-air missile is fired for the first time.

March 6, 1944 The first USAAF attack on Berlin takes place with 660 heavy bombers; 69 bombers and 11 escort fighters are lost.

March 10, 1944 The Blohm und Voss Bv 238 prototype debuts.

May 28–June 4, 1944 U.S. Navy airships K-123 and K-130 make the first non-rigid airship Atlantic crossing.

June 13, 1944 The first German V-1s are launched from France.

July 5, 1944 The Northrop MX-324, a rocket-powered plane, is flown for the first time by Harry Crosby.

July 28, 1944 The de Havilland Hornet, the fastest twin-engine fighter yet, makes its first flight.

August 4, 1944 A Gloster Meteor "tips" over a V-1 in the first jet success of the Allies.

August 4, 1944 The first *Aphrodite* mission is flown.

August 13, 1944 The USAAF uses GB-4 TV-guided bombs against E-boat pens on the European coast.

JUNKERS JU 290 The Junkers Ju 290 design began life as the Junkers Ju 89 four-engine bomber, which was roughly the equivalent of the Boeing B-17 prototype. The Ju 90 passenger transport was derived from the Ju 89 and was built in small quantities for both German and foreign use. The Ju 90 was redesigned into a military transport and then, as the Ju 290, into a maritime reconnaissance aircraft that was preferred to the Focke-Wulf Condor by its crews.

DOUGLAS C-47 SNATCHING WACO GLIDER Retrieving downed gliders was not easy, for they usually landed where a conventional aircraft could not follow. This hook-and-wire retrieval system was devised to permit pickups from such fields. The C-47 caught the line suspended between the two upright poles, which was connected to the towline. The towline was connected to the glider, which was snatched into the air—if all went well. It was a nerve-racking, hazardous task, especially in wartime.

REPUBLIC P-47, LIEUTENANT COLONEL GABBY GABRESKI This was a lethal combination for the Germans: a Republic P-47 Thunderbolt with Lieutenant Colonel Francis S. "Gabby" Gabreski at the controls. The top-scoring ace in Europe, with 28 victories and almost 200 combat missions, Gabreski made a low-level attack on a German airdrome. His propeller touched the ground, and he was forced to crash-land and be taken prisoner. During the Korean War, Gabreski flew the North American F-86 and gained 6½ more victories.

V-1 Buzz Bomb in Flight

The V-1 (for vengeance weapon) was a flying bomb, an early form of cruise missile devised by the Germans as a means of retaliating against Great Britain without losing bombers and crew members. Powered by an Argus pulse-jet engine, some 6,000 V-1s were launched against Great Britain, 3,400 against London alone. Had it been introduced six months earlier in the 8,000 per month quantities Adolf Hitler demanded, it might have interrupted Allied invasion plans.

FLIGHT TIMELINE

August 16, 1944 The Me 163 rocket fighter is used operationally for the first time.

September 7, 1944 The first V-2 rocket is launched against England.

September 8–9, 1944 V-2 operations begin against Paris and England.

September 10, 1944 The Fairchild XC-82 makes its first flight.

October 23, 1944 The Japanese introduce Kamikaze attacks in the Battle of Leyte Gulf.

November 12, 1944 Germany's *Tirpitz* is sunk by the RAF.

November 15, 1944 The Boeing XC-97 prototype flies for the first time.

November 24, 1944 The first major Boeing B-29 raid on Japan takes place.

December 6, 1944 The Heinkel He 162 *Volksjaeger* makes its first flight.

December 17, 1944 Major Richard Bong scores his final victory, number 40.

December 22, 1944 The uncrewed Bachem Natter vertical-launch rocket interceptor is launched for the first time.

January 1, 1945 Operation Bodenplatte takes place. It is the last major attack by the Luftwaffe.

January 3–4, 1945 RAF Mosquitos bomb Berlin, adding to the city's tension and despair.

NORTH AMERICAN P-51D MUSTANG The marriage of a great American airframe, the Mustang, with a great British engine, the Rolls-Royce Merlin, resulted in what many consider to be the best piston-engine fighter of World War II: the North American P-51. The Allies desperately needed a long-range escort fighter, and the Mustang, with two 75-gallon drop tanks, could accompany bombers all the way to Berlin and still defeat German fighters.

CURTISS SB2C-1 HELLDIVER
Curtiss had built a long series of biplane dive-bombers for the Navy and Marines, and the SB2C-1 was the company's first monoplane bomber. A big aircraft, powered by a 1,900-horsepower Wright R-2600 engine, the Helldiver initially had teething problems that delayed its entry into service, even though the first one flew on December 18, 1940. Its first operational sortie was made on November 11, 1943, but thereafter it became an effective warplane, with a top speed of 295 miles per hour.

BOEING B-29 Undoubtedly the best bomber of World War II, the Boeing B-29 represented a tremendous gamble, because it combined a new airframe, new engines, a new pressurized fuselage, and a new fire-control system with many other innovations. The program was more costly than the Manhattan Project. Had the B-29 failed, there would have been no way to deliver the atomic bomb. Of course, the B-29 did not fail; it defeated Japan from the air.

DE HAVILLAND HORNET Many consider the de Havilland D.H.103 Hornet to be the most elegant twin-engine fighter of all time. A development of the classic Mosquito, it was first flown by Geoffrey de Havilland, Jr., on July 28, 1944. The Hornet was powered by two 2,070-horsepower Merlin engines and had a top speed of 472 miles per hour. Overtaken by the jet age, the Hornet was the last RAF piston-engine fighter to see service.

LAST HURRICANE DELIVERED The 12,780th Hawker Hurricane was delivered in September 1944 and was labeled "The Last of the Many." Purchased by the Hawker Aircraft Company, it was maintained in full flying condition to fly with the historic RAF Battle of Britain Memorial Flight.

FLIGHT TIMELINE

January 20, 1945 Robert T. Jones formulates his swept-back wing theory.

January 24, 1945 Germany launches the A-9, a winged Intercontinental Ballistic Missile (ICBM) designed for use against New York.

January 26, 1945 The McDonnell XFD-1 makes its first flight.

February 1, 1945 The Bachem Natter is tested with a pilot. The aircraft crashes, and the pilot is killed.

February 3, 1945 One thousand bombers of the Eighth AF attack Berlin.

February 7, 1945 The Consolidated-Vultee XP-81 composite-power fighter makes its first flight.

February 13–15, 1945 The attack on Dresden takes place.

February 21, 1945 The Hawker Sea Fury debuts.

February 22, 1945 Allies launch Operation Clarion with several thousand bombers and fighters.

February 23, 1945 The Luftwaffe sinks its last ship of the war, the *Henry Bacon*.

March 3, 1945 V-1 attacks continue from Holland against England.

March 9–10, 1945 Boeing B-29 fire-raids take place against Tokyo.

March 14, 1945 The RAF drops a Grand Slam (22,000-pound) bomb on a key viaduct in Germany.

FAIRCHILD XC-82 PACKET The Fairchild XC-82 was designed for direct-access loading via a hydraulic ramp. The large, boxy fuselage could handle trucks, howitzers, half-tracks, and even some tanks. The Packet could carry 42 fully equipped troops or 34 stretchers when used for medical evacuation. Somewhat under-powered with its two 2,100-horsepower Pratt & Whitney R-2800 engines, the C-82 had a top speed of 248 miles per hour. Its first flight was on September 10, 1944.

C-47S AND CG-4S PREPARING TO LAUNCH By September 1944, the Allies could launch powerful airborne forces at the enemy but always with the risk of antiaircraft fire. These C-47s are lined up to take off sequentially, towing their Waco CG-4A gliders into the air. The operation was called Market Garden, the unsuccessful attempt to leapfrog German lines at Arnhem. Casualties were very heavy—the drop zone included an area where an SS division was refitting.

BOEING C-97 Boeing adapted B-29 technology to its C-97, retaining the wings and tail surfaces but adding a "double-bubble" pressurized crew and cargo compartment. First flown on November 15, 1944, the C-97 was developed over time, and later models were powered by the 28-cylinder "corncob" Pratt & Whitney R-4360 engines. The design really came into its own when converted to the tanker role as the KC-97.

HEINKEL HE 162 VOLKSJAEGER (PEOPLE'S FIGHTER) The tiny Heinkel He 162 *Volksjaeger* was designed, built, and flown (first flight: December 6, 1944) within 90 days, reflecting both the desperation and the genius of Germany's aviation industry. Mass production was envisaged from the start; the ultimate goal was to build 4,000 He 162s per month. Although originally intended for Hitler Youth pilots trained only on gliders, the He 162 proved tricky to fly. Its top speed was 521 miles per hour, and only a few saw combat.

FLIGHT TIMELINE

March 16, 1945 Organized resistance ends on Iwo Jima; Marine casualties: 6,891 dead, 18,070 wounded.

March 18, 1945 The Douglas XBT2D-1 Skyraider makes its first flight.

March 20–21, 1945 The last Luftwaffe raid on England takes place.

March 27, 1945 The last V-2 rocket falls on England at Orpington.

March 31, 1945 The British Commonwealth Air Training Plan, which produced 54,098 pilots, is terminated.

April 1, 1945 Ohka Kamikaze planes hit the battleship USS *West Virginia*.

April 7, 1945 B-29s are accompanied to Japan by long-range fighters for the first time.

April 10, 1945 The Luftwaffe makes a last reconnaissance sortie over England using the Arado Ar.234 jet.

April 12, 1945 Ohka Kamikaze planes sink the destroyer USS *Mannert L. Abele*.

April 23, 1945 A U.S. Navy PB4Y-1 Liberator launches a Bat missile attack against Japanese shipping in Balikpapan Harbor.

April 25, 1945 Berchtesgaden (Hitler's residence) is destroyed by RAF bombers.

April 30, 1945 Adolf Hitler commits suicide.

BACHEM BA 349 NATTER (VIPER) Germany desperately tried to regain control of its airspace with advanced weapons such as this rocket-propelled Bachem Ba 349 Natter (Viper). The Natter was launched from a vertical rail on a near-vertical 80-foot ramp, then it climbed to make one pass at a bomber formation with the 24 nose-mounted rockets, after which the pilot would bail out. The top speed of this suicide machine was 620 miles per hour. The Natter never saw combat. Its first vertical launch (unpiloted) took place on December 22, 1944.

ARADO AR.234B The world's first operational jet bomber, the Arado Ar.234 first flew on June 15, 1943, taking off from a trolley and landing on skids. Modified with a conventional landing gear, it became an invaluable reconnaissance plane, entering combat in September 1944. It was the only German aircraft able to do reconnaissance over the British Isles; at 460 miles per hour, it was difficult to intercept. The 234C had four engines and a top speed of 542 miles per hour.

SIKORSKY YR-4B The first American helicopter produced in quantity, the Sikorsky R-4 was powered by a 165-horsepower Warner R-500 radial engine and flew for the first time on January 14, 1942. Production models had a 180-horsepower engine and a maximum speed of 75 miles per hour. This aircraft is the first YR-4B and was field-tested in Burma and Alaska. The R-4 led to a glorious line of Sikorsky helicopters for military and civilian use.

CONSOLIDATED-VULTEE XP-81 The jet engine was still new and relatively unknown in 1943 when Convair submitted an escort fighter design calling for a General Electric TG-100 turboprop in the nose and an I-40-G turbojet in the tail. The XP-81's first flight was made with a Packard-built Merlin engine in the nose on February 7, 1945. The first flight with a turboprop was made on December 21, 1945—long after the war ended.

FLIGHT TIMELINE

May 7, 1945 The RAF sinks the last German U-boat of the war.

May 8, 1945 VE day: Germany surrenders.

May 22, 1945 Japanese balloon bombs hit the U.S. West Coast.

May 23–24, 1945 The United States continues heavy air raids on Tokyo.

May 27, 1945 Japanese Kamikaze attacks intensify at Okinawa.

June 11, 1945 The B-29s that will ultimately carry the atomic bomb land in the Mariana Islands.

June 22, 1945 Organized resistance on Okinawa ends; Kamikaze attacks end.

July 2, 1945 The Japanese announce that all but 200,000 people have evacuated Tokyo.

July 10, 1945 U.S. carrier-based aircraft attack land targets in Japan.

July 16, 1945 The world's first atomic bomb is detonated at Alamogordo, New Mexico.

July 26, 1945 The Potsdam Declaration calls for Japan's unconditional surrender.

August 6, 1945 The first atomic bomb is dropped on Hiroshima from the B-29 *Enola Gay*.

August 7, 1945 The first Japanese jet, Nakajima's Kikka, makes its first flight.

HAWKER SEA FURY The first Hawker Sea Fury prototype flew on February 21, 1945, and soon became the standard British carrier-based fighter. Some 615 were built—a large order in the postwar years—and they served with distinction in the Korean War as a fighter-bomber. In MiG-15 versus Sea Fury battles, the MiG was usually, but not always, the winner. The Sea Furies were ordered by a number of governments, including Iraq, Pakistan, Egypt, Burma, and Cuba. The aircraft had a top speed of 460 miles per hour.

DOUGLAS XBT2D-1 In classic fashion, Ed Heinemann, Leo Devlin, and Gene Root worked overnight in a hotel room to produce the preliminary sketches for the Douglas XBT2D-2 single-seat attack plane. Their efforts were rewarded with production contracts that ran to 3,180 aircraft over a 12-year period. This is the prototype, which made its first flight on March 18, 1945 and became famous as the workhorse Skyraider of the Korean and Vietnam wars.

JAPANESE YOKOSUKA MXY-7 OHKA Design work on the Yokosuka Ohka suicide aircraft began in August 1944. Ohkas were carried into battle by Japanese Betty bombers for rocket-powered gliding attacks against American targets. At full thrust, the Ohka could reach 403 miles per hour with its 2,646-pound warhead. Most Ohkas were lost when their mother ships were attacked by American fighters, though some successes were scored. On April 1, 1945, Ohka Kamikaze rockets damaged the battleship USS *West Virginia*.

BOEING B-29A More than 1,500 Boeing B-29s were ordered before the first flight on September 21, 1942. The B-29 was a much more advanced aircraft than the B-17, using the latest in construction techniques. Some 3,650 were built. Powered by the initially trouble-some 2,200-horsepower Wright R-3350 engine, the B-29 had a top speed of 358 miles per hour and was equipped with up to eleven .50-inch guns. The B-29 served again in the Korean War.

WRECKED GERMAN AIRCRAFT The airfields of Germany were littered with wrecked aircraft, unceremoniously piled off to the side and eventually salvaged for scrap metal. Here a Junkers Ju 88 and Focke-Wulf Fw 190 are seen in front of a Messerschmitt Me 262, which has had its swastika insignia cut away from its tail.

CONSOLIDATED B-24J LIBERATOR Consolidated was originally invited to build Boeing B-17s, but Reuben Fleet offered to build a better bomber instead. The XB-24 came into being in less than one year (from contract to first flight on December 29, 1939). The last Liberator, #18,188, was built on May 31, 1945.

THE *ENOLA GAY* The Boeing B-29 was specially modified to carry the atomic bomb and was the only aircraft in the USAAF inventory capable of doing so. The United States had obtained such air dominance over Japan that the *Enola Gay* flew its historic mission against Hiroshima on August 6, 1945, without any fighter escort.

BOMBING OF NAGASAKI

Shown here is the ominous mushroom cloud of the second atomic bomb, dropped on Nagasaki on August 9, 1945. Dropping nuclear weapons was believed to be the only way to influence the militarists leading Japan to sue for peace; had they not been dropped, an invasion probably would have been necessary. Estimates suggest the fighting would have cost the lives of hundreds of thousands of Americans and millions of Japanese.

FLIGHT TIMELINE

November 6, 1945 A Ryan Fireball, using jet power only, lands on the USS *Wake Island*. It's the first jet to land on a carrier.

November 7, 1945 The Gloster Meteor IV sets a world speed record of 606.25 miles per hour.

November 20, 1945 A USAAF B-29 flies nonstop from Guam to Washington, D.C.: 8,190 miles in 35 hours, 4 minutes.

December 2, 1945 The Bristol Freighter debuts.

December 3, 1945 A de Havilland Vampire becomes the first pure jet to land on a carrier, the HMS *Ocean*.

January 10, 1946 A Sikorsky R-5 helicopter sets an unofficial world altitude record of 21,000 feet.

January 16, 1946 The United States initiates its space program using V-2 rockets.

January 19, 1946 Jack Woolams pilots a Bell XS-1 in its first unpowered flight.

January 21, 1946 The United States announces that the USAAF has reduced its strength from a wartime peak of 2,400,000 troops to 900,000 and will go down to 400,000.

January 26, 1946 Colonel William Council flies an F-80 across the United States in 4 hours, 13 minutes, covering 2,470 miles nonstop at 584.6 miles per hour.

GLOSTER METEOR Britain was anxious to attain a position of primacy in the jet-fighter world and carefully prepared the first two Mark IV aircraft with a glossy high-speed finish. This Gloster Meteor IV, called the *Brittania,* was flown by Group Captain H. J. Wilson to set a world speed record of 606.25 miles per hour on November 7, 1945. More than 20 variants of the Meteor were produced, and they were used by dozens of countries.

LOCKHEED CONSTELLATION Unquestionably one of the most beautiful piston-engine airliners of all time, the Lockheed Constellation was a favorite of pilots and passengers. Initially designated the C-69 by the USAAF, it made its first flight on January 9, 1943. Both Pan Am and TWA put it into service; Pan Am used it for the New York-to-Paris route, on which regularly scheduled service began on December 4, 1945. Extensively developed over the years, the "Connie" served the military in many roles.

BELL A-13B One of Larry Bell's most astute moves was to direct his company's energies into the emerging helicopter market. They began with the magnificent Model 47, which first flew on December 8, 1945. It was developed through many civil and military versions and established Bell as a major player in helicopters. It was also used as an experimental test bed, and work with jet engines soon led to entirely new lines of Bell "choppers."

FLIGHT TIMELINE

February 4, 1946 Pan Am flies a Constellation from the United States to England in 14 hours, 9 minutes.

February 15, 1946 TWA introduces Constellations on transcontinental flights.

February 28, 1946 The Republic XP-84 Thunderjet fighter makes its first flight.

March 21, 1946 The USAAF establishes Strategic Air Command (SAC), Tactical Air Command (TAC), and Air Defense Command (ADC).

April–September 1946 The United States tests 64 V-2 missiles at White Sands, New Mexico.

April 1, 1946 The Bell Rascal guided missile program is started.

April 19, 1946 The USAAF and Consolidated-Vultee launch Project MX-774, which will later lead to the Atlas missile.

April 24, 1946 The first Soviet jet aircraft, the Yak-15 and MiG-9, make their first flights.

May 17, 1946 The Douglas XB-43, the first American jet bomber, debuts.

May 22, 1946 The de Havilland Chipmunk trainer makes its first flight powered by a 140-horsepower Gypsy Major engine.

June 22, 1946 Jets (two P-80s) carry mail for the first time in the United States.

B-17G This B-17G was assigned to the 91st Bomb Group. Its crew named it Shoo Shoo Baby and flew it for 24 missions, receiving flak damage seven times. On its last mission, the crew was forced to land in Sweden and was interned. The aircraft was returned to the United States in 1978 and has since been restored.

DOUGLAS C-54 SACRED COW The Douglas C-54 *Sacred Cow* was specially modified to accommodate President Franklin D. Roosevelt's wheelchair. The C-54 became the workhorse transport of the Military Air Transport Service and later the Military Airlift Command and did great work in the Berlin Airlift.

SIKORSKY R-5 The Sikorsky R-5 featured a 450-horsepower Pratt & Whitney R985 engine, giving it much greater performance than its predecessors. The S-51 commercial helicopter was derived from it, firmly establishing Sikorsky in the civil market. Primarily used for rescue work, the R-5 had a top speed of 106 miles per hour. On January 10, 1946, an R-5 set an unofficial altitude record of 21,000 feet.

REPUBLIC XP-84 PROTOTYPE After the great success of the P-47 Thunderbolt, the Republic firm was anxious to produce its jet equivalent and did so with Alexander Kartveli's magnificent XP-84 Thunderjet. This is the prototype, first flown on February 28, 1946. General Electric J35 engines gave production aircraft a top speed of 587 miles per hour. Many variants were introduced, including the swept-wing F-84F and RF-84F versions. The aircraft proved itself in Korea in close-air support and was used by many air forces.

BELL MODEL 47 AND BOEING C-97 A Bell Model 47 hovers near a Boeing C-97 transport, reflecting a typical flight-line scene of 1946. The prototype of this design was first flown on December 8, 1945, and from that point Bell never looked back as orders poured in from every branch of the service, as well as from civilian customers. The age of vertical flight had truly arrived.

DOUGLAS XB-43 The Douglas XB-43 was the United States' first jet bomber, and though no production contracts were issued, the aircraft was a valuable research tool. A modification of the earlier twin-piston engine, pusher propeller XB-42, the XB-43 had two General Electric TG-180 (J35) turbojets mounted where the Allison engines had been. Bob Brush made the first flight on May 17, 1946. Sleek looking despite its tall tail and "double-bubble" cockpit, the XB-43 had a top speed of 515 miles per hour.

NORTHROP XB-35 Long a dream of the great designer Jack Northrop, the Northrop XB-35 Flying Wing promised improved performance through reduced drag. The XB-35 made its first flight on June 25, 1946, arriving at a time when the jet engine was about to take over. The Flying Wings were modified with jet engines to become the YB-49 but were not a good bombing platform and never entered service.

FLIGHT TIMELINE

July 7, 1946 Howard Hughes is critically injured when his Hughes XF-11 aircraft crashes during a test flight.

July 11, 1946 A Lockheed Constellation crashes during a training flight. All remaining Constellations are grounded; two earlier accidents also involved this aircraft.

July 21, 1946 Congress posthumously awards Billy Mitchell a medal, which promotes him to Major General.

August 8, 1946 The Convair prototype XB-36 bomber makes its first flight.

September 2, 1946 The Air University is opened at Maxwell Field.

September 27, 1946 Geoffrey de Havilland, Jr., is killed when his de Havilland D.H.108 breaks up in a test flight over Thames Estuary.

October 1, 1946 A U.S. Navy PV2-1 Neptune "Truculent Turtle" flies nonstop from Perth, Australia, to Columbus, Ohio, (11,236 miles) in 55 hours, 15 minutes.

October 6, 1946 The *Pacusan Dreamboat*, a B-29, makes a 9,442-mile flight over the North Pole, from Honolulu to Cairo, Egypt, in 39 hours, 35 minutes.

October 11, 1946 Slick Goodlin makes an unpowered flight in a Bell XS-1.

December 1, 1946 An American Overseas Airways Connie flies from New York to London in 10 hours, 12 minutes, averaging 324 miles per hour.

HUGHES XF-11 This is the first prototype of the Hughes XF-11, in which Howard Hughes crashed when one of the counter-rotating propellers failed on July 7, 1946. A second prototype, with conventional four-blade propellers, was also test flown by Hughes, but no orders ensued. The handsome aircraft was intended for photo-reconnaissance, but the mission was ably handled by larger four-engine aircraft.

MCDONNELL FH-1 PHANTOM James McDonnell was a veteran in the business, but his company was not able to sell any production aircraft during World War II. His first jet design, the McDonnell FH-1 Phantom, first flew on January 26, 1945. The prototype XFD-1 (later XFH-1) landed on the USS *Franklin D. Roosevelt* on July 21, 1946, the first pure-jet American aircraft to land on a carrier. McDonnell went on to supply jet fighters to both the Navy and the USAF.

SUPERMARINE ATTACKER The Supermarine Attacker, first flown on July 27, 1946, was originally intended for the Royal Air Force but, suitably modified, was adopted for the Fleet Air Arm, for which 145 were built. Another 36 were sold to the fledgling air force of newly independent Pakistan. With a top speed of 590 miles per hour, the Attacker was comparable to other aircraft of the period but had a relatively short service life and was replaced by more advanced aircraft.

CONVAIR B-36 The need for the Convair B-36 became evident in 1941, when it appeared that Germany would dominate the entire European continent and would have to be attacked from bases in the United States. This is the prototype, the XB-36, which first flew on August 8, 1946. With six R-4360 pusher engines, the 230-foot wingspan, 328,000-pound gross weight bomber flew at 381 miles per hour. Later versions had four J47 jet engines added, considerably improving performance.

LOCKHEED NEPTUNE "TRUCULENT TURTLE" Unlike its predecessors the Ventura and the Harpoon, the Neptune was custom designed as a long-range patrol bomber. First flown on May 17, 1945, the P2V went on to a long career in the service of many countries. This specially modified aircraft, the "Truculent Turtle" set a world distance record of 11,236 miles on October 1, 1946. The aircraft was continually improved, with a later version, the P2V-7, boasting a top speed of 345 miles per hour.

FLIGHT TIMELINE

December 9, 1946 The Bell XS-1 makes its first powered flight.

December 12, 1946 A Gloster Meteor sets a London-to-Paris record of 23 minutes, 37 seconds.

January 26, 1947 Prince Gustav Adolf of Sweden is killed in a KLM DC-3 accident in Copenhagen.

March 17, 1947 The North American XB-45 Tornado jet bomber debuts. It is the first USAAF production jet bomber.

April 15, 1947 The Douglas D-558 Skystreak makes its first flight.

June 8, 1947 American Airlines begins transcontinental DC-6 services.

June 19, 1947 A Lockheed P-80R sets a world speed record of 623.738 miles per hour.

July 3, 1947 The Tupelov Tu-4, a Chinese copy of the B-29, makes its first flight.

July 8, 1947 The Boeing 377 Stratocruiser makes its first flight.

July 16, 1947 The Saunders-Roe SR.A/1 flying boat jet fighter debuts.

August 20, 1947 A Douglas Skystreak D-558-1, flown by Commander Turner Caldwell, sets a world speed record of 640.663 miles per hour.

August 23, 1947 Famous English designer Roy Chadwick is killed in the crash of an Avro Tudor airliner.

BELL XS-1 Theorists had predicted that aircraft would not be able to fly faster than the speed of sound, which is Mach 1 (or about 760 miles per hour at sea level), without encountering such turbulence that the plane would break up. The Bell XS-1, which made its first powered flight on December 9, 1946, was about to prove them wrong. On October 14, 1947, Captain Charles "Chuck" Yeager flew the Bell XS-1 (later X-1) to supersonic speeds.

LOCKHEED P-80R Shots this good and this revealing of an actual speed record flight are rare. This is Colonel Al Boyd flying the Lockheed P-80R "Racey" through the speed traps on one of its four runs necessary to set the world speed record of 623.738 miles per hour on June 19, 1947, at Muroc Dry Lake. The revelation is in the shape of the wings, which are modified from the standard wing platform with clipped tips and sharper leading edges.

NORTH AMERICAN B-45 TORNADO The North American B-45, which debuted on March 17, 1947, was a transitional jet bomber, retaining a straight wing but using four Allison J47 engines for power in production versions. The Tornado had its greatest success in the reconnaissance role as the RB-45, even engaging in overflights of Soviet territory long before the arrival of the Lockheed U-2. Although pleasant to fly, the B-45 was not popular with its crews because it was difficult to leave in an emergency.

DOUGLAS D-558 SKYSTREAK Project engineer Robert Donovan, working under Ed Heinemann's supervision, led the team designing the Douglas D-558-1 Skystreak, a research aircraft for the Navy and NACA. Quite conventional in appearance, the Skystreak was powered by an Allison J35 engine and made a short first flight on May 28, 1947. In August, the aircraft set two speed records in five days, with U.S. Navy Commander Turner Caldwell setting the first record of 640.663 miles per hour on August 20, 1947. Major Marion Carl flew at 650.796 miles per hour on August 25, 1947.

BOEING MODEL 377 STRATOCRUISER Although many manufacturers converted their civil aircraft to military purposes, Boeing was one of the few to use its military technology to build an airliner, the Model 377 Stratocruiser. Originally built as the C-97 Stratofreighter, the aircraft used the basic B-29 fuselage, wings, and tail. Later models adopted features from the Boeing B-50. The Stratocruiser first flew on July 8, 1947, and had a top speed of 375 miles per hour. Very luxurious, it was expensive to fly, and only 55 were built.

FLIGHT TIMELINE

August 25, 1947 Major Marion Carl raises the speed record of the Douglas Skystreak D-558-1 to 650.796 miles per hour.

September 18, 1947 The United States Air Force is established.

October 1, 1947 The North American XP-86 Sabre debuts.

October 1, 1947 The first scheduled helicopter services begin in Los Angeles with the Sikorsky S-51.

October 14, 1947 Chuck Yeager breaks the sound barrier in the Bell XS-1.

October 21, 1947 The Northrop YB-49 jet flying wing makes its first flight.

November 2, 1947 The Hughes Flying Boat makes its first and only flight.

November 14, 1947 The Avro AW-52 twin-jet flying wing makes its first flight.

November 24, 1947 The Consolidated-Vultee XC-99, a cargo version of the B-36, makes its first flight.

December 17, 1947 The Boeing XB-47 debuts.

December 30, 1947 The MiG-15 prototype makes its first flight.

January 15, 1948 BOAC withdraws Boeing 314 flying boats and substitutes Constellations between the United Kingdom and Bermuda.

January 30, 1948 Orville Wright dies.

SAUNDERS-ROE SR.A/1 FLYING BOAT FIGHTER First flown on July 16, 1947, the Saunders-Roe SR.A/1 was the first jet flying boat. Powered by two Metropolitan-Vickers jet engines of some 3,500 pounds of thrust, the "Squirt," as it was called, had an exceptionally good performance, with a top speed of 512 miles per hour. Two of the three prototypes were lost to accidents—through no fault of the design—but enthusiasm waned, and no production order was given.

DE HAVILLAND (CANADA) BEAVER Designed as a bush plane for Canadian and Alaskan service, the de Havilland DHC-2 Beaver made its first flight on August 16, 1947. The aircraft was a versatile delight from the start, performing as well on floats or skis as on its fixed gear. About 1,657 of the aircraft were built, and they served in more than 50 countries around the world. The top speed of 163 miles per hour was not as important as its outstanding short-field performance.

WAR TIME MEETING OF STETTINIUS, SPAATZ, WILLIAMS, AND DOOLITTLE From left, Secretary of State Edward R. Stettinius, Lieutenant General Carl "Tooey" Spaatz, Brigadier General Paul Williams, and Lieutenant General James Doolittle ("the master of the calculated risk"). Spaatz was said to be "the only general never to make a mistake" and the "best poker player in the Eighth Air Force." He became the first Chief of Staff of the new USAF in September 1947.

NORTH AMERICAN XP-86 SABRE This is the very first photograph released of the North American XP-86, which debuted on October 1, 1947. Originally planned as a straight-wing design, the aircraft was redesigned with a 35-degree wing sweep due to information received from Germany after the war. The result was a sensational fighter that would prove to be the answer to the Soviet Union's MiG-15 during the Korean War. Although pleasant to fly, the Sabre could be tricky, and many pilots lost their lives in the aircraft.

NORTHROP YB-49 Modified with eight Allison J35 jet engines, the YB-49 seemed to have everything necessary for success when it made its first flight on October 21, 1947. Unfortunately, it was not a good platform from which to bomb, and a decision was made to modify it to a reconnaissance role as the RB-49. Thirty were ordered, but the entire program was canceled in October 1949. Curiously, the YB-49 and the modern Northrop Grumman B-2A share the same 172-foot wingspan.

FLIGHT TIMELINE

January 30, 1948 An Avro Tudor IV disappears on a flight to Bermuda; Air Marshal Sir Arthur Coningham, the father of British ground-attack tactics, is on board.

February 4, 1948 Army Air Force and Navy Air Force transport services are merged to form Military Air Transport service.

February 4, 1948 The Douglas D-558-2 makes its first flight.

March 1, 1948 The last Curtiss fighter, the XF-87, makes its first flight.

March 23, 1948 Group Captain John Cunningham sets a world altitude record of 59,446 feet in a de Havilland D.H.100 Vampire.

April 5, 1948 A Soviet fighter collides with a British airliner over Berlin; 15 people are killed.

April 25, 1948 The XP-86 Sabre goes supersonic in a dive. It is the first jet to do so.

May 3, 1948 Howard C. Lilly dies in the crash of a Douglas D-558-1 Skystreak. He is the first NACA test pilot killed in the line of duty.

May 20, 1948 The Israeli Air Force goes into action for the first time.

June 26, 1948 The Berlin Airlift begins: 32 sorties by C-47s carry 80 tons of food.

July 12–14, 1948 Six de Havilland Vampires make the first jet crossing of the Atlantic.

HUGHES H-4 HERCULES FLYING BOAT The largest flying boat ever built at the time, the Hughes Flying Boat has been the subject of popular interest since its inception. Sometimes called the HK-1 (for Hughes Kaiser #1) or, colloquially, the "Spruce Goose," the 320-foot span Hercules was made entirely of Duramold. The eight-engine aircraft made its first and only flight on November 2, 1947, covering just one mile.

BOEING XB-47 The most important multijet aircraft in history, the Boeing XB-47 led to the purchase of more than 2,000 B-47 bombers and reconnaissance planes. It also led Boeing to build both the Boeing 707 and the KC-135 tanker. The B-47 was fast at 606 miles per hour and, with in-flight refueling, had an unlimited range. It was demanding to fly but was a superb warplane.

MiG-15 The Soviet Union was determined to catch up with the West in the development of jet aircraft. It pulled off a political coup when it persuaded Sir Stafford Cripps of Great Britain to sell 55 Rolls-Royce Nene jet engines to the Soviet Union. Using these as models, the Soviet Union designed the Klimov RD-45 jet to power the superb swept-wing MiG-15, which dueled with U.S. North American F-86s in MiG Alley in Korea.

SAAB-21R Sweden's decision to produce its own warplanes resulted in the Saab-21, powered by a Daimler Benz DB 606 engine, first flown on July 30, 1943. To meet the jet age, Saab substituted a 3,000-pound thrust de Havilland Goblin turbojet, modifying the structure to match the increased power. Sixty were built as fighters and later converted for ground attack. The jet's top speed of 497 miles per hour was 100 miles per hour faster than the piston-engine version.

FLIGHT TIMELINE

July 13, 1948 The first MX-774 is launched. It is the predecessor of the Atlas ICBM.

July 16, 1948 Two USAF B-29 groups go to England for temporary duty as an implied threat to the Soviet Union.

July 16, 1948 The Vickers Viscount, the world's first turboprop airliner, makes its first flight.

July 20, 1948 Sixteen Lockheed F-80s fly the Atlantic.

August 16, 1948 The Northrop XF-89 Scorpion makes its first flight.

September 1, 1948 The Saab J-29 Flying Barrel, the first European swept-wing jet fighter, debuts.

September 5, 1948 The Martin *Caroline Mars* lifts 68,282 pounds, the heaviest load ever lifted by an aircraft.

September 6, 1948 A de Havilland D.H.108 breaks the sound barrier in a dive.

September 15, 1948 Major R. L. Johnson sets a world speed record of 670.98 miles per hour in a F-86A that is fully equipped with guns and ammunition.

September 18, 1948 The Convair XF-92 delta-wing prototype debuts.

October 20, 1948 The McDonnell XF 88A Voodoo flies for the first time.

CURTISS XF-87 BLACKHAWK

The initial German successes in the Battle of the Bulge convinced the USAAF that an all-weather fighter was needed. Curtiss responded with the handsome XF-87 Black-hawk, a four-jet aircraft that initially was to have automatic nose and tail turrets. First flown on March 1, 1948, the 49,900-pound Blackhawk was underpowered by its 3,000-horsepower Westinghouse XJ34 engines. The last of a long line of Curtiss fighters, the XF-87 could top 600 miles per hour.

SPECIAL DE HAVILLAND VAMPIRE Group Captain John Cunningham, perhaps the RAF's greatest night fighter and a superb test pilot, is shown in a special de Havilland D.H.100 Vampire. The third production aircraft was fitted with a test de Havilland Ghost engine and a pressure cabin, and four feet were added to each wing. On March 23, 1948, Cunningham set a new altitude record of 59,446 feet. Had the pressure cabin failed, Cunningham would have been killed, because he was not equipped with a pressure suit.

LOCKHEED F-80 In June 1948, the USAF changed the "P" for pursuit designation to "F" for fighter, and the Lockheed P-80 became the F-80. The aircraft did yeoman work in Korea as a close-air support and reconnaissance aircraft. For pilots familiar with the Mustang or Thunderbolt, the F-80 came as a revelation, for it was quiet, vibration free, and very fast.

BERLIN AIRLIFT On June 22, 1948, the Soviet Union announced that all surface traffic in Berlin would be cut off. It hoped to drive the Allies from the city. The United States responded with a humanitarian airlift called "Operation Vittles" and on June 26, 1948, began supplying fuel, food, medicine, and other necessities to the people of Berlin. The airlift was an immediate success, and children often gathered to watch aircraft bring in supplies. The embarrassed Soviet Union lifted the blockade.

FLIGHT TIMELINE

November 22, 1948 England announces the sale of ten Rolls-Royce Nene engines to the Soviet Union; 55 engines are supplied in all. The engine becomes the basis for one used in the MiG-15.

November 30, 1948 Curtiss-Wright demonstrates new reversible-pitch propellers on a C-54.

December 15, 1948 A new airlift base is opened at Celle, Germany.

December 16, 1948 The Northrop X-4 tailless research plane makes its first flight.

January 3, 1949 USAF SAC bombers begin 90-day rotational training in England.

January 7, 1949 The Israeli Air Force attacks RAF reconnaissance planes, shooting down four Spitfires and one Tempest.

February 8, 1949 Russ Schleeh flies an XB-47 from Moses Lake, Washington, to Bolling Air Field, Washington, D.C., in 3 hours and 46 minutes at 607 miles per hour.

February 25, 1949 A two-stage V-2/WAC Corporal missile is launched from White Sands, New Mexico, setting a 244-mile altitude record.

February 26–March 2, 1949 The USAF Boeing B-50A *Lucky Lady II* completes the first nonstop round-the-world flight in 94 hours and 1 minute, with four in-flight refuelings.

VICKERS VISCOUNT Powered by the excellent Rolls-Royce Dart turboprop engines, the Vickers Viscount was perhaps the most successful postwar British airliner and became the world's first turboprop commercial airliner. A total of 444 Viscounts were built, and U.S. passengers loved them. With a maximum speed of 350 miles per hour and a capacity of 59 passengers, the Viscount was a perfect short-haul airliner from the time of its first flight on July 16, 1948.

NORTHROP XF-89 SCORPION With the proud tradition of the P-61 Black Widow behind it, Northrop seemed a natural to build the all-weather fighter that the Air Force needed. It faced stiff competition, however, from the time of its first flight on August 16, 1948. After some agonizing development problems, the 636-miles-per-hour Scorpion went into widespread service, with more than 1,050 built. Later versions were armed with the Genie nuclear rocket.

MCDONNELL XF-85 GOBLIN Because jet fighters were short-ranged, several experiments were made with "parasite fighters" that could be carried along by the bombers and released to repel attacks. One of these was the McDonnell XF-85 Goblin, which was to have been carried by the B-36. First flown on August 23, 1948, the tiny 21-foot wingspan fighter was too difficult to handle, and the program was dropped.

SAAB J-29F Quick quiz: Why was this aircraft called the flying barrel? A glance at this photograph will reveal the answer. The portly Saab J-29 was a sensation when it debuted on September 1, 1948, as it was the first swept-wing fighter in Europe. Some 661 were built, and the fighter, with a speed of 658 miles per hour, was fully equivalent to its MiG-15 and F-86 counterparts for much of its career. Note the "saw-tooth" wing, a refinement introduced in 1953.

DE HAVILLAND D.H.108 The beautiful little de Havilland D.H.108 research aircraft brought both joy and sorrow to the company. On the positive side, it provided important research information on high speeds, swept wings, and tailless aircraft. Unfortunately, the designer's son, Geoffrey de Havilland, Jr., was killed when the aircraft broke up in flight on September 27, 1946. He had previously set a speed record of 616 miles per hour in the aircraft (August 23) and demonstrated the aircraft in air shows. The D.H.108 broke the speed of sound in a dive on September 6, 1948.

FLIGHT TIMELINE

March 7–8, 1949 Captain Bill Odom flies a Beech Bonanza nonstop from Hawaii to Teterboro, New Jersey: 4,957 miles.

March 25, 1949 A Bell XH-12 claims a speed record for helicopters: 133.9 miles per hour.

April 21, 1949 The French fly the Leduc ram-jet powered research aircraft for the first time.

April 26, 1949 *Sunkist Lady*, an Aeronca lightplane, sets an endurance record of 1,008 hours; it is refueled by gasoline passed by hand from a jeep.

May 12, 1949 The Berlin blockade is rescinded by the Soviets; the airlift wins.

May 13, 1949 English Electric Canberra, a British jet bomber, makes its first flight.

June 2, 1949 H. H. Arnold is given the permanent five-star rank of General of the Air Force.

July 27, 1949 The de Havilland Comet prototype makes its first flight. It is powered by four de Havilland Ghost engines.

August 9, 1949 The first American emergency use of an ejection seat is carried out by J. L. Fruin after he loses control of a U.S. Navy Banshee aircraft.

September 4, 1949 The giant eight-engine Bristol Brabazon makes its first flight.

September 30, 1949 Allies formally end the Berlin Airlift.

NORTH AMERICAN FJ-4 FURY The U.S. Navy was eager to enter the jet age but uncertain as to the shipboard qualities of a swept-wing fighter. The North American FJ-2/4 series swiftly proved that they were more than qualified for the task. The FJ-4 was developed into an attack fighter, capable of carrying a wide variety of ordnance. The Navy Fury fighters were very similar to USAF Sabres, with the addition of normal equipment required for carrier operation.

BOEING B-50A LUCKY LADY II Here, a Boeing KB-29 tanker is shown using the British hose-type refueling system to refuel the Boeing B-50A on the first nonstop round-the-world flight, completed on March 2, 1949. The *Lucky Lady II* made the trip of 23,453 miles in 94 hours and 1 minute. Boeing later developed the much more efficient "flying boom" refueling system, which became the standard method. Today it is absolutely vital for fighters, bombers, and transports.

CONVAIR XF-92A The radical delta-wing Convair XF-92A was first flown by the great test pilot Sam Shannon on September 18, 1948. Although easy to fly and land, the aircraft was unable to reach supersonic speeds in level flight. Major Frank K. "Pete" Everest took it past Mach 1 in a dive on one occasion. The XF-92A provided valuable research information on delta wings and led directly to the development of the F-102 and 106 fighters.

MARTIN JRM-1 MARS The largest operational flying boat in the world when it entered service in December 1943, the Mars had a long and successful career extending to the present day (it now operates as a fire-bomber). Five of the 200-foot-wingspan aircraft were built, and they served well as transport aircraft, on one occasion carrying a total of 308 people. In this picture, the *Caroline Mars* is flying 90 Annapolis cadets on a summer air-cruise.

DOUGLAS D-558-1 SKYROCKET The crash of the second Skyrocket, which killed Howard C. Lilly on May 3, 1948, delayed the flight of the third aircraft until April 22, 1949. It then made 82 more flights to investigate handling at high subsonic speeds. The aircraft's maximum speed at sea level was 651 miles per hour.

FLIGHT TIMELINE

November 2, 1949 The Piascecki HRP-2 helicopter makes its first flight.

December 22, 1949 The North American YF-86D Sabre Dog makes its first flight.

March 16, 1950 Group Captain John Cunningham flies a de Havilland Comet from England to Italy and back: 1,832 miles in four hours and six minutes at an average speed of 450 miles per hour.

April 4, 1950 A Gloster Meteor flies from England to Denmark in one hour and five minutes at 541.43 miles per hour.

May 12, 1950 The Bell XS-1 makes its last flight (for a motion picture).

June 3, 1950 The Republic F-84F prototype (YF-96A) makes its first flight.

June 25, 1950 The Korean War begins.

June 27, 1950 A North American F-82, flown by Lieutenant William G. Hudson, shoots down a Yak 9 fighter in the first U.S. victory of the Korean War.

July 3, 1950 A Grumman Panther, flying off the USS *Valley Forge*, is the first Navy jet in combat.

July 29, 1950 A prototype Vickers Viscount enters passenger service.

September 15, 1950 General Douglas MacArthur lands at Inchon in Korea.

ENGLISH ELECTRIC CANBERRA One of the most successful of all the British bombers was the English Electric Canberra, designed by W.E.W. Petter and intended to be a jet replacement for the highly successful de Havilland Mosquito. From its first flight on May 13, 1949, the 518-miles-per-hour Canberra was a sensation and went on to fill bombing and reconnaissance duties for the RAF and many other air forces. Built by Martin, the aircraft became the B-57 in U.S. service.

SOVIET UNION GIVES UP BLOCKADE OF BERLIN The Soviet Union tried to force the Western Allies out of Berlin with a ground blockade in June 1948. Unable to confront the more than 30 Soviet divisions on the ground, the United States resorted to an airlift that flew more than two million tons of fuel, food, and supplies into the same Berlin it had been bombing four years before. This is the first bus to arrive after the blockade was lifted on May 12, 1949.

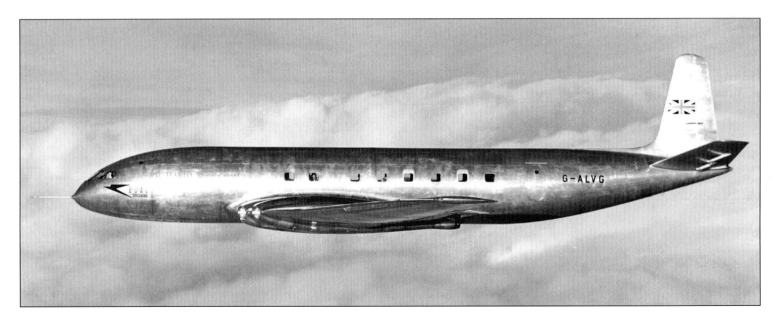

DE HAVILLAND D.H.106 COMET Beautiful, serene, and revolutionary but harboring a fatal flaw, the prototype of the de Havilland Comet flies over England. After building some of the great warplanes of World War II, de Havilland rocked the industry with its sensational Comet airliner, powered by four de Havilland Ghost jet engines. Years ahead of all other transports, the 36-seat Comet would have three fatal crashes when metal fatigue caused them to explode in flight. The aircraft's top speed was 450 miles per hour.

AVRO 707 Great Britain was interested in delta-wing flight, and Avro led the experimental path with its 707, intended to investigate low-speed flight. The Avro 707 was a development model for the projected Vulcan jet bomber, which became the most successful British heavy bomber of the post-World War II period. Three 707s were built, and one crashed.

BRISTOL BRABAZON One of the all-time great miscalculations, the 180-passenger, eight piston-engine Bristol Brabazon came at a time when turboprops (which were intended to be used) and turbojets were just coming in. The huge 230-foot wing and 290,000-pound gross weight made it the largest British aircraft of its time. Intended for transoceanic service, the Brabazon made its first flight on September 4, 1949. Structural problems led to project cancellation.

FLIGHT TIMELINE

September 22, 1950 Colonel David C. Schilling leads the flight of two F-84E aircraft for the first nonstop transatlantic jet crossing.

September 29, 1950 Captain R. V. Wheeler makes a record parachute jump from 42,449 feet.

October 9, 1950 The Soviet government protests a U.S. attack on a Soviet airfield near the Korean border.

October 20, 1950 Three thousand U.S. paratroopers are dropped near Seoul.

November 7, 1950 The British end use of flying boats in BOAC.

November 8, 1950 A Lockheed F-80C, piloted by Lieutenant Russell J. Brown, shoots down a MiG-15 in the first jet-versus-jet combat.

November 8, 1950 B-29s bomb North Korean bridges across Yalu.

December 17, 1950 The first F-86s go into action in Korea, claiming four MiG-15s.

December 31, 1950 The world's airlines have carried 31.2 million passengers.

January 16, 1951 The first Consolidated-Vultee B-36D bombers land in England on a training flight from a base in Texas.

January 23, 1951 Republic F-84 Thunderjets (straight wing) shoot down four MiG-15s near Sinuiji.

FAIREY GANNET Disproving the cliché that an aircraft that doesn't look right won't fly right, the bulky Fairey Gannet turned out to be an excellent antisubmarine aircraft. Powered by an Armstrong-Siddeley Double Mamba turboprop engine driving counter-rotating propellers, the Gannet first appeared in flight on September 19, 1949. About 370 of the aircraft were built, and they proved to be the last of a long line of Fairey aircraft to serve the Royal Navy. The Fairey Gannet had a top speed of 310 miles per hour.

RAF BOEING B-29 The Royal Air Force swallowed its pride in 1950 to acquire the Washington (Boeing B-29) to strengthen its aging Avro Lincoln bomber force until such time as the new jet bombers were available. A total of 88 B-29s were acquired from U.S. stocks. RAF crews liked the pressurized B-29s, which were more comfortable than the Lincolns and had far better performance. Most were returned to the United States by 1954.

BLACKBURN BEVERLY Blackburn was a relatively small firm that dated back to the early days of flight and was always noted for its distinctive designs, such as the Skua. The huge 162-foot span Beverly was actually a design of General Aircraft, which had built Hamilcar gliders during World War II. First flown in 1950, the Beverly was a fixed-gear, unpressurized aircraft with a top speed of 238 miles per hour. About 49 were built, and they served until replaced by Lockheed Hercules transports in 1967.

GRUMMAN F9F-2 Grumman's F9F-2 Panther flew first on November 24, 1947, starting an uninterrupted line of aircraft that led to the F-14 Tomcat. A total of 437 were built, and their 6,250-pound thrust Pratt & Whitney J48s pushed them to a top speed of 587 miles per hour. The Panther was the first Navy jet to be used in combat, flying off the USS *Valley Forge* on July 3, 1950, and shooting down a MiG-15 on November 9.

SHORT SUNDERLAND The Short Sunderland, which performed so valiantly as a patrol and antisubmarine plane during World War II, did equally well during the Korean War, flying 1,647 sorties and totaling 13,380 hours flying time. The Sunderland was the last of a long line of flying boats to serve with the RAF and did so from 1938 to 1959. Its top speed was just 213 miles per hour, but it could fly for 13½ hours at a cruising speed of 134 miles per hour.

FLIGHT TIMELINE

January 31, 1951 Charles Blair flies a P-51 Mustang from New York to London, averaging 450 miles per hour for 3,500 miles.

February 6, 1951 The USAF announces the loss of 223 aircraft in Korea; only ten are due to enemy action, the rest were accidents.

February 14, 1951 The Republic F-84F makes its first flight.

February 21, 1951 An English Electric Canberra is the first jet to fly the Atlantic nonstop without refueling, making the flight in 4 hours, 37 minutes, at an average speed of 449.46 miles per hour.

February 23, 1951 The Dassault Mystère makes its first flight.

March 6, 1951 The USAF announces that Martin will build the Canberra.

March 15, 1951 A KC-97 tanker refuels a B-47 for the first time.

April 1–2, 1951 B-29s attack bridges across Yalu.

April 12, 1951 Two B-29s are shot down by MiG-15s in heavy fighting.

May 18, 1951 The first British V-bomber, the Vickers Valiant, flies. It is powered by four Rolls-Royce Avon engines.

May 20, 1951 The first U.S. jet ace, Captain James Jabara, gets his fifth and sixth victories of the Korean War when he shoots down two MiGs.

REPUBLIC F-84 THUNDERJETS AND NORTH AMERICAN F-86 SABRES

The Korean War began on June 25, 1950, with the invasion of South Korea by North Korean troops who were well equipped and well trained by the Soviet Union. The invasion had been undertaken with the belief that the United States would not intervene, but President Harry S. Truman secured United Nations support and announced the United States would resist the invasion. Initially the North Koreans swept all before them, but U.S. airpower eventually halted them. It was not until MiG-15s appeared in November 1950 that a decision was made to send North American F-86 Sabres and Republic F-84 Thunderjets to fight in Korea.

The F-86s quickly secured air superiority, battling the enemy to a standstill in MiG Alley, but the F-84s proved to be the unsung hero of the war, carrying the battle to the enemy daily.

Republic F-84 Thunderjet

North American F-86 Sabre

KB-29 REFUELING F-84 A man used to making history, World War II ace Colonel David C. Schilling had scored 22½ victories during the war. He achieved postwar fame on September 22, 1950, with a nonstop jet crossing of the Atlantic in his Republic F-84E. The aircraft was refueled in flight three times. Schilling won the Harmon International Trophy for the flight. After facing combat, transatlantic crossing, and many other dangers, he, ironically enough, died in a car accident in 1956 at age 38.

NORTH AMERICAN F-86D "SABRE DOG" With the Soviet Union's development of the atomic bomb and the Tupolev Tu-4 bomber, the United States had to prepare defenses against an attack. Several interceptors were developed including this North American F-86D, which featured nose radar, a more powerful afterburning G.E. J47 engine, and a tray of two dozen 2.75-inch rockets. Some 2,500 F-86Ds were produced. Lieutenant Colonel William F. Barnes piloted an F-86D on July 16, 1953, to set a speed record of 715.6 miles per hour.

CHANCE VOUGHT F7U-1

Radical designs have great appeal but are usually difficult to execute. The tailless design promised great speed and a high rate of climb, but the aircraft had a high accident rate. Approximately 290 were built, but even though the Vought F7U-1 was flown briefly by the Blue Angels, it never gained a place in the hearts of naval aviators. The top speed of later models was 680 miles per hour.

DASSAULT MYSTÈRE II France was determined to maintain an indigenous aircraft industry producing first-line products, and the Dassault firm obliged with one great design after another. Dassault aircraft always maintained performance parity with Soviet and U.S. counterparts. This is the Mystère II, part of a line of fighters that not only defended France but provided a tremendous income through sales to other countries. Israel became a particularly good customer of France for Dassault fighters.

VICKERS VALIANT On May 18, 1951, the Royal Air Force's V-bombers made their brilliant debut. The clean, swept-wing Vickers Valiant had its four jet engines mounted in the wing, rather than on pods like U.S. jet bombers. Its top speed was Mach .84 at 30,000 feet. The Valiant saw combat in the Suez conflict in 1956 and dropped the first British atomic bomb during 1956 tests. It was withdrawn from service in 1964.

BELL X-5 The Bell X-5 variable-sweep aircraft was based on German Messerschmitt P.1101 aircraft. The Bell version, first flown by Jean "Skip" Zeigler on June 20, 1951, provided for sweeping the wing in flight from 20 degrees to 60 degrees in 20 seconds. A total of 149 flights were made by the two prototypes. Unfortunately, the aircraft had terrible spin character-istics. Major Ray Popson died in the crash of the second example.

A BOEING KB-29P REFUELS A NORTH AMERICAN RB-45 The North American B-45 Tornado first flew on March 17, 1947, becoming the USAF's first operational jet bomber. More than 100 of the bomber version were built, along with 33 of the successful RB-45 reconnaissance planes, some of which flew covert missions over the Soviet Union. The Tornado engaged in one of the first combat in-flight refuelings in Korea on July 14, 1951, and made the first nonstop jet flight from Alaska to Japan on July 29, 1952.

FLIGHT TIMELINE

August 17, 1951 Colonel Fred Ascani sets a world speed record of 635.686 miles per hour for 100 kilometers in an F-86E during the National Air Races.

September 13, 1951 The first USAF guided missile squadron is formed with Matadors.

September 26, 1951 The de Havilland D.H.110 Sea Vixen two-seater all-weather fighter makes its first flight.

October 3, 1951 The Soviet Union explodes its second atomic bomb.

November 26, 1951 The Gloster Javelin, a twin-jet delta-wing interceptor, makes its first flight.

December 12, 1951 The de Havilland Otter makes its first flight.

December 16, 1951 The Kaman K-225, a gas-turbine helicopter, completes tests.

January 3, 1952 The Bristol Type 173 prototype heli-copter makes its first flight.

January 5, 1952 Pan Am begins the first all-cargo transatlantic service with DC-6A aircraft.

April 15, 1952 The Boeing YB-52, powered by eight Pratt & Whitney J57 engines, makes its first flight.

May 2, 1952 The first sched-uled jet airline service begins with de Havilland Comet flights from London to Johannesburg.

SUPERMARINE SWIFT The first British swept-wing fighter jet, the Supermarine Swift, set a world speed record of 737 miles per hour in 1953 but was a total failure as an operational fighter. It eventually served relatively well when modified into a photo-reconnaissance plane as the Swift F.R.5, but it was a happy day when the Hawker Hunter arrived to replace it. Only 36 of the fighter version were built.

HAWKER HUNTER One of the most beautiful and useful fighters ever built, the Hunter was flown by 22 foreign countries. A total of 1,972 were manufactured. The last of a long line of Sir Sydney Camm's fighters, which included the Fury, Hurricane, and Tempest, the Hunter was a delight to fly and capable in both the air superiority and ground attack roles. Fast, at 700 miles per hour, it was also easy to maintain.

GLOSTER JAVELIN Gloster had come a long way from the Gladiator or even the Meteor to create its delta-wing, T-tail Javelin, shown here in the prototype's first flight on November 26, 1951. The Javelin went through a long series of models, and the Mark 9 had a maximum speed of 701 miles per hour at sea level and a service ceiling of 52,000 feet. Some 436 were built, and they served the RAF very well.

KAMAN K-225 The Kaman K-225 was powered by the Boeing YT-50 turbine engine. Charles Kaman founded his company in 1945 and was a pioneer in the jet-powered helicopter field. The K-225 was built in small numbers as the YH-22 from 1949 on. The helicopter benefitted more from the introduction of the jet engine than from any other technological advance.

FLIGHT TIMELINE

June 16, 1952 Soviet MiGs shoot down a Swedish Catalina on a rescue mission.

June 17, 1952 ZPN-1, the world's largest nonrigid airship, is delivered to the Navy by Goodyear Aircraft Company. It is 324 feet long and 35 feet high.

July 14–17, 1952 Fifty-eight Republic F-84s, led by Colonel David C. Schilling, fly with seven stops from Turner Air Force Base, Georgia, to Yokota, Japan.

July 15–31, 1952 Two Sikorsky S-55s make the first helicopter crossing of the North Atlantic in 42 hours, 25 minutes, with four stops.

July 29, 1952 A North American RB-45C Tornado completes the first nonstop transpacific flight from Elmendorf AFB, Alaska to Yokota, Japan.

August 16, 1952 The Bristol Britannia makes its first flight.

August 22, 1952 The Saunders-Roe S.E.45 *Princess*, a ten-engine flying boat, makes its first flight.

August 30, 1952 The Avro Vulcan delta-wing bomber makes its first flight. It will be the mainstay of the RAF for the next three decades.

September 6, 1952 A de Havilland D.H.110 breaks up in flight, killing 30 people in an air-show crowd.

October 6, 1952 A de Havilland Comet is severely damaged during a takeoff accident in Rome.

BRISTOL TYPE 173 The Bristol Aeroplane Company called on gyroplane expert Raoul Hafner to design their first helicopter, the Type 171 Sycamore, of which a small number were made. The next step was the twin-rotor Type 173, powered by two Alvis Leonides engines of 575 horsepower each. Either engine could drive both rotors if one engine failed. An improved version, the Type 192, had Napier Gazelle turboshaft engines. In 1960, Bristol's Helicopter department was acquired by Westland Aircraft.

BOEING XB-52 STRATOFORTRESS The Boeing XB-52 was the first prototype, but the YB-52 was the first to fly, taking to the air on April 15, 1952. No one at Boeing could ever have imagined that B-52s would still be in first-line service more than 50 years later. The XB- and YB-52 aircraft differed from production versions primarily by their tandem cockpit arrangement, which followed B-47 practice. The last B-52H came off the production line in 1962.

GOODYEAR ZPN-1 The U.S. Navy used blimps to great advantage during World War II in the battle against German U-boats. After the war, it did not seem probable that blimps would be useful in the jet age, but the requirement for radar warning capability made them invaluable again as aerial radar sites. This ZPN-1 became a ZPG-2W with a designation change and was followed by the larger ZPG-3W.

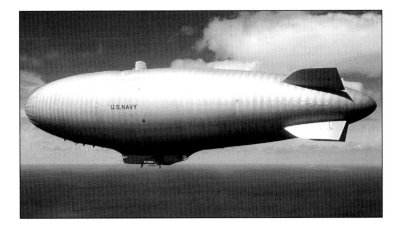

BRISTOL BRITANNIA Powered by Proteus turboprop engines, the Bristol Britannia was a good aircraft but was sold in small numbers. First flown on August 16, 1952, the aircraft was developed with more powerful engines as they became available. Later versions of the Britannia carried up to 133 people at a top speed of 397 miles per hour. A total of 83 were built in Great Britain and a further 33 CL-Argus types were built in Canada.

MARTIN PB5M The Martin PB5M Marlin was the last of a long series of Martin flying boat patrol planes, the role being overtaken by long-range land-based aircraft such as the Lockheed Neptune and Orion. Some 287 of the PB5Ms were built, and though they resembled the famous Mariner, they were a larger, more powerful aircraft. Later aircraft had a T-tail and a top speed of 251 miles per hour.

FLIGHT TIMELINE

October 7, 1952 A USAF Boeing B-29 is shot down by Soviet fighters six miles off Hokkaido in Northern Japan.

October 8, 1952 Soviet MiG-15s attack a U.S. ambulance aircraft near Berlin.

October 23, 1952 The gigantic Hughes XH-17 Flying Crane makes its first flight.

October 28, 1952 The Douglas Skywarrior, XA3D-1, makes its first flight. It is the heaviest aircraft yet to enter service on carriers.

November 3, 1952 The Saab Lansen, a two-seat, all-weather attack plane, makes its first flight.

November 26, 1952 A Northrop B-62 Snark missile is launched from a zero-length launcher.

December 3, 1952 Soviet fighters force down a USAF C-47 aircraft in Hungary.

December 24, 1952 The Handley Page Victor makes its first flight.

January 12, 1953 The U.S. Navy's first angled deck carrier, the *Antietam*, begins flight trials.

February 1, 1953 Chance Vought delivers the last F4U Corsair (of 12,571 built since 1940).

February 16, 1953 Two Japanese pilots of Japan's Self Defense Force, flying F-84s, shoot down two Soviet piston-engine fighters over Hokkaiddo.

AVRO VULCAN The most advanced of the British "V-bombers" was the delta-wing Avro Vulcan, which combined a top speed of 645 miles per hour with superb maneuverability and long range. The Vulcan first flew on August 30, 1952, and served in the Falklands War of May 1982. Like the Boeing B-52, the Vulcan changed from high- to low-altitude missions in the 1960s. The Vulcan performed very well in the Strategic Air Command bombing competitions.

SUD-EST SO 4050-03 VAUTOUR One of the most versatile aircraft in the French air force, the Sud-Est SO 4050 Vautour was designed for all-weather fighting, close-air support, and bombing. After the first prototype flew on October 16, 1952, some 170 production aircraft were built, distinguished by their swept wings and bicycle-style landing gear arrangement. With a maximum speed of 686 miles per hour, the Vautour was a formidable aircraft and was used with distinction by Israel in combat.

DOUGLAS A3D SKYWARRIOR The Navy's first twin-jet nuclear bomber, the Douglas A3D Skywarrior was the largest and heaviest aircraft ever designed for use from an aircraft carrier. The Skywarrior made its maiden flight on October 28, 1952. Later aircraft were powered by the reliable Pratt & Whitney J57 engine and had top speeds of 610 miles per hour. The A3D matured into a conventional bomber, electronic reconnaissance plane, and tanker, and was used by the USAF as the RB-66.

HANDLEY PAGE VICTOR The third of the RAF's "V-bombers," the Handley Page Victor was also the most radical in appearance, with its "crescent wing," T-tail, and unusual fuselage shape. The first flight took place on December 24, 1952, and the Victor began a career of more than 40 years as nuclear-bomber, standoff missile carrier, maritime reconnaissance plane, and finally, as a tanker. Eighty-four were built, and later models had a top speed of 640 miles per hour.

March 2, 1953 French aviation shows advances with the first flight of the Sud-Ouest SO 9000 Trident jet.

March 3, 1953 The Comet *Empress of Hawaii* crashes on takeoff from Karachi, killing all 11 on board. It is the first Comet accident with fatalities.

March 15, 1953 The last propeller-driven bomber, the RB-50H, is delivered to the USAF.

March 24, 1953 A Czech C-47 is hijacked and flown to an American zone in Germany; six highjackers are granted political asylum.

April 3, 1953 The BOAC inaugurates weekly London to Tokyo service with the Comet.

April 9, 1953 The Convair Sea Dart, a hydro-ski, delta-wing, twin-engine, sea-based fighter, makes its first flight.

May 2, 1953 One year after beginning operations, a Comet crashes near Calcutta, India; 43 are killed.

May 12, 1953 The first Bell X-2 rocket plane explodes during captive flight, killing Jean Zeigler, the test pilot.

May 18, 1953 The DC-7C, the ultimate Douglas piston-engine airliner, debuts.

May 18, 1953 Captain Joseph McConnell, a leading Korean ace, shoots down 3 MiG-15s to bring his total to 16.

SUD-EST SO 9000 TRIDENT

After World War II, France made desperate attempts to leap ahead technologically with bold experiments, including the Mach 1.5 Sud-Est SO 9000 Trident, which made its first flight on March 2, 1953. Ten were ordered, and one set an altitude record of 79,452 feet in May 1958. The project was canceled, perhaps because of asymmetric control problems if one of the jet engines failed and the promise of the more conventional Dassault Mirage III.

CONVAIR F2Y SEA DART

Convair was a beehive of experiments in the early 1950s, with turboprop patrol planes, vertical takeoff fighters, and the radical water-based F2Y Sea Dart fighter. Of classic Convair delta-wing design, the Sea Dart was first flown by Sam Shannon on April 9, 1953. The airplane performed well in the air, going supersonic in a dive (it was not area-ruled), but the hydroskis had protracted problems, and the Navy eventually lost interest.

NORTH AMERICAN F-100 SUPER SABRE The first operational U.S. fighter to have a supersonic capability in level flight, the North American F-100 went through a long and troubling development period before emerging as a workhorse ground-attack and reconnaissance plane in the Vietnam War. First flown on May 25, 1953, the Super Sabre set a speed record of 754.98 miles per hour on October 29 of that year. More than 1,600 F-100s were built, and they were also used by Denmark, France, and Turkey.

LOCKHEED **F-94C** STARFIRE The ultimate development of the original P-80 design, the Lockheed F-94C Starfire interceptor had twenty-four 2.75-inch rockets in the nose and twelve more in each wing pod. Its top speed was 585 miles per hour, and more than 850 of the Starfire series were built.

HAWKER HUNTER MK 3 One of the best-liked jets in RAF history, the Hawker Hunter was widely exported. This special all-red aircraft was flown by the famous test pilot Squadron Leader Neville Duke to set a speed record of 727.48 miles per hour on September 7, 1953. Two years later, the aircraft was relegated to ground instruction duties for mechanics. Some 1,972 Hunters were made, and they served 22 air forces.

FLIGHT TIMELINE

May 19, 1953 Jacqueline Cochran becomes the first woman to break Mach 1 in a Canadian-built F-86E, powered by an Avro Orenda engine.

May 25, 1953 The USAF's first operational supersonic fighter, the North American F-100 Super Sabre, makes its first flight.

June 18, 1953 The Douglas C-124 Globemaster crashes on takeoff in Japan, killing 129 people. It is the worst air disaster to date.

July 16, 1953 Lieutenant Colonel William F. Barnes flies a North American F-86D Sabre at 715.6 miles per hour, setting a world speed record.

July 17, 1953 Lieutenant Guy Bordelon, flying a vintage Vought F4U Corsair, shoots down his fifth aircraft to become the first Navy ace of the Korean War.

July 27, 1953 The Korean Armistice is signed.

August 21, 1953 Marion Carl reaches 83,235 feet in an airdropped Douglas D-558-2.

August 25, 1953 The USAF announces that the B-36 can successfully launch and recover an F-84F in flight.

September 1, 1953 A B-47 is successfully refueled in flight by a jet tanker, a KB-47B.

September 7, 1953 Famous test pilot Neville Duke sets a world speed record in a Hawker Hunter: 727.48 miles per hour.

CONVAIR **YF-102A** When it made its first flight on October 24, 1953, the Convair YF-102A had everything but the high speed that it had promised. The problem was drag, and the solution was the application of Dr. Richard Whitcomb's area rule, which resulted in a redesigned Coke-bottle style fuselage. With the new "wasp-waisted" fuselage, the aircraft went supersonic on its first flight and began an era of delta-wing interceptors. Total procurement was 899 single seaters and 111 two-seat trainers, all carrying a heavy missile armament.

CAPTAIN CHARLES "CHUCK" YEAGER The success of the Bell XS-1 (later X-1) in breaking the sound barrier on October 14, 1947 was a highly classified secret—until the news leaked out. Then on January 17, 1948, the record-breaking pilot, Captain Charles "Chuck" Yeager, was allowed to reveal that he had flown as many as 30 flights faster than the speed of sound in the Bell rocket plane. On December 12, 1953, Yeager flew the Bell X-1A at 1,650 miles per hour (Mach 2.5) to 70,000 feet.

SIKORSKY S-56 The first twin-engine Sikorsky helicopter, the S-56 made its flying debut on December 18, 1953, as the XHR2S-1 for the U.S. Marines. Powered by two Pratt & Whitney R-2800 engines, the heavy lifter could accommodate 26 troops, and some 60 were ordered. A further 94 went to the Army as the H-37A Mojave. The long landing gear was retractable, another first for the S-56.

BOEING STRATOJETS Pictured here are two rare aircraft: a Boeing KB-47G tanker and a YB-47F receiver using probe and drogue refueling techniques. This "buddy-refueling" was not feasible; the tanker B-47 could not carry sufficient fuel to make it worthwhile, and the probe and drogue system could not transfer fuel swiftly enough. The solution, of course, was the Boeing KC-135 and the flying boom—both of which are still being used today.

FLIGHT TIMELINE

September 21, 1953 Lieutenant Noh Keun-suk, a North Korean pilot, defects with a MiG-15 jet fighter; he is given political asylum and a $100,000 reward.

September 25, 1953 Mike Lithgow sets a world speed record of 737.7 miles per hour in a Supermarine Swift.

October 3, 1953 Lieutenant Commander James Verdin sets a world speed record of 752.94 miles per hour in a Douglas XF4-D Skyray.

October 16, 1953 Robert O. Rahn flies a Douglas XF4-D Skyray to 728.11 miles per hour for a closed-course record.

October 24, 1953 The Convair F-102 makes its first flight; the aircraft can't go supersonic until its fuselage is redesigned with "Coke-bottle" effect. It is the first U.S. delta-wing aircraft to go into service.

October 29, 1953 Lieutenant Colonel F. K. Everest flies a North American F-100A to 754.98 miles per hour over a 15-kilometer course.

November 20, 1953 Scott Crossfield reaches 1,327 miles per hour in a Douglas D-558-2 Skyrocket, the first Mach 2 flight.

November 29, 1953 The DC-7 enters commercial service with American Airlines.

December 12, 1953 Chuck Yeager flies an X-1A at 1,650 miles per hour (Mach 2.5) to 70,000 feet.

CHAPTER SIX

1954 to 1963:

Jets and Rockets, Speed and Space

The end of the Korean War found the world locked in an uneasy peace. The Cold War continually threatened to get hot, particularly when minor or major rebellions against the oppressive Soviet Union took place in East Germany, Hungary, or Czechoslovakia.

Lockheed U-2

Tupolev Tu-104   One benefactor of the tension was the arms industry, which, among other products, fielded a seemingly endless series of ever more capable warplanes. These included the Century Series fighters, such as Lockheed's F-104 Starfighter, known as the "Missile with a Man in It"; the Republic F-105 Thunderchief; and the McDonnell F-4, which was briefly known as the F-110 in the USAF. Larger aircraft were not neglected; the Boeing B-52 entered service to replace its formidable older brother, the B-47, and the KC-135 filled the indispensable air refueling role. Air refueling began as an essential tool for bombers but soon adapted to fighters and eventually to cargo planes and helicopters. All found it equally indispensable.

The B-52 and the KC-135 would become the backbone of the Strategic Air Command (SAC), the most powerful armed force in history. General Curtis E. LeMay commanded the SAC, and it was his goal to make the United States so unquestionably powerful that no nation would dare attack it with nuclear weapons. He succeeded remarkably.

The Soviet Union experienced a similar explosion of new military types. MiG fighters and Tupolev bombers were produced in great numbers and exported to all the Soviet satellite countries. The Soviet Union also demonstrated its military prowess in a continuing series of tests of both atomic and thermonuclear bombs.

The jet age came to passengers as well. There was an initial dark cloud when an unforeseen metal-fatigue problem led to the crash of three de Havilland Comet transports, prompting their subsequent removal from service. But Boeing, which had significant experience with pressurized aircraft such as the B-29 and B-50, had no problems with the introduction of its revolutionary 707. The Soviet Union used technology derived from captured B-29s to design their first passenger liner, the Tupolev Tu-104. The airline world was bowled over by the comfort, performance, and economy of the new jets. A revolution in travel was set in motion as both railroads and ocean liners were eclipsed by jet airliners.

The jet engine would affect every area of aviation, with the exception of the light aircraft, and was particularly important in spurring both the capability and the sale of helicopters. Rotary-wing aircraft could now fly at higher altitudes and speeds and embodied far greater lift capability. The same measure of performance would be true of executive aircraft as jet engine designs were introduced. Jet engines were also the harbinger of vertical flight for fixed-wing aircraft, a difficult task that is still not routine.

On October 4, 1957, the entire world, but most especially the United States, was rocked with both admiration and fear of a new Soviet achievement called *Sputnik*. This tiny satellite, beeping its simple beep as it orbited the earth, demonstrated how far Soviet scientists had come in the advanced rockets necessary to orbit a satellite. It was the first Soviet space triumph, but it was far from the last, as one new achievement followed another.

The implications of the satellite were abundantly clear, but Soviet Premier Nikita Khrushchev emphasized that a rocket that could put a satellite into orbit could also place a nuclear warhead on targets anywhere on Earth.

There had already been a great race for aerial supremacy, one in which the United States had a clear lead. There were now two additional races: to achieve supremacy in the field of intercontinental ballistic missiles and to achieve supremacy in space. The best minds in both the Soviet Union and the United States would be marshaled to achieve supremacy in all three areas. The race for space was decided in the following decade, and the

heed SR-71. And, before long, satellites would be conducting reconnaissance from space.

In 1962, the Soviet Union and the United States came closer to war than ever before or since with the Cuban missile crisis. A USAF U-2 reconnaissance plane discovered Soviet medium-range ballistic missiles being emplaced in Cuba. The United States, under President John F. Kennedy, reacted with a vigor that caused Khrushchev to back down, stating that any attack from Cuba would be regarded as a direct attack on the United States by the Soviet Union and would be met with overwhelming retaliatory force. Later, in his memoirs, Khrushchev would

United States was able to maintain its lead in aviation. But the race for supremacy in intercontinental ballistic missiles went on for the rest of the century and, indeed, continues at a lower level today. The Soviet Union succeeded in building larger, more accurate missiles with bigger warheads. The United States was able to build an almost equivalent missile force while maintaining a growing and prosperous economy. The misdirected management methods of the Soviet Union could not, and while it became a military giant, the Soviet Union's economy self-destructed from within on December 25, 1991.

Reconnaissance became extremely important during this period, beginning with the celebrated overflights of the Lockheed U-2, one of which resulted in a major national crisis when Captain Francis Gary Powers was shot down over the Soviet Union on May 1, 1960. The anticipation of this incident also laid the groundwork for the greatest reconnaissance aircraft of all time, the Lock-

confess that the thought of nuclear armed B-52s orbiting his borders caused him to call off the crisis.

As the decade wound down, yet another confrontation was facing the two superpowers, this time in Vietnam. Here, as in Korea, the Soviet Union and its sometime ally, sometime enemy China preferred to have a client state engage in warfare with the United States. Although actual warfare would not come until 1965, the United States became involved in the early 1960s and found itself on a slippery downward slope that would not reach its bottom until January 1973.

Despite the terrible external pressures of war, the world still needed heroes. Aviation was still the home of heroes, and the beginning siren call of space elicited a new breed, from Scott Crossfield and the North American X-15 to Joe Kittinger and his incredible parachute jumps from balloons at the edge of space.

Boeing 707

LOCKHEED **F-104** The advent of the MiG-15 in Korea came as a shock to the U.S. military, and Lockheed was tasked to come up with an aircraft that would not only be superior to the MiG-15 but also to any successor. Kelly Johnson, leading the famed Lockheed "Skunk Works," came up with the Mach 2 Lockheed F-104 Starfighter, which made its first flight on February 27, 1954. Although too short-ranged for the USAF, the aircraft became very popular with NATO countries.

GOODYEAR **ZPG-2** In May 1954, this Goodyear ZPG-2 airship flew 6,200 miles over Arctic regions to within 600 miles of the North Pole. It was equipped with external fuel tanks (visible just below the U.S. Navy markings)—just like a jet fighter.

BOEING 367-80 (707 PROTOTYPE) The revolutionary Boeing 367-80 rolled out to an appreciative crowd on May 14, 1954. Using experience derived from the B-47 and B-52 bombers and the C-97 transport, Boeing set the standard for the future with the sole 367-80. First flown on July 15, 1954, the 367-80 was used by Boeing as a test aircraft for many years, paving the way for the 707 airliner and the KC-135 tanker. The 367-80 had a maximum speed of 582 miles per hour.

VICKERS VISCOUNT The world of American aviation was shaken when Capital Airlines ordered three Vickers Viscounts in June 1954. It was the first time a non-American manufacturer had gained U.S. sales. Capital ultimately bought 60 Viscounts; Continental soon followed with an order for 15. The airliner sold well all over the world, with some 60 operators ultimately using them. The last production version, the Type 810, could carry up to 65 passengers at 357 miles per hour.

FLIGHT TIMELINE

January 10, 1954 A BOAC Comet breaks up in the air near Elba, Italy; 35 people are killed.

February 25, 1954 The Convair R3Y-1 Tradewind makes its first flight; engine problems keep it from becoming more successful.

February 27, 1954 The Lockheed XF-104 Starfighter makes its first flight.

March 1, 1954 The first hydrogen bomb is exploded in the Marshall Islands.

April 8, 1954 A BOAC Comet breaks up in the air south of Naples, Italy; an investigation shows fatigue cracks around the windows.

June 2, 1954 Soviet MiG-15s attack a Belgian DC-3 carrying a cargo of pigs.

June 22, 1954 The Douglas A-4 Skyhawk makes its first flight.

July 15, 1954 The Boeing 367-80, a 707 prototype, makes its first flight. It will have a profound influence on civil jet designs.

July 23, 1954 A British-owned Douglas DC-4 is shot down by Chinese fighters off Hainan Island.

July 26, 1954 U.S. Skyraiders shoot down two Chinese fighters that attacked them while they searched for DC-4 survivors.

August 1, 1954 James "Skeets" Coleman flies a Convair XFY-1 in vertical takeoff and landing.

ED HEINEMANN AND DOUGLAS XA4D-1 SKYHAWK PROTOTYPE Great aircraft designers like Ed Heinemann have the capacity to reach within themselves to develop aircraft that meet the needs of the service—but might not be what they asked for. He did that with the Douglas AD-1 and again with the magnificent Douglas A-4 Skyhawk, a lightweight attack bomber of enormous capability that made its first flight on June 22, 1954. With a top speed of 670 miles per hour, it was invaluable in the Vietnam War, the Arab-Israeli wars, and elsewhere.

BOAC COMET After the series of tragic crashes that grounded the original Comet, both de Havilland and BOAC attempted to come back with improved versions that solved the structural fatigue problem. The Comet 3 made its first flight on July 19, 1954, and the next year flew around the world in an attempt to generate sales. It was the first jet airliner to fly the Pacific and the first to circumnavigate the globe.

CONVAIR XFY-1 "POGO" A vertical takeoff and landing (VTOL) fighter that could operate from any deck, not just an aircraft carrier, was a dream of all navys. In 1951, the innovative Convair firm combined delta-wing and advanced turboprop technology to create the XFY-1 "Pogo." James "Skeets" Coleman made a successful transition flight on August 1, 1954, but landing vertically was deemed too difficult for the average service pilot, and the project was canceled.

August 3, 1954 An XF2Y-1 Sea Dart exceeds the speed of sound in a dive. It is the first water-based plane to do so.

August 4, 1954 The English Electric Lightning flies.

August 23, 1954 The Douglas X-3 Stilleto makes its first flight.

August 26, 1954 Major Arthur "Kit" Murray reaches 90,440 feet in a Bell X-1A rocket plane.

September 29, 1954 The McDonnell F-101A Voodoo, a development of the XF-88, makes its first flight. It has two J57 engines.

October 6, 1954 The Fairey Delta 2 research aircraft makes its first flight.

October 17, 1954 The Sikorsky XH-39 sets a helicopter altitude record of 24,500 feet. It is piloted by Army Warrant Officer Billy I. Wester.

November 1, 1954 The last B-29 bomber is withdrawn from service.

February 26, 1955 George Smith makes the first supersonic ejection from an F-100.

March 2, 1955 The Boeing KC-135 is judged to be the winner of the tanker competition.

March 17, 1955 BOAC announces that it will purchase 20 de Havilland Comet 4s, a redesign of the original ill-fated Comet.

MAJOR ARTHUR "KIT" MURRAY AND THE BELL X-1A The Bell X-1A had experienced roll-coupling at high speeds and was then dedicated to exploring flight at high altitudes. On August 26, 1954, Major Arthur "Kit" Murray set an altitude record of 90,440 feet in the X-1A. He is shown here in the protective pressure suit of the time, difficult to don and tiresome to wear but imperative in the event of a cabin decompression.

ENGLISH ELECTRIC LIGHTNING The unorthodox Lightning was not exactly a supersonic sensation on its August 4, 1954, first flight. However, later models, fitted with Rolls-Royce Avon engines with afterburning, exceeded Mach 2. The unusual engine configuration, one mounted atop another, led to maintenance problems, but these were nothing compared to those encountered with the electronic systems. The final version, the Lightning F.53, had an improved wing and larger tanks and was a very useful interceptor.

MCDONNELL F-101A VOODOO James McDonnell wanted to sell aircraft to both the Navy and the USAF and found the means to do so with the very advanced McDonnell F-101A Voodoo, the second of the "Century Series" fighters. Originally intended as an escort fighter for the Strategic Air Command (SAC), the Voodoo served in a number of roles, including reconnaissance, tactical nuclear strike, and interception. After making its first flight on September 29, 1954, the F-101 served for more than 20 years. Its top speed was 1,134 miles per hour.

PAYEN PA-49 DELTA WING Roland Payen was one of those indomitable designers who followed his own path regardless of circumstance. The Payen Pa-49 was a strange looking, tiny little delta-wing jet powered by a 330-pound Turbomeca Palas turbojet. Despite the limited thrust, the Payen achieved 249 miles per hour and led to the construction of a small number of larger aircraft.

LOCKHEED YC-130 HERCULES Sometimes even the great ones get it wrong, for Kelly Johnson told designer Willis Hawkins, "If you send this in (to the Air Force) you'll destroy the Lockheed Company." Fortunately, Johnson was very wrong, and the Hercules became a great success. The principal external differences between this prototype on its first flight on January 21, 1955, and a later C-130 are the lack of a radome, external tanks, and the use of three-blade propellers.

FLIGHT TIMELINE

March 23, 1955 Sweden sets an unusual speed record for formation flying: two Saab J-29s flying in formation over a 621-mile closed course at 560 miles per hour.

March 25, 1955 The Vought XF8U-1 exceeds the speed of sound on its first flight.

April 1, 1955 Lufthansa Airlines begins its first regular operations.

April 6, 1955 A B-36 launches an air-to-air missile with a nuclear warhead and explodes it over Yucca Flats, Nevada.

April 20, 1955 The McDonnell XV-1 convertiplane transitions from vertical to horizontal flight.

May 10, 1955 The GE XJ79 turbojet engine makes its first flight. It is later used on the F-104, B-58, and F-4, among others.

May 17, 1955 The first of 60 Vickers Viscounts is delivered to Continental Air Lines.

May 27, 1955 The Caravelle Jet airliner makes its first flight; it will become the first French airliner ever to be adopted for service in the United States.

June 7, 1955 Douglas announces its decision to build the DC-8 with four J57 engines in direct competition to the Boeing 707.

June 15, 1955 The Tupolev Tu-104 makes its first flight. It is the first jet for Aeroflot.

HUNTING PERCIVAL JET PROVOST The piston-engine Hunting Percival Provost became the standard basic trainer of the RAF in 1953. In the same year, nine examples of the Jet Provost were ordered for test, and in 1957, it became the standard basic trainer. It incorporated a tricycle landing gear, ejection seats, and a 1,750-pound thrust Bristol Siddeley Viper engine that gave a top speed of 326 miles per hour. Some Jet Provosts are flying as private aircraft in the United States today.

SUD AVIATION/AEROSPATIALE ALOUETTE (LARK) II JET The jet engine was important because helicopters had always been chronically short on power. The introduction of turbines enabled helicopters to lift greater loads, fly at greater speeds, and operate at higher altitudes. Powered by the 350 shaft-horsepower Turboméca Artouste engine, the Alouette II first flew on March 12, 1955. It soon became a commercial sensation and is shown here being demonstrated in Baltimore, Maryland. More than 1,300 were sold.

GEORGE SMITH AND NORTH AMERICAN F-100 The North American F-100 Super Sabre had many teething problems, one of which required an ejection at supersonic speeds by veteran test pilot George F. Smith on February 26, 1955. Smith was injured but survived. The F-100 went on to a troubled career in which many aircraft were lost (some 500 between 1956 and 1970), but it distinguished itself in combat in Vietnam. The aircraft's top speed was 892 miles per hour.

FLIGHT TIMELINE

June 29, 1955 The first Boeing B-52 enters operational service with the 93rd Bomb Wing at Castle Air Force Base.

July 14, 1955 The Martin P6M SeaMaster, a jet seaplane, makes its first flight.

August 20, 1955 Colonel Horace A. Hanes sets a world speed record of more than 822 miles per hour in a North American F-100A Super Sabre.

August 23, 1955 An RAF Canberra reconnaissance plane makes a round-trip transatlantic flight of 6,920 miles in 14 hours, 21 minutes, including a 35-minute stop at Floyd Bennett Field for refueling.

August 29, 1955 A Canberra sets a world altitude record of 65,876 feet for nonrocket airplanes.

September 3, 1955 The ground-level ejection seat is tested successfully in the Gloster Meteor.

October 8, 1955 The USS *Saratoga*, a new aircraft carrier, is launched.

October 13, 1955 Pan Am announces orders for 25 Douglas DC-8s and 20 Boeing 707s.

October 15, 1955 The Douglas A4-D Skyhawk sets a 500-kilometer record of 695.13 miles per hour.

VOUGHT F-8 CRUSADER One of the most beloved aircraft of the Vietnam War, the Vought F-8 Crusader was known as the "last of the gunfighters" for its ability to shoot down MiGs. First flown on March 25, 1955, the Crusader featured an unusual variable incidence wing to improve lift on takeoff. Armed with four 20-mm cannons at a time when many fighters had only missiles, the Mach 1.8 Crusader was at its best in a dogfight.

SUD EST CARAVELLE France stunned the world with the introduction of its Sud Est Caravelle twin-engine jet. The first flight took place on May 27, 1955, and the aircraft was the first to feature engines mounted aft on the fuselage, which insured a quiet passenger cabin. A total of 280 were sold, and they were used by 35 different airlines. The largest model carried 104 passengers at 513 miles per hour over short- to medium-range routes.

BOEING B-52 On June 29, 1955, the first B-52 entered operational service with the 93rd Bomb Wing at Castle Air Force Base. First flown on April 15, 1952, the Boeing B-52 has been in continuous service ever since and will probably still be in service in 2040. The eight-engine giant was originally intended to be a high-altitude nuclear bomber but gradually became a tactical bomber using conventional weap-ons. Armed with new precision-guided munitions and cruise missiles, it retained its status as a first-line war plane in the Persian Gulf War and in Afghanistan.

LIEUTENANT GENERAL ANDREI TUPOLEV AND V. GRIZO-DUBOVA A photographer arranged for Lieutenant General Andrei Tupolev to sit with aviatrix V. Grizodubova to watch an air show at Tushino outside of Moscow on July 25, 1955, when the Tupolev Tu-104 airliner was introduced to the public. Grizodubova had set a distance record in the Tupolev ANT-37*bis* in September 1938. Shortly before his death, Joseph Stalin had personally approved the conversion of the Tupolev Tu-16 design to that of the Tu-104.

LOCKHEED T-33 The Lockheed T-33 was built in Canada by Canadair. Some 656 were built, all powered by Rolls-Royce Nene jet engines, which provided a top speed of 600 miles per hour. The first Canadair Silver Star was flown on December 22, 1952. Japan also built the T-33. The Kawasaki company produced 210 aircraft, which served for more than 20 years with the Japanese Air Self Defense Force.

COLONEL HORACE A. HANES AND F-100 On August 20, 1955, Colonel Horace A. Hanes set a speed record of just over 822 miles per hour in a North American F-100A Super Sabre, flying over a course at Edwards Air Force Base, California. This was the first official speed record set above Mach 1.

NORD GRIFFON France produced some fascinating prototypes after World War II in an effort to bring its industry back up to world standards. The Nord Griffon was well in advance of its time, intended from the start to employ a combined turbojet/ramjet power plant. Two aircraft were built, and the Griffon II had a 7,800-pound thrust Atar jet engine built integral with the ramjet. About 200 flights were completed before the program was canceled.

BOEING 707 No matter how good an airliner is, it still has to be purchased in sizable numbers before it can be launched into production. Pan American Airways made history on October 13, 1955, by buying 20 Boeing 707s and 25 Douglas DC-8s to enter the jet age with a bang.

REPUBLIC **F-105D**

The Republic F-105D Thunderchief was unofficially termed the "Thud" because of early development problems in which there were many crashes. Intended as a long-range nuclear bomber, it instead served brilliantly in the Vietnam War as a strike plane and as a Wild Weasel enemy defense suppression aircraft. The F-105 was fast, capable of 1,390 miles per hour, and it could carry an enormous 14,000-pound ordnance load.

The veterans of F-105 operations in Vietnam are extremely proud of their work on the aircraft and celebrate it at meetings where the missions—and the parties—are reenacted. These meetings always include a solemn toast to the many F-105 crew members who were killed in action.

SAAB 35 DRAKEN (DRAGON) Sweden has manufactured a series of excellent fighters, and the Saab 35 Draken was perhaps the most unusual of all, with its unique double-delta configuration. The first European supersonic fighter, the Mach 2 Draken made its first flight on October 25, 1955. Able to operate from Sweden's dispersed airfields, it appeared in a long series of models, each more effective than the last. Some 606 Drakens were built, and they were also used by Finland, Austria, and Denmark.

FLIGHT TIMELINE

May 21, 1956 The first U.S. air-dropped hydrogen bomb is exploded in the Bikini Islands.

May 27, 1956 Soviets announce that the Tupolev Tu-104 passenger jet has a cruising speed of 500 to 560 miles per hour and a range of 3,000 miles.

June 21, 1956 Orders are announced for 30 Convair 600 Golden Arrow jets. It will be the biggest commercial jet failure in history.

June 30, 1956 A United DC-7 and a TWA Super Connie collide over the Grand Canyon; 128 people are killed.

July 23, 1956 The long-lived French Dassault Etendard IV makes its first flight.

August 9, 1956 The Fiat G.91 prototype—a "Mini-Sabre"—makes its first flight.

August 23–24, 1956 The Hiller H-21 twin-rotor aircraft makes a nonstop transcontinental flight from San Diego to Washington, D.C.

August 31, 1956 The first production Boeing KC-135A tanker makes its first flight.

September 2, 1956 The H-13 helicopter sets an endurance record of 57 hours, 40 minutes.

September 20, 1956 The United States announces that the Bell X-2 has reached 1,900 miles per hour and 126,000 feet altitude.

DOUGLAS DC-6 The mighty Douglas Aircraft Company reacted to the Lockheed Constellation with its own pressurized airliner, the DC-6, which could carry from 48 to 86 passengers at a cruising speed of 315 miles per hour. The DC-6 was well liked by pilots, passengers, and maintenance personnel. USAF DC-6 aircraft were designated C-118, and one, the *Independence,* became President Harry Truman's Air Force One.

FOKKER F27 FRIENDSHIP
Fokker mated its F27 with the Rolls-Royce Dart turboprop to come up with this prototype, which made its first flight on November 24, 1955. Fairchild was also looking for a product and entered into an agreement to manufacture the F27 in the United States, the first twin-turboprop to be built there. Almost 800 were built, and they served airlines all over the world. Seating grew over time to 60, and top speed was more than 300 miles per hour.

RYAN X-13 VERTIJET There are many approaches to vertical takeoffs and landings, all of them difficult, but Ryan came up with an ingenious compromise—a vertical descent but a lateral landing against a stand instead of trying to touch down vertically. The X-13, which made its first flight on December 10, 1955, was perhaps the most successful of all the VTOL aircraft of the period, but the real problem was building an operational aircraft with enough fuel to perform a combat mission. Only two were built.

FLIGHT TIMELINE

September 20, 1956 Another order for Lockheed T-33 trainers is announced. Ultimately 5,691 of the trainers will be built by Lockheed; they will remain in service for more than 40 years.

September 27, 1956 Captain Milburn Apt is killed in the crash of a Bell X-2 after setting a Mach 3.196 speed record (2,094 miles per hour).

October 1956 The last of the Connies, the 1649A Starliner, makes its first flight.

November 6, 1956 Morton Lewis and Malcolm Ross set an altitude record of 76,000 feet in a balloon.

November 11, 1956 The Convair XB-58 Hustler supersonic bomber makes its first flight.

November 15, 1956 The North American F-107 reaches Mach 2 in test flights.

November 17, 1956 The Mirage III, a delta-wing fighter, makes its first flight.

November 28, 1956 The Ryan X-13 Vertijet makes its first jet vertical takeoff and transition into level flight.

December 17, 1956 The Short SC-1 VTOL research plane makes its first flight.

December 26, 1956 The Convair F-106 Delta Dart prototype makes its first flight.

DOUGLAS DC-7C The Douglas DC-7C (shown here on its December 20, 1955, first flight) and the Lockheed Starliner were the peak of piston-engine airliner development, with intercontinental range and cruising speeds of 360 miles per hour. Their 3,250-horsepower Curtiss Wright R-3350 turbo-compound engines were not reliable, however, and both aircraft were jokingly called "the fastest trimotors in the world." Fortunately for airline passengers, the jet engine was on its way to save the day.

WILLIAM JUDD AND CESSNA 180 Emulating Charles Lindbergh's immortal New York-to-Paris flight of 1927, William Judd flew his Cessna 180 from Rye, New York, landing in Paris on February 6, 1956, for a flight time of 25 hours and 15 minutes.

FAIREY DELTA 2 Flown by famed test pilot Peter Twiss, the Fairey Delta 2 raised the world absolute speed record to 1,132 miles per hour on March 10, 1956, the first time it had exceeded 1,000 miles per hour. The Fairey Delta 2 was later used in experiments that led directly to the Concorde airliner. The Delta 2 was not an easy aircraft to fly and was the last Fairey fixed-wing aircraft, ending a saga that began in 1915.

VISCOUNT TRENCHARD Marshal of the Royal Air Force Hugh Trenchard was considered the father of the Royal Air Force. "Boom"—so called because of his deep voice—fostered the aggressive tactics that became the hallmark of British flyers. After World War I, Trenchard returned as Chief of Air Staff and supervised the "air control" tactics the RAF used to maintain order in the Middle East. He died on February 10, 1956.

DE HAVILLAND COMET 2 The Comet 2 was being developed for transatlantic work when the Comet 1 tragedies occurred. Comet 2 fuselages were rebuilt with stronger metal and round windows. Airlines were not interested in the aircraft, and all 15 built were ultimately adopted by the RAF as transports with the No. 216 Squadron. Its top speed was 490 miles per hour, with a range of 2,100 miles.

BELL X-2 The relatively tiny size of the Bell X-2, a swept-wing development of the Bell X-1 series, is seen here, with Lieutenant Colonel Frank "Pete" Everest posed in the cockpit. Everest made the X-2's first powered flight on November 11, 1955, following a long and troubled test program. He gained the title "fastest man alive" by flying the X-2 at 1,900 miles per hour (Mach 2.87) on July 23, 1956.

DASSAULT ETENDARD IV One must admire the Dassault company for fiercely remaining independent and competitive in the postwar years. A steady series of great fighters emerged from Dassault's factories including a private venture, the Etendard IV, which ultimately led to a line of French Aéronavale fighters. The Etendard IV first flew on July 23, 1956, and led to a production order for about 70 aircraft.

BOEING KC-135A STRATOTANKER The Boeing KC-135 was structurally similar to the 707 passenger liner but had the military equipment required for in-flight refueling, including the Boeing-designed flying boom system. The first flight on August 31, 1956, initiated a new era in the United States Air Force, for aerial refueling soon spread from SAC bombers to tactical fighters to transports. KC-135s were a force multiplier, enabling other aircraft to do their missions.

GENERAL CURTIS E. LEMAY
The Commander in Chief of the SAC, General Curtis E. LeMay salutes after receipt of the Distinguished Flying Cross for a record flight from Buenos Aires to Washington. Perhaps the greatest air combat leader in history, LeMay shaped the SAC, which was vitally important to winning the Cold War, in his image.

FLIGHT TIMELINE

May 16, 1957 The Boeing Bomarc interceptor is ordered into production.

June 6, 1957 Two U.S. Navy Skywarriors fly from the USS *Bon Homme Richard* to the USS *Saratoga* in the first carrier-to-carrier nonstop transcontinental flight.

July 16, 1957 Future astronaut and senator John Glenn breaks the transcontinental speed record in a Vought F8U-1P Crusader by flying 3 hours, 22 minutes, 50.05 seconds, at an average speed of 723.517 miles per hour.

July 16, 1957 Two Douglas A3D Skywarriors make a record flight from Moffet Field in California to Honolulu in 4 hours, 45 minutes.

July 19, 1957 An F-89J fires an air-to-air Genie rocket, with nuclear warhead, over Yucca Flats, Nevada.

August 1957 The R.7, the first Soviet intercontinental ballistic missile, is launched.

August 12, 1957 A Douglas F3D-1 Skynight makes an automatic landing on board the USS *Antietam*.

August 18, 1957 Paul Bikle establishes a glider speed record of 55.02 miles per hour over a 300-kilometer triangular course.

August 19–20, 1957 Major David G. Simons sets a balloon altitude record of 101,516 feet.

August 28, 1957 A Canberra sets a jet aircraft altitude record of 70,308 feet.

LOCKHEED STARLINER Competition in the airline transport business has always been fierce, and Lockheed never made a profit on any of their civilian airliners. The profits came when the civilian airliners were converted for military purposes. The Lockheed Starliner shown here was the prototype of the last of the series, the 1649, which made its first flight in October 1956. With its Wright turbo-compound engines, the 1649 had a maximum speed of 377 miles per hour. Jets were on the horizon, and piston-engine transports were just about obsolete.

CONVAIR XB-58 HUSTLER The world's first supersonic bomber, Convair's delta-wing XB-58 Hustler stunned the Soviet Union when it debuted on November 11, 1956, with Beryl A. Erickson as pilot. The XB-58 was unique because its area-ruled fuselage carried a 57-foot-long weapons pod. Three times as expensive as the Boeing B-52, the B-58 had a high accident rate and was withdrawn from service in 1969. Its top speed was 1,321 miles per hour.

CONVAIR F-106A DELTA DART The wing of the Convair F-106A Delta Dart was similar to its predecessor, the F-102 Delta Dagger, but the fuselage was better streamlined. The F-106A flew first on December 26, 1956. A total of about 400 Delta Darts were built, and they were continually modified to stay in service until 1988. Despite its complexity and difficult mission, the F-106A had the lowest accident rate of any single-engine aircraft in USAF history. Its top speed was 1,328 miles per hour.

DR. RICHARD WHITCOMB
Aviation engineers and scientists rarely get recognition for their contributions, primarily because such work is largely a team effort. One young man who deservedly received early recognition was Dr. Richard Whitcomb, whose concept of the area rule for supersonic aircraft design proved to be invaluable. Whitcomb was also the driving force behind the creation of the supercritical airfoil. Here he receives an award.

NORTHROP SNARK The Northrop Snark, Project MX-775A, was a subsonic, turbojet-powered missile with a 6,325-mile range and a top speed of 610 miles per hour. It was part of the first intercontinental missile program in the world, after the aborted German A-10 effort. The first flight took place on August 6, 1953, and featured a Nortronics stellar-inertial guidance system. Carrying up to a 20-megaton nuclear payload, the Snark was operational from 1957 to 1961, when it was replaced by the Atlas ICBM.

BELL X-14 Bell was an innovative company, and it took up the challenge of vertical flight with the Model 65 VTOL, then followed with the X-14, which borrowed the wing from a Bonanza and the rear fuselage and tail surfaces from a Beech T-34. The thrust from two 1,750 pound Armstrong Siddeley Viper engines was vectored to lift the aircraft, and its February 19, 1957, first flight was followed by a full transition in May.

WESTLAND WESSEX HELICOPTER Westland wisely entered the helicopter business by building the Sikorsky S-51 under license as the Dragonfly. It led the way to a long line of successful Westland helicopters, including the Wessex. Essentially a Sikorsky S-58 with a Napier Gazelle turboshaft engine, the Wessex made its first flight on May 17, 1957. There followed another 381 Wessex choppers in 11 models. Their maximum speed was around 130 miles per hour; maximum range was approximately 310 miles.

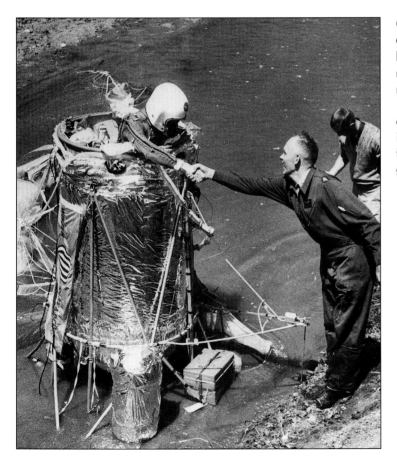

CAPTAIN JOE KITTINGER Captain Joe W. Kittinger shakes hands with Major David G. Simmons after piloting a balloon to a record 96,000 feet on June 2, 1957. Kittinger went on to make even higher ascensions, parachuting out of one balloon at 102,800 feet on August 16, 1960, and going supersonic in his free fall.

FLIGHT TIMELINE

December 28, 1957 J. E. Woman, in a Cessna YH-41, reaches 30,335 feet to set a world helicopter record.

January 14–20, 1958 Qantas Airways flies the first scheduled round-the-world route using Lockheed's Super Constellations.

January 31, 1958 The first successful U.S. satellite, *Explorer I*, is launched from Cape Canaveral.

March 27, 1958 A Boeing KC-135 flies nonstop from California to New Zealand.

April 8, 1958 A USAF KC-135 flies nonstop from Tokyo to Azores, Portugal, a distance of 10,228 miles. Brigadier General W. E. Eubank piloted the aircraft, setting a world speed record of 13 hours, 45 minutes, and 46 seconds between Tokyo and Washington, D.C. (492.262 miles per hour).

April 9, 1958 A Canberra blows up at 56,000 feet, necessitating the highest ejection to date.

April 18, 1958 The Grumman F11F-1 Tiger, piloted by Lieutenant Commander George C. Watkins, sets a world altitude record of 76,932 feet.

May 2, 1958 Rene Carpentier flies the mixed-powerplant Trident to 78,452 feet.

May 7, 1958 The Lockheed F-104A reclaims the altitude record when Major Howard C. Johnson pilots it to 91,243 feet.

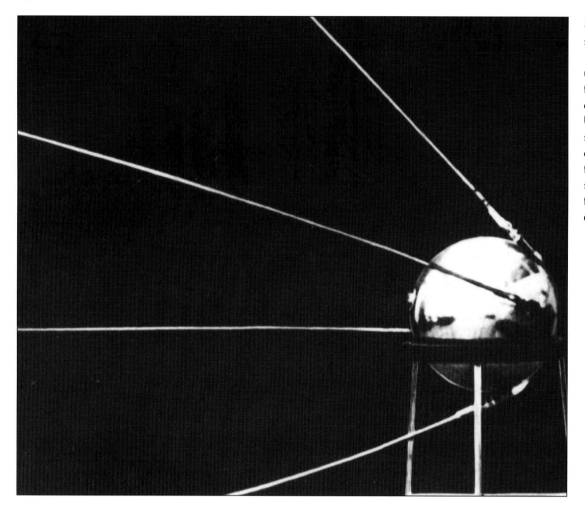

SPUTNIK The Soviet Union shocked the world on October 4, 1957, when it demonstrated an unexpected scientific prowess with the launch of the world's first artificial satellite, *Sputnik*. The United States in particular was shocked, and *Sputnik* brought about a space race that continued through the Cold War. The simple satellite emitted a haunting "beep" that will forever be remembered by all who heard it.

MIL MI-6 FIRST FLIGHT The Mil Mi-6 was the largest and fastest helicopter in the world at the time of its record-breaking flight on October 31, 1957, when it flew at 7,500 feet with 24,000 pounds of cargo. Some 800 of the transports, which had a top speed of 186 miles per hour, were built. The rotor had a diameter of just under 115 feet, and the maximum gross takeoff weight approached 94,000 pounds.

FAIREY ROTODYNE Intended to be the first vertical takeoff airliner, the Fairey Rotodyne roared into its first flight on November 6, 1957. The Rotodyne used a power-driven rotor for vertical flight, propellers for forward propulsion, and an auto-rotating rotor for cruising flight. The sizable 46-foot-span wing shared the lifting duties with the 90-foot-diameter rotor. Although there was both commercial and military interest in the aircraft, project delays brought about cancellation in 1962.

BOEING 707 Using the experience gained in building the B-47, the Boeing company took a colossal risk by entering the jet transport market with an entirely new design, the 707, which made its first flight on December 20, 1957. Pan American ordered 20 (and also ordered 25 Douglas DC-8s), and this was the beginning of a revolution in air transport. Jet airliners were faster, larger, and more economical than piston-engine airliners, and the public loved them. The 707 established Boeing as the premier manufacturer of airliners.

FLIGHT TIMELINE

May 16, 1958 Captain Walter W. Irwin flies an F-104A at 1,403 miles per hour, setting a world speed record.

May 17, 1958 Four McDonnell F3H Demons and four Vought F8U Crusaders fly nonstop across the Atlantic.

May 22–23, 1958 Major E. N. LeFaivre, USMC, sets five time-to-climb altitude records in a Douglas F4D-1.

May 27, 1958 The McDonnell F4H-1 Phantom II makes its first flight with Robert Little as the pilot.

June 12, 1958 A KC-135 sets an unofficial coast-to-coast record of 3 hours, 42 minutes, 45 seconds.

July 3, 1958 A Boeing 707 commercial airliner sets a Los Angeles to Mexico City record: three hours, nine minutes.

July 26, 1958 Captain Ivan Kincheloe, a famous test pilot, is killed in the crash of a Lockheed F-104.

July 27, 1958 Commanders Malcom Ross and Morton Lewis set a balloon endurance record of 34 hours and 20 minutes.

August 1, 1958 Captain Marion Boling sets a record of 6,979 miles in a Beechcraft Bonanza, flying from Manila to Pendleton, Oregon.

August 7, 1958 A de Havilland Comet 4 sets a west-east transatlantic record, flying from New York to Hatfield, England, in 6 hours and 27 minutes.

SIKORSKY S-58 (HSS-1) I The Sikorsky S-58 was used with great success by the United States Navy, Marines, Coast Guard, and Army, as well as by civilian organizations. A total of 1,820 S-58s were built. The aircraft was also built under license in Great Britain and France, and some were converted from reciprocating engines (Wright R-1820) to turboshaft engines (G.E. T58).

LOCKHEED JETSTAR Larry Bell used to say that in the aviation business, it was usually better to be second than first, because you avoided some of the problems. This was the case with the Lockheed JetStar, one of the first "business jets." (Only 204 were produced.) This is the twin-engine prototype, which first flew on September 4, 1957. Later models had four engines and a top speed of 547 miles per hour.

VANGUARD SATELLITE The successful launch of the rocket that carried the *Vanguard I* gave the morale of the United States a badly needed shot in the arm. It lifted off on March 17, 1958, after two previous well-publicized failures. The miniature test-satellite (it was six inches in diameter) was the first to employ solar cells to recharge mercury batteries. It measured atmospheric density and revealed the earth to be pear-shaped. The satellite weighed only 3.25 pounds and was referred to by the Soviet press as a "grapefruit." *Vanguard I* is still in orbit today.

LIEUTENANT COMMANDER GEORGE C. WATKINS The old-fashioned pressure suit was extremely uncomfortable to wear, but Lieutenant Commander George C. Watkins needed it for protection on his record-setting April 18, 1958, flight in a Grumman F11F-1 Tiger. He zoomed to an altitude record of 76,932 feet. At 750 miles per hour, the Tiger was the Navy's first supersonic fighter, but it was too short-ranged and was superseded by the Vought F8U Crusader by 1959.

CAPTAIN WALTER W. IRWIN Another member of Hamilton Air Force Base's 83rd Fighter Interceptor Wing, Captain Walter W. Irwin climbs out of his F-104A after flying at 1,403 miles per hour—twice the speed of sound—a world record set on May 16, 1958.

LOCKHEED X-7 Lockheed's X-7 missile is dropped from a B-29 over the Holloman Air Development Center at Alamagordo, New Mexico. The spindly X-7 was one of the most important contributions by Lockheed engineers because it generated data about high Mach number flight, as well as the characteristics needed for reentry of space vehicles into the atmosphere. The X-7 hit Mach 4 on this flight. It was recovered by parachute, landing on a spike in its nose.

MAJOR HOWARD C. JOHNSON The armed services competed against each other to set records because they gained publicity and helped get a bigger share of the budget. Here USAF Major Howard C. Johnson is congratulated for setting a world altitude record of 91,243 feet on May 7, 1958, in the red-hot Lockheed F-104A Starfighter. At left is Captain Walter Irwin, with Korean War ace Captain James Low at the right. The F-104 was too short-ranged for the Air Force and served best in foreign air forces.

McDonnell F4H-1 Phantom II The McDonnell Aircraft Corporation hoped to sell as many as 200 or 300 of its F4H-1 Phantom II fighters to the U.S. Navy. Robert Little was at the controls in this first flight photo of May 27, 1958, by which time interest was growing even in the USAF. More than 5,000 of the aircraft were built for use in 11 air arms. They were powered by twin GE J79 engines and had a top speed of 1,485 miles per hour.

Douglas DC-8 Douglas responded quickly to Boeing's challenge, announcing on June 7, 1955, that it would build the DC-8, which flew on May 30, 1958. Externally, the two aircraft were difficult to tell apart, and both were equally well liked by passengers. Douglas was beginning to have management problems, however, and would not be able to compete with Boeing in introducing new models. Douglas eventually became part of McDonnell Douglas, which in turn was acquired by Boeing.

FLIGHT TIMELINE

January 25, 1959 American Airlines starts 707 transcontinental service.

February 12, 1959 The last Convair B-36 is withdrawn from service.

March 10, 1959 The first captive flight of an X-15 is made with Scott Crossfield in the cockpit.

April 2, 1959 Seven astronauts are selected for Project Mercury: L. Gordon Cooper, Jr.; Virgil I. "Gus" Grissom; Donald K. "Deke" Slayton; Scott Carpenter; Alan B. Shepard, Jr.; Walter M. Schirra, Jr.; and John H. Glenn, Jr.

April 23, 1959 The Hound Dog Missile makes its first flight with B-52s.

May 27, 1959 The Bomarc undergoes its first test flight.

May 28, 1959 Two monkeys, Able and Baker, are launched in the Jupiter nose cone; both will be recovered safely.

June 4, 1959 Max Conrad sets a lightplane distance record of 7,683 miles in a Piper Comanche.

June 8, 1959 Scott Crossfield makes the first glide flight in a North American X-15.

June 16, 1959 Soviet MiGs attack a Martin P4M Mercator, shooting out both starboard engines and wounding two crew members.

June 17, 1959 The Dassault Mirage IV-A bomber makes its first flight.

FAA CREATED On August 23, 1958, the Federal Aviation Administration (FAA) was created when President Dwight D. Eisenhower signed the Federal Aviation Act of 1958. The new law brought together all the disparate agencies that had grown up over the years and combined them into the FAA and the Civil Aeronautics Board.

FAIREY ROTODYNE Advertised by Fairey as "the world's first vertical takeoff airliner" the Rotodyne made its first flight on November 6, 1957, and set a world speed record for convertiplanes of 190.9 miles per hour on January 5, 1959. With its four-bladed, 90-foot-diameter rotor and two Napier Eland turboprop power plants, the Rotodyne could carry up to 48 passengers. Despite a promising start, excess noise and weight doomed the project, which was canceled in 1962.

ARMSTRONG WHITWORTH ARGOSY The Armstrong Whitworth Argosy first flew on January 8, 1959, powered by four Rolls-Royce Dart turboprop engines of 2,020-shaft horsepower. A big aircraft, with a 115-foot span and 88,000-pound gross weight, the Argosy, like so many British aircraft of the time, was built in too few numbers to be profitable; only about 73 were made. The Argosy was easy to load through its large rear entrance and fairly fast at 280 miles per hour.

CONVAIR B-36 PEACEMAKER The last Convair B-36 was retired on February 12, 1959. This RB-36E was photographed over Travis Air Force Base, California, in August 1952. The huge B-36 was a controversial aircraft from the start, one that the U.S. Navy unfairly attacked as a "billion-dollar blunder." The name Peacemaker was justified; although it never dropped a bomb in anger, its intercontinental nuclear capability kept the Soviet Union in check during the early days of the Cold War.

VANGUARD II On February 17, 1959, the U.S. Navy launched *Vanguard II,* a weather satellite, into orbit from Cape Canaveral, Florida. The satellite was carried into space by a Viking-derived launcher, also called Vanguard. The satellite itself was 21 inches long and weighed only 21 pounds, a far cry from today's behemoths.

CANADA AVRO CF-105 ARROW One of the most advanced fighter planes in history, the Avro CF-105 Arrow made its first flight on March 25, 1958. The delta-wing interceptor was capable of Mach 2.3. Only six of the aircraft were made before the Canadian government canceled the Arrow program on February 20, 1959.

PAYLOAD PACKAGE While the Soviet Union preferred huge rockets to lift its spacecraft, the United States sought ways to minimize the weight and size of space vehicles. This is the payload package for the *Pioneer 4* space probe launched by a Juno II rocket for a moon flyby on March 3, 1959. The probe flew within 37,300 miles of the moon before it passed into an orbit around the sun.

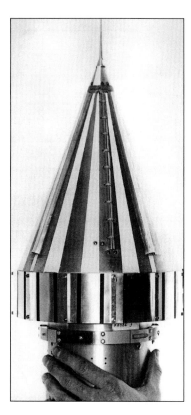

ANDRE TURCAT In France, test pilot Andre Turcat occupied a position of prestige equivalent to Chuck Yeager in the United States. Here Vice President Richard Nixon presents him with the Harmon Trophy for setting a speed record of 1,018 miles per hour on February 25, 1959, in the Nord Griffon II, which used a turbojet-ramjet engine for the purpose. Ironically, work is still ongoing with ramjet engines, which were used successfully in drones but not yet in production aircraft.

FLIGHT TIMELINE

December 11, 1959 Brigadier General J. H. Moore, flying a Republic F-105B, sets a 100-kilometer closed-course speed record of 1,216.48 miles per hour.

December 14, 1959 Captain J. B. Jordan, in a Lockheed F-104C, sets an altitude record of 103,389 feet.

December 15, 1959 Major Joseph W. Rogers, in a Convair F-106A Delta Dart, sets a straightaway course record of 1,525.9 miles per hour.

March 1, 1960 A ZPG-3W airship stays on patrol for 49.3 hours, spending 58 hours in the air—a new record.

April 1, 1960 The first weather satellite, *Tiros 1*, is launched.

May 1, 1960 Captain Francis Gary Powers is shot down over the Soviet Union in a Lockheed U-2.

May 21, 1960 The last North American B-25 is withdrawn from USAF service.

July 1, 1960 The first Carrier On-Board Delivery (COD) squadron is activated.

August 12, 1960 Major Robert White pilots a North American X-15 to 136,500 feet.

August 12, 1960 *Echo 1*, the first passive communication satellite, is launched.

August 16, 1960 Joe Kittinger breaks his own record with a leap from a balloon at 102,800 feet and a free fall of 84,700 feet.

FIRST SEVEN ASTRONAUTS The nation was cheered and heartened by the selection of the first seven astronauts on April 2, 1959. The challenge of space had to be met, and these seven men seemed best qualified to meet it. Front row, from left: Walter M. Schirra, Jr.; Donald K. "Deke" Slayton; John H. Glenn, Jr.; and Scott Carpenter. Back row, from left: Alan B. Shepard, Jr.; Virgil I. "Gus" Grissom; and L. Gordon Cooper, Jr. They would make history.

B-52 WITH HOUND DOG MISSILE On April 23, 1959, the Hound Dog Missile made its first flight with B-52s. The AGM-28 A (Air to Ground Missile) Hound Dog entered operations in 1961 to assist in penetrating the Soviet Union's tough air defenses. Designed for the new B-52G aircraft, one Hound Dog was carried on pylons beneath each wing. With its 7,500-pound thrust Pratt & Whitney J52 engine, the Hound Dog could fly at Mach 2.1 with a one Megaton thermonuclear warhead. Some 693 were bought, all were phased out by 1975.

BOEING NB-52A AND NORTH AMERICAN X-15 One of the first three production Boeing B-52s was designated NB-52A and assigned to flight test duty at Edwards Air Force Base, where it carried experimental aircraft like the North American X-15 to launch altitudes. The X-15 was perhaps the most successful and productive of the entire X series of experimental aircraft.

MONKEY ABLE Using animals for space flight experiments was a precursor to crewed space flight. Here, Monkey Able sits on top of the chamber in which it took a ride into space on May 28, 1959, at 10,000 miles per hour. His colleague, Monkey Baker, also survived the ride in the Jupiter rocket.

FLIGHT TIMELINE

September 5, 1960 Major Tom Miller, USMC, sets a 500-kilometer closed course speed record of 1,216.78 miles per hour in a McDonnell F4H-1 Phantom II.

September 21, 1960 The first Republic F-105A is accepted by Tactical Air Command.

September 25, 1960 Commander J. F. Davis sets a 100-kilometer closed course record of 1,390.21 miles per hour in a Phantom II, exceeding the existing record by more than 200 miles per hour.

October 14, 1960 A catastrophic accident occurs at Baikonur cosmodrome in the Soviet Union during the purported launch of a rocket to Mars.

October 16, 1960 The de Havilland Comet 4 is withdrawn from commercial passenger service.

December 10, 1960 A C-119 catches a 300-pound capsule from *Discoverer XVIII*.

December 13, 1960 A North American YA3J-1 sets a world altitude record of 91,450.8 feet with a 1,000-kilogram payload.

December 20, 1960 The Martin Company, founded in 1911 by Glenn L. Martin, delivers its last airplane, a P5M-2 flying boat, to the Navy. Martin will later develop experimental aircraft related to the space program.

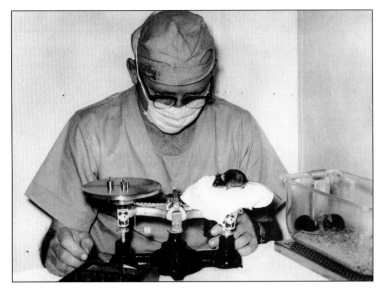

DISCOVERER III LAUNCHED WITH "SPACE MICE" You are looking at the James Bond of the rodent world. A technician weighs a mouse prior to a flight in *Discoverer III*, ostensibly an experiment to learn about space flight conditions. The *Discoverer* series was the beginning of spy-satellite operations, and when *Discoverer XIV* at last succeeded in its mission, the Soviet Union became a virtual open book to U.S. intelligence services.

MAX CONRAD LANDS AFTER RECORD FLIGHT A beloved figure in general aviation, Max Conrad steps from his Piper Comanche after setting a lightplane distance record of 7,683 miles on June 4, 1959. Conrad took off from Casablanca and flew direct to Los Angeles in just a little more than 58 hours.

SCOTT CROSSFIELD IN X-15
Scott Crossfield was not only a test pilot but also a great, visionary engineer who was the catalyst for the entire North American X-15 program. Crossfield, who worked for North American, flew the first X-15 flight suspended from the wing of the B-52 carrier plane, making his first gliding flight on June 8, 1959. The flight ran into a little difficulty with pilot-induced pitch oscillation, but Crossfield quickly got it under control and landed successfully.

MIRAGE IV On June 17, 1959, yet another of Marcel Dassault's magnificent creations took to the air. This was the Mirage IV, powered by two SNECMA Atar 9 turbojets of 13,000 pounds of thrust. The Mach 2.2 bomber was intended to carry the flag of France's proud *la force de frappe,* its own nuclear deterrent force. More than 60 were procured, and they, like the SAC, maintained an instant nuclear alert force.

TUPOLEV TU-114 The Soviet Union liked nothing better than to stun the West, particularly the United States, with its aeronautical achievements. It succeeded on June 28, 1959, when a magnificent Tupolev Tu-114 flew from Moscow to New York in 11 hours. A derivative of the Tu-95 Bear, the turboprop Tu-114 was for years the largest, heaviest, and longest-range transport in the world. Its top speed was 547 miles per hour, and the range was 6,040 miles.

FLIGHT TIMELINE

January 12, 1961 Major H. J. Deutschendorf establishes a world speed record of 808 miles per hour over a 2,000-kilometer closed course in a Convair B-58.

January 14, 1961 Major H. E. Confer sets a 1,000-kilometer closed course speed record of 1,284.73 miles per hour in a Convair B-58.

January 31, 1961 After a suborbital flight in a *Mercury* spacecraft, the chimpanzee Ham is recovered.

February 25, 1961 A Schwiezer I-23-E sailplane, piloted by Paul F. Bickle, sets an altitude record of 46,267 feet.

March 8, 1961 Max Conrad sets a lightplane round-the-world record: 8 days, 18 hours, and 35 minutes.

March 17, 1961 The first supersonic pilot trainer, the Northrop T-38, is delivered to Randolph Air Force Base.

March 30, 1961 Joe Walker sets an altitude record of 169,600 feet in a North American X-15.

April 10, 1961 A Navy Lockheed C-130BL makes a winter flight to and from Antarctica to bring out a stricken Soviet scientist.

April 12, 1961 Soviet Yuri Gagarin becomes the first person in space and completes one orbit of the earth in 108 minutes.

QANTAS FIRST JET TO LAND IN HONOLULU Sir Hudson Fysh of Qantas is warmly welcomed by Mae Beimes at Honolulu International Airport on June 30, 1959. The Qantas Airlines 707 arrived from San Francisco without any tourists but was recognized for being the first transpacific passenger jet crossing. The tourists came later—by the millions!

JACQUELINE AURIOL IN MIRAGE III Like her American rival, Jacqueline Cochran, France's Jacqueline Auriol was determined to be the fastest woman on Earth. On August 26, 1959, Auriol flew a Mirage III to become the first woman to fly at Mach 2. She is quoted as saying: "In the case of pilots, it is a little touch of madness that drives us to go beyond all known bounds. Any search into the unknown is an incomparable exploitation of oneself."

LOCKHEED F-104 Another product of Kelly Johnson and the "Skunk Works," the tiny 21-foot, 11-inch wingspan Lockheed F-104 was so fast they called it the "missile with a man in it." On December 14, 1959, Captain J. B. Jordan used a Lockheed F-104C to set an altitude record of 103,389 feet. Capable of Mach 2 speeds, the only failing of the F-104 in USAF terms was its lack of range. It became very popular in foreign markets, however, and both the F-104G and F-104S were built in Europe for service in Germany and Italy, respectively.

CONVAIR F-106 Major Joseph W. Rogers prepares to climb out of the cockpit of his Convair F-106 Delta Dart after setting a straightaway speed record of 1,525.9 miles per hour on December 15, 1959. The F-106 proved to be a remarkable interceptor and served the nation well for decades.

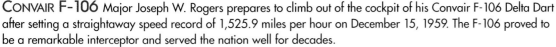

FLIGHT TIMELINE

April 21, 1961 The North American X-15, piloted by Major Robert White, reaches 3,074 miles per hour and 105,100 feet altitude in its first flight at full throttle.

April 28, 1961 The Soviet Union reclaims the altitude record with a 118,898-foot flight by a Mikoyan Ye-66A.

May 4, 1961 A world balloon record of 113,739.9 feet is set in a two-place open gondola balloon by Commander Malcolm Ross and Lieutenant Commander V. A. Prather. Unfortunately, Prather was killed when he fell from the sling of a recovery helicopter.

May 5, 1961 Alan B. Shepard, Jr., makes the first U.S. suborbital flight in the *Freedom 7* Mercury spacecraft.

May 10, 1961 Major Elmer E. Murphy flies a Convair B-58 to 1,302 miles per hour over a closed course of 669.4 miles, earning the United States permanent possession of the Blériot trophy.

May 17, 1961 The Avro "flying saucer," a circular aircraft, has its first test flight.

May 17, 1961 The Sikorsky HSS-2 helicopter sets a world-class speed record of 192.9 miles per hour at Windsor Locks, Connecticut.

May 24, 1961 Lieutenant R. F. Gordon and Lieutenant B. R. Young fly a Phantom F-4H fighter at 870 miles per hour for 2,421.1 miles to win the Bendix Trophy.

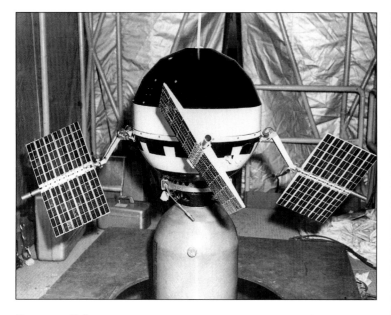

PIONEER 5 SATELLITE The *Pioneer 5* satellite is shown here mounted on the third stage of a Thor-Able rocket. A total of 4,800 solar cells, shown on the deployed paddles, converted the sun's rays to electricity. *Pioneer 5* was designed to provide the first map of the interplanetary magnetic field. The vehicle was launched on March 11, 1960, and functioned for a record 106 days. It communicated with Earth from a record distance of 36.2 million kilometers.

GRUMMAN A-6 INTRUDER The first flight of the Grumman A-6 Intruder took place on April 19, 1960, piloted by Robert Smythe. Shown here undergoing field testing on a carrier, the Intruder turned out to be another one of the "Iron Works" successes, flying as a bomber, tanker, and now as an electronic countermeasures aircraft.

TIROS I SATELLITE The 270-pound *Tiros I* satellite was launched from Cape Canaveral, Florida, on April 1, 1960, to test experimental television techniques, which led to a worldwide system of meteorological satellite information. It operated in space for only 78 days but proved that satellites were essential for surveying global weather conditions from space.

BOEING AIR INDIA 707 The Boeing Company eventually won its long competition with the Douglas company because it was able to produce more aircraft suited to particular needs. A case in point is the 707-437, a long-range aircraft specially suited to the requirements of Air India. It is shown here on its first nonstop flight from London to Bombay. Six were purchased, all using Rolls-Royce Conway engines with 17,500 pounds of thrust.

ECHO 1 SATELLITE The *Echo 1* satellite was launched on August 12, 1960. Thirty meters in diameter, *Echo 1* was essentially a large balloon made of plastic film coated with aluminum. It was capable of reflecting radio waves from Earth. A signal was successfully transmitted between the United States and France on August 18, and on August 19, a photograph of President Dwight Eisenhower was transmitted between Iowa and Texas. *Echo 1* continued in orbit until 1968.

FLIGHT TIMELINE

May 25, 1961 President John F. Kennedy commits the United States to placing a person on the moon before 1970.

May 26, 1961 A Convair B-58, flown by Lieutenant Colonel William Payne, sets a New York-to-Paris record of 3 hours, 19 minutes, at 1,089.36 miles per hour. (Payne is subsequently killed in an accident in a B-58 in Paris.)

June 9, 1961 The first Boeing C-135 is delivered.

July 10, 1961 The Republic F-105D flies 1,520 miles nonstop on instruments at 500 feet altitude to test radar navigation.

July 21, 1961 Virgil "Gus" Grissom makes a suborbital flight in the Mercury *Liberty Bell 7*.

August 6–7, 1961 Soviet Major Gherman S. Titov completes 17 Earth orbits in the *Vostok 2*.

August 10, 1961 The Republic F-105 lifts a seven-ton armament load, the heaviest load ever lifted by a single-engine aircraft.

August 17, 1961 A Bomarc-B SAM destroys a drone B-47 at 50 miles distance, 5,000 feet altitude.

August 21, 1961 Douglas test pilots take a DC-8 supersonic in a dive.

August 24, 1961 Jacqueline Cochran sets a women's speed record in a Northrop T-38 Talon.

BOEING MINUTEMAN MISSILE LAUNCH The Boeing Minuteman missile proved to be a tremendous step forward, as it was the first solid-fuel ICBM. The Minuteman was easier and safer to build, store, and launch than its liquid-fueled predecessors, the Atlas and the Titan, had been. A total of 1,000 Minutemen were deployed in silos in six locations.

DISCOVERER XIV SATELLITE
Men of a C-130 cargo plane unload a container holding the capsule ejected from the *Discoverer XIV* satellite. They are almost certainly unaware that they are handling the most significant event in intelligence history. In its one passage, *Discoverer XIV* revealed more about the Soviet Union than all previous U-2 flights combined, setting the stage for the myriad intelligence satellites in use today.

LOCKHEED U-2 It is difficult to recall now how little the United States knew of the Soviet Union during the early years of the Cold War. The Lockheed U-2 was designed to overfly the Soviet Union and determine exactly how advanced its bombers, missiles, and other offensive weapons were. Designed by Kelly Johnson and built in the "Skunk Works," the U-2 was a difficult aircraft to fly, demanding extreme concentration and good technique.

FLIGHT TIMELINE

August 28, 1961 Lieutenant Hunt Hardisty (pilot) and Lieutenant Earl H. DeEsch (RIO) set a low-altitude speed record of 902.769 miles per hour in a McDonnell Phantom II.

October 7, 1961 The Soviet Union's Kamov Ka-22 helicopter sets a 221.4 miles per hour speed record for its class.

October 18, 1961 A Kaman H-43B Huskie helicopter sets an altitude record of 32,840 feet for its class.

November 1, 1961 A Sikorsky HSS-2 helicopter sets new speed records for 100, 500, and 1,000 kilometers at 182.8, 179.5, and 175.3 miles per hour, respectively.

November 9, 1961 Robert White takes a North American X-15 to 101,600 feet and 4,093 miles per hour.

November 19–20, 1961 Constance Wolf sets 15 world records for women balloonists with a 40-hour, 13-minute flight, reaching 13,000 feet in altitude.

November 22, 1961 The McDonnell F4H Phantom II, flown by Lieutenant Colonel Robert B. Robinson, USMC, sets a world speed record of 1,605.51 miles per hour.

January 10–11, 1962 A Boeing B-52H sets a non-stop, unrefueled distance record of 12,532 miles.

January 23, 1962 Eighteen Vought F8U-2N Crusaders make the first transpacific flight by a complete Marine Corps jet squadron.

SPACE CHIMP HAM As cruel as it sounds, chimpanzees were required for experimentation during the early days of space flight. Ham won his animal astronaut status with a 420-mile ride through space aboard a Redstone rocket fired from Cape Canaveral, Florida, on January 31, 1961.

YURI GAGARIN Major Yuri Gagarin became the first man to orbit the earth, blasting off in a *Vostok 1* rocket on April 12, 1961. The 108-minute flight was one in a succession of Soviet triumphs that seemed to leave the U.S. space program in the dust. Gagarin lost his life in the crash of a two-seat MiG-15 trainer on March 27, 1968.

ALAN SHEPARD The Mercury spacecraft *Freedom 7* carried the first American into space when U.S. Navy Commander Alan B. Shepard, Jr., flew 115 miles above the earth on May 5, 1961. The 15-minute, 22-second flight was less dramatic than Yuri Gagarin's, but the American space effort was more solidly grounded and would lead to a human on the moon a little more than eight years later.

TRIPLE SATELLITE PAYLOAD Putting satellites in space was expensive, and if you could place three at once, as with the *Transit 4* satellite, you were doing the public a service. The Thor-Able launch vehicle had a rocky start but eventually served well.

FLIGHT TIMELINE

February 5, 1962 The Sikorsky HSS-2 Sea King is the first helicopter to officially exceed 200 miles per hour in a time trial, clocking 210.6 miles per hour.

February 14, 1962 Major Walter F. Daniel sets a 12,000-meter time-to-climb record of 1 minute, 35.74 seconds in a T-38 Talon.

February 20, 1962 Marine fighter pilot and future senator John H. Glenn, Jr., makes the first U.S. orbital flight of Earth in *Friendship 7*, completing three orbits.

February 21, 1962 A McDonnell Phantom II establishes new time-to-climb records to 3,000 and 6,000 meters in 34.52 and 48.78 seconds, respectively.

February 28, 1962 A Convair B-58 ejection capsule is tested at 565 miles per hour at 20,000 feet by Warrant Officer Edward J. Murray, who spends 26 seconds in a free fall and 8 minutes in a parachute.

March 1, 1962 A Phantom II, flown by Lieutenant Colonel W. C. McGraw, USMC, sets time-to-climb records to 9,000 and 12,000 meters in 61.62 and 77.15 seconds.

March 3, 1962 Climbing records continue to fall; a Phantom II piloted by Lieutenant Commander D. W. Nordberg gets to 15,000 meters in 114.54 seconds.

March 31, 1962 Lieutenant Commander F. Taylor Brown flies to 20,000 meters in 178.5 seconds in a Phantom II.

HINDUSTAN HF-24 MARAT The Hindustan Aircraft Ltd. was formed to build aircraft for the Indian market in Bangalore in May 1940. Over the years, its capability increased, and famous Focke-Wulf designer Kurt Tank was employed to create the Hindustan HF-24 Marat, shown here on June 17, 1961, the day of its first flight. About 130 of the supersonic aircraft were produced. It was moderately successful and, though underpowered, it demonstrated India's manufacturing prowess.

GUS GRISSOM NEXT TO LIBERTY BELL 7 Astronaut Virgil "Gus" Grissom sits smiling besides the *Liberty Bell,* in which he made the United States' second suborbital flight on July 21, 1961. The *Liberty Bell 7* sank during the recovery process, setting off a controversy as to whether Grissom had made a technical error after splashdown. The spacecraft was recovered 38 years later. Grissom died in the tragic fire on *Apollo I* in 1967.

GHERMAN S. TITOV On August 6, 1961, cosmonaut Gherman S. Titov made a 17-orbit flight in his *Vostok 2* space capsule. Each orbit took 89 minutes, and Titov initially reported being ill. Despite this he carried on, radioing greetings to the people of the world. The space sickness was natural enough, for the lack of gravity upset the normal sense of equilibrium provided by the eyes and ears.

FLIGHT TIMELINE

April 3, 1962 Lieutenant Commander John W. Young flies a Phantom II to 25,000 meters in 230.44 seconds.

April 12, 1962 All world time-to-climb records are held by the Phantom II as Lieutenant Commander D. W. Nordberg climbs to 30,000 meters in 371.43 seconds.

April 17, 1962 Major David W. Craw sets a world altitude record in a Boeing C-135B. He climbs to 47,171 feet with a 66,138-pound payload.

April 22, 1962 Jacqueline Cochran takes 49 world records in a 5,120-mile, three-stop flight in a Lockheed JetStar from New Orleans to Hanover, Germany.

May 10, 1962 A Phantom II fires a Sparrow III missile at supersonic speeds in a head-on attack of the Regulus II target missile, also supersonic. This is the first successful head-on attack of an air-launched missile against a surface-launched missile.

May 24, 1962 Scott Carpenter completes a three-orbit flight in *Aurora 7.*

June 1, 1962 Captain William Stevenson sets a closed-course distance record of 11,336.92 miles in a Boeing B-52H.

June 13, 1962 Captain Richard H. Coan sets a world-class closed-course distance record for type in a Kaman H-43B Huskie, 655.64 miles.

BELL UH-1F HUEY The Bell Model 205 UH-1C "Huey" was one of the most important helicopters in history. The Huey made its first flight on August 16, 1961, and was produced both in a civilian version and under license by Agusta in Italy and Fuji in Japan. The workhorse helicopter of the Vietnam War, the Huey was powered by an Avco Lycoming turboshaft engine and had a top speed of 127 miles per hour. This is a UH-1F model.

CESSNA SKYMASTER Twin-engine aircraft are generally considered safer than single-engine aircraft—as long as both engines are running. But when one stops, a conventional twin-engine aircraft presents problems of asymmetric thrust, which is sometimes hard to control. Cessna solved the problem with its "push-pull" centerline thrust Skymaster. Later models of the aircraft served as forward air control O-2s in Vietnam.

CONVAIR B-58 HUSTLER One of the most beautiful bombers ever built, the Convair B-58 Hustler was the finest expression of the Convair delta-wing stable of aircraft. With a speed of 1,385 miles per hour at 40,000 feet, the Hustler was virtually immune to interception by enemy aircraft. However, it was a dangerous aircraft to fly. Serious accident rates and high operating costs caused it to be removed from service in 1969.

ROBERT ROBINSON SETS
SPEED RECORD Lieutenant
Colonel Robert B. Robinson sits in
the McDonnell F4H Phantom II
fighter in which he has set a world
speed record of 1,605.51 miles per
hour on November 22, 1961, at
Edwards Air Force Base. The
Phantom set dozens of records for
speed, time to climb, and altitude.

PILATUS PC-6C-2 (FAIRCHILD PEACEMAKER) The original 340-horsepower Lycoming piston-engine Pilatus
Porter made its first flight on May 4, 1959, and proved to be a commercial success. More than 450 were sold all
around the world. Performance was vastly improved when a 532-shaft horsepower Turboméca Astazou turboprop engine was installed in the PC-6A. Fairchild licensed the aircraft for manufacture in the United States, and it
served the CIA well in Southeast Asia, using the 650-shaft horsepower Garrett engine.

FLIGHT TIMELINE

June 27, 1962 Joe Walker
reaches 4,159 miles per
hour in a North American
X-15, an unofficial speed
record.

July 5, 1962 The Kaman
H-43B, piloted by Captain
Chester R. Radcliffe, Jr.,
breaks its own distance
record with a flight of 888.4
miles.

July 7, 1962 The Lockheed
XV-4A VTOL research
aircraft makes its first flight.

July 10, 1962 NASA
launches *Telstar 1*, the first
privately financed satellite.

August 11–15, 1962 Soviet
Major Andrian Nikolayev, in
Vostok 3, completes 64
revolutions and communi-
cates via television with
Earth, a space first.

August 27, 1962 NASA
launches *Mariner 2* spacecraft for a Venus flyby, to
take place in December.

August 31, 1962 A Navy
airship flies for the last time
at Lakehurst, New Jersey. It
is the end of an era; airships
had been used by the Navy
since 1917.

September 12, 1962 A
Grumman Albatross UF-2G
sets a world altitude record
for amphibians with a
1,000-kilogram load at
29,640 feet.

September 14, 1962 Fitz
Fulton sets a world altitude
record for payloads of 4,409
and 11,023 pounds in a
Convair B-58 at 85,360.8
feet.

OXIDIZER TRAILERS

2 MISSILE TRANSPORTERS

OXIDIZER TRAILER

6 MISSILE TRANSPORTERS

PROB IRBM PROPELLANT TRAILERS

ERECTOR

3 MISSILE TRANSPORTERS

CUBAN MISSILE CRISIS The world edged toward the brink of nuclear war during the 1962 Cuban Missile Crisis. USAF Lockheed U-2 aircraft brought back photos proving that the Soviet Union was building Intermediate Range Ballistic Missile sites in Cuba. This led to a confrontation between the two superpowers. When President John F. Kennedy ordered a "quarantine" of Cuba and put the U.S. military on full alert, the Soviet leaders reconsidered the situation and had the missiles removed.

HAWKER SIDDELEY TRIDENT The Hawker Siddeley Trident, first flown on January 9, 1962, is a perfect illustration of the problem Great Britain encountered in attempting to compete with the United States in the manufacture of jet passenger airliners. Although comparable in size, configuration, and performance to the Boeing 727, which made its first flight 13 months later, the Trident never gained a comparable market share. Only 117 were built compared to 1,831 Boeing 727s.

SIKORSKY **S-64A** The remarkable Sikorsky S-64A made its first flight on May 9, 1962, with its massive six-bladed rotor driven by two 4,800-shaft horsepower Pratt & Whitney T73 turboshaft engines. The U.S. Army bought the S-64As, designating them the CH-54A Tarhe, and using them for heavy-lift work in Vietnam. The Tarhe could recover entire aircraft from crash sites. Only 94 were purchased by the Army during the program.

SCOTT CARPENTER COMPLETES THREE-ORBIT MISSION The Navy paramedic waves to the helicopter as he maneuvers his life raft close to the one containing Astronaut Scott Carpenter, who has just completed three orbits of the earth in his *Aurora 7* spacecraft. The May 24, 1962, liftoff was flawless, and Carpenter was amazed to find he had no sense of speed as he moved at approximately 17,000 miles per hour around the earth. The splashdown was nearly 180 miles from the original target.

FLIGHT TIMELINE

September 15, 1962 A Grumman Albatros UF-2G sets a 5,000-kilometer speed record for amphibians with a 1,000-kilogram load at an average speed of 151.4 miles per hour.

September 19, 1962 The Pregnant Guppy, a converted Boeing 377 Stratocruiser, makes its first flight. It was designed by Aero Spacelines to carry missile and aircraft components.

October 17, 1962 A flight of 16 Douglas A4-C Skyhawks complete a two-way crossing of the Atlantic, refueling from Marine KC-130F Hercules tankers.

October 22, 1962 The Cuban Missile Crisis begins.

October 29, 1962 The Douglas DC-8F Trader all-cargo jet makes its first flight.

November 2, 1962 The Lockheed XH-51A rigid-rotor helicopter makes its first flight.

December 8, 1962 The Bell OH-4A light observation helicopter prototype debuts.

December 13–14, 1962 Project Stargazer balloon, piloted by Joe Kittinger, takes a civilian astronomer to 82,000 feet for the clearest celestial view ever experienced by an astronomer.

December 24, 1962 The Nord 262 pressurized light transport makes its first flight. It will have a troubled service history for years until reengined.

BOEING B-52H A total of 744 B-52s were built; the last 106 consisted of the B-52H model shown here. It is powered by eight 17,000-pound thrust Pratt & Whitney TF33-P-3 turbofan engines. The first YB-52 flew on April 15, 1952; the last rolled out of the factory on June 22, 1962. The aircraft is still in front-line service, conducting a variety of missions it was never intended for, including the use of precision-guided munitions.

TELSTAR 1 The world was knit ever closer together with the launch of *Telstar 1* by a Thor-Delta rocket on July 10, 1962. This was the West's first commercial communications satellite, designed by Bell Laboratories to relay television signals, telephone calls, and data messages.

VICKERS VC-10 The beautiful VC-10 was the last aircraft designed and built solely by Vickers. BOAC specifications called for an aircraft that could land and take off from airfields in hot climates and at higher altitudes. Fulfilling these requirements meant that the VC-10's performance could not compete with that of the Boeing 707, and only about 50 were built. The RAF bought 14 VC-10s for use as transports and as a tanker.

FLIGHT TIMELINE

January 7, 1963 The Short Skyvan prototype flies.

January 7–13, 1963 U.S. Navy helicopters fly extensive rescue missions in flooded areas in Morocco, rescuing 320 people.

January 17, 1963 Joe Walker earns astronaut wings by flying a North American X-15 to 271,000 feet, essentially out of Earth's atmosphere.

January 26, 1963 The Hiller OH-5A helicopter makes its first flight.

January 29, 1963 A Walleye television-guided bomb demonstrates automatic homing; the device will be used extensively in Vietnam and beyond.

February 22, 1963 An LC-130F Hercules makes the longest flight in history over Antarctica: 3,470 miles from McMurdo Station over the South Pole to the Shackleton Mountains.

April 10, 1963 American Airlines pilot Wylie H. Drummond sets a national record for commercial jets by flying from Los Angeles to New York (2,474 miles) in 3 hours and 38 minutes at a speed of 680.9 miles per hour.

April 18, 1963 The Northrop X-21A (modified Douglas B-66) makes its first flight.

April 30–May 12, 1963 Betty Miller becomes the first woman to fly the Pacific solo, in four hops from Oakland, California, to Brisbane, Australia.

DE HAVILLAND D.H.125 The first flight of the de Havilland D.H.125 executive jet on August 13, 1962, came 53 years after the first de Havilland aircraft. The D.H.125 was the last aircraft to bear the de Havilland name before the company was absorbed by the Hawker Siddeley group. Initially called the "Jet Dragon"—an interesting name for an executive jet—the aircraft met with great success, and variants of the original design are still flying.

BOEING MODEL 377-PG, THE PREGNANT GUPPY A Boeing 377 Stratocruiser was modified into the Pregnant Guppy for Aero Spacelines, which needed to transport large spacecraft sections from the West Coast to Cape Canaveral. The modification was done by the On-Mark Engineering company after an intense feasibility study. Despite its unusual look, the plane flew well on its September 19, 1962, first flight. The entire aft section of the aircraft unbolts for easy loading.

McDonnell F-101C During the 1962 Cuban Missile Crisis, airfields in Florida and the southeastern United States filled with warplanes ready for any eventuality. The record-setting Voodoo was there in all its varieties, including this F-101C and many RF-101C reconnaissance planes. The F-101/RF-101 series had the lowest accident rate of any fighter during their first year of service. The Voodoo also served well in the Vietnam War.

Joe Walker After flying the North American X-15 to a record height of 271,000 feet on January 17, 1963, Joe Walker described the flight as "a cliff-hanger all the way." Walker was awarded astronaut wings for the flight into space.

FLIGHT TIMELINE

May 1, 1963 Jacqueline Cochran flies a TF-104G (two-seat) Starfighter to set a 100-kilometer closed-course record for women at 1,203.686 miles per hour.

May 7, 1963 Famed aviation and space pioneer Theodore von Karman dies in Aachen, Germany, just before his 82nd birthday.

May 8, 1963 Two squadrons of Douglas A-1E Skyraiders are added to the First Air Commando Group at Hurlburt Air Force Base for use in Vietnam.

May 19–21, 1963 Colonel James B. Swindal, in a VC-137C (Air Force One) sets 30 world records in flight from Washington to Moscow and back.

May 27, 1963 The first USAF version of the Phantom II, the F-4C, makes its first flight.

June 13, 1963 A Phantom II and a Crusader make the first fully automatic, hands-off carrier landings on the USS *Midway*.

June 14–19, 1963 The first woman in space, Soviet Junior Lieutenant Valentina V. Tereshkova completes 48 Earth orbits in *Vostok 6*.

June 20, 1963 The Navy ends seaplane pilot training with a last flight in a Martin Marlin.

June 27, 1963 Colonel Robert Rushworth takes a North American X-15 to 285,000 feet, earning his astronaut's wings.

AGENT ORANGE Operation Ranch Hand was one of the most controversial operations of the Vietnam War. Fairchild C-123 aircraft were modified to carry equipment (pictured here) to spray chemical defoliants on the jungle areas concealing enemy forces. Ground force commanders demanded use of the defoliant to avoid ambushes, and it was highly successful, but environmentalists argued against its use.

BOEING 727 On February 9, 1963, the 727 made its first flight. Despite its success with the 707 series, Boeing literally gambled its company's future on the 727. Jack Steiner, who led the design team, had to use the most advanced engineering to create the 727 and enable it to operate successfully over shorter routes. Flying the 727 required special training because of the T-tail.

THEODORE VON KARMAN

One of the greatest figures in aviation engineering history, Theodore von Karman died on May 7, 1963, after a brilliant career that began in his native Hungary and included work for the Austro-Hungarian Air Force in World War I. Between the wars he was a consultant, but in 1940, he helped found Aerojet Engineering Corporation and headed General Hap Arnold's vitally important Scientific Advisory Group. He is shown here at age 80, working for NATO.

FLIGHT TIMELINE

July 19, 1963 Joe Walker flies a North American X-15 to 347,000 feet at 3,710 miles per hour.

August 7, 1963 Ben Greene establishes a record for Class D gliders with a 457.97 mile flight from Texas to Idaho.

August 20, 1963 The BAC 111 twinjet transport makes its first flight.

September 3, 1963 Milt Thompson lands a wingless M-2 lifting body reentry glider after a drop at 13,000 feet.

October 1, 1963 Admiral James R. Reedy makes the first transpolar nonstop flight in a Lockheed C-130.

October 16, 1963 Major Sidney J. Kubesch sets three world records in a Convair B-58 during a flight from Tokyo to London. He makes the flight in 8 hours and 35 minutes, averaging 692.7 miles per hour.

December 17, 1963 The Lockheed C-141A transport debuts in a 55-minute flight at Dobbins Air Force Base, Georgia.

December 21, 1963 The Hawker Siddeley Andover transport debuts.

ILYUSHIN IL-62 TRANSPORT The handsome Ilyushin Il-62 transport was first flown in January 1963 and by 1967 had become the first Soviet four-engine jet airliner to operate on a transatlantic route. Powered by aft-mounted Soloviev D-30KU turbofans of 24,500 pounds thrust each, it cruised at 560 miles per hour. Approximately 210 were built, and some were supplied to Soviet satellite nation airlines—which probably would have preferred to buy Boeing 707s because the Il-62s were expensive to operate.

TRANSALL C.160D Aerospatiale and MBB created a consortium to build the Transall C.160, which first flew on February 25, 1963. About 200 were built, and they served the air forces of West Germany, Turkey, France, and South Africa. The aircraft was quite versatile, equally at home in troop transport, cargo, tanker, medevac, intelligence gathering, and maritime reconnaissance roles. Its top speed was about 360 miles per hour, and it could carry up to 35,000 pounds of cargo.

JACQUELINE COCHRAN AND SEVERSKY P-35 It was a long way from this Seversky AP-7 (similar to the Air Corps P-35), shown here, to the red-hot Lockheed TF-104G Starfighter in which Jacqueline Cochran set a 100-kilometer closed-course speed record for women at 1,203.686 miles per hour on May 1, 1963. Oddly enough, the TF-104G was probably easier to land than the tricky AP-7!

DASSAULT MYSTÈRE-FALCON 20 Dassault knew that it could not rest on its military laurels and decided to enter the new and promising executive jet market with its Mystère-Falcon 20 (it was called the Mystère in France, the Falcon in the United States). First flown on May 5, 1963, it became an instant success. Later models were powered by General Electric CF700 turbofans of 4,500 pounds thrust each. American manufacturers were stunned when the Coast Guard selected the Falcon as its HU-25 Guardian surveillance aircraft.

JET COMMANDER Ted Smith's Aero Commander had been an instant success. One was even used as a Presidential aircraft. The configuration of the aircraft lent itself to development into an executive jet. The designs of the original company were taken over by Rockwell, then sold to Gulfstream America, and finally to Israeli Aircraft Industries, where it was known as the Westwind. While economical, the Jet Commander/Westwind never offered the performance of the more popular Learjet.

BRITISH AIRWAYS CORPORA-
TION **BAC 111** After suffering
the embarrassment of the Comet
disasters, Great Britain desperately
wished to gain a large share of the
jet transport business. The BAC 111
was one of its greatest successes. It
flew for the first time on August 20,
1963. The BAC 111 featured such
innovations as engines mounted at
the rear and a T-tail. After 230
were built, production was moved
to Romania where additional
examples have been completed.

VALERY BYKOVSKY On June
14–19, 1963, Cosmonaut Valery
Bykovsky flew *Vostok 5* for 119
hours and 16 minutes. Premier
Nikita Khrushchev himself
announced the liftoff, hinting that
Bykovsky might be joined in orbit
by another astronaut. This was a
clear statement of Soviet space
supremacy, and it was aimed
directly at the United States.

VALENTINA TERESHKOVA

When Valery Bykovsky lifted off in *Vostok 5*, Premier Nikita Khrushchev hinted that he would be joined in orbit by another astronaut. This hint was fulfilled when the first woman cosmonaut, Valentina Tereshkova, was launched from the Baikonva complex in *Vostok 6*, arriving in orbit only about three miles from Bykovsky's spacecraft. Tereshkova had come from a humble factory job to become a parachutist and then a cosmonaut. Not really properly conditioned, she did not do well in training and suffered badly from nausea and disorientation in space. She parachuted from her spacecraft after reentry, landing at 11:20 A.M. on June 19 to become the latest hero of the Soviet Union, a symbol of the emancipation of Soviet women.

It was only later revealed that her primary mission was to provide the Soviet Union with data on the effect of radiation on cells. She was married to the pilot of *Vostok 3*, Andrian Nikolayev, in November 1963. Their child, Yelena, was born the following June. Yelena grew up with no trace of side effects from the cosmic radiation her parents had received.

LOCKHEED C-141 STARLIFTER It is difficult to imagine the joy with which Military Airlift Command pilots received the beautiful, fast, powerful Lockheed C-141 StarLifter after years of flying "Old Shaky," the piston-powered Douglas C-124. The C-141, which made its first flight on December 17, 1963, was invaluable during the Vietnam War, and 270 of them were later "stretched" to become the C-141B, effectively increasing the fleet by 87 aircraft. The C-141B was also given an in-flight refueling capability. Its top speed was 566 miles per hour.

SAAB 105 Saab became a tremendous innovator, often leading the industry with its new designs. One of these, the Saab 105 twin-jet trainer/attack plane made its first flight on June 29, 1963. The aircraft, with a top speed of 600 miles per hour and a range of 510 miles with full ordnance, was perfect for Sweden, which ordered 150 copies. Austria also bought 40. The shoulder-wing, T-tailed Saab was relatively inexpensive to buy and maintain.

LOCKHEED C-130 HERCULES
The Lockheed C-130 Hercules is undoubtedly the best turboprop transport aircraft in history, built in greater numbers than any other and fulfilling more missions. It was a workhorse in combat in Vietnam, flying into airstrips under fire, and it has been a leader in the many flights made by the USAF to disaster areas. This C-130 was among several carrying relief supplies—including a complete hospital—to Skopje, Macedonia, after an earthquake.

MCDONNELL F-4C PHANTOM The United States Air Force would have preferred to design its own fighter plane, but the performance of the Navy's McDonnell F-4C Phantom was so superior that using it was unavoidable. And the USAF did not make the mistake of redesigning the Phantom to Air Force specifications, accepting it in its pure Navy configuration to speed up delivery. The Phantom was the primary fighter for both the Navy and the USAF in the Vietnam War.

CHAPTER SEVEN

1964 to 1973:

Moon Landings Amidst a Fragile Peace and Dangerous New Wars

The revolution in flight after World War II accelerated progress everywhere, including flight. The new tools, including massive computers; new materials, such as titanium; and new techniques of manufacture, all spurred development not only of space efforts but also consumer products. The public was not quite ready to demand personal computers, but for the first time, slide rules began to take a back seat to still clumsy mainframe computer programs.

Grumman F-14 Tomcat

Every nation raced forward with new aircraft designs, some of them seemingly suited to national backgrounds. The Soviets, for example, tended toward gigantic aircraft such as the Antonov An-22 and the Mil Mi 10 and Mi 12 helicopters. They were also determined to be first wherever possible and rushed the Tupolev Tu-144 supersonic transport (SST) into production so that it could fly before its elegant—and expensive—competitor, the Anglo-French Concorde. The United States, for both economic and environmental reasons, opted out of the SST competition, a move that proved to be very intelligent indeed. In air transport, it was time for smaller, more economic jet airliners to fly the shorter routes, and there appeared the Douglas DC-9, Boeing 737, and British Aircraft Corporation 111. The process would continue for years. Thousands of transports would be manufactured, and accumulated passenger miles would become astronomical.

All was not completely serene in the airline industry. The practice of terrorists hijacking airliners became ever more common. Things would get worse over the years.

The increasing effectiveness of SAMS (surface-to-air missiles) was devastating both in Vietnam and in the recurring wars in the Middle East. They also affected bombing strategy, because they forced the cancellation of the Mach 3 North American XB-70 bomber.

The rocket technology for SAMS was relatively primitive; it derived from that of the German World War II Wasserfall. Rockets for ICBMs and for spacecraft became increasingly advanced, however. Under the leadership of General Bernard Schriever, the United States went through four generations of ICBM development, starting with the Atlas and working through the Titan, Minuteman, and Peacekeeper. The Soviets had their counterpart series of rockets, which were usually more powerful than those of the United States.

It was upon these rockets that the race to the moon was based. The Soviet Union kept its efforts cloaked in secrecy, as was its national habit, whereas the United States portrayed its plan for reaching the moon as a scientific experiment—open to all. Three massive, integrated programs, Mercury, Gemini, and Apollo, led to the first successful moon landing on July 20, 1969. As things worked out, the Soviet Union never reached the point where it could challenge the United States in the moon race, and it turned to other things, including deep

Bell Huey Cobra

space probes of remarkable capability. In time, the race would turn into international cooperation.

Throughout this period, the agony of the Vietnam War dragged on, with a curious inversion dictated by U.S. political leaders, including President Lyndon Johnson and Secretary of Defense Robert McNamara. The inversion called for U.S. strategic B-52s to be employed in a tactical role in South Vietnam, while U.S. tactical fighters (McDonnell F-4s and Republic F-105s) were employed in a strategic role against North Vietnam. But it was not until strategic bombing was used during Operation Linebacker II in December 1972, that the North Vietnamese succumbed to pressure and agreed to a peace treaty.

The United States' involvement in the Vietnam War had been long, longer still for the Vietnamese. But wars were shorter in the Middle East. Faced with Arab invasion threats, Israel made a surprise attack on the Arab forces surrounding it in June 1967, decisively defeating them and extending its borders to their present configuration. The SAMS intervened in the next few years, as the Soviet Union supplied Egypt and Syria with massive amounts of antiaircraft equipment. A surprise attack by the Arab nations in October 1973 came within hours of defeating Israel, which, in turn, was within hours of using its nuclear missiles as a last line of defense. Israel managed to survive and, sustained by a massive airlift of arms and aircraft from the United States, was just able to defeat the Arabs. Even though Middle Eastern wars were shorter, events would prove that peace is not easily distinguishable from warfare.

The United States, having passed on the SST, startled the air transport world with a gigantic gamble by Boeing and Pan American—the leviathan Boeing 747 airliner. After some initial problems with engines, the 747 turned the industry upside down as fares were lowered and more and more people traveled. Airline travel was no longer just for business people and the wealthy, nor was it reserved for citizens of the United States. Now average citizens from all over the world could—and did—travel.

Helicopters began to take on new jobs all over the world, delivering supplies to oil rigs, covering sporting events, and acting as indispensable medical and police stalwarts. Interest in fixed-wing vertical takeoff and landing aircraft also increased. In Great Britain, the Hawker Sid-

Lockheed SR-71 Blackbird

deley Harrier promised great things for the future with vectored thrust technology, while in the United States there were a whole range of experiments including tilt rotor, tilt fan, and tilt wing.

All of these advances were being made under the umbrella of the most interesting acronym in history: MAD. This acronym stood for "Mutual Assured Destruction" and meant that if either the Soviet Union or the United States of America launched an ICBM attack, the other nation would still have sufficient power for a devastating counterstrike. Under MAD, nuclear weapons were built at a tremendous rate on either side, yet somehow the unusual logic held, and there was no massive nuclear exchange.

SHORT BELFAST The Short Belfast came at a time when the venerable company realized that cargo aircraft might be the most profitable path to the future. Studies for what became the Belfast went on for more than ten years before the first prototype flew from Sydenham, England, to Aldergrove, Canada, on January 5, 1964. The largest aircraft to enter the RAF until that time, the Belfast could cruise at 358 miles per hour carrying a 77,000-pound cargo.

SATURN LAUNCH VEHICLE This historic photo, taken December 15, 1963, shows the first fully mated Saturn launch vehicle, which would have so important a history in space flight. The United States had come a long way since 1945 when it was busy gathering V-2 missiles in Germany to find out what made a ballistic missile tick.

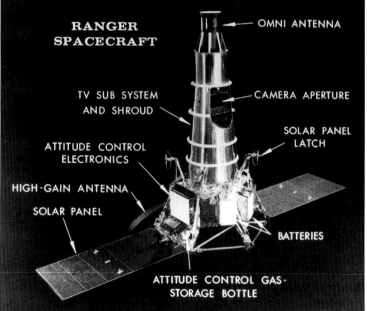

RANGER SPACECRAFT People's fascination with the moon was enhanced, not diminished, by space exploration. The *Ranger 2* was the first of the standardized spacecraft, equipped for varied missions including orbiting and impacting the moon. *Ranger 4* was tracked to a crash landing on the "dark side" of the moon.

NORTHROP F-5B

The supersonic Northrop F-5B was backed by a vigorous Northrop sales organization that exhibited the aircraft at air shows all over the world, with notable success. The relatively low-cost aircraft had a superb performance and was used by 35 air forces. The first USAF F-5Bs entered service in April 1964. The F-5 type was also built in Spain and Canada, and 2,622 were delivered. Top speed was Mach 1.64.

One of the surprising consequences of F-5 sales was the growth of many "aftermarket" companies who specialized in providing updates to the aircraft to keep it competitive with large, more modern types.

DE HAVILLAND DHC-5 BUFFALO The Buffalo was developed from the DHC-4 Caribou and featured General Electric turboprop engines for much improved performance. First flown on April 9, 1964, the Buffalo was also used for a series of experiments including vectored thrust and an air-cushion landing system. The aircraft was used in small numbers by several air forces because of its load-carrying capacity and short field capability.

FLIGHT TIMELINE

January 5, 1964 The Short Belfast, a four-turboprop transport, makes its first flight.

February 24, 1964 The Northrop F-5B, a two-seat version of the F-5, makes its first flight.

February 29, 1964 President Lyndon Johnson reveals the existence of the Lockheed A-11 version. The aircraft is later designated the YF-12A.

April 9, 1964 The de Havilland (Canada) DHC-5 Buffalo makes its first flight.

April 17, 1964 Geraldine Mock becomes the first woman to fly around the world solo. She covers 23,103 miles in 29 days.

May 1, 1964 A Lockheed P-3A Orion, piloted by Captain R. P. Ruehrmund, makes an 18-day, 26,550-nautical mile flight around the world.

May 7, 1964 The British Aerospace Super VC-10 makes its first flight.

May 11, 1964 Jacqueline Cochran sets a women's 15/25 kilometer course record at 1,429.2 miles per hour.

May 11, 1964 The North American XB-70 is rolled out.

May 25, 1964 The Ryan XV-5A makes its first flight.

June 4, 1964 Jacqueline Cochran sets two women's speed records: 1,302 miles per hour (100 kilometers) and 1,135 miles per hour (500 kilometers).

GERALDINE MOCK Shown here is Geraldine "Jerry" Mock, about to take off on a successful solo round-the-world flight, the first by a woman. She made the flight in a Cessna 180, the *Spirit of Columbus*, taking off on March 19, 1964, from Columbus, Ohio, and returning on April 17, 1964, after flying 23,103 miles around the world.

JACQUELINE COCHRAN Probably the most accomplished female pilot in history, Jacqueline Cochran is shown with the Lockheed F-104G Super Starfighter in which she set two women's speed records on June 4, 1964. She flew at 1,302 miles per hour for the 100-kilometer record and at 1,135 miles per hour for the 500-kilometer record. On May 11, 1964, she flew at 1,429.2 miles per hour for the 15/25 kilometer straightaway event. At the time, she held 85 world records, more than anyone else.

RYAN XV-5A VERTIFAN The first flight of the XV-5A took place on May 25, 1964. Two prototypes were built; both were damaged, and one was rebuilt as the XV-5B. The aircraft was powered by two GE J85 engines of 2,650 pounds of static thrust and lifted by jet-driven fans in the nose and wings, with the nose fan also being used to control yaw. The principle worked, but the engine and fan placement required too much room to be practical.

RANGER *7* The checkout of a satellite has, from *Sputnik* on, been a matter of excruciating detail. This is *Ranger 7* in Hangar A-M in the John F. Kennedy Space Center. *Ranger 7* weighed 806 pounds, including a 382-pound scientific experiment consisting of six TV cameras. *Ranger 7,* launched on July 28, 1964, televised sharp images of the moon before impact; *Ranger 8* and *9* mapped larger areas.

FLIGHT TIMELINE

July 16, 1964 A Ryan XV-5A research aircraft, which uses a "fan in wing" principle, makes a vertical takeoff, flies conventionally, hovers, and lands vertically. The aircraft will go on to an extensive test program, but no production type aircraft will ensue.

July 28–31, 1964 The *Ranger 7* is launched to take photos of the moon. After 68 hours of flight, it crash-lands on the lunar surface.

August 2, 1964 North Vietnamese torpedo boats attack the USS *Maddox* in the Gulf of Tonkin.

August 5, 1964 U.S. Navy planes from the USS *Constellation* and USS *Ticonderoga* attack North Vietnamese torpedo boat bases.

September 21, 1964 The North American XB-70A Valkyrie makes its first flight.

September 27, 1964 The British Aerospace TSR.2, the British equivalent of the F-111, makes its first flight.

September 28, 1964 Polaris A-3, a fleet ballistic missile, becomes operational.

September 29, 1964 The LTV-Hiller-Ryan XC-142 tilt-wing four-engine transport research airplane makes its first flight.

September 30, 1964 A Lockheed C-130 flies from Australia to Williams Field, McMurdo Station—the first flight over the Pole from Australia.

BRITISH AEROSPACE TSR.2

This is the maiden flight of the British Aerospace TSR.2, which took place on September 27, 1964. This Mach 2.05 attack and reconnaissance bomber could fly completely automatic sorties in all weather conditions and was canceled by the British government for budgetary reasons and the prospect of buying the General Dynamics F-111.

Several books and articles have been written on canceled projects, and the TSR.2 and the Avro-Canada Arrow always head the list as having had the most promise for success.

LTV-Hiller-Ryan XC-142 Makes First Public Transition Flight This is not a formation of XC-142s but a photo-montage of the transition from vertical takeoff to horizontal flight by the LTV-Hiller-Ryan XC-142 tilt-wing aircraft. Note that the elevator angle matches the wing angle. The first flight took place on September 29, 1964, and the first test transition was made on January 11, 1965. Five aircraft were produced, and four were damaged in heavy landings. About 420 hours were flown before the project was canceled.

Cosmonauts Yegorov, Feoktistov, and Komarov The Soviet Union was anxious to beat the United States in the publicity race as well as the space race and sent the hastily cobbled *Voskhod 1* (just a reworked Vostok) into a 16-orbit flight on October 12, 1964. Carrying flowers, from left, Vladimir Komarov, crew commander; Boris Yegorov; and Konstantin Feoktistov are welcomed by Soviet leaders Anastas Mikoyan, Leonid Brezhnev, and Alexi Kosygin.

Sikorsky CH-53A The Sikorsky CH-53A was first flown on October 14, 1964. More than 20 versions have entered production and have been invaluable in air-sea rescue, special operations, antimine warfare, NASA spacecraft rescue, and more. The later CH-53E is powered by three GE T64 turboshafts of 4,380 shaft horsepower and has a maximum speed of 196 miles per hour with up to 55 troops.

GENERAL DYNAMICS F-111A One of the most controversial warplanes in history, the swing-wing General Dynamics F-111A was the product of Secretary of Defense Robert McNamara's demand for commonality in USAF and Navy fighters. The Navy version was not built, but the USAF F-111A flew first on December 21, 1964. A total of 563 were built, and they became a uniquely effective strike aircraft. FB-111s served the Strategic Air Command. The F-111F had a top speed of 1,650 miles per hour.

LOCKHEED SR-71 No aircraft in history ever had such a tremendous advantage over its contemporaries as the SR-71 Blackbird, which test pilot Robert Gilliand flew for the first time on December 22, 1964. Nor did any aircraft maintain that superiority for so long; the SR-71 still holds many of the records it set. The Mach 3 beauty has become a cult airplane, beloved by its fans, who regret its retirement for "reasons of economy."

FLIGHT TIMELINE

October 14, 1964 The Sikorsky CH-53A Sea Stallion makes its first flight

November 28, 1964 NASA launches the *Mariner 4* spacecraft for a Mars flyby (achieved July 14, 1965).

December 21, 1964 The General Dynamics F-111A Aardvark, a low-altitude supersonic bomber, makes its first flight.

December 22, 1964 The Lockheed SR-71 Blackbird reconnaissance aircraft makes its first flight.

January 11, 1965 The LTV-Hiller-Ryan XC-142 makes successful transitions from vertical to forward flight and back.

February 16, 1965 The Saturn launch vehicle with payload debuts.

February 25, 1965 The Douglas DC-9 makes its first flight.

March 23, 1965 The two-person *Gemini 3* spacecraft makes its first flight. Virgil "Gus" Grissom and John Young make three orbits in the first flight mission that moves from one orbit to another.

April 6, 1965 The first commercial communications satellite *Early Bird* is launched into a 22,300-mile synchronous orbit.

May 1, 1965 Colonel Robert L. Stephens pilots a Lockheed YF-12A to establish a world speed record of 2,062 miles per hour at Edwards Air Force Base.

DC-9 The Douglas DC-9 made its maiden flight on February 25, 1965, and proved to be a tremendous asset to Douglas, and later McDonnell Douglas, for it was an economical aircraft that operated well over short routes. The design of the aircraft lent itself to modification, and several different versions appeared over the years, each one carrying more passengers. One version, the C-9A Nightingale, serves the armed forces as a medical evacuation aircraft.

COSMONAUTS LEONOV AND BELYALYEV Soviet Cosmonauts Alexi Leonov and Pavel Belyalyev await blastoff in their *Voskhod II* spacecraft from the super-secret Soviet equivalent to Cape Canaveral, the Baikonur Cosmodrome, on March 18, 1965. Leonov did the first EVA (extravehicular activity) in history on this flight and had considerable difficulty getting back into his spacecraft. Their landing on March 19 was far off course, and they suffered hardships waiting two days in the deep snow for their eventual rescue.

LIEUTENANT COLONEL DANIEL ANDRE, COLONEL ROBERT L. STEPHENS, AND YF-12 The Lockheed SR-71 began life as the Mach 3 Lockheed A-11, which first flew on April 26, 1962. Four A-11s were modified as YF-12 interceptors, in which Colonel Robert L. Stephens (right) and Lieutenant Colonel Daniel Andre set two records on May 1, 1965. The first record was for absolute sustained altitude (80,258 feet); the other was a speed record of 2,062 miles per hour for the 15/25-kilometer closed-circuit course. The square cases are air-conditioning boxes.

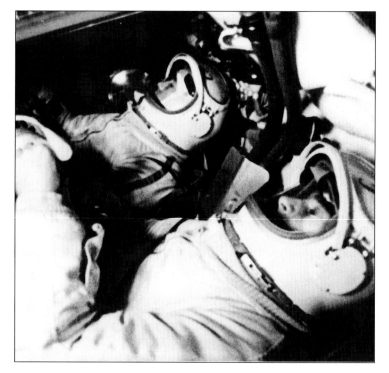

CANADAIR CL-84 The Canadair CL-84 VTOL/STOL aircraft used the tilt-wing formula with two turboprop engines. First hovered on May 7, 1965, the CL-84 had an impressive maximum speed of 321 miles per hour and a 340-mile range. Four were built, two crashed, and all suffered from the difficulty VTOL/STOL aircraft have: carrying enough fuel and equipment while still maintaining an adequate range.

ASTRONAUT EDWARD WHITE IN EVA Astronaut Edward White made a 20-minute EVA flight from the *Gemini 4* spacecraft on June 3, 1965, while his fellow astronaut, James McDivitt, photographed him. White holds an oxygen "space gun" to help him maneuver. Sadly, White was killed in the fire on *Apollo 1* on January 27, 1967, along with Virgil "Gus" Grissom and Roger Chaffee.

FLIGHT TIMELINE

June 3–7, 1965 James A. McDivitt and Edward White complete 62 orbits in *Gemini 4;* White is the first American to walk in space.

June 13, 1965 The unusual-looking Britten-Norman BN-2 Islander makes its first flight.

September 7, 1965 The Bell Model 209, which will become the Huey Cobra, makes its first flight.

September 27, 1965 The LTV A-7A Corsair attack aircraft makes its first flight.

November 15, 1965 A Flying Tiger Boeing 707 becomes the first to fly around the world across the poles.

December 4–18, 1965 Frank Borman and James Lovell complete 206 orbits in *Gemini 7* and rendezvous with *Gemini 6.*

January 10, 1966 The Bell Model 206A Jet Ranger helicopter makes its first flight.

January 31, 1966 *Luna 9* is launched to the moon.

February 8, 1966 Freddie Laker announces the formation of Laker Airways.

March 16, 1966 *Gemini 8* achieves the first space docking.

March 17, 1966 The Bell X-22A makes its first flight.

April 3, 1966 *Luna 10* becomes the first artificial moon satellite.

BRITTEN-NORMAN BN-2 ISLANDER While great things were going on in space, great things were going on in general aviation with the advent of the first flight of the Britten-Norman BN-2 Islander on June 13, 1965. More than 1,100 of the highly functional cruise utility transports were sold, and they worked in 120 different countries. A variety of military versions were proposed, and a three-engine Trislander was developed.

GEMINI 5 AND TITAN II ICBM technology was transferred directly to space flight, and astronauts Gordon Cooper and Charles Conrad were well aware of the power of the *Titan II* launcher lifting their *Gemini 5* toward their eight days in orbit on August 21, 1965. Their mission marked the exact point when U.S. space exploration began to surpass Soviet space exploration. After overcoming numerous problems that threatened to end the mission early, *Gemini 5* splashed down successfully after 120 orbits.

BELL HUEY COBRA If ever an aircraft looked like, and lived up to, its name, it was the Bell Huey Cobra. First flown on September 7, 1965, the Huey was an aerial fire support system with a narrow, tandem-seat fuselage and small stub wings for additional lift and an armament platform. The Huey Cobra was immensely successful in the Vietnam War and, when equipped with TOW antitank missiles, became a prime tank killer.

LTV A-7A CORSAIR II Perhaps not as handsome as the F-8 Crusader that preceded it, the A-7A Corsair II won the hearts of both the Navy and the USAF with its speed, accurate strike capability, bomb load, and ruggedness. Flown first on September 27, 1965, it was ideally suited for operations in Southeast Asia, where it flew 90,000 missions for the Navy. Although slated for retirement, two squadrons of the veteran Corsair II saw service in the Persian Gulf War.

FLIGHT TIMELINE

May 18, 1966 The LTV XC-142A triservice V/STOL transport makes carrier takeoffs and landings on the USS *Bennington*.

May 18–June 20, 1966 Englishwoman Shelia Scott completes a record solo round-the-world flight for women in a Piper Comanche, flying 29,005 miles.

June 16, 1966 Navy A-4s make the first carrier strike since 1964 against North Vietnam, hitting oil storage facilities at Thanh Hoa.

July 12, 1966 The Northrop M2-F2 lifting body, predecessor to the Space Shuttle, flies. It has a wingless design, using its fuselage to generate lift.

August 10, 1966 *Lunar Orbiter 1* is launched by NASA to photograph the moon and survey Apollo landing sites.

August 31, 1966 The Hawker Siddeley AV-8A VTOL development aircraft makes its first hovering flight.

September 8, 1966 The Phoenix missile, to be the heart of the F-14 weapon system, undergoes a successful full-function test launch from an A-3A Skywarrior.

September 15, 1966 Reinhold Platz, Fokker's top designer in World War I, dies at age 80.

October 21, 1966 The Yakovlev Yak-40 trijet makes its first flight.

FLYING TIGER BOEING 707
The Flying Tiger Line was founded in 1945 by Robert Prescott, a veteran "Hump" flyer supplying the famous Flying Tigers of Claire Chennault. Prescott's venture successfully entered the jet age in 1965 when it leased two Boeing 707s. On November 15, 1965, a Flying Tiger Line 707, sponsored by Colonel W. F. Rockwell, made the first polar flight around the earth in 51 hours, 27 minutes. The pilots were Fred Austin and Harrison Finch.

GEMINI 6 A AND TITAN II The Soviet Union space program was closed; failures were not revealed and successes announced only after the fact. However, the U.S. space program was open, revealing to the public both successes and failures. Consequently, when this *Titan II* rocket ignited, then shut down on December 13, 1965, leaving astronauts Tom Stafford and Wally Schirra sitting on top of a potential fireball in their spacecraft, all the world was watching. They launched successfully in the *Gemini 6* spacecraft two days later for a flight of just under 26 hours.

SIR GEOFFREY DE HAVILLAND

Sir Geoffrey de Havilland made his first flight in an aircraft of his own design on September 10, 1910. He went on to become one of the most distinguished aircraft designers and manufacturers in history, producing a wide range of aircraft from this Hornet Moth to the Mosquito to a line of jet fighters and airliners. He died on May 26, 1965, respected by his peers and honored by his country.

FLIGHT TIMELINE

November 11, 1966 The last Gemini mission is flown by Edwin "Buzz" Aldrin and James Lovell. They complete 59 orbits, and Aldrin spends 5½-hours in extravehicular activity (EVA).

December 6, 1966 The Luftwaffe grounds the Lockheed F-104 fleet after the 65th accident.

December 23, 1966 The Dassault Mirage F1 makes its first flight.

January 2, 1967 Boeing is awarded the contract for the design of a supersonic transport; the design will eventually be canceled.

January 27, 1967 *Apollo 1* astronauts Virgil "Gus" Grissom, Edward White, and Roger Chaffee die in a tragic fire during a preflight test.

February 10, 1967 The Dornier Do 31E flies for the first time.

February 26, 1967 Grumman A-6 Intruders conduct the first aerial mining of the Vietnam War, laying mine-fields in the mouths of the Song Ca and Son Giang rivers.

March 8, 1967 The all-metal Slingsby T.53 glider makes its first flight.

March 11, 1967 The Bede BD-2, an all-metal sailplane, makes its first flight.

April 9, 1967 The Boeing 737 twin-jet debuts.

April 18, 1967 Aeroflot begins Moscow to Tokyo service with a Tupolev Tu-114.

NUCLEAR INCIDENT WITH B-52 AT PALOMARES, SPAIN In-flight refueling is terribly hazardous, as the collision and crash of a Boeing B-52 with a KC-135 tanker illustrated on January 17, 1966. Seven of the eleven crew members were killed in the accident. Four unarmed nuclear bombs fell away from the B-52. All were eventually recovered amid a storm of controversy.

LUNA 9 EXHIBIT IN MOSCOW
Luna 9 was launched on January 31, 1966, and made the first successful soft landing on the moon, sending back television pictures and radiation data for four days. This is an exhibition celebrating the Soviet space triumph in Moscow.

DOUGLAS DC-8 Douglas had dominated the air transport world from the time of the DC-3's debut in 1935, but it was caught short by the Boeing 707 and had to hurry to catch up with the handsome DC-8. It matched the 707 in performance, but Douglas did not match Boeing in management or marketing, and only 556 were sold.

BERNIE FISHER True heroism can never be explained, and anyone who flew in Vietnam knows just how much courage it took for Major Bernard Fisher to land his A-1E at the Ashau Special Forces Camp under enemy fire to rescue Major Stafford W. Myers (left). Myers had crash-landed his aircraft on the airstrip that was held by the North Vietnamese. Fisher received the Medal of Honor for his March 10, 1966, rescue effort.

DAVID SCOTT AND NEIL ARMSTRONG IN GEMINI 8 The small size of the Mercury and Gemini spacecraft is surprising. One must salute the astronauts, who managed to stay in confined quarters in their uncomfortable pressure suits for long periods of time, enduring the discomfort of high G forces, weightlessness, and danger. Launched on March 16, 1966, with David Scott (left) and Neil Armstrong, the *Gemini 8* rendezvoused with an *Agena* for the first-ever docking in orbit.

SHEILA SCOTT Sheila Scott waves from the wing of her advertisement-bedecked Piper Comanche 260B aircraft, before leaving on the first leg of her round-the-world flight on May 18, 1966, from Heathrow Airport in London. She landed there on June 20, flying 29,005 miles en route.

FLIGHT TIMELINE

April 27, 1967 A-6 Intruders and A-4 Skyhawks raid Kep Airfield in North Vietnam, striking MiGs on the ground.

May 9, 1967 The Fokker F28 Friendship makes its first flight.

May 23, 1967 The Hawker Siddeley Nimrod, a development of the de Havilland Comet 4, makes its first flight.

June 8, 1967 Israeli forces sink the USS *Liberty*.

June 14, 1967 NASA launches *Mariner 5* for a Venus flyby (achieved October 19, 1967).

September 2, 1967 The Lockheed AH-56A Cheyenne attack helicopter, which features a rigid rotor and pusher propeller, makes its first flight.

October 3, 1967 Major William Knight flies a North American X-15 to the fastest speed of its career: 4,534 miles per hour (Mach 6.72).

October 23, 1967 The Canadair CL-215 water bomber makes its first flight.

November 18, 1967 The swing-wing Dassault Mirage G makes its first flight.

March 10, 1968 Lockheed selects the Rolls-Royce RB.211 engine to power its L-1011.

March 17, 1968 U.S. F-111s begin operation in Vietnam. The aircraft prove to be disastrous, and they are withdrawn from service.

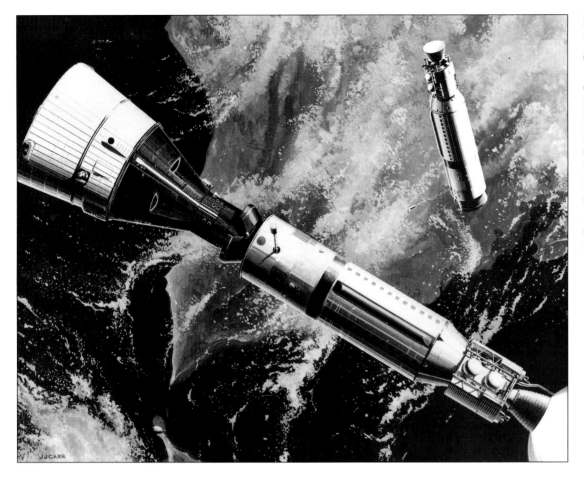

DOUBLE RENDEZVOUS FOR GEMINI 10 John Young and Michael Collins launched in *Gemini 10* on July 18, 1966, at 5:20 P.M., docking with their *Agena* target (GATV-5005) after 5 hours and 52 minutes of flight. The *Agena* then powered up to lift them into an orbit with a 763-kilometer apogee, the highest yet. Collins made two more EVAs, one before and one after the rendezvous with *Gemini 8's Agena,* illustrated here. Splashdown was 70 hours and 10 minutes after blastoff.

REINHOLD PLATZ Reinhold Platz, shown here with Tony Fokker (in the Fokker Dr I cockpit), died on September 15, 1966, at the age of 80. Relatively unknown for many years, Platz later was celebrated as the real creative design genius behind Tony Fokker's later designs in a book, *Fokker, the Creative Years,* by A. R. Weyl. More recently, scholars have disputed this, attributing good welding, manufacturing, and management skills to Platz but not design genius.

LOCKHEED C-130 WITH FULTON RESCUE SYSTEM The Fulton Rescue System was developed to pick up personnel stranded behind enemy lines. This HC-130H is just another example of the versatility of the Lockheed Hercules, which can be adapted to virtually any role. In the Fulton System, a balloon carries a cable upward, and the cable is attached to the person being rescued. The HC-130H has a device at its nose that snares the cable, allowing the rescued person to be reeled in.

GRUMMAN GULFSTREAM II Grumman had already scored a tremendous coup with its original Gulfstream turboprop twin transport, which immediately became one of the most sought after executive planes in the business. It upped the ante in the Gulfstream II, which first flew on October 2, 1966. With a Mach .85 cruise, a 3,800-mile range, and a short-field capability, the Gulfstream II's utter luxury put it in a class by itself.

FLIGHT TIMELINE

March 27, 1968 The first Soviet cosmonaut, Yuri Gagarin, is killed in the crash of a two-seat MiG-15.

May 5, 1968 A Grumman Gulfstream II lands at London, completing the first nonstop transatlantic flight by an executive jet.

June 8, 1968 Barnes Wallis dies at the age of 80. He invented the "Dam Buster" raid bombs and geodetic airframes; he also designed dirigibles.

June 30, 1968 The world's largest airplane, the Lockheed C-5A Galaxy, makes its first flight.

July 6, 1968 Marine Corps North American OV-10A Broncos arrive in Vietnam.

September 8, 1968 A Consortium of French and English manufacturers results in the first flight of the Jaguar E-01 prototype; the aircraft will serve well in the Gulf War.

October 11, 1968 Wally Schirra, Donn Eisele, and Walter Cunningham make 163 orbits in the *Apollo 7*, the first crewed Apollo mission.

December 21-27, 1968 *Apollo 8*, with Frank Borman, James Lovell, and William Anders, orbits the moon ten times.

December 31, 1968 The Tupelov Tu-144 SST makes its first flight, becoming the world's first SST to fly.

January 7, 1969 The USAF accepts the 1,000th T-38 trainer from Northrop.

SAAB 37 VIGGEN (THUNDER-BOLT) Like Dassault, Saab manages to bring out a new and very advanced aircraft at regular intervals. The Saab 37 Viggen, with its unique double-delta configuration, made its first flight on February 8, 1967, and rapidly became Sweden's primary military aircraft, fulfilling ground-attack, interceptor, photo-reconnaissance, maritime-reconnaissance, and training roles. With a Mach 2+ speed capability and the ability to operate from Sweden's widely dispersed airfields, the Viggen is reportedly a delight to fly.

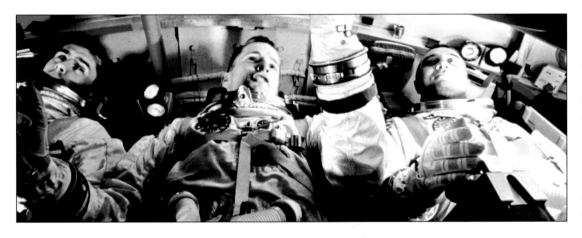

APOLLO 1 A tragedy in the making, astronauts Roger Chaffee (left), Edward White (center), and Virgil "Gus" Grissom (right) practice in their *Apollo 1* spacecraft. They were killed on January 27, 1967, at Cape Kennedy (Canaveral), Florida, when an electrical short ignited the 100 percent oxygen atmosphere of the spacecraft, burning them to death. Subsequent *Apollo* spacecraft did not have a similar pure-oxygen atmosphere.

BOEING 737 Aircraft manufacturers like to have a complete line of products so that airlines can buy aircraft to suit their routes. The Boeing 737 was introduced on April 9, 1967, as a short-haul airliner and soon became the most popular of its type in history, with 5,000 orders taken to date. A Boeing 737 is said to take off every 5.6 seconds from airports all over the world.

COSMONAUT VLADIMIR KOMAROV Veteran Cosmonaut Vladimir Komarov launched on April 23, 1967, in *Soyuz 1,* the first Soviet spacecraft capable of moving from one orbit to another by firing onboard propulsion systems. Komarov ran into problems on his 15th orbit. Reentry was successful, but when the parachutes deployed, they twisted. Komarov died when his spacecraft smashed into the earth near Orenburg in the Soviet Union.

FLIGHT TIMELINE

January 14, 1969 Exhaust from a starter generator unit detonates a Zuni rocket warhead onboard the USS *Enterprise;* 27 people are killed.

January 14–17, 1969 Colonel V. Shatalov in *Soyuz 4* joins with *Soyuz 5* and achieves the first docking between two piloted spacecraft.

February 3, 1969 The U.S. Navy issues a contract to Grumman for the F-14A.

February 9, 1969 The Boeing 747 makes its first flight.

February 24, 1969 *Mariner 6* is launched for a Mars flyby (achieved July 31, 1969).

March 2, 1969 The prototype Concorde supersonic airliner makes its first flight.

March 3–13, 1969 *Apollo 9,* with James A. McDivitt, David R. Scott, and Russell L. Schweickart as crew, completes 151 Earth orbits and tests the Lunar module in flight.

March 5, 1969 The existence of the Mil-12 helicopter, the largest ever flown, is announced.

April 9, 1969 The second Concorde (British-built) makes its first flight.

April 14, 1969 A North Korean aircraft shoots down an unarmed Lockheed EC-121 Constellation, killing the 31 crew members.

April 28, 1969 The Hawker Siddeley Harrier makes a transatlantic crossing.

HAWKER SIDDELEY (BRITISH AEROSPACE) NIMROD The basic design of the de Havilland Comet was too good to waste, so Hawker Siddeley (later part of British Aerospace) translated the design into the Nimrod, a very efficient maritime patrol aircraft that flew for the first time on May 23, 1967. Essentially a beefed-up and improved Comet 4, the 535-miles-per-hour Nimrod has added antisubmarine warfare and intelligence gathering to its roles.

MAJOR WILLIAM KNIGHT The North American X-15 was probably the most productive of the "X-plane" series, and only the most elite pilots—Scott Crossfield, Jo Walker, Bob Rushworth, Joe Engle, William Knight—flew it. On October 3, 1967, Knight flew it to Mach 6.72, or 4,534 miles per hour, faster than any plane in history. Knight would later win his astronaut wings with a flight to 280,000 feet.

SHIN MEIWA SS-2 FLYING BOAT The Kawasaki firm was one of Japan's biggest producers of military aircraft during World War II, reentering the arena as Shin Meiwa Industry doing maintenance and repair work. Its first major aircraft project was the Shin Meiwa SS-2 flying boat designed for search-and-rescue work as well as maritime reconnaissance. The SS-2 first flew on October 5, 1967. An amphibian version, the SS-2A, first flew in 1974. A 1,500-shaft horsepower gas turbine is used to provide compressed air for a boundary layer control system.

FLIGHT TIMELINE

May 11, 1969 Lieutenant Commander Brian Davis, Royal Navy, wins the *Daily Mail* transatlantic race in 4 hours, 17 minutes.

May 18–26, 1969 NASA launches *Apollo 10* with Thomas P. Stafford, John W. Young, and Eugene A. Cernan.

June 1, 1969 The Marine OV-10A Bronco sets a 2,539.78-mile distance record for turboprop aircraft.

June 15, 1969 Aeroflot and Pan Am begin Moscow to New York services.

July 14, 1969 The first Vought A-7E Corsair II is delivered to the Navy.

July 20, 1969 In the *Apollo 11* mission, Neil Armstrong and Edwin "Buzz" Aldrin walk on the moon.

July 24, 1969 Neil Armstrong, Michael Collins, and Edwin "Buzz" Aldrin, the *Apollo 11* astronauts who went to the moon, are recovered by helicopters off the USS *Hornet*.

August 4, 1969 The U.S. Navy orders $461 million worth of a new antisubmarine warfare plane, the Lockheed S-3A.

September 15, 1969 The Cessna Citation business jet makes its first flight.

October 2, 1969 The first Hawker Siddeley Nimrod, a development of the original de Havilland Comet, is delivered to the RAF.

CANADAIR CL-215 WATER BOMBER The first specially designed water bomber (previous aircraft had been adaptations of former fighters, bombers, and transports) to fight forest fires, the Canadair CL-215 created a sensation after its first flight on October 23, 1967. Able to scoop water into its tanks from a lake or river, the CL-215 can drop its 1,200-gallon load every ten minutes, far more than is possible with a conventional aircraft. About 125 were built, and they serve in 8 countries.

MCDONNELL F-4K PHANTOM II A number of major modifications had to be made to the McDonnell F-4J to make it suitable for operations from the smaller British aircraft carriers. This included the use of Rolls-Royce Spey turbofans with 20,515 pounds of thrust in afterburner. The first YF-4K flew on June 27, 1966, and 48 more were delivered to the Royal Navy as the FG-1. Some were later transferred to the RAF on January 4, 1968.

YURI GAGARIN One of the most likable, personable heroes of the Soviet Union, Yuri Gagarin, the first man to fly in space, went through some still unknown difficulty later in his career. He died in a two-seat MiG-15 on March 27, 1968, under circumstances that have always been described as mysterious.

TUPOLEV TU-144 SST The Soviet Union created the Tupolev Tu-144 supersonic transport. Chief Designer Yuri N. Popov beat his Concorde rivals into the air, flying for the first time on December 31, 1968. Cruise speed was Mach 2.285 with 121 passengers, but the aircraft was flawed by high fuel consumption and safety problems and was withdrawn from service.

SEPECAT JAGUAR A joint product of British Aerospace and Breguet Aviation, the *Société Européenne de Production de l'Avion ECAT* (SEPECAT) Jaguar is a twin-jet attack aircraft used by the French and British air forces in four different versions. It has also been exported and manufactured under license in India. Fast at Mach 1.6 and capable of low-level operations, the Jaguar is a versatile aircraft that has proved itself in combat. The first prototype flew on September 8, 1968.

JUAN TRIPPE Juan Trippe forged new routes for his airlines by calling new aircraft into being. He pioneered his Caribbean routes with Consolidated and Sikorsky flying boats, then did the same for the Pacific with Sikorsky and Martin flying boats. He backed the development of the Boeing 314 for transatlantic work. He bought early Boeing 707 and Douglas DC-8 jets. But his biggest triumph was joining with Bill Allen of Boeing to bring the 747 into existence.

MAJOR JERAULD GENTRY Major Jerauld "Jerry" Gentry, one of the top USAF test pilots at Edwards Air Force Base, talks to his wife before his April 17, 1969, flight in the Martin Marietta X-24A lifting body. Dropped from the wing of an N52-52A, the X-24A glided to the ground, paving the way for later aircraft like the Space Shuttle. Under rocket power, the X-24A achieved supersonic flight. Despite its unusual wingless configuration, the X-24A was reportedly pleasant to fly.

BOEING 747 IN PAN AM MARKINGS Unquestionably the most important jet airliner since the 707, the Boeing 747 revolutionized the travel industry with its gigantic size and high speed. First flown on February 9, 1969, the big jet had some teething problems, particularly with engines, but soon dominated the world's airways. Able to carry 400 to 500 passengers (depending on the airline) at 600 miles per hour, the 747 changed the world. It set the pattern for the jumbo jet and still leads the way.

October 12, 1969 The first SEPECAT Jaguar strike fighter to be completed in Britain makes its first flight.

November 10, 1969 Master showman Jim Bede sets an unrefueled closed-circuit course distance record of 8,973.4 miles in his radical BD-2.

November 14–24, 1969 *Apollo 12* makes a second lunar mission with Charles (Pete) Conrad, Jr.; Richard F. Gordon, Jr.; and Alan L. Bean as the crew.

December 17, 1969 The first Lockheed C-5A Galaxy is handed over to the Air Force; this controversial aircraft will have tremendous importance in several wars.

December 23, 1969 McDonnell Douglas is chosen to build the F-15 air-superiority fighter.

January 22, 1970 The Boeing 747 begins Pan Am transatlantic service.

February 15, 1970 Air Chief Marshal Lord (Hugh) Dowding dies at age 87; he was the Commander of Fighter Command during the Battle of Britain.

March 2, 1970 The General Electric CF-6 engine is tested on a Boeing B-52 test bed; the engine is intended for the McDonnell Douglas DC-10.

March 16, 1970 A Lockheed EC-121 crashes at Da Nang, Vietnam; 23 people are killed.

CONCORDE Two longtime rivals, enemies, and allies, Great Britain and France teamed up to create the Aerospatiale/British Aerospace Concorde, the only successful (technically if not economically) supersonic transport to date. The first French Concorde flew on March 2, 1969, and the British Concorde on April 9. The enormous development costs could never be recovered as the production run was limited to nine aircraft. Top speed was Mach 2.04.

APOLLO 10 CREW PORTRAIT The three primary crew members for the *Apollo 10* mission (launched on May 18, 1969) pose in front of a large map of the lunar surface. From the left are astronauts Eugene A. Cernan, lunar module pilot; Thomas P. Stafford, mission commander; and John W. Young, command module pilot.

APOLLO 11 Astronaut Edwin "Buzz" Aldrin poses for a photograph besides the U.S. flag deployed on the moon during the *Apollo 11* mission of July 20, 1969. Aldrin and his fellow astronaut Neil Armstrong were the first to walk on the lunar surface, where temperatures ranged from 234 degrees above zero to 274 degrees below zero. *Apollo 11* was launched by a Saturn V launch vehicle on July 16, 1969.

FLIGHT TIMELINE

March 19, 1970 Major Jerauld Gentry makes the first piloted and powered flight in a Martin Marietta X-24A lifting body vehicle, a research tool for the shuttle.

March 28, 1970 A Navy Phantom II downs a MiG-21 to resume air combat after a bombing halt.

April 10, 1970 The Douglas A-4M Skyhawk, a much more advanced version of the original aircraft, makes its first flight.

April 11–17, 1970 The *Apollo 13* mission is aborted after an explosion on board.

May 2, 1970 A Navy helicopter rescues 26 people from a DC-9 ditched in the Caribbean.

May 9, 1970 Navy helicopters and OV-10A Broncos combine with boats to attack in the Mekong Delta region.

May 26, 1970 The Tupolev Tu-144 reaches Mach 2 in test flights.

June 1, 1970 The first Lockheed C-5A goes into operational service.

June 9, 1970 A New York to Washington, D.C., speed record for helicopters is set—1 hour, 18 minutes at 156.43 miles per hour—in a Marine Corps Ch-53D flown by James Wright and Colonel Henry Hart.

June 10, 1970 A New York-to-Boston helicopter speed record is set (same crew and helicopter as above): one hour, nine minutes at 162.72 miles per hour.

CESSNA CITATION JET Clyde Cessna liked fast airplanes, and he would approve heartily of the Cessna Citation, which flew for the first time on September 15, 1969. The Citation paved the way for a complete line of ever larger and more powerful Cessna business jets. The Citation II has two 2,500-pound thrust engines, a cruising speed of 440 miles per hour, and a range of 2,000 miles.

AERMACCHI MB 326 Italy's aviation industry was also resurgent, and the Aermacchi MB 326 had the classic beautiful lines that always characterized Macchi aircraft. On its first flight on December 10, 1957, it was powered by 1,750-pound static-thrust Viper turbojets, accounting for its tiny jet intake. Later aircraft had larger engines. More than 700 were sold as trainers and close-air support aircraft.

McDonnell Douglas DC-10 The three-engine McDonnell Douglas DC-10 made its first flight on August 29, 1970, from Long Beach, California, to Edwards Air Force Base. The DC-10 had been rushed into production to compete with the Lockheed L-1011 for the wide-body jet airliner market. Neither aircraft was a commercial success; the market was too small for two aircraft. The DC-10 was sold as the KC-10 tanker to the USAF.

Terrorists Blow up Hijacked Aircraft in Jordan "Skyjack Sunday" took place on September 19, 1970, at Dawson Field, in Jordan. TWA, Swissair, and BOAC aircraft, along with more than 400 passengers, were hijacked by the Popular Front for the Liberation of Palestine and taken to the Jordanian airport. The airliners were blown up on the ground. This is the remains of a Vickers VC-10 airliner.

FLIGHT TIMELINE

July 17, 1970 Lockheed P-3A Orions begin operation with the Navy.

August 17, 1970 The Soviets launch *Venera 7*, which lands on Venus on December 15, 1970.

August 22, 1970 Two Sikorsky HH-53C helicopters fly a 9,000-mile nonstop transpacific flight refueled by Lockheed KC-130s.

August 29, 1970 The McDonnell Douglas DC-10 makes its first flight.

September 25, 1970 The television-guided Condor missile is test fired.

October 24, 1970 Bill Dana makes the last flight in a North American X-15.

November 10, 1970 The Soviet Union lands the first remote-controlled moon rover *Luna 17*.

November 12, 1970 Japan reenters military aircraft building with the first flight of the NAMC XC-1 jet transport.

November 16, 1970 The Lockheed L-1011 TriStar makes its first flight.

November 21, 1970 The United States attempts to rescue U.S. prisoners of war from Son Tay prison in North Vietnam, only to learn that the prisoners have been moved.

December 21, 1970 The Grumman F-14A Tomcat makes its first flight.

GRUMMAN F-14A TOMCAT Grumman's answer to the abominable F-111B fiasco was its magnificent F-14A Tomcat, the most formidable fleet defense fighter in history. The first Tomcat flew on December 21, 1970, only to be lost nine days later due to hydraulic failure. The Tomcat quickly became the Navy's top fighter and remained so for almost 30 years. A speed of Mach 2.34 and its Phoenix missile system make it a deadly opponent.

HAWKER SIDDELEY AV-8A HARRIER The Marines wanted a VTOL fighter desperately, and they got one with the Harrier, the first of which they accepted on January 6, 1971. The Hawker Siddeley AV-8A Harrier first flew on August 31, 1966. A Mark III Harrier has a 21,500-pound thrust Rolls-Royce Bristol Pegasus vectored thrust turbofan, a maximum speed of 740 miles per hour at sea level, and an initial rate of climb of 22,500 feet per minute. The battlefield support fighter performed beautifully in the Falklands War.

LOCKHEED P-3 ORION Lockheed turned to its Electra II turboprop for the basic Orion airframe and engine combination, but the interior of the aircraft is loaded not with passenger seats but with the most sophisticated antisubmarine warfare equipment in history. The first Orion flew on August 19, 1953, and was quickly ordered in large numbers by a wide variety of air forces. On January 27, 1971, an Orion set a world-class speed record for turboprop aircraft: 501.44 miles per hour over a closed course.

APOLLO 14 CREW This is the crew of *Apollo 14*, which made the third moon landing. From left, Command Module Pilot Stuart Roosa, Commander Alan Shepard, and Lunar Module Pilot Edgar Mitchell. The mission launched on January 31, 1971, and splashed down on February 9, 1971.

CASA 212 Aviocar Although CASA's name is unfamiliar to most Americans, the firm dates back to 1923. It has produced many significant aircraft, including this handsome 212 Aviocar, a 19-passenger airliner first flown on March 26, 1971. The two 900-shaft horsepower Garrett-AiResearch Turboprops give the aircraft a cruising speed of 240 miles per hour. The 212 is a modern equivalent of the DC-3/C-47, though its sales (about 500) are much smaller.

Dassault Falcon 20 Used by Federal Express Everyone from his college professors to his family told Fred Smith that he was wrong when he founded Federal Express as the potential airborne replacement for the venerable Railway Express. But Smith, personable and persistent, knew he was right, even on April 17, 1971, the first day of operation when Federal Express carried fewer than 20 packages. Hard work and fine service changed that, and FedEx became the profitable giant upon which everyone now depends—even the Post Office.

MARINER 9 Mariner 9 was launched on May 30, 1971. It orbited Mars for 14 hours, becoming the first spacecraft to orbit another planet. The 2,200-pound, windmill-shaped satellite took 7,000 television pictures of the Martian surface, stored them on an onboard tape recorder, then beamed them back to the 210-foot dish antennae at Coldstone, California. Mars was revealed to be a magnificent spectacle of canyons and volcanoes.

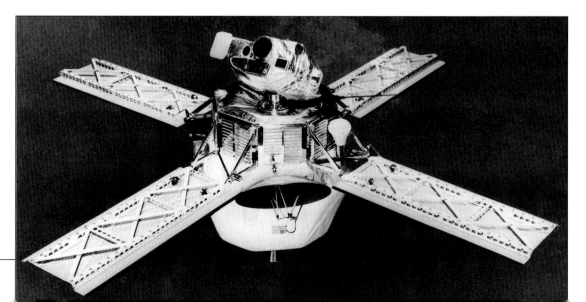

SHEILA SCOTT Sheila Scott flew from equator to equator via the North Pole in her Piper Aztec between June 11 and August 3, 1971. The 43-year-old British pilot is shown here in London prior to departing on her grueling trip.

SOUTHWEST AIRLINES BEGINS OPERATION On June 18, 1971, Southwest Airlines began operation with a saucy inauguration featuring miniskirted, booted beautiful young stewardesses. Under Herb Kelleher's brilliant leadership and a fleet of bright orange Boeing 737s, Southwest became one of the most efficient and most profitable airlines in history. Where other companies fell to deregulation, Southwest prospered and expanded by offering courteous low-fare service while keeping tight control of costs.

FLIGHT TIMELINE

June 18, 1971 Southwest Airlines begins operations.

June 29, 1971 *Soyuz 11* docks with the Soviet space station *Salyut 1*. The crew is killed upon entering the earth's atmosphere on the return trip because of equipment failure.

July 7, 1971 The Navy A-1 Skyraider is retired.

July 20, 1971 Japan makes its first indigenous supersonic aircraft, the Mitsubishi XT-2 jet trainer.

July 26–August 7, 1971 *Apollo 15* uses a lunar rover vehicle.

January 5, 1972 President Richard Nixon announces the Space Shuttle program.

January 21, 1972 The Lockheed S-3A Viking antisubmarine warfare aircraft makes its first flight. It has twice the speed and range of the Grumman S-2 Tracker it replaces.

February 6, 1972 Lyle Shelton sets a time-to-climb record in an F8F2 Bearcat: 3,000 meters in 1 minute, 31 seconds.

February 14–25, 1972 The Soviets send *Luna 20* to the moon; it digs samples and rockets them back to the Soviet Union.

March 24, 1972 The first McDonnell Douglas QF-4B target drone is delivered.

March 29, 1972 The Ryan BQM-34E, a supersonic Firebee II, is used in missile defense exercises for the first time.

BRIGADIER GENERAL JEANNE M. HOLM Jeanne M. Holm was born in Portland, Oregon, in 1921, and enlisted in the Army in 1942. Commissioned in 1943, she held various important posts before becoming the first female Brigadier General in the USAF on July 16, 1971. She was promoted to Major General on June 1, 1973, and retired in that rank.

APOLLO 15 MOON LANDING The moon's Hadley Delta forms the background for this view of the Lunar Roving Vehicle. Astronaut James B. Irwin stands near the Rover, which extended the capabilities of the *Apollo 15* crew that included Irwin, David Scott, and Alfred Worden. Launched on July 26, 1971, Scott and Irwin would explore the moon while Worden manned the Command Module. Splashdown took place on August 7, after one of the most productive Apollo missions.

LOCKHEED S-3A VIKING The versatility of the Lockheed company was never better illustrated than with the S-3A Viking antisubmarine warfare aircraft, first flown on January 21, 1972. With the SR-71, C-5A, and L-1011 all in operation, Lockheed created a carrier-borne jet antisubmarine aircraft to meet the Soviet sub challenge. The Viking had a top speed of 518 miles per hour and an endurance of more than four hours and was soon employed in maritime recon-naissance, refueling, and electronic intelligence work. About 185 were procured.

FAIRCHILD-REPUBLIC A-10A THUNDERBOLT II (WARTHOG) Form follows function, but beauty does not always follow form, for the Fairchild A-10 Warthog makes up in efficiency what it lacks in looks. The Fairchild-Republic Thunderbolt II is far more versatile and powerful than its famous ancestor, the P-47 Thunderbolt. First flown on May 10, 1972, the 439-miles-per-hour A-10A won a hard-fought competition over the Northrop YA-9A. Nineteen years later it distinguished itself in the Persian Gulf War with its antiarmor capability.

MCDONNELL DOUGLAS F-15 EAGLE The first flight of the most important fighter plane of the last three decades of the twentieth century, the McDonnell Douglas F-15 Eagle, took place on July 27, 1972. Although the McDonnell F-4 had performed well, it had not been optimized as an air superiority fighter. The F-15 was, and it dominated conflicts throughout the world, particularly in the Middle East. Since its debut, the Mach 2.5 Eagle has added an air-to-ground capability.

FLIGHT TIMELINE

April 6, 1972 The Navy conducts heavy air strikes against North Vietnam.

April 16–27, 1972 The *Apollo 16* mission sets up a lunar astronomical observatory.

May 6, 1972 U.S. Navy pilots down two MiG-21s and two MiG-17s.

May 9, 1972 Operation Pocket Money, the mining of principal North Vietnamese ports, begins.

May 10, 1972 The Fairchild-Republic A-10 Thunderbolt II prototype ground-support aircraft debuts.

May 10, 1972 Navy pilots shoot down 10 MiGs; Lieutenant Randall Cunningham and RIO William Driscoll become aces with a triple victory over MiGs at Haiphong.

May 26, 1972 Cessna rolls out its 100,000th aircraft; no other company has approached this figure in total production.

May 30, 1972 The Northrop A-9A makes its first flight.

May 31, 1972 The Navy announces it has flown 3,949 sorties against North Vietnam during the month of May.

June 20, 1972 A new helicopter class altitude record of 40,820 feet is set by Jean Boulet in an Aerospatiale Lama.

July 26, 1972 Rockwell International wins the competition to build the Space Shuttle.

STEVE RITCHIE AND CHARLES DEBELLEVUE On August 28, 1972, Captain Steve Ritchie shot down his fifth MiG-21 to become the first USAF ace of the Vietnam War. At left is his Weapons Systems Officer, Captain Charles "Chuck" DeBellevue. Ritchie was the only USAF pilot ace of the Vietnam War. DeBellevue, who flew with other pilots, was the leading ace with six victories. Ritchie might be the last USAF pilot ace, given the changing nature of aerial conflict.

APOLLO 17 The last crewed spacecraft to reach the moon, the *Apollo 17* lunar module is tested prior to being placed in the adapter housing it will use for the initial stages of the December 7, 1972, flight. Astronauts Eugene Cernan and future senator Harrison Schmitt landed in the moon's Taurus-Littrow region. Ronald Evans piloted the lunar orbiter.

AIRBUS INDUSTRIE A300 A consortium of aircraft manufacturers from France, Germany, the United Kingdom, Spain, the Netherlands, and Belgium formed Airbus in December 1970. Their first product was the A300 wide-body twin jet, which became the foundation for an industrial giant that is now competing on equal terms with Boeing in the airline business. The A300's first flight took place on October 28, 1972, and the aircraft became an instant hit that led to a distinguished line of airliners.

ANDREI TUPOLEV The famous Soviet aircraft designer, Andrei Tupolev, died on December 23, 1972. His career spanned small all-metal monoplanes to the supersonic Tu-144. In the process, he had been placed in prison by Joseph Stalin but was allowed to go on designing aircraft. When "rehabilitated," he came to the forefront of Soviet bomber and transport production.

MCDONNELL F-4F PHANTOMS IN LUFTWAFFE The postwar German Federal Republic selected an insignia similar to the Cross Patée used on World War I German aircraft for its new Luftwaffe. The F-4F was a development of the F-4E and was intended for the air superiority role. The German government received 175 F-4Fs that it continually modernized to improve combat effectiveness.

FLIGHT TIMELINE

July 27, 1972 The McDonnell Douglas F-15 Eagle makes its first flight.

August 5, 1972 An F-4J Phantom makes the first fully automated landing aboard a carrier, the USS *Ranger*.

August 11, 1972 The Northrop F-5E makes its first flight.

October 28, 1972 The Airbus Industrie A300 makes its first flight.

December 7–19, 1972 *Apollo 17*, the last flight in the program, is launched with Eugene Cernan, Ronald Evans, and Harrison Schmitt as crew.

December 18, 1972 Linebacker II bombing raids begin to bring the North Vietnamese to the negotiating table in Paris.

December 29, 1972 Heavy raids take place on Hanoi. The North Vietnamese go to the peace table.

January 12, 1973 The last Navy kill of the war is scored when an MiG-21 is shot down, bringing the total to 57 MiGs shot down.

January 27, 1973 The Vietnamese cease-fire is in effect.

March 29, 1973 The United States' participation in the Vietnam War officially ends.

April 6, 1973 NASA launches *Pioneer 11* on a flyby to Jupiter and Saturn.

April 10, 1973 The Boeing T-43A, a navigator trainer version of the 737, debuts.

BOEING B-52 BOMBING The Boeing B-52 was designed as a strategic long rifle, able to fly alone or in cells of three deep into the Soviet Union with powerful nuclear weapons. During the Vietnam War it became a tactical artillery barrage, dropping tons of conventional bombs on the instruction of Sky Spot radar sites. It became the most feared weapon of the Vietnam War—there was no warning of an attack until the bombs exploded.

LOCKHEED C-5A GALAXY IN OPERATION NICKEL GRASS Israel was almost defeated in the 1973 Yom Kippur War when a plea for an emergency airlift from the United States to provide moral support and munitions was heeded. The previously much-maligned Lockheed C-5A Galaxy did superb work, with its sister ship, the Lockheed C-141, in supplying vital munitions that saved Israel during Operation Nickel Grass. Ammunition still cold from the flight over was slammed into the hot breeches of Israeli guns.

SIR ALAN COBHAM On October 21, 1973, the pioneer of aerial refueling, Sir Alan Cobham, passed away at the age of 79. Sir Alan had founded Flight Refueling, Incorporated, which brought out the trailing hose system of refueling.

SKYLAB With the moon-landing behind it, the United States looked for new space adventures to conquer, creating its first space station, the *Skylab Orbital Workshop*. The third *Skylab* mission ran from November 16, 1973, through February 8, 1974, and was crewed by Gerald P. Carr, Edward G. Gibson, and William R. Pogue.

SIR ROBERT WATSON-WATT

The Scottish physicist, Sir Robert Alexander Watson-Watt was Scientific Advisor on Telecommunications at the Ministry of Aircraft Production. On February 12, 1935, Sir Robert had submitted a paper entitled "Detection and Location of Aircraft by Radio Methods." This led directly to the creation of the radar system that was so important in winning the Battle of Britain. Patriot that he was, he seems to be quite proud of his Buick car in this photo. Watson-Watt died on December 5, 1973, at the age of 81.

FLIGHT TIMELINE

May 14, 1973 NASA launches the *Skylab 1* space station; crews are sent up separately later.

May 25–June 22, 1973 Charles Conrad, Joseph Kerwin, and Paul Weitz, the first Skylab crew, board *Skylab*.

June 1, 1973 The first General Dynamics F-111Cs are delivered to the Royal Australian Air Force.

July 25, 1973 The Mikoyan Ye-266 sets a new altitude record of 118,898 feet.

August 1, 1973 The Martin X-24B lifting body, piloted by John Manke, makes a glide flight after being dropped from a Boeing B-52 mother ship.

August 16, 1973 A Grumman F-14 shoots down a QT-33 target drone with a Sparrowhawk missile.

October 6, 1973 Surprise air attacks by Arab forces open the Yom Kippur War.

October 19–24, 1973 Twenty-four Douglas A-4s are supplied to Israel.

October 21, 1973 The pioneer of aerial refueling, Sir Alan Cobham, dies at age 79.

October 26, 1973 The Alpha Jet trainer prototype makes its first flight; it is manufactured jointly by Dornier and Dassault/Breguet.

November 3, 1973 The United States launches *Mariner 10* to go to Venus and Mercury.

CHAPTER EIGHT

1974 to 1983:

New Worlds to Conquer in Air and Space

In a global economy, wars in the Middle East can affect gas prices everywhere. Increased prices were a shock at the gas station pump for the average driver, but they became a matter of life or death for airlines. Where in the past fuel economy had been just one of the performance factors to consider when designing or buying a new airliner, it now became paramount. But, regardless of the cost of fuel, both the Concorde and the Tupolev Tu-144 supersonic transports entered passenger service.

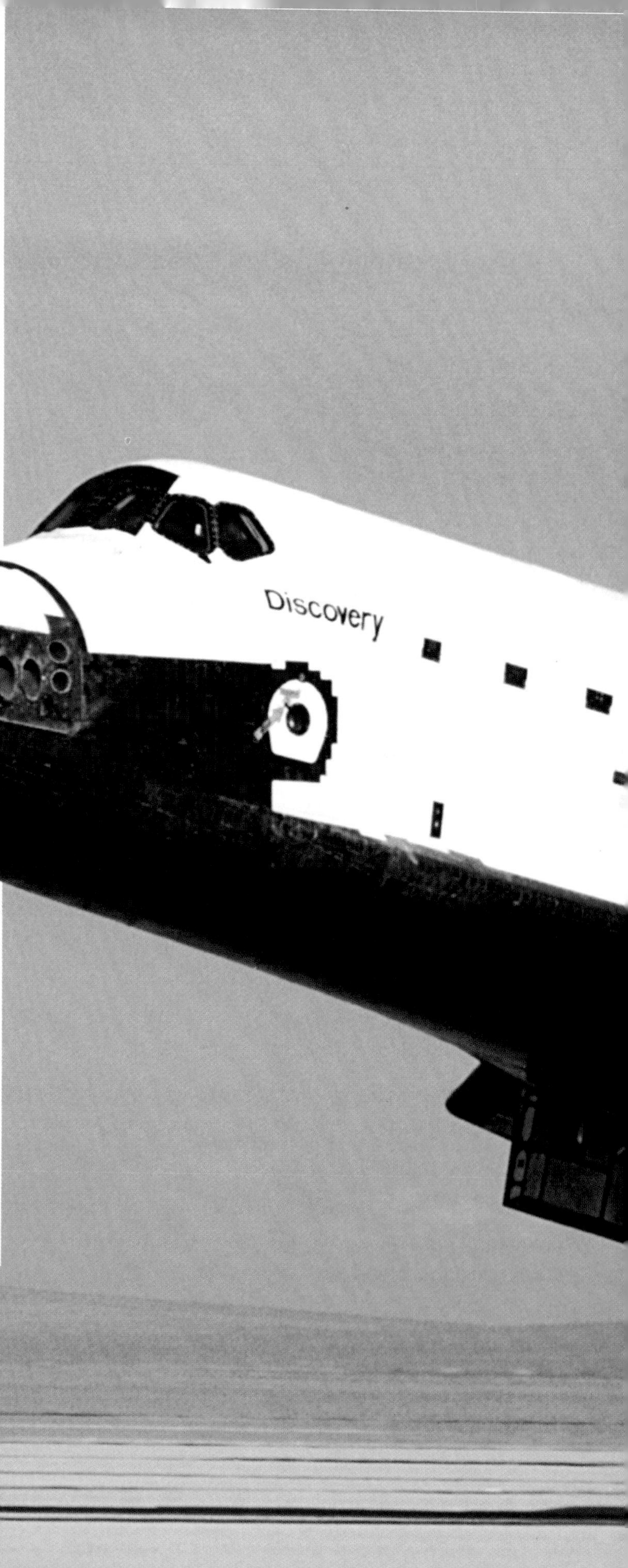

Space Shuttle *Discovery*

McDonnell F-15 Eagle

neers would pass on. Charles Lindbergh died at the age of 72 and Willy Messerschmitt at age 80.

But even as the famous passed on, other new names emerged. Dr. Paul MacCready and his team created the *Gossamer Condor* to win the Kremer Prize for piloted aircraft. Piloted by Bryan Allen, the shimmering aircraft flew a figure-eight course around two points one half mile apart. The flight had far more than human-interest value. It would lead to a steady series of solar-powered research aircraft.

The taking of hostages by terrorists took on a more international flavor on July 3–4, 1976, when 100 crew and passengers aboard an Air France Airbus A300B were hijacked and, with President Idi Amin's permission, were brought to the airport at Entebbe, Uganda, by their Palestinian and East German captors. An Israeli commando unit stormed the airport and rescued the hostages, setting a precedent for the war against terrorism.

A sad mission for helicopters occurred in Vietnam in 1975. The North Vietnamese violated the 1973 peace treaty and invaded South Vietnam, reaching the capital, Saigon, in late April 1975. On April 30, U.S. helicopters evacuated staff members and refugees from the roof of the embassy and adjacent buildings, ending all U.S. presence in Vietnam.

The high fuel prices hit the military, too, and flying times were cut all over the world. Older aircraft were being retired by the thousands. The U.S. military, in the midst of considering the lessons learned in Vietnam, came up with the requirement for two new fighters: the expensive McDonnell Douglas F-15 Eagle for air superiority work and the less expensive General Dynamics F-16 Fighting Falcon for ground attack and other tasks. Both would serve the United States well for decades to come, and both would be used by many allied nations around the world. The Soviet Union responded, as usual, with its own excellent MiG and Sukhoi designs, while France, also as usual, continued to develop and expand their line of Dassault fighters.

International cooperation was in the wind, and the effort proven in the building of the Anglo-French Concorde spread to other types including the Panavia Tornado and the SEPECAT Jaguar. Ultimately the idea would result in the fantastic line of Airbus Industrie transports.

As the century of flight progressed into its eighth decade, it was natural that some of the great pio-

There were other wars, of course, the most significant being the eight-year struggle between Iraq and Iran in which ballistic missiles and chemical weapons were used with abandon. In the South Atlantic, Argentina attempted to take back what it calls the Malvinas from Great Britain. A short intense war followed that resulted in a British victory but at considerable cost. The territory remained the Falkland Islands and was not recovered by Argentina. In the same decade, the Soviet Union became involved in a war in Afghanistan, which would have uncanny parallels to the planning, execution, and outcome of the U.S. involvement in Vietnam.

Politically, the Cold War seemed to be less dangerous. It was true that both the United States and the Soviet Union each had aircraft, ICBMs, and Submarine Launched Ballistic Missiles (SLBM) aimed at each other, but the rhetoric became a little less violent. One reason was the comprehensive information that each side was gaining from the other by means of satellite intelligence systems. Satellites were in the process of changing everything, including navigation, communication, meteorology, and intelligence, and the rockets that were brought into being to deliver nuclear warheads were now pumping satellites into the sky with increasing regularity.

A new, more efficient Airborne Warning and Control System (AWACS) emerged with the arrival of the Boeing E-3A Sentry. The AWACS became a force multiplier, able to identify enemy airborne

possible. The ultraluxurious jets now featured intercontinental range and speeds that were in the high-subsonic range.

Another new phenomenon was arising out of the brain, sweat, and energy of Paul Poberzney, whose Experimental Aircraft Association (EAA) had grown from a few friends gathered in his basement into the most important general aviation organization in history. The EAA, with its annual Fly-In at Oshkosh, Wisconsin, promoted every aspect of general aviation, including ultra-lights, home-builts, classics, war-birds, and more. It began by essentially offering private flyers an alternative to purchasing a used Piper Cub but became a leader in aviation

targets and direct friendly assets to them. With satellites and AWACS, the possibility of a surprise attack was reduced, and both the United States and the Soviet Union became more comfortable with each other.

Among the great advances in business was the proliferation of executive jet aircraft. What had begun with the Lockheed JetStar, North American Saberliner, and Learjet now turned into a competitive race between Gulfstream, Dassault, Learjet, Cessna, and others to produce the most luxurious and most cost-effective executive jet transports

business, education, and research. The home-built industry became a phenomenon in itself, with more and more kits being offered and more and more aircraft being completed and flown.

This was also the decade of the Space Shuttle, the fantastic rocket-borne glider that would take astronauts into orbit for experiments, national defense, and, ultimately, to build the International Space Station. The path to the Space Shuttle was taken deliberately and with great care. Piloted space flight had captured the public's imagination in a way even the most fantastic satellite never could.

Airbus A300

TOM GATCH A sad photo, in retrospect, for it shows Colonel Tom Gatch receiving last-minute handshakes prior to his flight from the Harrisburg, Virginia, International Airport. On February 18, 1974, Gatch's gondola was lifted by ten helium-filled balloons for his attempt to fly across the Atlantic. Unfortunately he disappeared en route. The Atlantic was not conquered by balloon until the flight of the *Double Eagle II* in August 1978.

MCDONNELL DC-10 CRASH The DC-10 was plagued by a series of crashes that shook public confidence in the aircraft. This crash, at Orly, France, took place on March 3, 1974. More than 300 lives were lost—the world's worst air disaster to that date.

HAWKER SIDDELEY (BRITISH AEROSPACE) HAWK In modern times, aircraft had longer lives than companies, and what started as the Hawker Siddeley P.1182 Hawk on August 21, 1974, became a British Aerospace Hawk and then a McDonnell Douglas (now Boeing) T-45A Goshawk. Of the hundreds built, many have been exported to countries around the world, where they serve both as trainers and attack aircraft. Its top speed is about 650 miles per hour, and service ceiling is 50,000 feet.

AIRBUS A300

The Airbus A300 prototype surprised everyone with its advanced features. As its sales success grew, Boeing protested that Airbus was being subsidized by European governments and was offered for sale at unfairly low prices. Airbus countered that Boeing was in effect subsidized by the United States because of its military business. Both arguments were valid, and it was left for the marketplace to decide—and it decided in favor of Airbus. And, while Airbus plunged ahead with its A380, a giant airplane that would surpass the 747 in capacity when it entered the market, Boeing toyed with its Sonic Cruiser for months before deciding against its production.

DASSAULT ETENDARD Despite the company's relatively small size, Dassault came up with an amazing variety of aircraft, including the Etendard, first flown on July 23, 1956, and intended to be an inexpensive lightweight fighter. This aircraft lost a NATO competition to the F-86-like Fiat G.91. The basic design was developed into the Super Etendard, which flew on October 28, 1974.

FLIGHT TIMELINE

February 2, 1974 The General Dynamics YF-16 makes its first "official" flight.

February 18, 1974 Tom Gatch takes off to cross the Atlantic in an unusual balloon/capsule system; he is lost at sea.

February 22, 1974 Lieutenant, Junior Grade, Barbara Ann Allen becomes the first female Navy Aviator.

March 1, 1974 The Sikorsky YCH-53 turboshaft transport makes its first flight.

March 3, 1974 A Turkish Douglas DC-10 crashes after takeoff from Orly, France; 346 are killed.

April 2, 1974 The last Douglas C-54 Skymaster is retired.

May 20, 1974 The ATS-6 satellite is launched.

June 4, 1974 Second Lieutenant Sally D. Woolfolk becomes the first female Army aviator.

June 9, 1974 The Northrop YF-17 prototype makes its first flight.

August 3, 1974 The world's largest (volume of 50.3 million cubic feet) unpiloted balloon is launched from Fort Churchill in Manitoba, Canada; it rises to 155,000 feet.

August 9, 1974 The first EC-130 Hercules TACAMO aircraft is accepted by the U.S. Navy.

August 21, 1974 The Hawker Siddeley P.1182 Hawk makes its first flight.

SR-71 MAKES RECORD FLIGHT Looking relaxed and pleased, Captain Harold B. Adams (left), the pilot, and Major William C. Machorek (right), the reconnaissance systems officer, have just landed at Beale Air Force Base, California, after a record flight between London and Los Angeles. They made the 5,645-mile flight in just 3 hours and 47 minutes, averaging 1,480 miles per hour. They had flown to Farnborough on September 1, 1974, crossing the Atlantic in just 1 hour, 55 minutes, and 42 seconds.

ROCKWELL INTERNATIONAL B-1B The original Rockwell International B-1 supersonic bomber prototype first flew on December 23, 1974, but the program was canceled by President Jimmy Carter in favor of the air-launched cruise missile. When President Ronald Reagan revived the program in October 1981 with an order for 100 B-1B bombers, the original prototypes were modified and pressed into service as test vehicles. This is the second B-1 prototype, 74-0159. The production swing-wing B-1Bs had a top speed of 792 miles per hour.

GENERAL DYNAMICS F-16 FIGHTING FALCON This is a December 13, 1973, roll-out shot of the General Dynamics YF-16 prototype at the Fort Worth plant. (The fighter division of General Dynamics was subsequently purchased by Lockheed.) The Mach 2.0 F-16 would win a hard-fought competition with the Northrop YF-17 on January 13, 1975, and then go on to become one of the most versatile and popular fighters in the world. The YF-17 was subsequently developed into the McDonnell Douglas F/A-18.

FLIGHT TIMELINE

DE HAVILLAND CANADA DHC-7 DASH 7 Although descended from the DHC-4 Caribou, the DHC-7 is a far more elegant aircraft, with four of the reliable Pratt & Whitney PT6A turboprops. The Dash 7 made its first flight on March 27, 1975. The aircraft has a top speed of 270 miles per hour as well as an STOL capability deriving from a sophisticated flap system operating within the slipstream of the propellers. About 113 were built.

LEARJET 35 On April 5, 1975, a Learjet 35 flew nonstop from Hawaii to Wichita, Kansas, a distance of 3,833 miles, proving the utility of the swift, sleek executive aircraft. The Learjet 35 could cruise with eight passengers at 530 miles per hour.

August 22, 1974 The Short SD3-30 makes its first flight.

August 25, 1974 Charles Lindbergh dies at age 72.

September 11, 1974 The Bell Model 206L Long Ranger makes its first flight.

September 25, 1974 The Northrop F-5F makes its first flight.

October 17, 1974 The Sikorsky YUH-60A helicopter makes its first flight.

October 28, 1974 The Dassault Super Etendard carrier-based fighter makes its first flight.

November 20, 1974 The first crash of a Boeing 747 "Jumbo Jet" occurs; 59 people die.

December 23, 1974 The Rockwell International B-1A prototype makes its first flight.

January 13, 1975 The General Dynamics F-16 wins the lightweight fighter contest over the F-17.

January 16–February 1, 1975 A McDonnell Douglas F-15 "Streak Eagle" sets eight world time-to-climb records.

January 17, 1975 The first production version of the Lockheed P-3C Orion is delivered to the Navy.

March 7, 1975 The Yak 42 trijet transport makes its first flight.

March 27, 1975 The de Havilland DHC-7 Dash 7 transport makes its first flight.

HELICOPTERS EVACUATE SAIGON EMBASSY In the spring of 1975, the North Vietnamese broke the agreements made in the 1973 peace treaty and invaded South Vietnam. Without U.S. air power to support them, the South Vietnamese troops fell back, and on April 29–30, 1975, the U.S. embassy in Saigon was evacuated by helicopter. It was a tragic end to U.S. involvement in Southeast Asia.

STAFFORD AND LEONOV The world took a step closer to peace between July 15–24, 1975, when the Apollo–Soyuz space rendezvous took place and the crew exchanged greetings. Here American astronaut Thomas P. Stafford and Soviet cosmonaut Alexei A. Leonov move through the hatchway between the *Apollo* and the *Soyuz*. The two spacecraft were docked in Earth's orbit.

HUGHES MODEL YAH-64 APACHE On September 30, 1975, the Hughes Model YAH-64 Apache made its first flight. It was selected as the winner of the Advanced Attack Helicopter competition on December 9, 1976, and since then has been the U.S. Army's most advanced helicopter. Ownership of the design first passed to McDonnell Douglas and then to Boeing. The Apache is powered by two General Electric T700 engines and has a top speed of 192 miles per hour.

BOEING 747 SP (SPECIAL PERFORMANCE) The great strength of the Boeing Company was its ability to react to market demand and supply the aircraft the customer wanted, when they wanted it. In this, Boeing far outstripped Douglas but has been matched quite well by Airbus. The SP was a lightweight, long-range 747 with a shortened fuselage, which could still carry up to 440 passengers for 6,800 miles.

CONCORDE The Concorde entered passenger service on both Air France and British Airways January 21, 1976, but despite the esteem in which the passengers held them, no further orders ensued. The Concorde's nose is in its drooped position for takeoff and landing; in supersonic flight it is raised to be perfectly streamlined.

FLIGHT TIMELINE

April 4, 1975 More than 100 orphans and adult escorts are killed in the first crash of a Lockheed C-5 Galaxy while evacuating Saigon.

April 29–30, 1975 Naval and Marine Corps helicopters evacuate U.S. citizens and South Vietnamese refugees from Saigon as the North Vietnamese storm the city.

June 3, 1975 The Mitsubishi F-1 supersonic single-seat fighter debuts; it is a development of an earlier T-2 trainer.

June 22, 1975 Svetlana Savitskaya flies a Mikoyan Ye-133 at 1667.42 miles per hour to set a women's speed record.

July 15–24, 1975 U.S. astronauts and Soviet cosmonauts dock their spacecraft during the Apollo/Soyuz Project.

August 20, 1975 The *Viking 1* spacecraft is launched to Mars to transmit pictures from the surface. It releases the lander on July 20, 1976, and pictures are transmitted on August 7, 1976.

August 26, 1975 The McDonnell Douglas YC-15 STOL transport makes its first flight.

September 9, 1975 The *Viking 2* is launched to Mars and lands on September 3, 1976.

September 30, 1975 The Hughes YAH-64 Apache prototype helicopter debuts.

October 1, 1975 The Bell YAH-63, competitor to the YAH-64, flies for the first time.

Dassault Mirage F1-B

Whereas the Mirage III series were delta-wing fighters, the successor version, the Mirage F1-B, had a swept wing. The original F1 first flew on December 23, 1966, and soon demonstrated a Mach 2 capability. A two-seat trainer, the F1-B followed on May 26, 1976. Both seats were equipped with the very effective fire-control radar system. Of the almost 800 produced, about 60 percent were sold to foreign countries.

Raid on Entebbe One of the most thrilling antiterrorism strikes in history took place on July 3–4, 1976, when four Israeli Lockheed C-130 transports made a 5,000-mile round-trip to Entebbe, Uganda. Filled with Israeli special forces, the Lockheed C-130s landed to rescue the 103 surviving hostages being held by Palestinian terrorists from hijacked Air France Flight 139. Only 53 minutes after landing, the C-130s took off for the return flight to a joyous Israel.

Lockheed SR-71 Blackbird

The product of the combined genius of Kelly Johnson, Ben Rich, and their brilliant "Skunk Works" teams, the Lockheed SR-71 could have set records on virtually any flight it made. On this flight, which took place on July 28, 1976, Captain E. W. Joersz and Major G. T. Morgan set a speed record of 2,193.1 miles per hour. The aircraft has such a sculptural beauty that it is a work of art as well as engineering.

BOEING YC-14 AMST The Advanced Military STOL Transport (AMST) competition pitted the Boeing YC-14 against the McDonnell Douglas YC-15. The Boeing design was considerably more sophisticated with a supercritical wing, upper-surface blowing, and complex flaps. It proved to be a terrific aircraft, but funds dried up, and no AMST transport was procured. The YC-14 prototype made its first flight on August 9, 1976.

VIKTOR BELENKO Lieutenant Viktor I. Belenko defected to the West with a Soviet MiG-25 fighter on September 6, 1976. He is shown here, heavily disguised as a "Blues Brother," at the Los Angeles airport. Belenko has since become a citizen of the United States, giving inspirational talks and contributing his engineering and flying knowledge. The MiG-25 was returned to the Soviet Union after a quick but thorough analysis.

FLIGHT TIMELINE

October 3, 1975 The first KC-130R Hercules tanker is delivered.

December 26, 1975 A Tu-144 completes the first supersonic airmail service between Moscow and Alma Ata, Kazakhstan.

January 21, 1976 The Concorde begins supersonic passenger service.

February 10, 1976 *Pioneer 10* crosses the orbit of Saturn on its way out of the solar system.

March 24, 1976 A Boeing 747 SP sets a world record by flying 10,290 miles nonstop from Paine Field, Washington, to Capetown.

April 5, 1976 Aviation pioneer and reclusive billionaire Howard Hughes dies at the age of 70.

May 20, 1976 The Bell AH-IT Sea Cobra makes its first flight.

May 26, 1976 The Dassault Mirage F1-B makes its first flight.

June 5, 1976 A Tomahawk missile undergoes its first in-flight launch; it is released from the wing of an A-6 Intruder.

June 24, 1976 The Navy accepts the first Beech T-34C turboprop trainer.

July 3–4, 1976 The Israelis rescue hostages in a raid on Entebbe, Uganda, destroying 11 MiGs.

July 20, 1976 The indigenous Israeli fighter, Kfir, is demonstrated publicly.

DASSAULT-MYSTÈRE FALCON 50 The success of the Dassault-Mystère Falcon executive jets led to a demand for one with transatlantic range. The inventive Dassault engineers took the basic Falcon 50, replaced its two engines with three 3,700-horsepower Garrett turbofans, and installed a supercritical wing and bigger fuel tanks. The result was the 3,915-mile range Falcon 50, which made its first flight on November 7, 1976. Its top speed was 545 miles per hour, with eight passengers carried in luxury.

BOEING E-3A AWACS On March 24, 1977, the first operational Boeing E-3A Airborne Warning and Control System (AWACS) was delivered to the USAF. The E-3A Sentry is a militarized version of the Boeing 707-320B, with a 30-foot diameter rotor-dome rotating above the fuselage. The AWACS is a force multiplier; it can oversee the direction of an air battle and direct resources to where they are most needed.

LOCKHEED C-141B One of the most useful transports of all time, the Lockheed C-141 was a dream come true when it was first received by USAF pilots used to flying the old Douglas C-124. The C-141B, which debuted on March 24, 1977, was a "stretched" version, some 23.3 feet longer than the original StarLifter, with an increased productivity of 45 percent. The C-141B cruised at 566 miles per hour and served brilliantly.

BELL XV-15 No other company has had experience in as many varied forms of vertical flight as the Bell Aircraft Corporation. This is the Bell XV-15 tilt-rotor, which made its first hovering flight on May 3, 1977. The engines tilt forward to provide an aircraft's forward speed combined with a helicopter's vertical capability. The XV-15's success led directly to the development of the V-22 Osprey.

CESSNA CITATION II A bare-bones Cessna Citation II makes its first flight on January 31, 1977; production aircraft would have gorgeous paint jobs and luxurious interiors. A succession of evermore capable aircraft flowed from the Cessna plant, all retaining the delightful flight characteristics for which Cessnas were noted. The Citation II was certified for single-pilot operation, but most users prefer to have two pilots for safety reasons.

FLIGHT TIMELINE

July 28, 1976 A Lockheed SR-71, piloted by Captain E. W. Joersz and Major G. T. Morgan, sets a world speed record of 2,193.1 miles per hour.

July 28, 1976 A Lockheed SR-71 sets an altitude in sustained/level flight record of 85,069 feet; it is piloted by Captain Robert Helt and Major Larry Elliot.

August 9, 1976 The Boeing YC-14 prototype flies; it will compete with the YC-15.

September 6, 1976 Lieutenant Viktor I. Belenko flies a MiG-25 to Japan, defecting from the Soviet Union.

September 17, 1976 The Space Shuttle *Enterprise* is rolled out in Palmsdale, California.

October 6, 1976 The AV-8 Harrier is deployed overseas for the first time on the USS *Franklin D. Roosevelt*.

October 12, 1976 The Sikorsky Model 72 prototype debuts.

November 7, 1976 The Dassault-Mystère Falcon 50 executive jet transport makes its first flight.

December 2, 1976 The Shuttle Carrier Aircraft, a modified Boeing 747, makes its first flight.

December 22, 1976 The Ilyushin Il-86 wide-body transport makes its first flight.

December 23, 1976 The Sikorsky S-70 wins the U.S. Army competition; it will be designated the UH-60A.

SPACE SHUTTLE *ENTERPRISE* AND NASA 747 Boeing engineers had never envisaged the 747 as part of a composite aircraft, intended to let the Space Shuttle *Enterprise* be launched for glide flights to the ground. The first approach and landing test of the Space Shuttle *Enterprise* was carried out on August 12, 1977, with astronauts Fred Haise and C. Gordon Fullerton flying the 75-ton glider to a beautiful landing.

DR. PAUL MACCREADY The soft-spoken Dr. Paul MacCready is an aeronautical genius of the first order, besides being a superb model maker and an expert glider pilot. On August 23, 1977, Mac-Cready celebrated his 52nd birthday with the news that his friend Bryan Allen had won the £50,000 Kremer Prize for human-powered aircraft. Allen was flying the MacCready-designed *Gossamer Condor*. MacCready went on to establish an industry in such unconventional aircraft.

FAIRCHILD REPUBLIC A-10 The Fairchild Republic A-10 is called the Warthog for its less than aesthetic looks, but it is beloved by pilots because of its rugged structure and lethal armament. Its principal weapon is the General Electric GAU-8/A Avenger 30-mm seven-barrel cannon, firing depleted uranium rounds that have tremendous impact. It was about to be retired, but it did so well in the Gulf War that it was given a new lease on life. The Warthog entered operational service on June 10, 1977.

MiG-29 FULCRUM The MiG-29, an advanced twin-jet fighter with a Mach 2.35 top speed at altitude, made its first flight on October 6, 1977. It entered widespread service in the Soviet Union and with its Warsaw Pact allies and was also exported to many other countries. In a unique twist of fate, former East German MiG-29s are now operated by a united Germany and are in demand by many air forces for "aggressor" training exercises.

SEPARATION! THE SPACE SHUTTLE DEPARTS THE 747 A tremendous amount of engineering was necessary to make the 747 and the Space Shuttle compatible in flight and able to separate without difficulty. Stability required 200 square feet of additional vertical surface to be added to the 747's horizontal surfaces. This flight took place on October 12, 1977. The *Enterprise* became a static test vehicle at the conclusion of the gliding flights.

FLIGHT TIMELINE

January 13, 1977 AV-8 Harriers make the first bow-on, downwind landings in carrier history on the USS *Franklin D. Roosevelt*, illustrating the operation flexibility of VSTOL-type aircraft.

January 21, 1977 Tie-down tests begin on the Bell XV-15 tilt-rotor; it will lead to the V-22 Osprey.

January 31, 1977 The first Vought TA-7C two-seat version of the Corsair is delivered to the Navy.

January 31, 1977 The Cessna Citation II makes its first flight.

February 17, 1977 Beech-craft produces the 10,000th Bonanza.

February 18, 1977 The Space Shuttle *Enterprise* flies aboard the Shuttle Carrier Aircraft.

March 16, 1977 The Army accepts the first production Bell AH-1S Cobra with TOW capability; it will be important in the Gulf War.

March 24, 1977 The first Boeing E-3A AWACs are delivered to the USAF.

March 24, 1977 The stretched Lockheed C-141B Starlifter debuts.

March 27, 1977 In the worst air disaster to date, Pan Am and KLM Boeing 747s collide on the runway at Tenerife in the Canary Islands; 575 people are killed.

April 5, 1977 The Navy takes delivery of the first Beech T-44A trainer.

AIRLINE DEREGULATION ACT President Jimmy Carter signed the Airline Deregulation Act on October 24, 1978, allowing immediate fare reductions of up to 70 percent without Civil Aeronautic Board (CAB) approval. The CAB was to be entirely phased out by 1983. By the end of 1978, 248 new airline routes had been awarded to applicants. Fares dropped and travel boomed but many airlines encountered financial difficulty and went out of business.

VLADIMIR REMEK On March 2, 1978, the first Czechoslovakian astronaut, Vladimir Remek joined the crew of *Soyuz 28*. The pilot-cosmonaut was a highly decorated engineer, and his flight was a Soviet attempt to symbolize the close political ties of the two countries. The reality was different: The Czechs wanted their freedom, which would come 11 years later.

BRITISH AEROSPACE FORMED WITH HAWKER SIDDELEY AS COMPONENT The consolidation of the American aerospace industry in recent years was foreshadowed by similar mergers in Great Britain. In 1977, the British Aircraft Corporation, Hawker Siddeley Aviation, Hawker Siddeley Dynamics, and Scottish Aviation all came together to form British Aerospace. One of Hawker Siddeley's great contributions to the new mix was its unique Harrier VTOL/STOL fighter.

DASSAULT MIRAGE 2000 Before World War II, the Bloch firm manufactured fighters for France. Marcel Bloch's resistance fighter code name was d'Assault, and after the war, he used that name to set up Avions Marcel Dassault. When the French government asked for a fighter similar to the General Dynamics F-16, Dassault responded with the Mach 2.2 Mirage 2000, a single-seat, delta-wing, fly-by-wire fighter with a 56,000-foot altitude ceiling. Its first flight was on March 10, 1978.

EASTERN AIRLINES A300S Former Astronaut Frank Borman, then head of Eastern Airlines, broke with tradition when he opted for 25 Airbus A300s on April 6, 1978, opening up the U.S. market to Airbus and dealing American airliner builders a body blow. He did it because Eastern was in severe financial trouble, and Airbus offered a good airplane at an unbeatable price.

FLIGHT TIMELINE

April 8, 1977 The first E-2C Automatic Radar Processing System aircraft is delivered to the Navy.

May 3, 1977 The Bell XV-15 tilt-rotor makes its first hovering flight.

June 10, 1977 The Fairchild A-10 Republic Warthog is introduced into operational service.

June 16, 1977 Rocket pioneer Wernher von Braun dies.

June 22, 1977 OV-10 Broncos are tested with Forward Looking Infra-Red (FLIR) Sensor, which gives the Bronco additional night capability.

June 30, 1977 President Jimmy Carter announces the cancellation of the B-1A bomber. A principal reason behind this decision—the new stealth technology to come—is kept secret.

August 12, 1977 The Space Shuttle *Enterprise* makes its first free-flight (glide) from the 747 Shuttle Carrier Aircraft.

August 20, 1977 *Voyager 2* is launched on a multiplanet flyby mission.

August 23, 1977 The *Gossamer Condor*, designed by Dr. Paul MacCready, wins the Kremer Prize for a human-powered flight around a course slightly longer than a mile.

August 26, 1977 The Rockwell International XFV-12 VSTOL fighter debuts; it will be short-lived.

DOUBLE EAGLE II Former astronaut Senator Harrison "Jack" Schmitt (left) escorts balloonist Maxie Anderson through the crowds celebrating the August 12–17, 1978, balloon-duration record of 137 hours and 5 minutes established when the *Double Eagle II* made the first crossing of the Atlantic by balloon. Anderson was accompanied by Ben Abruzzo and Larry Newman.

DORNIER TURBO SKYSERVANT There was no end to the adaptability of the basic Dornier Do 28 design; the stub pylons on which engines were mounted made a change of powerplants easy. The TurboSky version used two Pratt & Whitney PT6A turboprops, giving it amazing STOL performance.

DAVID COOK On May 9, 1978, David Cook made the first hang-glider crossing of the English Channel in his Revell VJ-23 powered glider. The 37-year-old Cook reversed Louis Blériot's direction flying from the beach near Walmer Castle at Deal and touching down at Calais, France, about an hour later. The VJ-23 was powered by a nine-horsepower engine.

August 31, 1977 Alexander Fedotov flies a Mikoyan Ye-266M to set a world altitude record for air-breathing engined aircraft of 123,524 feet.

September 5, 1977 *Voyager 1* is launched on a multi-planet flyby mission.

December 10, 1977–March 16, 1978 Soviets in *Soyuz 26* dock with *Salyut 6* space station, breaking U.S. records for time in space with a 96-day, 10-hour stay.

December 13, 1977 Eastern Airlines begins preliminary Airbus service.

January 10–16, 1978 Soviets achieve the first docking of three spacecraft at once with *Soyuz 26*, *Soyuz 27*, and *Salyut 6*.

January 20–February 8, 1978 The Soviet space station *Salyut 6* is resupplied by the uncrewed vehicle *Progress*.

January 31, 1978 The RAF buys 30 Boeing Vertol CH-47 Chinooks.

February 2, 1978 A Tomahawk missile is launched from the USS *Barb*, a submarine.

March 10, 1978 The Dassault Mirage 2000 fighter makes its first flight.

April 6, 1978 Eastern Airlines orders 25 Airbus A300s.

April 10, 1978 The Sikorsky S-72 compound helicopter flies.

AEROSPACE SEA HARRIER The modification of the standard Royal Air Force Harrier for Royal Navy use as the "Sea Harrier" proved to be absolutely vital to the British victory in the Falklands War of 1982, where 28 Sea Harriers, operating off HMS *Hermes* and HMS *Invincible* were able to defeat the Argentine air force in combat, shooting down 22 aircraft and a helicopter with no loss to themselves. The Sea Harrier resembles its successor, the McDonnell Douglas AV-8B. The Sea Harrier made its first flight on August 20, 1978.

PROFESSOR WILLY MESSERSCHMITT Willy Messerschmitt, a German designer, died on September 15, 1978, at the age of 80. He started his designing career with a glider, then branched out into sports planes and transports before designing the Messerschmitt Bf 109 fighter, the primary German fighter of World War II. After the war, Messerschmitt designed aircraft for Spain and Egypt, then returned to resume his business in Germany.

McDonnell Douglas AV-8B The first flight of the McDonnell Douglas YAV-8B Advanced Harrier II was made on November 9, 1978, with test pilot C. A. Plummer at the controls. The AV-8B has a top speed of 661 miles per hour and fills the Marine Corps need for a fighter that can land and rearm close to the front lines. Great Britain, Spain, and Italy have also opted for the Advanced Harrier.

McDonnell Douglas F/A-18 Hornet The McDonnell Douglas F/A-18 Hornet was designed to replace both the F-4 Phantom and the A-7 Corsair. Its first flight took place on November 18, 1978. Test pilot Jack Krings flew from St. Louis, Missouri, to Springfield, Illinois, reaching 300 knots and 24,000 feet. The Mach 1.8 Hornet has seen a great deal of combat, including the Persian Gulf War where it engaged in air-to-air combat, then conducted close-air support attacks on one mission.

McDonnell Douglas KC-10 Extender Refueling F-15 Fighter Russ Schleeh, a top-notch test pilot, powerboat driver, and motorcyclist was also a persistent salesperson, and he labored long and hard to sell the USAF a tanker version of the Douglas DC-10. He succeeded at last on November 20, 1978, with an order for 60, and they have been an invaluable addition to the KC-135 fleet. The Extender, with a maximum speed of 560 miles per hour, also has a cargo capability. It has performed well in the Middle Eastern crises.

BOEING E-3A SENTRY (AWACS) The Boeing E-3A Airborne Warning and Control System grew from two original missions (warning of air or missile attack and mobile air control center) to many times that number as its tremendous utility was demonstrated. A basic Boeing 707-320B commercial airliner was modified with the rotating 30-foot dome and equipped with an ever-changing array of electronic equipment. Since its 1972 operational debut, the indispensable Sentry has been a true force multiplier. The AWACS entered duty with the USAF on January 1, 1979.

McDONNELL DOUGLAS A-4 SKYHAWK PRODUCTION ENDS Douglas's ace designer, Ed Heinemann, used the phrase "simplicate and add lightness" to describe his design philosophy. On one of his great landmark designs, he led his team to create the tiny, swift Douglas A-4 Skyhawk. The A-4 remained in production for 26 years, ending only after a phenomenal (for peacetime) 2,960 aircraft were delivered. The last A-4 was delivered to the Navy on February 27, 1979.

FLIGHT TIMELINE

May 9, 1978 David Cook pilots the first hang glider, a Revell VJ-23, across the English Channel, following Louis Blériot's route.

May 20, 1978 McDonnell Douglas delivers the 5,000th F-4 Phantom II, the most important western fighter of the Cold War.

June 6, 1978 Tu-144 SST service is suspended.

June 15–November 2, 1978 The Soviets set a record for space duration: 139 days, 14 hours in *Salyut 6*.

July 14, 1978 Boeing announces it will begin production of the model 767.

August 8, 1978 *Pioneer 13* is launched by NASA; on December 9, 1978, it will drop five probes into the Venusian atmosphere.

August 12–17, 1978 Maxie Anderson, Ben Abruzzo, and Larry Newman set a balloon duration record of 137 hours, 5 minutes in the *Double Eagle II*. It is the first transatlantic crossing of a gas balloon.

August 20, 1978 The BAE's Sea Harrier makes its first flight.

September 15, 1978 Professor Willy Messerschmitt dies at age 80.

October 24, 1978 President Jimmy Carter signs the Airline Deregulation Act.

November 8, 1978 The Canadair CL-600 "widebodied" business jet debuts.

DASSAULT MIRAGE G8 The highly inventive, two-seat, swing-wing Dassault Mirage G8 made its first flight on May 8, 1971, and was intended as an experimental variable geometry aircraft. With its twin Atar turbojet engines, it had a top speed of Mach 2+. Although not chosen for production, the Mirage G8 was influential in later Dassault designs.

CRASH OF DC-10 AT O'HARE The salability of the McDonnell Douglas DC-10 was virtually ended when the aircraft was grounded after the May 25, 1979, crash at Chicago's O'Hare airport. The American Airlines DC-10 crashed during takeoff for a flight to Los Angeles, killing 272 people.

GOSSAMER ALBATROSS Brian Allen may look slender, but the professional bicyclist was immensely strong and had the endurance necessary to pedal the *Gossamer Albatross* from Folkestone, England, across the English Channel to France on June 12, 1979. The aircraft was designed by a team led by Dr. Paul MacCready. The fragile *Gossamer Albatross* had a wingspan of 96 feet and weighed only 55 pounds.

U.S. SKYLAB REENTRY REMAINS The United States placed a true space station, *Skylab,* into orbit in May 1973. *Skylab* housed three 3-person crews, the last remaining aboard for 84 days, which was a record for continuous residency in space. *Skylab* fell to Earth in July 1979, showering debris over uninhabited parts of Australia and the Indian Ocean. This recovered portion was brought home to the United States on July 25, 1979.

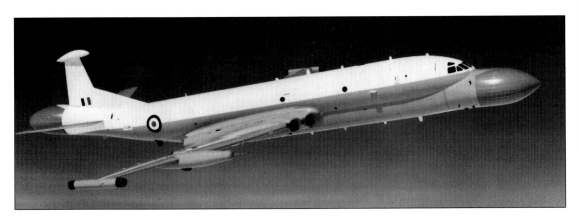

BRITISH AEROSPACE NIMROD AEW.3 As aircraft became larger and faster, they also became more expensive and necessarily more long-lived. Aircraft came to be regarded as "platforms" into which (and in some cases onto which) equipment could be placed for missions far different from those originally intended. Thus the beautifully slim lines of the original de Havilland Comet were "desecrated" with the bulging dual-frequency antenna required by the radar for early warning work.

FLIGHT TIMELINE

November 9, 1978 The McDonnell Douglas AV-8B Advanced Harrier II makes its first flight.

November 18, 1978 The McDonnell Douglas F/A-18 Hornet debuts.

November 20, 1978 After ten years of trying, McDonnell Douglas gets the go-ahead for the KC-10 tanker version of the DC-10.

December 19, 1978 The *Solar One,* the first solar-powered aircraft, flies.

January 1, 1979 AWACS goes to duty with the USAF.

January 6, 1979 The USAF accepts the first F-16A.

January 29, 1979 The Northrop RF-5E makes its first flight.

February 25–August 19, 1979 The Soviets set another space endurance record: *Soyuz 32* docks with *Salyut 6,* and cosmonauts spend 175 days, 6 minutes in space.

February 27, 1979 McDonnell Douglas delivers the last A-4 Skyhawk to the Navy.

March 5, 1979 *Voyager 1* gathers vast information during a flyby of Jupiter.

March 9, 1979 The Dassault-Breguet Super Mirage 4000 makes its first flight.

March 11, 1979 The U.S. *NavStar* Global Positioning System (GPS) satellite is used for the first time on a transatlantic flight.

SIKORSKY SH-60B SEAHAWK
The Sikorsky Model S-70 was manufactured in almost 40 variations and in great quantity, with almost 2,000 built. The variants include the UH-60A Blackhawk and SH-60B Seahawk, which won a Navy competition for Light Airborne Multi-Purpose System (LAMPS). The first Seahawk prototype flew on December 12, 1979. The aircraft has both a maritime surveillance and an antisubmarine capability.

EDGLEY OPTICA With its unique helicopterlike cockpit bubble and ducted fan configuration, the Edgley Optica gained worldwide attention at the time of its first flight on December 14, 1979. Despite a promising performance, the plane seemed to be cursed, suffering crashes, business failures, arson, and other mishaps, so that only a handful were ever produced. Able to fly as slow as 57 miles per hour, it was an ideal observation aircraft.

NASA AD-1 SWING-WING
Designed by one of the United States' finest scientist/engineers, Dr. Robert T. Jones, the NASA AD-1 offered a unique configuration for supersonic flight, an oblique wing that was fixed at conventional position for takeoff but swung to a fore-and-aft position for high-speed flight. In 1944, Dr. Jones had put forward his ideas about the advantages of the swept wing to NACA but was told his concepts were erroneous. The aircraft made its first flight on December 21, 1979.

SIR BARNES WALLIS One of the great British aircraft designers, Sir Barnes Wallis died at age 90 on October 30, 1979. He was the principal designer of the most successful British dirigible, the R-100, and created the geodetic construction that was used in the Vickers Wellington bomber. He was perhaps most famous for designing the spinning, bouncing "Dam Buster" bomb used to destroy German dams during World War II.

FLIGHT TIMELINE

March 22, 1979 The Lockheed CP-140 Aurora makes its first flight for the Canadian Armed Forces.

March 23, 1979 Boeing orders the 757 into production.

March 26, 1979 An AV-8B tests a new ski-ramp technique developed by the British; it cuts takeoff distance from 930 to 230 feet.

April 15, 1979 The Dassault Mirage 50 multimission fighter debuts.

April 17, 1979 The world's second solar-powered aircraft, the *Solar Riser*, flies.

April 20, 1979 The last Concorde makes its first flight.

April 30, 1979 The first Lockheed L-1011 is delivered to British Airways.

May 11, 1979 The Boeing Vertol YCH-47D makes its first flight.

May 25, 1979 A DC-10 loses its engine and pylon on takeoff at Chicago killing 272 people.

June 1, 1979 The United States agrees to train Egyptian pilots to fly 35 Phantom F-4Es supplied to them.

June 5, 1979 The first production of the Panavia Tornado is rolled out. It will distinguish itself in the Gulf War.

June 6, 1979 All DC-10s are grounded due to the accident in Chicago on May 25.

IRAN HOSTAGE RESCUE FIASCO One of the greatest fiascos in U.S. military history was the April 24, 1980, Operation Eagle Claw, the disastrous attempt to rescue embassy hostages being held in Iran. The operation fell apart, and eight U.S. personnel were killed in a terrible mishap caused by equipment failures in the Iranian desert. The rescue mission was quickly aborted.

ILYUSHIN IL-86 On September 20, 1980, an Ilyushin Il-86 wide-body transport captured the speed for a 2,000-kilometer closed circuit at 526 knots. The aircraft made its first flight on December 22, 1976, and 100 were ordered. Although the Il-86 is fast, it is not economical, because it is burdened by engines that were developed more for military use than commercial use.

JAPANESE PHANTOM Japan entered the aviation business after World War I, building the designs of other countries before creating its own industry. It did the same thing after World War II with the McDonnell F-4EJ Phantom II, shown here on its January 14, 1971, first flight. A total of 139 were built, 126 in Japan by Mitsubishi and Kawasaki for the Japanese Air Self Defense Force, with the last deliveries in 1980 and 1981.

BEECHCRAFT C99 Beechcraft is noted for the beauty and reliability of its aircraft, qualities found in the Commuter C99, first flown on June 20, 1980. A progressive development of the Queen Air-based Model 99, the C99 featured the dependable Pratt & Whitney PT6A turboprops and could carry up to 15 passengers at 287 miles per hour.

INDIAN SATELLITE More and more nations require their own independent access to space, and this is India's first Satellite Launching Vehicle and its payload, the Rohini Satellite (RS-1). The Indian Space Research Organization planned and funded the test effort, which took place on July 18, 1980.

June 12, 1979 Dr. Paul MacCready's *Gossamer Albatross* makes the first human-powered flight across the English Channel.

June 20, 1979 Lieutenant Dona Spruill, flying a C-1A trader onto *Independence*, becomes the first woman qualified in fixed-wing aircraft on carrier landings.

July 9, 1979 *Voyager 2* achieves flyby of Jupiter.

July 11, 1979 The American Space Station *Skylab* reenters the atmosphere and burns up.

July 13, 1979 The FAA lifts the grounding of DC-10s.

July 24, 1979 The Bell XV-15 makes a successful transition from a helicopter to a fixed-wing mode of flight.

August 30, 1979 The prototype Sikorsky SH-60B Seahawk is rolled out at Stratford, Connecticut.

September 1, 1979 *Pioneer 1* flies by Saturn and sends photographs to Earth. New outer rings are discovered.

September 15, 1979 The first Navy version of the Beech Super King Air, the UC-12B, arrives at Patuxent Naval Air Station for tests.

September 28, 1979 The last RA-5C Vigilante squadron (RVAH-7) is disbanded.

October 30, 1979 The F/A-18 begins carrier qualification trials.

October 30, 1979 Aircraft designer Sir Barnes Wallis dies at the age of 90.

JANICE BROWN This is the MacCready *Gossamer Penguin*, piloted by Janice Brown, the world's first totally solar-powered aircraft to be piloted by a person. The flight took place on a dry lake bed in the Mojave Desert on August 7, 1980. The pilot flew the plane at a speed with which bicycles could keep pace and reached an altitude of 12 feet. The science had application in MacCready's later *Helios*, a huge aircraft that acts as a satellite.

FOKKER F27 The Fokker F27 was one of the most successful turboprop airliners of its time, and this 1980 version marks its 25th anniversary, with 600 already built. In configuration not unlike the trimotor F.XX of 1933, the F27 was aptly named the Friendship. Another 186 would be built before production ended. The F27 served in widely varying roles, including airliner, cargo-carrying, and maritime reconnaissance.

DASSAULT-BREGUET/DORNIER ALPHA JET Too many cooks did not spoil the broth of the Dassault-Breguet/Dornier Alpha Jet, which flew first on October 26, 1973, to meet the requirements for a new training plane with close-air support capability. The design was one of many featuring international cooperation at the December 12, 1980, debut of this particular aircraft, an Alpha Jet with a supercritical wing. A production Alpha Jet had a top speed of 570 miles per hour.

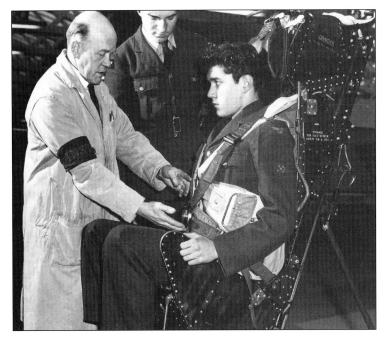

SIR JAMES MARTIN Sir James Martin designed some handsome aircraft, including the Martin-Baker MB-5, which many think would have been the best piston-engine fighter of World War II if it had been produced. But after his death on January 5, 1981, Martin would probably prefer to be remembered for his Martin-Baker ejector seats, which have saved so many thousands of lives. Here RAF Cadets receive ejector seat training at the RAF Apprentice School.

DONALD DOUGLAS The early years of aviation were sparked by the genius of young engineers. Sadly, the later years are marked by the death of the members of that hardy band of engineering entrepreneurs. Donald Douglas went from his first aircraft, the Cloudster, to become the major producer of military and commercial aircraft. Unfortunately, when age forced his retirement, the Douglas company went into an irreversible decline. Douglas died on February 1, 1981, at age 88.

FLIGHT TIMELINE

November 4, 1979 Iranians seize hostages at the American Embassy in Teheran.

November 16, 1979 The Lockheed L-1011-500 Tristar debuts.

November 20, 1979 The RA-5C Vigilante makes its last flight.

December 21, 1979 NASA's AD-1 swing-wing research aircraft makes its first flight.

March 28, 1980 Learjet, produces its 1,000th aircraft.

April 9–October 11, 1980 The *Soyuz 35* crew sets a new space record at *Salyut 6*: 184 days, 20 hours, and 12 minutes.

April 24–25, 1980 Eight RH-53D Sea Stallion helicopters from the USS *Nimitz* attempt to rescue U.S. hostages, but efforts are aborted. One of the helicopters later collides with a C-130.

May 18, 1980 The People's Republic of China launches a prototype ICBM.

June 4, 1980 A Japanese F-15 Eagle makes its first flight in St. Louis. Most will be manufactured in Japan.

June 20, 1980 The Beech C99 commuter airliner debuts.

July 12, 1980 The McDonnell Douglas KC-10 Extender tanker makes its first flight.

July 18, 1980 India becomes the seventh nation to launch an artificial satellite, called the *Rohini 1*.

BELL MODEL 222 After producing fighters and research planes, Bell turned to helicopters after World War II and became a leading producer. On January 18, 1981, Bell delivered its 25,000th helicopter, a Model 222. The Model 222 first flew on August 13, 1976, and was designed from the start as a twin-jet engine commercial helicopter suitable for executive travel at 165 miles per hour cruise speed or for rough-work as an offshore oil-rig service aircraft.

JOHN K. "JACK" NORTHROP
On February 18, 1981, John K. "Jack" Northrop died at the age of 86. Northrop is remembered for his Lockheed Vega and his flying wings. Shortly before his death, the Northrop company briefed him on the super-secret Northrop B-2 stealth bomber. It too is a flying wing, validating Jack's theories, and has a 172-foot wingspan—the same as his XB-35.

DORNIER 228-100 The most unusual view of the Dornier Do 228 is from directly above or below, so that its uniquely Dornier-shaped "TNT" wing can be seen. The Do 228-100 made its first flight on March 28, 1981, and about 35 production aircraft were built, despite the loss of the prototype in a crash. The Do 228-200, a larger version, carried 19 passengers and was built in greater quantities. Garrett turboprops of 776-shaft horsepower enable a cruise of 270 miles per hour.

SPACE SHUTTLE COLUMBIA ON TEST MISSION April 12, 1981, saw the first flight of the powered Space Shuttle. Astronauts Robert Crippen (left) and John Young were at the controls, with Young serving as commander. On the first orbital flight by a winged spacecraft, the team completed 36 orbits. Both men had powerful personalities, and there are legions of stories on how they operated, but both were personable and created a fine public image that was captured in IMAX films.

ISRAELI F-16S BOMB IRAQ NUCLEAR REACTOR In what was perhaps one of the most providential air raids in history, eight Israeli General Dynamic F-16 Fighting Falcons bombed the Iraqi nuclear reactor at Osirak on June 7, 1981, with McDonnell Douglas F-15 Eagles providing cover. Worldwide reaction to this raid was negative. It was widely reported that one of the pilots in the raid was Ilan Ramon, who would later die in the break up of the Space Shuttle *Columbia*.

LOCKHEED F-117A NIGHTHAWK Almost as amazing as the stealth quality of the Lockheed F-117A Nighthawk was the perfect security that kept it secret from the world at large from its June 18, 1981, first flight until 1988. It was used with blinding success in the Gulf War. Top speed of the Nighthawk is just under Mach 1, but its greatest asset is its stealthy ability to be invisible to radar and infrared seeking detectors.

FLIGHT TIMELINE

July 21, 1980 The F-16 is formally named the Fighting Falcon in honor of the Air Force Academy.

August 7, 1980 The Mac-Cready *Gossamer Penguin* makes its first solar-powered flight.

August 9, 1980 Famous American pilot Jacqueline Cochran dies. She was the first woman to fly faster than the speed of sound.

September 25, 1980 The Cameron D-38, a hot-airship, makes its first flight.

November 12, 1980 *Voyager 1* flies within 77,000 miles of Saturn.

November 18–21, 1980 Judith Chisholm establishes a record for women between England and Australia, with a flight of 3 days, 13 hours in a Cessna Turbo Centurion.

November 20, 1980 The MacCready *Solar Challenger* makes its first flight on solar power alone.

December 3, 1980 Judith Chisholm sets a women's solo round-the-world record: 15 days, 22 minutes.

December 5, 1980 The *Solar Challenger*, piloted by Janice Brown, flies for 1 hour, 32 minutes, under solar power.

December 9, 1980 Boeing rolls out its 500th 747.

December 12, 1980 The Alpha Jet, produced by a consortium of Dassualt-Breguet/Dornier, makes its first flight.

GRUMMAN/GENERAL DYNAMICS EF-111 RAVEN The sensational Grumman/General Dynamics EF-111 Raven made its first flight on June 26, 1981, bringing to the USAF an immensely powerful electronic countermeasures aircraft. This 366th Tactical Fighter Wing Raven is approaching a tanker for refueling. The swing-wing fighter, which had a top speed of 1,380 miles per hour, provided invaluable service during the Gulf War. The Ravens were retired in the 1990s because they were too expensive to operate.

LOCKHEED TR-1A On August 1, 1981, the first model of the new Lockheed TR-1A made its debut flight. Essentially a modernized U-2, the TR-1A was ordered back into production 12 years after the U-2 line had been shut down. The aircraft had greatly improved systems and much more sophisticated sensors. In 1992, all U-2s and tactical TR-1As were given the designation U-2R. The first U-2 had been given a useful life expectancy of about two years.

VOYAGER 2 PHOTOS OF SATURN'S RINGS

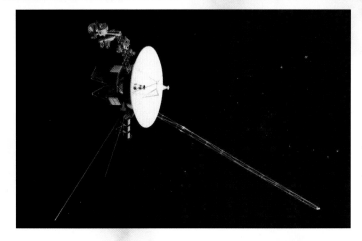

The *Voyager 1* and *Voyager 2* satellites were perhaps the greatest bargains in space history. This is an August 17, 1981, photo of Saturn's rings, taken by *Voyager 2*.

Voyager 1 (image at left) was launched September 5, 1977, and flew past Jupiter on March 5, 1979, and by Saturn on November 12, 1980. *Voyager 2* was launched August 20, 1977 (before *Voyager 1*), and flew by Jupiter on July 9, 1979; by Saturn on August 25, 1981; by Uranus on January 25, 1986; and by Neptune on August 25, 1989.

Voyager 2 took advantage of a rare once-every-189-years alignment to slingshot its way from outer planet to outer planet. Between the two probes, the world's knowledge of the four giant planets, their satellites, and their rings has become immense. *Voyager 1* and *Voyager 2* discovered that Jupiter has complicated atmospheric dynamics, lightning, and auroras. Three new satellites were discovered. Two of the major surprises were that Jupiter has rings and that Io (one of Jupiter's moons) has active sulfurous volcanoes, with major effects on the Jovian magnetosphere. If no unforeseen failures occur, the United States will be able to maintain communications with both spacecraft until at least the year 2030.

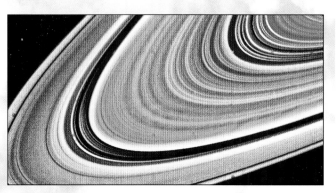

4,000TH BOEING 727 AIRLINER DELIVERED Boeing had been ousted from the commercial airline business by the Douglas DC-3 and had made only partial comebacks with its piston-engine 307 Stratoliner, 314 Clipper, and 377 Stratocruiser. It hit the jackpot with the jet age, however, and by 1981 had delivered its 4,000th airliner, a Boeing 727.

FLIGHT TIMELINE

January 5, 1981 Sir James Martin, designer of fighter prototypes and the Martin-Baker ejection seat, dies at age 87.

January 26, 1981 Pan Am retires the last of its 707s.

February 1, 1981 Donald Douglas dies at age 88.

February 18, 1981 John K. "Jack" Northrop dies at age 86.

April 3, 1981 Juan Trippe, founder of Pan Am, dies at age 81.

April 12–14, 1981 The Space Shuttle *Columbia* conducts its first orbital test flight.

June 1, 1981 The Short Brothers 360 makes its first flight.

June 5, 1981 Dick Rutan sets a straight-line distance for class record in a Rutan Long-Ez: 4,563.7 miles.

June 7, 1981 Israeli F-16s bomb the Osirak nuclear reactor near Baghdad.

June 18, 1981 The Lockheed F-117A Nighthawk stealth fighter makes its first flight.

June 26, 1981 The Grumman/General Dynamics EF-111A Raven makes its first flight.

July 7, 1981 The *Solar Challenger* crosses the English Channel.

August 1, 1981 The Lockheed TR-1A, a development of the U-2, makes its first flight.

DOUGLAS DC-9 While Boeing was moving ahead with an ever increasing number of airliners specialized to fit niche markets, the floundering Douglas company managed to field only one truly successful airliner after the DC-8, the workhorse Douglas DC-9. On September 7, 1981, McDonnell Douglas delivered its 1,000th DC-9, and the aircraft continues today in slightly modified form as the Boeing 717.

ED LINK On September 7, 1981, Ed Link, the father of the simulator, died at age 77. Link originated the "blue box synthetic trainer," which trained thousands of pilots over the years and gave birth to the aircraft simulator industry that is so vital to aviation now. Flying the Link Trainer was a lot like balancing a pool ball on a needle—but it taught pilots instrument procedures. Here Link is shown with Anne Morrow Lindbergh and Francis L. Kellogg (seated inside the Link Trainer), president of the Charles A. Lindberg Fund.

BOEING 767 Boeing was thrust into the forefront of the airliner industry by two factors, the decline of U.S. competition with the weak output from McDonnell Douglas and the increase of foreign competition from Airbus. It responded by creating a whole series of new aircraft, each of which could be carefully tailored to airline needs. The wide-body 767 was announced at the same time as the narrow-body 757, but the 767 flew first on September 26, 1981.

SPACE SHUTTLE COLUMBIA On November 12, 1981, Joe Engle and Richard Truly flew 36 orbits for the STS-2 mission in the *Columbia.* The Remote Manipulator System was tested for the first time. STS-2 was also the last time a flight was made with an "all-rookie" flight crew aboard. The first flight of the *Columbia,* shown here, took place on April 12–14, 1981.

DOUBLE EAGLE V On November 13, 1981, a balloon called the *Double Eagle V* landed after its flight across the Pacific from Japan to Covelo, California. From the left are Ron Clark, Larry Newman, Captain Ben Abruzzo, and Rocky Aoki. They are showing off the good luck charms they brought with them—which apparently worked.

BOEING 757 On February 19, 1982, the Boeing 757 took off on its first flight. The narrow-body airliner found wide acceptance. Intended as a replacement for the wildly popular 727, the 757 carried up to 224 people at a Mach .80 cruising speed.

August 3, 1981 More than 13,000 U.S. Air Traffic controllers illegally go on strike; President Ronald Reagan will later fire them.

August 4, 1981 Boeing rolls out the first model 767.

August 25, 1981 *Voyager 2* passes within 63,000 miles of Saturn.

August 26, 1981 The first Japanese-assembled F-15J Eagle debuts.

September 7, 1981 Ed Link, inventor of the original pilot simulator trainer, dies at 77.

September 7, 1981 McDonnell Douglas delivers the 1,000th DC-9 series airliner.

September 26, 1981 The Boeing 767 makes its first flight.

October 2, 1981 The Rockwell International B-1B will go into production; 100 aircraft are ordered.

October 9, 1981 *The Super Chicken III,* a helium-filled balloon, completes the first nonstop balloon flight across America, from California to Georgia, in 55 hours, 25 minutes.

November 12–14, 1981 The Space Shuttle *Columbia* makes its second orbital flight.

November 13, 1981 The *Double Eagle V*—piloted by Ben Abruzzo, Larry Newman, Ron Clark, and Rocky Aoki—makes a transpacific balloon flight.

BRITISH VULCAN ATTACKS FALKLAND ISLANDS Argentina invaded their "Malvinas"—the Falkland Islands, on April 2, 1982, expecting to force their return from Great Britain. Instead, Prime Minister Margaret Thatcher mobilized Britain's strength, sending Avro Vulcan bombers to bomb the critically important Port Stanley runway. The Vulcans had to be refueled several times by VC-10 tankers. The biggest threats of the Argentine air forces were the Douglas A-4 Skyhawk (like these) and the Dassault Super Entendards with Exocet missiles.

PRINCE ANDREW VISITS FALKLAND ISLANDS The Argentine government ordered an invasion of the Falkland Islands on April 2, 1982, launching a surprisingly bitter war that lasted until June 14, 1982, when the British managed to defeat Argentine forces. Prince Andrew (second from right) visited Port Stanley, the scene of some tough fighting, in July.

BRITISH AEROSPACE 146 Originally the Hawker Siddeley HS 146, this four-jet high-wing aircraft has had a long history and is still being revamped for the modern market. The first flight of the prototype was made on August 1, 1981, and performance was pleasing, with the wide body providing comfort for about 70 passengers cruising at 435 miles per hour. Larger variants followed, and the aircraft now has a new lease on life as the Avro RJ (regional jet) 146 aircraft.

NORTHROP F-20 TIGERSHARK Famous test pilot Paul Metz is shown in the cockpit of the Northrop F-20 Tigershark, which first flew on August 30, 1982. A private venture, Northrop hoped that the F-20 would repeat the success of its F-5 and become the preferred lightweight fighter in foreign nations. Unfortunately, the availability of the proven Lockheed F-16 and some untimely F-20 crashes prevented this.

FLIGHT TIMELINE

January 10, 1982 A Gulfstream III, *Spirit of America*, completes a round-the-world flight in 43 hours, 39 minutes, for a new record.

January 27, 1982 The 1,000th Cessna business jet is delivered.

February 19, 1982 The Boeing 757 makes its first flight from the plant at Renton, Washington.

March 1, 1982 A descent module from the *Venera 13* spacecraft lands on Venus; it transmits data for 127 minutes, taking photos and analyzing soil samples.

March 22–30, 1982 The Space Shuttle *Columbia*, with Jack Lousma and Gordon Fullerton as pilots, makes its third flight.

April 2, 1982 Argentina invades the Falkland Islands to force their return from Great Britain.

April 3, 1982 The Airbus 310 debuts.

April 19, 1982 The Soviets launch the *Salyut 7* space station into orbit.

April 25, 1982 British helicopters go into action in the Falkland Islands to repel the Argentine invaders.

May 1, 1982 An Avro Vulcan, designed as a nuclear bomber, bombs Port Stanley airfield in the Falklands.

May 1, 1982 The British score their first victory with a Sea Harrier when it shoots down an Argentine Mirage IIIEA with a Sidewinder.

THE SPIRIT OF TEXAS On September 30, 1982, H. Ross Perot, Jr. (left), and Jay Coburn completed the first circumnavigation of the globe by helicopter. Flying a modified Bell 206L Longranger, *The Spirit of Texas,* the duo averaged 117 miles per hour during their 246.5 hours of flight time. The trip started and ended in Fort Worth, Texas, but covered 26 nations and approximately 26,000 miles.

SALLY RIDE Sally Ride became the first American woman in space when she launched in the Space Shuttle *Challenger* on June 18, 1983, for a 97-orbit flight in which the first Shuttle rendezvous was conducted. Robert Crippen was the captain on the flight.

AVRO VULCAN The British and the general flying public formed a strong attachment to the beautiful Avro Vulcan bomber, and when age dictated their retirement from service in 1984, there were strong protests. At least one organization attempted to keep a Vulcan flying, but as might be expected, the cost and the risk were too great. Designed as a high-altitude nuclear bomber, it wound up its days as a maritime reconnaissance and low-level bomber.

DASSAULT MIRAGE 2000 The fly-by-wire Dassault Mirage 2000 was an attempt to get maximum performance from a lightweight aircraft powered by a 21,835-pound thrust SNCEMA turbofan. This photo shows the classic Dassault delta-wing configuration, which provides great maneuverability even at relatively low speeds.

DE HAVILLAND DHC-8 De Havilland of Canada followed up its successful DHC-7 Dash 7 with a smaller version, the Dash 8, and met with even more success after the first flight of the prototype on June 20, 1983. A smaller, twin-engine aircraft of 36 seats, the DHC-8 cruises at 308 miles per hour. Boeing has since acquired the company, which had almost 400 of the aircraft on order.

FLIGHT TIMELINE

May 4, 1982 The British destroyer HMS *Sheffield* is sunk by an Exocet missile launched by an Argentine Super Etendard fighter.

May 13, 1982 Braniff International ceases operations, becoming the first major casualty of deregulation.

May 13–December 10, 1982 A two-person Soviet crew joins *Salyut 7*. They stay for 211 days, 8 hours, and 5 minutes.

May 17, 1982 Soviets make the first launch of a satellite from a space station.

May 20, 1982 The U.S. army accepts the first Boeing-Vertol CH-47D Chinook helicopter.

May 25, 1982 Argentine Skyhawks sink the British destroyer HMS *Coventry*.

June 3, 1982 Soviets test *Cosmos 1374*, a winged spacecraft that is the forerunner of the Soviet shuttle.

June 14, 1982 The war in the Falklands ends with Argentine surrender.

June 27–July 4, 1982 The Space Shuttle *Columbia* makes a fourth test flight.

June 30, 1982 The Space Shuttle *Challenger* is rolled out at Palmdale, from the Rockwell factory.

July 29, 1982 The Soviet Union sends *Salyut 6* back into the atmosphere, burning it up.

August 1, 1982 The British Aerospace Model 146 Series 200 makes its first flight.

1,000TH GENERAL DYNAMICS F-16 PRODUCED By July 8, 1983, the General Dynamics Corporation had exceeded its wildest dreams with the production of the 1,000th F-16 Fighting Falcon. The aircraft had found acceptance all over the world, and Dan Tellep, Chairman and CEO of Lockheed, pronounced it "a good franchise" when Lockheed acquired the fighter division of General Dynamics in 1993. It was a typical Tellep understatement, for sales of the (now) Lockheed Martin F-16 surpassed 4,250 by September 2000.

LOCKHEED L-1011 TRISTAR The Lockheed L-1011 TriStar was a far more sophisticated aircraft than its rival trijet wide-body, the Douglas DC-10. Pilots and passengers loved it from its first flight on November 16, 1970, but it faced a market too small for two competitors. Some 250 TriStars were sold at such a tremendous loss to Lockheed that it came close to bankruptcy. The last of the L-1011s was rolled out on August 19, 1983.

FIRST NIGHT SPACE SHUTTLE LAUNCH No one who has ever witnessed a night Space Shuttle launch will ever forget it as a spectacle of light and power. If you are fortunate enough to be up close, you get not only the light but the incredible vibrations that literally shake the earth. This is *Challenger* on August 30, 1983, on the first night launch; after 97 orbits, it made the first night Space Shuttle landing. Richard Truly was the Commander.

FLIGHT TIMELINE

August 11, 1982 The first McDonnell Douglas KC-10 Extender is delivered to the USAF.

August 19–27, 1982 Soviets launch *Soyuz T-7* to go to *Salyut 7* space station; Svetlana Savitskaya, the second woman in space, is on board.

August 30, 1982 The Northrop F-20 Tigershark makes its first flight.

September 3, 1982 The Beech Commuter aircraft, Model 1900, makes its first flight.

September 9, 1982 The Conestoga, the first U.S. private-venture space rocket, is launched by Space Services Inc. It does not make it to orbit, and the venture eventually fails.

September 30, 1982 H. Ross Perot, Jr., and Jay Coburn complete the first round-the-world flight by a helicopter.

October 15, 1982 Northrop delivers the 1,000th of its F-5 fighter series.

November 11–16, 1982 The Space Shuttle *Columbia* makes its first operational flight.

December 23, 1982 The Short Sherpa makes its first flight.

January 25, 1983 The IRAS (Infrared Astronomical Satellite) is launched by NASA.

January 25, 1983 The Saab-Fairchild 340 twin turbo-prop makes its first flight.

KOREAN AIRLINES FLIGHT 007 SHOT DOWN BY SOVIET FIGHTER Korean Airlines Flight 007, with its 269 passengers and crew, strayed off course over a Soviet missile installation in the far Pacific and was shot out of the sky by Major Gennady Osipovich, in his Sukhoi Su-15 fighter on September 1, 1983. All 269 people on board the airliner were killed.

AGUSTA MANGUSTA ANTI-TANK HELICOPTER The venerable Agusta firm entered the helicopter business by building Bell 47s under license. In the intervening years, it has developed its own line, and on September 15, 1983, the Agusta *Mangusta (Mongoose)* antitank helicopter flew for the first time. It was ordered first by the Italian air force and has been used in the wars in what was formerly Yugoslavia. With a top speed of nearly 200 miles per hour, the agile *Mangusta* is an effective weapon.

1,000TH BOEING 737 DELIVERED "Fat Albert" is not a particularly attractive nickname, but the wide-body Boeing 737 proved itself to be attractive enough to sell 1,000 aircraft by December 9, 1983. It has since added to its total, with sales of more than 4,000 by the end of 2002.

BEECH STARSHIP Determined to create a new line of executive aircraft, Beech turned to Burt Rutan for the design of the Beech Model 2000 Starship. Rutan's 85 percent scale version, produced by his Scaled Composites firm, was successful, and the first preproduction Starship flew on February 15, 1986. The performance of the full-size aircraft did not live up to expectations, however, and it was withdrawn from production.

FLIGHT TIMELINE

February 3, 1983 A nuclear-attack version of the Dassault Mirage 2000N makes its first flight.

March 23, 1983 President Ronald Reagan announces the Star Wars antimissile system.

March 23, 1983 The prototype Rockwell International B-1A resumes testing in preparation for the B-1B program.

April 4–9, 1983 The Space Shuttle *Challenger* is launched for the first time.

April 25, 1983 The Dornier Do 24TT amphibian makes it first flight.

June 18, 1983 Sally Ride becomes the first American woman in space, aboard the Space Shuttle *Challenger.*

June 20, 1983 The de Havilland DHC-8 Dash 8 transport debuts.

July 8, 1983 General Dynamics delivers the 1,000th F-16 fighter.

July 22, 1983 The world's first solo round-the-world helicopter flight is completed by Dick Smith.

August 30–September 6, 1983 Space Shuttle *Challenger* makes its third operational mission.

November 28–December 8, 1983 Space Shuttle *Columbia* is launched with the European Spacelab on board.

December 9, 1983 The 1,000th Boeing 737 is rolled out.

CHAPTER NINE

1984 to 1993:

A Time of Turbulence and Change

As the eighth decade of the twentieth century began, the world's political situation seemed to have stabilized. The Cold War contenders, the United States and the Soviet Union, though still armed to the teeth with enough weaponry to destroy civilization, were somehow becoming, if not friendly, at least not as overtly hostile. There were new players on the world scene—Japan and a slowly unifying Europe and China—but, for the most part, the main concern was that no war break out between the United States and the U.S.S.R.

Lockheed F-117A Nighthawk

The Soviet Union was continuing its long and outstanding series of space flights. Cosmonauts were spending lengthy periods in space, shuttling back and forth on their *Soyuz* vehicles as if they were space commuters. New Soviet aircraft were introduced, including advanced versions of the superb Sukhoi Su 27 and MiG-29, and Soviet vertical-lift fighters operated off a Soviet aircraft carrier. Then on December 25, 1991, the Soviet Union was split apart, dissolving like a cube of sugar in hot coffee. The communist system that had led the world in space, whose military might was renowned, never learned how to feed, clothe, or house its people, and, ultimately, the people spoke. Fortunately for the world, the Soviet Union went out with a whimper—not with a nuclear bang.

While the collapse of the Soviet Union might have been the defining event of the decade, it was only one of the many dramatic and exciting situations that kept people everywhere glued to their television sets as good and bad news poured forth.

On the good side, women achieved an ever increasing prominence in aerospace occupations. Captain Lynn Ripplemeyer flew a 747 across the Atlantic for People's Express. Sheila Widnall became the first female Secretary of the Air Force. Svetlana Savitskaya made the first EVA by a woman from the *Salyut7/Soyuz T-12* for three hours. She was also the first woman to fly twice in space. The United States quickly countered when Sally Ride became the first American woman to go into space twice and Kathryn Sullivan made the first EVA by an American woman, both onboard the Space Shuttle *Challenger*. The ebullient Jeana Yeager set a world record with Dick Rutan in their epochal nonstop, unrefueled flight around the world in the *Voyager*. But such progress was not without its costs. In a moment that remains etched in memory, the Space Shuttle *Challenger* blew up on January 28, 1986. Among the crew were veteran astronaut Judith Resnik and teacher Christa McAuliffe. Then, in 1991, Major Mari T. Rossi crashed in a Chinook helicopter, becoming the first American woman to die in aerial combat.

The speed of aeronautical progress accelerated as the world of flight eagerly seized upon computers, integrating them into every phase of air and space operations, from design to actual flying of air and spacecraft. The tremendous growth in computer technology was force-fed by the demand of aerospace companies, who pushed the envelope of computer development at a rate that no one would have believed and that ultimately benefitted everyone, including personal computer users.

Lockheed X-35

The Airbus Industrie A320 was a Computer Aided Design (CAD) and a Computer Aided Manufacture (CAM), and this would be the way of the future. Gone were wooden mock-ups and the absolute need for a prototype; with CAD/CAM the first aircraft made could be a production version, if desired.

Computers were also invaluable for the proliferation of simulators so lifelike they could be used for the transition training of airline and military crews. Simulators grew in importance as the cost of flying time went up; they would soon substitute for the actual use of aircraft for familiarization flying and flight checks.

Terrorism became more and more prevalent, with airliners being blown up on the ground and in the air. The most appalling incident was the destruction of Pan Am Flight 103 over Scotland on December 21, 1988. One decisive action against terrorists took place when President Ronald Reagan authorized Operation El Dorado Canyon, a swift strike by General Dynamics F-111s and Navy A-6 and A-7E aircraft that punished—and reportedly terrorized—Libya's Colonel Moammar Gadhafi.

In August 1990, Saddam Hussein sent his armies into Kuwait, annexing it as an Iraqi province. He next threatened Saudi Arabia, which was vulnerable to Iraq's military might. The United States led a U.N. force to intervene first with Operation Desert Shield and then to counterattack with Operation Desert Storm. Both operations revealed to the world the unprecedented might of the United States with conventional weapons. Stealth aircraft; precision-guided munitions; airborne command and control; and the use of space-based navigation, meteorological, communications, and intelligence systems overwhelmed the Iraqis.

The combination of Lockheed Martin F-117A Nighthawk stealth fighters and precision-guided munitions revealed, in real time, some of the most spectacular bombing results in history. All over the world, people watched in awe as crosshairs were aligned on a target—the window of a bunker, the cockpit of a parked aircraft—followed by a bomb dropping to strike the target. In the meantime, no Nighthawk was even hit by enemy fire.

Voyager

Many of those television sets were in the Soviet Union, where both military and political leaders were forced to realize that the U.S.S.R. was no longer in any way competitive with the United States and, in its desperate economic situation, never could be again. This important factor hastened the Soviet Union's breakup and, perhaps more importantly, insured that it was a peaceful one.

In the aftermath of Desert Storm, the United States did what it has always done—it demobilized and stopped spending on defense. The three greatest air commands in history, SAC, TAC, and ADC were abolished, and in their place came the Air Mobility Command and Air Combat Command.

In the meantime, there was progress on many fronts, including the introduction of the Northrop Grumman B-2A Spirit stealth bomber and the new stealth fighter, the Lockheed Martin F-22 Raptor. Nor were foreign manufacturers idle, as France produced the Dassault-Breguet Rafale, Great Britain and Germany the Eurofighter, Israel the Lavi, and Sweden the Saab Gripen. The tilt-rotor Bell/Boeing V-22 Osprey flew, and a wave of huge aircraft company mergers began when Lockheed acquired the General Dynamics Military Aircraft Division and the following year merged with Martin Marietta to become Lockheed Martin.

Unfortunately, wars were not going away, they were going to become what was called "asymmetric," and the unfathomable world of terrorism would become the nemesis of the next decade.

CHALLENGER MISSION 41B
The Space Shuttle *Challenger* successfully executed the tenth Space Shuttle mission, launching on February 3, 1984, with Vance Brand as commander and Robert L. "Hoot" Gibson as pilot. Here mission specialist Bruce McCandless flies untethered in his Manned Maneuvering Unit (MMU). The landing came on February 11 after 127 orbits.

PANAVIA TORNADO With aircraft expensive and orders infrequent, it was necessary in the latter part of the century for European manufacturers to band together in consortiums to cut expenses. Panavia was formed by the British Aircraft Corporation, Messerschmitt-Boelkow, and Fiat, all of which subsequently changed corporate names. The production Panavia Tornado F. Mk 2 Interceptor flew for the first time on March 5, 1984. The Mach 2.2 Tornado served well in the Gulf War.

EMBRAER AMX Despite the difficulty in selling combat aircraft, an able new competitor emerged unexpectedly from Brazil, where EMBRAER offered first the Tucano trainer and then, with Aeritalia and Aermacchi, the AMX attack plane, of which 192 were built. Its first flight was on May 15, 1984.

VOYAGER Burt Rutan is already one of aeronautical engineering's immortal designers, ranking with Ed Heinemann and Kelly Johnson for his many unorthodox solutions to difficult flight problems. This is his *Voyager,* an all-composite aircraft in which his brother Dick flew for the first time on June 22, 1984. Two years later, Dick Rutan and Jeana Yeager would break all records with a nonstop, unrefueled flight around the world.

FLIGHT TIMELINE

January 12, 1984 The U.S. Marines get the first McDonnell Douglas AV-8B Harrier IIs, which will be used in the Persian Gulf War.

January 21, 1984 The Air Force successfully fires an ASAT (antisatellite) missile from an F-15 over the Pacific.

January 25, 1984 In his State of the Union address, President Ronald Reagan calls for building a space station.

February 3–11, 1984 Space Shuttle *Challenger* is launched. It tests the Manned Maneuvering Unit, in which astronaut Bruce McCandless orbits, untethered, around the shuttle.

February 24, 1984 The General Dynamics F-16XL is defeated by the McDonnell Douglas F-15E Strike Eagle in competition.

March 6, 1984 The comeback of lighter-than-air craft is signaled by the first flight of the British Airship Industries Skyship.

March 31, 1984 The last Avro Vulcan is removed from RAF service.

April 6–13, 1984 The Space Shuttle *Challenger* mission makes the first on-orbit satellite repair of *Solar Max.*

May 15, 1984 A consortium of Aeritalia/Aermacchi/EMBRAER creates the AMX close-support aircraft, which makes its first flight. On a subsequent flight 15 days later, it crashes, killing the pilot.

RICHARD BRANSON AND VIRGIN AIRLINES Not everyone had confidence in the ultimate success of Virgin Airlines when it was launched by entrepreneur Richard Branson on June 22, 1984. Anyone who has flown the airline knows that it is a first-rate success.

LAST BOEING 727 ROLLED OUT The 1,832nd—and last—727 was rolled out of the Boeing plant on August 14, 1984, painted in Federal Express colors, purple and orange. The aircraft represented a tremendous success to a program that had been considered a risky gamble at its start, but the combination of three engines instead of four (which means less inventory costs) and the superlative high-lift wing (which permitted operation out of short, high-altitude fields) insured the 727's success.

KATHRYN SULLIVAN The first U.S. woman to walk in space, Kathryn Sullivan is a trained geologist. Her space walk came on the 13th Space Shuttle flight aboard the *Challenger*. Robert Crippen was the commander, Jon McBride the pilot, and Sally Ride was a mission specialist. The flight launched on October 5, 1984, and landed on October 13 after 133 orbits.

ATR-42 TRANSPORT Avions de Transport Regional (ATR) was formed by a joint venture of Aerospatiale of France and Aeritalia (now Alenia) of Italy in 1980. British Aerospace later merged its commuter aircraft division with ATR. The first design to result from this was the ATR-42, first flown on August 16, 1984. About 285 have been built. The high-wing aircraft is powered by Pratt & Whitney turboprops of 3,600 shaft horsepower and can carry 42 to 52 passengers.

ROCKWELL B-1B One of the most controversial bombers of its time, the Rockwell B-1B also had one of the longest development periods, beginning in 1970 and extending through the original B-1 of 1974, which was canceled by Jimmy Carter. President Ronald Reagan reinstated the B-1B, of which 100 were built. The first production aircraft flew on October 18, 1984. After a rocky start, the swing-wing Mach 1.25 B-1B has done an outstanding job in Kosovo and Afghanistan.

GRUMMAN X-29 Germany had experimented with forward swept wings on its Junkers Ju 287 jet bomber, but it was not until the late 1970s that new developments, including fly-by-wire systems, composite materials, and the supercritical airfoil made further research rewarding. The first of the two X-29s built lifted on December 14, 1984, beginning a highly successful test program. The Mach 1.8 X-29 was particularly valuable in testing the high angle of attack flight regimes.

FLIGHT TIMELINE

June 22, 1984 *Voyager* flies for the first time.

June 22, 1984 Virgin Airlines launches operations.

July 17–19, 1984 The 100th human space flight occurs with the launch of the Soviet *Soyuz T-12*.

July 25, 1984 Svetlana Savitskaya becomes the first woman to make a space walk, from *Salyut 7*.

August 4, 1984 European space flight exploration continues with the launch of *Ariane 3* from French Guinea.

August 14, 1984 The last of 1,832 Boeing 727s is rolled out in Renton, Washington.

August 29, 1984 A Rockwell International B-1A crashes.

August 30, 1984 The Space Shuttle *Discovery* is launched on its maiden flight.

September 14–18, 1984 Joe Kittinger, famous for high-altitude parachute drops, makes the first nonstop solo balloon flight across the Atlantic.

October 5, 1984 The Space Shuttle *Challenger* is launched.

October 18, 1984 The Rockwell International B-1B makes its first flight. One hundred are ordered.

November 8–16, 1984 The Space Shuttle *Discovery* makes its second flight. For the first time, an orbiting satellite is retrieved and returned to Earth.

LOCKHEED C-5A GALAXY On December 17, 1984, the 81st anniversary of the Wright brothers' first flight, the Lockheed C-5A Galaxy made a record heavy-weight takeoff of 920,836 pounds, about 920,068 pounds more than the Kitty Hawk Flyer. The C-5A was controversial because of cost and wing structural problems, but it has been an indispensable asset to the United States for more than 30 years. It has served valiantly in combat and in compassionate missions all over the world.

BOEING 767 Airlines constantly seek to lower operating costs with new technology (for example, replacing the familiar three-person cockpit with one that two pilots could operate successfully). In the same way, they wished to have twin-engine aircraft with trans-atlantic capability, a goal that was fulfilled when the Boeing 767 was reworked to have three pilots in the cockpit instead of two. A 767 made the first crossing on February 1, 1985.

EMBRAER TUCANO The EMBRAER firm was formed in 1969 and was an instant success with a wide variety of aircraft, including the familiar Bandeirante and Brasilia turboprop transports. The company expanded its range with the Tucano, a trainer originally intended for the Brazilian Air Force. It sold to many other air forces as well, including the Royal Air Force, which replaced its Jet Provosts with Tucano on March 21, 1985. Its first flight took place on August 16, 1980, and it had a top speed of 278 miles per hour.

ANTONOV AN-124 CONDOR TRANSPORT The largest aircraft in the world at the time, the Antonov An-124 flew into Le Bourget, France, on May 29, 1985, astounding the Western world. Powered by four 51,000-pound thrust turbofan engines and capable of a cruise speed of 537 miles per hour and a range of 10,000 miles, the An-124 was a tour-de-force. "Condor" is the NATO code name for the aircraft. Three years later the An-124 was followed by the even larger Antonov An-225.

IRANIAN GUERILLAS HOLD PASSENGERS HOSTAGE

Flight 847 of a TWA Boeing 727 was hijacked by two Shiite terrorists. Initially 153 people were held hostage. Women, children, and the elderly were released. One American hostage was killed. The remaining passengers were held in various parts of Beirut. After Israel released 31 of its Shiite prisoners, the Iranian-held hostages were freed. Here American hostages are returning home on July 2, 1985.

FLIGHT TIMELINE

December 14, 1984 The Grumman X-29 technology demonstrator, with forward swept wings, makes its first flight.

January 24–27, 1985 The Space Shuttle *Discovery* conducts a classified defense assignment; military aviation has melded with space flight.

March 21, 1985 The RAF selects EMBRAER Tucano as its new basic trainer.

April 12–19, 1985 The Space Shuttle *Discovery* carries Senator Jake Garn into orbit.

April 29–May 6, 1985 The Space Shuttle *Challenger* launches with *Spacelab 3*.

May 29, 1985 The Soviet Union unveils the world's largest airplane, the Antonov An-124 heavy transport, at the Paris air show.

June 11, 1985 The Soviet *Vega-1* spacecraft is sent to rendezvous with Halley's Comet.

June 17–24, 1985 The Space Shuttle *Discovery* is launched with two foreign astronauts, Patrick Baudry of France and Sulton Abdelaz-izi Al-Saud of Saudi Arabia.

July 29–August 6, 1985 The Space Shuttle *Challenger* is launched; it experiences the first major in-flight emergency of shuttle history when one main engine shuts down during ascent.

JAPAN AIR LINES BOEING 747 CRASH On August 12, 1985, a Japan Air Lines Boeing 747SR crashed into a ridge near Mount Osutaka, northwest of Tokyo, killing all 520 on board. This is the highest number of casualties for any single aircraft accident. The victims of this crash had a particularly difficult time, for the aircraft remained in the air for almost 30 minutes after it was certain that it was going to crash.

DELTA TRISTAR CRASH A microburst caused the crash of a Delta Lockheed L-1011 TriStar on approach to the Dallas Fort Worth Regional Airport, killing 133 people on August 2, 1985. The microburst, though previously known to meteorologists, was a new phenomenon for most people. Several incidents prompted government action to provide equipment at airports to predict microbursts.

LOCKHEED C-5B GALAXY The original controversies over the Galaxy limited the USAF purchase to just 81 aircraft, far fewer than were needed. The oversight was partially corrected on September 10, 1985, when the first of 50 Lockheed C-5Bs made its debut. The aircraft can carry some outsize cargo that the later Boeing C-17A cannot.

McDonnell Douglas F-15 Eagle The capable McDonnell Douglas F-15 Eagle added another mission to its capability on September 13, 1985, when it fired an antisatellite missile, destroying an inert satellite. The program was not continued because it was considered "destabilizing"—no one wanted antisatellite capability proliferated.

Giuseppe Garibaldi Italy badly needed aircraft carriers during World War II but possessed none because Benito Mussolini insisted that "all of Italy is an aircraft carrier." This is the helicopter and aircraft carrier *Giuseppe Garibaldi,* named after a great Italian hero; it became part of the Italian Navy on September 30, 1985.

FLIGHT TIMELINE

August 12, 1985 The world's worst aircraft disaster to date occurs when a Japan Air Lines Boeing 747 crashes into the mountains. Japan Air Lines later faults Boeing quality control for the accident.

August 18, 1985 The Japanese launch a space probe for a flyby of Halley's Comet.

August 27–September 3, 1985 Space Shuttle *Discovery* is launched; it deploys three satellites and repairs another.

September 10, 1985 The Lockheed C-5B Galaxy makes its first flight.

September 13, 1985 An ASAT missile fired from an F-15 successfully intercepts an orbiting satellite.

September 30, 1985 Italians acquire a new aircraft carrier for helicopters and VSTOL aircraft, the *Giuseppe Garibaldi.*

October 3–7, 1985 The Space Shuttle *Atlantis* is launched on its maiden flight; it sets a new shuttle altitude record with an orbit of 1,725,000 miles.

October 30–November 6, 1985 Space Shuttle *Challenger* is launched with German and Dutch astronauts as part of the largest (eight-member) crew in history.

November 15, 1985 The last independant general aviation manufacturer—Cessna—is purchased by General Dynamics.

EXPLOSION OF *CHALLENGER*

The United States space program suffered its worst setback ever in full view of a waiting crowd and a television audience of millions on January 28, 1986. Pictured from the left, front row: Mike Smith, Dick Scobee, Ron McNair. Rear row, from the left: Ellison S. Onizuka, Sharon Christa McAuliffe, Gregory B. Jarvis, Judith A. Resnik. All died in the aftermath of the explosion.

Rubber O-rings in the right solid rocket booster failed because of the cold temperature, allowing an explosion to take place 72 seconds after launch. The possibility of such failure had been known but was discounted. The network television cameras caught the tragedy of the explosion live, then registered the myriad emotions of the crowd, some of whom were related to the crew members. It was a sad day for space.

BEECH STARSHIP The Beech Starship made its first flight on February 15, 1986, a significant landmark in the history of general aviation. In the early days of the Experimental Aircraft Association, "experimental aircraft" were generally slightly modified versions of contemporary light aircraft. This changed with the advent of the Rutan series of composite structure and advanced configuration aircraft, beginning with his VariEze in the late 1960s. From that point, experimental aircraft led the way for general aviation.

HALLEY'S COMET, 1986 The success of space program initiatives, particularly the space probes, has sparked a widespread interest in astronomical events. One of the most fervently awaited was the passage of Halley's Comet in 1986, as seen in this Ford Observatory photo. Incredibly, the European Space Agency's *Giotto* satellite intercepted Halley's Comet on March 13–14, 1986.

NAJEEB HALABY AND MARCEL DASSAULT In this earlier photo, Marcel Dassault, President of Avions Marcel Dassault, has just pinned Najeeb E. Halaby (left), then President of Pan American Airways, with the award of Knight of the Legion of Honor. Dassault was the name adopted by Marcel Bloch as a resistance fighter; he kept it after the war. He died on April 18, 1986, at the age of 94.

FLIGHT TIMELINE

November 26–December 3, 1985 Space Shuttle *Atlantis* is launched in an experiment with space station structures.

December 17, 1985 On the 82nd anniversary of the Wright Brothers flight, the Douglas DC-3 celebrates its 50th birthday. Approximately 400 are still in use.

December 28, 1985 The U.S. *Pioneer 12* probe passes within 25,000,000 miles of Halley's Comet.

January 8, 1986 The first Lockheed C-5B transport is delivered to the Air Force.

January 12–18, 1986 Space Shuttle *Columbia* is launched.

January 24, 1986 The U.S. planetary spacecraft *Voyager 2* makes a Uranus flyby (passes within 66,500 miles) and encounters moons and ring system, then is redirected toward Neptune.

January 28, 1986 The Space Shuttle *Challenger* blows up 72 seconds into liftoff; teacher Christa McAuliffe is on board. Seven astronauts perish; the Shuttle fleet is grounded for 30 months.

February 15, 1986 The futuristic Beech Starship 1 business aircraft makes its first flight.

March 9, 1986 Soviet comet probe *Vega 2* observes Halley's Comet from a distance of 4,990 miles.

March 13–14, 1986 The European Space Agency's *Giotto* satellite flies within 335 miles of Halley's Comet.

JUNKERS JU 52/3M The great German airline Lufthansa looked to its heritage and restored a Junkers Ju 52/3m transport like this one, flying it again for the first time on April 6, 1986. The sturdy trimotor was the equivalent of the American DC-3 and served all over the world in both civil and military capacities. Its ability to get in and out of small fields was invaluable.

BOEING B-52H AND AGM-86B ALCM General Curtis E. LeMay had to fight hard to get a fleet of B-52s; at a cost of $3 to $6 million each, they were expensive. The B-52s proved to be a good investment because the last of them, a B-52H, was delivered in 1962. They are still a first-line combat platform. This is the first flight of a B-52H carrying a full load of AGM-86B ALCMs (air-launched cruise missiles).

BOEING AWACS The Boeing E-3A Sentry AWACS (Airborne Warning and Control System) is always in short supply in the USAF, being a "high-demand/low-density" asset. So it was with goodwill that the United States approved the sale of five AWACS to Saudi Arabia, the first being turned over on June 30, 1986. This is a USAF aircraft on patrol during Operation Desert Shield.

DASSAULT-BREGUET RAFALE (SQUALL) Dassault extended its mastery of the fighter domain with the July 4, 1986, first flight of its remarkable Rafale. Designed from the start to operate from runways or aircraft carrier decks, the Rafale will be the primary fighter for both the French Air Force and French Navy, with some 220 on order. It will also be a contender for contracts with other nations seeking a twenty-first century fighter.

JEANA YEAGER AND DICK RUTAN IN VOYAGER Against all odds, Dick Rutan and Jeana Yeager made a 11,336.9-mile test flight on July 10, 1986, to set a new world distance record for unrefueled flight. The flight was a preliminary test for their proposed round-the-world nonstop unrefueled flight, which many considered to be impossible.

FLIGHT TIMELINE

April 14–15, 1986 The United States strikes Libya in retaliation for terrorist activities. Attacking aircraft include EF-111As and F-111s from the United Kingdom (France won't allow flight over its airspace), as well as Navy A-6s and A-7s.

July 1, 1986 The first close look at MiG-29 fighters occurs on a goodwill visit to Finland. The aircraft closely resemble F-15s and have similar performance.

July 4, 1986 The Eurofighter, the Dassault-Breguet Rafale, makes its first flight.

July 10–14, 1986 On a test flight, the *Voyager* flies 11,336.9 miles nonstop, unrefueled.

July 11, 1986 Reports of the crash of the second Lockheed F-117A stealth fighter give rise to unfounded concerns that it is too unstable for pilots.

August 11, 1986 The Westland Lynx becomes the world's fastest production helicopter, flying at 249.09 miles per hour.

September 2, 1986 An unusual combination hot-air/helium balloon makes a record flight from Amsterdam to St. John, Newfoundland, in 50 hours, piloted by Henk and Evelyn Brink of the Netherlands.

September 23, 1986 The Piaggio Avanti twin turboprop makes its first flight; it is a potential competitor to the Beech Starship.

FOKKER 100 The Fokker 100 was a significant step up from the familiar eight-seat F28 Fellowship, of which some 241 had been built. The Fokker 100 made its first flight on November 30, 1986, and was a much more modern aircraft than its predecessor. The sleek-looking twin-jet was an immediate success. Its 107-passenger capacity and 585-miles-per-hour speed made it ideal for short routes in Europe and the United States.

VOYAGER MAKES NONSTOP FLIGHT AROUND THE WORLD The adventurous nature of modern American youths was illustrated with the round-the-world, nonstop, unrefueled flight of *Voyager*. Taking off on December 14, 1986, the *Voyager* flew 24,986 miles, landing at Edwards Air Force Base on December 23.

BOEING E-6A HERMES FOR THE TACAMO PROGRAM TACAMO stands for "Take Charge and Move Out," a Navy program for maintaining the vital communications between naval headquarters and the fleet of submerged Trident submarines. The Boeing E-6A comprises a basic 707 airframe equipped with highly classified communications gear and CFM F108 turbofans of 24,000 pounds thrust. (The original 707 engines were of 9,500 pounds thrust.) The Hermes made its first flight on February 19, 1987, with a top speed of 610 miles per hour.

MATHIAS RUST LANDS CESSNA IN MOSCOW On May 29, 1987, Mathias Rust, a 19-year-old German, flew his Cessna 172 from Finland, crossing through the Soviet defense systems undetected, and landed his aircraft in Red Square in Moscow. Rust was tried and sentenced to four years in jail but was freed in 1988. Soviet Defense Minister Marshal Alexander Koldunov was dismissed, and there were shake-ups in the armed services.

McDONNELL DOUGLAS AV-8B HARRIER The U.S. Marines were delighted with the prospect of a VTOL fighter that could operate close to the front, and the Harrier filled the bill. McDonnell Douglas obtained a license to build the advanced AV-8B. Changes included a supercritical wing, a new high-lift system, and twin-Aden 30-mm cannon. This night-attack version first flew on June 26, 1987. The 750-miles-per-hour Harrier is also armed with Sidewinder missiles and can carry up to 7,000 pounds of ordnance.

FLIGHT TIMELINE

November 6, 1986 Forty-five people are killed in the crash of a Chinook helicopter near Scotland. It is the worst civilian helicopter crash in history.

November 30, 1986 The Fokker 100 twin-turboprop passenger liner makes its first flight.

December 4, 1986 The McDonnell Douglas MD-87, a smaller version of the older DC-9 airliner, makes its first flight.

December 11, 1986 The McDonnell Douglas F-15E Eagle, a combination air superiority/ground support fighter, makes its first flight.

December 14–23, 1986 Burt Rutan's specially designed *Voyager* makes the first nonstop, unrefueled circumnavigation of the world.

January 21, 1987 Lois McCallan sets a human-powered record for women in MIT's *Michelob Light Eagle.*

February 6–July 30, 1987 *Soyuz TM-2* is launched; it uses a new automatic docking system to dock with space station *Mir.* The Soviet Union provides full television coverage.

February 6, 1987 The Aerospatial Super Puma helicopter flies.

February 19, 1987 The Boeing E-6A TACAMO relay aircraft makes its first flight.

February 22, 1987 The Airbus 320, with fly-by-wire system, makes its first flight.

RICHARD BRANSON Being a multimillionaire, a flamboyant entrepreneur, and an airline owner is not enough for Richard Branson. Along with Per Lindstrand, he made the first transatlantic crossing by hot-air balloon in the *Virgin Atlantic Flyer* on June 26, 1987.

ROCKWELL B-1B The much-maligned Rockwell (now Boeing) B-1B has in fact always been a formidable aircraft. On July 4, 1987, a B-1B set four world records for speed, distance, and payload. The aircraft has been criticized because its defensive electronic suite was long delayed in reaching its specified requirements, but the highly trained crews performed well without it, distinguishing themselves in the Kosovo and Afghanistan conflicts. The B-1B now has a tremendous conventional weapon capability.

TUPOLEV TU-160 BLACKJACK BOMBER In 1988, the Soviet Union was still flexing its military muscles. In January of that year, it formed the first unit of the formidable Tupolev Tu-160 Blackjacks, the world's largest bomber, roughly equivalent to the American Rockwell B-1B. The Mach 1.88 Blackjack was a tremendous threat with its 7,500-mile range, but economic difficulties and political strategy limited production to about 20 aircraft.

INDIA LAUNCHES *PRITHVI* MISSILE On February 25, 1988, India debuted its *Prithvi* tactical surface-to-surface missile. On December 12, 2001, it test fired a longer-range version, which is believed to be nuclear capable and is undoubtedly deployed against Pakistan and possibly China.

T-45A GOSHAWK The product of a cooperative effort between British Aerospace and McDonnell Douglas (now Boeing), the T-45A Goshawk made its first flight on April 16, 1988. The Goshawk is considered the heart of a totally integrated training system for the U.S. armed services. Maximum level speed is 540 knots.

FLIGHT TIMELINE

March 1987 Patrice Francheske makes the first microlight round-the-world flight.

April 26, 1987 The first prototype of the Saab JAS 39 Gripen is unveiled.

May 29, 1987 Mathias Rust lands a Cessna 172 in Red Square.

June 26, 1987 Richard Branson and Per Lindstrand cross the Atlantic by hot-air balloon for the first time. They reach 153 miles per hour in a jet stream.

September 30, 1987 A NASA report indicates that there are 18,400 trackable artificial objects in space.

October 9, 1987 The pre-production EH 101 helicopter makes its first flight.

November 19, 1987 Northrop is awarded a $2 billion contract to develop the B-2 stealth bomber.

November 29, 1987 A Korean Airlines Boeing 707 is blown up by a terrorist bomb.

December 29, 1987 Soviet cosmonaut Yuri Romanenko sets a new human space duration record of 326 days, 11 hours, and 38 minutes.

January 1988 The first Low Level Wind Shear Alert System is installed.

January 1988 Tupelov Blackjacks enter operational service with the Soviet Air Force.

CHRONICLE OF FLIGHT

BELL/BOEING V-22 OSPREY The controversy swirling around the Bell/Boeing V-22 Osprey, which debuted on May 23, 1988, exceeds that of all previous aircraft, including the Lockheed C-5 and the Rockwell B-1B. The big tilt-rotor aircraft promises to be the perfect replacement for helicopters, for it combines vertical lift capabilities with high dash-speeds. Unfortunately, its flight test program has been plagued by crashes, and despite unwavering Marine and Air Force support, its future is in doubt.

USS VINCENNES This is a photo of the combat center aboard the USS *Vincennes,* which shot down Iranian Airbus Flight 655 with 290 people onboard on July 3, 1988. The accidental shoot-down occurred when the airliner strayed too close to two U.S. Navy warships. The crew on the *Vincennes* mistook the aircraft for an incoming Iranian F-14 fighter.

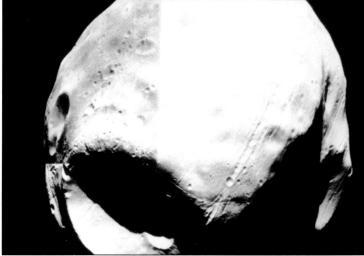

PHOBOS The Soviet Union launched *Phobos 1* on July 7, 1988, but it was lost en route by command error. *Phobos 2* was launched on July 12, 1988, and was inserted into Mars orbit on January 29, 1989. The orbiter moved within 800 kilometers of the Martian satellite Phobos, took photos of it (including the one shown here) and then failed, apparently never making a landing on the Martian moon.

JET TEAM CRASHES One of the most spectacular air show crashes in history occurred on August 28, 1988, when the Aermacchi MB-339A aircraft of the Italian Tricolori aerobatic collided above Ramstein Air Base, Germany, killing 39 on the ground and 3 pilots. The European air show was not conducted under the strict ground rules that apply to similar events in the United States.

ILYUSHIN IL-96 The Ilyushin Il-96, first flown on September 28, 1988, was handicapped by the performance of the Soviet Perm PS90 engines that equipped it. About 15 Il-96-300s were built, most of which were delivered to Aeroflot. After the demise of the Soviet Union, Ilyushin developed a stretched version of the Il-96 equipped with U.S.-built Pratt & Whitney PW2237 jet engines and Western electronics. It is marketed in a passenger version, the Il-96M, and a freighter version, the Il-96T.

FLIGHT TIMELINE

January 29–30, 1984 A 747SP sets a round-the-world record of 36 hours and 54 minutes.

February 8, 1988 The Department of Defense begins SDI (Star Wars) experimentation with the launch of the Delta 181.

March 1988 Germany revives a World War II idea of using the Sänger concept to "skip" a reusable aerospace plane through upper levels of atmosphere.

April 15, 1988 A modified Tupelov Tu-154, the first aircraft fueled by liquid hydrogen, flies for the first time.

April 16, 1988 The British Aerospace/McDonnell Douglas T-45A Goshawk trainer makes its first flight.

April 23, 1988 Smoking is banned on U.S. domestic airline flights.

May 23, 1988 The first Bell/Boeing V-22 Osprey prototype is rolled out.

May 27, 1988 The McDonnell Douglas F-4 Phantom celebrates the 30th anniversary of its first flight.

June 26, 1988 An Airbus Industries A320 airliner flies into the ground; questions are raised concerning the fly-by-wire concept.

July 3, 1988 An Airbus 300 of Iran Air is shot down by the guided missile cruiser USS *Vincennes;* there are 290 casualties.

LOCKHEED F-117A NIGHTHAWK In an age when secrets are difficult to keep, the USAF did a magnificent job with the Lockheed F-117A Nighthawk stealth fighter, which first flew on June 18, 1981. The aircraft remained shrouded in secrecy until the Air Force announced its existence on November 10, 1988. The Nighthawk went on to do spectacular work in the Gulf War, dominating the skies over Baghdad.

SOVIET SPACE SHUTTLE BURAN The Soviet Space Shuttle *Buran* is pictured here on the launching pad with its huge Energia booster rocket. On November 15, 1988, the *Buran* was launched from the Baikonour Cosmodrome for the first time. It was unpiloted and followed an automatic flight path through its landing. Similar to the American Space Shuttle in appearance, two more *Burans* were planned but no more launches were made, and the program was canceled.

NORTHROP B-2 SPIRIT STEALTH BOMBER The secrecy around the Northrop B-2A Spirit stealth bomber was unprecedented, but rising program costs made an early disclosure politically necessary, and on November 22, 1988, the astounding flying wing was rolled out. The most expensive bomber ever built, it is also the most capable and may, in the long run, be the most economical, because it is able to fly long-range missions without the "packages" of electronic-support aircraft and refuelers other bombers require.

ANTONOV AN-225 The Antonov An-225 *Mriya* is currently the world's largest aircraft, with a maximum gross takeoff weight of 1,322,750 pounds and a wingspan of 290 feet. It was designed to carry the *Buran* shuttle orbiter and is shown here arriving at the Paris Air Show on June 18, 2001. The prototype made its first flight on December 18, 1988, and in the following year set an amazing 106 world records.

FLIGHT TIMELINE

July 7, 1988 The Soviet *Phobos 1* spacecraft is launched to study Mars; communications are lost on August 29, 1989.

July 12, 1988 *Phobos 2*, the companion spacecraft to *Phobos 1*, is launched to study Mars, arriving on January 29, 1989.

August 17, 1988 President Zia of Pakistan is killed in the crash of a Lockheed C-130.

August 28, 1988 Three Aermacchi MB-339s from an Italian air demonstration team collide during an air show at Ramstein Air Base in Germany.

September 28, 1988 The Ilyushin Il-96 wide-body transport makes its first flight.

September 29, 1988 The Space Shuttle *Discovery* is launched in the first shuttle flight since the *Challenger* disaster.

November 5, 1988 Soviets unveil the Antonov An-225 *Mriya* transport. It is the largest aircraft in the world, weighing more than 1,000,000 pounds when fully loaded.

November 10, 1988 The U.S. Air Force confirms the existence of the Lockheed F-117 stealth fighter.

November 15, 1988 Soviets launch their counterpart to the Space Shuttle, the *Buran*; it is totally automatic, no humans are onboard. The program is later canceled.

PAN AM BLOWN UP OVER LOCKERBIE On December 21, 1988, Pan Am Flight 103, a Boeing 747, was blown up over Lockerbie, Scotland, killing its 258 passengers and crew as well as 11 Lockerbie residents. Two Libyans, Abdelbaset Ali Muhammad Al-Megrahi and Al Amin Khalifa Fhimah, were charged with planting an explosive-packed cassette recorder onboard the aircraft.

DAEDALUS 88 AIRCRAFT
A team led by Dr. John S. Langford created *Daedalus 88,* a human-powered aircraft that flew from Crete to Santori, Greece, on April 23, 1988. The effort required the most advanced aerodynamics and structural techniques.

TUPOLEV TU-204 Influenced by the modern 757/767 series from Boeing, Tupolev countered with the Tu-204, powered by two Perry/Soloviev turbofans of 35,000 pounds thrust each. With its supercritical wing, winglets, and fly-by-wire controls, the Tu-204 is a state-of-the-art airliner, with seats for up to 214. The Tu-204 made its first flight on January 2, 1989.

GPS SATELLITE SENT INTO ORBIT Strangely enough, the military ICBM program led directly to civilian space programs. A McDonnell Douglas (now Boeing) Delta II space launcher, launched from Cape Canaveral, Florida, put the first Ground Positioning System (GPS) satellite, called *NavStar,* into orbit on February 14, 1989. This is the March 24 launch of the *Delta Star* satellite used for tracking missiles.

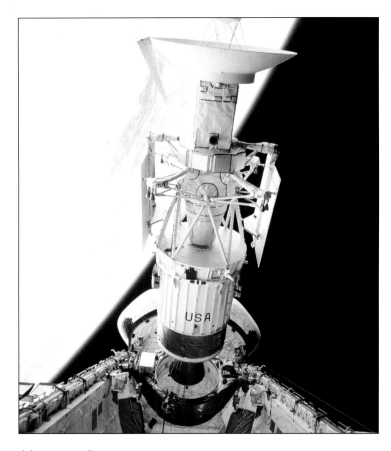

MAGELLAN PROBE On May 4, 1989, Major Mark C. Lee released the *Magellan* probe from the Space Shuttle *Atlantis,* so it could create a map of Venus. The *Magellan* mapped more than 70 percent of the surface of Venus.

ALEXANDER YAKOVLEV Alexander Sergeyevich Yakovlev died on August 22, 1989, at the age of 84. He built his first glider in 1923 and later became a protégé of Andrei Tupolev. Unlike Tupolev, he maintained Joseph Stalin's trust and built a series of Yak fighters that were numerically and qualitatively the most important Soviet Union fighters during World War II. The Yak-9 pictured here was equal to its German counterparts, and almost 17,000 of them were built.

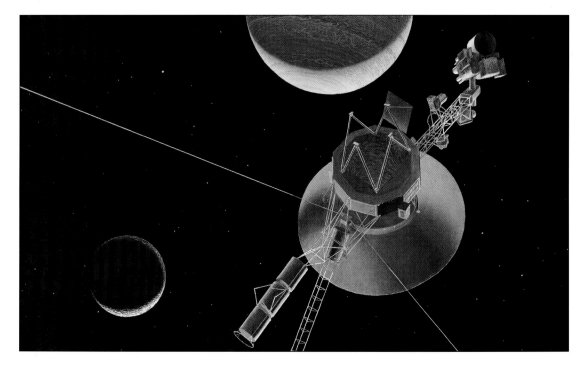

VOYAGER 2 Here is a painting of the *Voyager 2* as it looks back upon Neptune and its moon, Triton. On August 25, 1989, the *Voyager 2* space probe completed a grand tour of our solar system, coming within 3,000 miles of Neptune.

ANTONOV AN-225 MRIYA WITH BURAN Just as the modified Boeing 747 carries the American Space Shuttle, so did the huge Antonov An-225 carry the *Buran* on June 7, 1989. The deterioration of the Soviet Union's economy and its subsequent dissolution prevented large-scale production of the An-225 or further use of the *Buran*.

QANTAS 747 A Qantas 747 airliner flew nonstop from London to Sydney, a distance of 11,100 miles, in 20 hours, landing on August 18, 1989. It was the longest nonstop commercial airline flight to that date, and it was reported that even the first-class passengers were exhausted.

F-117A OPERATION JUST CAUSE The first combat use of the Lockheed F-117A Nighthawk stealth fighter took place on December 20, 1989, as Operation Just Cause began in Panama. That debut was considered inauspicious. The bombing was not as precise as that achieved by the Nighthawk during the Gulf War.

SR-71 BLACKBIRD RETIRED The Lockheed SR-71 Blackbird retired from Strategic Air Command service on January 25, 1990. The most advanced aircraft in history, SR-71s continued on with NASA as test beds and briefly returned to active duty before being retired again. On its first flight and its last, the Mach 3+ Blackbird was the most advanced aircraft in the world—and it still is.

POND RACER Reminiscent of the World War II Lockheed P-38 but made of composite construction and using Japanese engines, the radical Pond Racer was designed for the unlimited racing class at the Reno National Air Races. Round-the-world pilot Dick Rutan was at the controls on its March 22, 1990, first flight. The Pond Racer crashed before it was fully developed.

PEGASUS Young companies thrived in the space age, when new research ideas could be funded and realized in a way never possible in the past. One of these was Orbital Sciences, whose air-launched space booster *Pegasus* is shown being launched on April 5, 1990.

FLIGHT TIMELINE

April 24–29, 1990 The Space Shuttle *Discovery* carries the Hubble Space Telescope into orbit.

August 2, 1990 Iraq seizes Kuwait.

September 6, 1990 A Boeing 747 becomes the new Air Force One.

September 29, 1990 The Lockheed Martin YF-22 Raptor supersonic stealth fighter debuts.

October 29, 1990 Boeing gives the formal go-ahead for the 777, a twin-engine jet with a wider body than the 767. It is designed to compete with the Airbus A330 and A340.

November 9, 1990 Kansai Airport, built on a human-made island, becomes Japan's first 24-hour airport.

December 21, 1990 Famed aircraft designer Clarence L. "Kelly" Johnson dies at age 80. He designed the P-80, F-104, U-2, and SR-71.

1991 Mil-Brooke Helicopters in Miami becomes the support organization for Mil aircraft in North America.

January 15–19, 1991 Richard Branson and Per Lindstrand fly the first transpacific balloon flight, covering 6,700 miles.

January 17, 1991 Operation Desert Storm begins: The technology of modern warfare is unveiled.

February 13, 1991 The Swearingen SJ-30 small business jet makes its first flight.

EC-135C Ends "Looking Glass" Mission For 29 years, the Strategic Air Command kept EC-135Cs in the air continually. Looking Glass crews were to direct the launching of aircraft and missiles if ground control became impossible. Looking Glass began on February 3, 1961, and ended on July 24, 1990. Looking Glass ceased continuous airborne alert but remained on ground alert 24 hours a day. Crews accumulated more than 281,000 accident-free flying hours, an aviation feat.

Lockheed YF-22A Prototype Flying for the first time on September 29, 1990, the Mach 1.7 Lockheed YF-22A Raptor won a hard-fought competition against the Northrop YF-23A to become the USAF's premier fighter for the twenty-first century. Designed to combine stealth, supercruise, and extreme agility, the Raptor's designation was recently changed to F/A-22 to reflect its acquisition of an air-to-ground capability. Only 339 of the estimated 750 Raptors required for a Global Strike Task Force have been ordered.

BOEING 727 RETIRED FROM UNITED On January 13, 1991, the very first Boeing 727 ever built retired after more than 64,292 hours of flying time and carrying more than 3,000,000 passengers.

F-15CS OVER BURNING OIL WELLS

On August 2, 1990, six Iraqi divisions invaded Kuwait. Five days later, U.S. military forces began deploying to Saudi Arabia. Among the first of these were 48 McDonnell Douglas F-15 Eagles from the 1st Tactical Fighter Wing at Langley Air Force Base, Virginia. Their presence was sufficient to restrain Saddam Hussein from advancing into Saudi Arabia. An immense build up of personnel and supplies ensued, and on January 17, 1991, Operation Desert Storm began with a whirlwind attack that incapacitated Iraqi defenses. Total air superiority, supplemented by stealth aircraft and precision-guided munitions, wore the Iraqi forces to the ground. The air war continued for five weeks, with 109,000 combat sorties, 40,000 of them against Iraqi ground forces. Only 38 Coalition aircraft were lost, which is below the normal peacetime accident rate. Of the 88,500 tons of ordnance dropped, 6,500 tons were precision guided, and these gutted the Iraqi ability to resist.

AIRBUS A340 Airbus threw down the gauntlet to Boeing's 747 and 777 aircraft with its A340 series of aircraft, which made its first flight on October 25, 1991. The later models of the A340 are powered by 56,000-pound thrust Rolls-Royce Trent engines and can carry up to 380 passengers over a 7,500 nautical mile range. Airbus emphasizes the commonality of its line, which makes it easy for pilots to be checked out in several different Airbus models.

PAN AMERICAN AIRWAYS ENDS OPERATIONS

Boeing 727

Juan Trippe guided Pan American Airway's progress from its 1927 inception until his retirement almost 40 years later. During that period, Pan Am became America's national carrier, establishing international routes that set standards for airline speed, comfort, and safety. Using the giant Sikorsky, Martin, and Boeing clipper flying boats in the early years, Pan Am transitioned first to the four-engine landplane and then to the jet, always with success. With Bill Allen of Boeing, Trippe brought the gigantic Boeing 747 into being. Then, the Airline Deregulation Act allowed Pan Am to obtain domestic airline routes through an unwise merger with National Airlines. From this point on, despite desperate efforts by management to reduce costs and increase revenue, the fortune of Pan Am declined. On December 4, 1991, the company filed for bankruptcy, ending a golden era of airline travel.

One of the great values of Pan American was spurring not only its airline competition, but also aircraft manufacturers who fought for its business—being flown by Pan Am was an accolade that led to further sales. Such was the case with the famous Douglas DC-7 rivalry aircraft, which made transatlantic flights. *Clipper Jupiter Rex* (below left), was one of seven DC-7Bs proudly operated by Pan Am.

The *China Clipper* will always be indelibly associated with Pan American. Only three of the beautiful M-130s were built, but when they debuted, they startled the world. The $417,000 *China Clipper* inaugurated transpacific airmail service on November 22, 1935. It was lost ten years later in an accident at Port of Spain, Trinidad. The *Hawaiian Clipper* disappeared under mysterious circumstances on July 28, 1938, and the *Philippine Clipper* crashed on January 21, 1943.

Douglas DC-7B

Pan American Martin M-130 *China Clipper*

LOCKHEED C-5 IN OPERATION PROVIDE HOPE When the Soviet Union dissolved on December 25, 1991, it was in terrible economic difficulty. In Operation Provide Hope, its former enemy, the United States, sent 65 C-5 and C-141 missions with 2,363 tons of food and medical supplies to 24 locations in the Commonwealth of Independent States. Ultimately, the United States supplied a total of 25,000 short tons of supplies to 33 cities in the former Soviet Union.

GRUMMAN A-6 On January 21, 1992, the last variant of the venerable Grumman A-6 left the line, closing out 31 years of production of one of the most valuable and versatile aircraft ever built. Not a pretty plane, the A-6 was a workhorse, serving as attack plane, tanker, and electronic countermeasures aircraft. Only 660 were built and are in short supply today.

FLIGHT TIMELINE

March 23, 1992 Beechcraft (now part of Raytheon) delivers their 50,000th aircraft, a King Air 90B.

May 12, 1992 Lockheed Martin delivers the 2,000th C-130.

May 18, 1992 The first production McDonnell Douglas C-17 makes its first flight.

June 11, 1992 McDonnell Douglas delivers the 2,000th DC-9/MD-80/MD-90 series aircraft.

September 1992 The existence of the National Reconnaissance Office is declassified.

September 12, 1992 Dr. Mae C. Jemison becomes the first African American woman in space when she is launched onboard the Space Shuttle *Endeavor.*

September 25, 1992 NASA launches *Mars Observer* to study the Red Planet. Communication with the craft will be lost August 22, 1993.

November 2, 1992 The Airbus A330 335-passenger twin makes its first flight.

December 16, 1992 The McDonnell Douglas (Boeing) C-17 sets altitude records.

March 4, 1993 The Saab JAS 39B Gripen (a multirole aircraft) makes its first flight.

March 12, 1993 Lockheed acquires General Dynamics' Fort Worth division, the builder of the F-16.

ROCKWELL (BOEING) B-1B Few aircraft have been more badly maligned than the Rockwell (now Boeing) B-1B, but it is a sensational plane, as demonstrated on February 28–29, 1992, when it set 12 time-to-climb records. The swing-wing B-1B Lancer (the crews call it the Bone) has done brilliant work in Afghanistan.

LOCKHEED HC-130H The best estimate Lockheed originally had for sales of its new C-130 in 1954 was 400 or 500, with perhaps another 200 in foreign sales. By May 12, 1992, it produced the 2,000th C-130, and they are still coming off the assembly line. The aircraft are amazingly versatile, used as cargo planes, gunships, intelligence aircraft, special forces planes, and for search and rescue (as is the case with this HC-130H).

SAC UNDERGROUND COMMAND POST On June 1, 1992, the USAF did away with three important commands that had been first formed in 1946. They were the Strategic Air Command, Tactical Air Command, and Military Airlift Command. Their forces were recombined into Air Combat Command and Air Mobility Command. This is a photo of SAC's underground command center at Offutt Air Force Base, Nebraska.

FLIGHT TIMELINE

June 8, 1993 The first Saab JAS 39 Grippen is handed over to the Swedish Air Force.

June 26, 1993 The *NavStar* Global Position System (GPS) satellite constellation is completed.

August 6, 1993 Sheila Widnall becomes Secretary of the U.S. Air Force.

August 17, 1993 NASA selects Boeing as its prime contractor for the International Space Station.

December 2–13, 1993 The Hubble's optical flaw is repaired by the *Discovery* Shuttle crew.

LOCKHEED C-5 AND SOMALI RELIEF One of the most advanced features of the Lockheed C-5A Galaxy was the huge visor opening in the nose to permit loading of cargo. This C-5 has just brought food and medical supplies into Somalia, where they were vitally needed. Unfortunately, as is so often the case with relief supplies, insuring their distribution to the neediest people was not as easy as flying them in. Local warlords often seized the material to sell for profit.

2,000TH DC-9 (MD-83) In an effort to improve sales and remove the tarnished image of the McDonnell Douglas DC-10, the line of transports was relabeled. The familiar DC-9 became the MD-83. Customers knew what it was and continued to buy it. This MD-83 is the 2,000th example of the line.

USS GEORGE WASHINGTON The sixth of the *Nimitz*-class aircraft carriers to come in service on July 4, 1992, the USS *George Washington* (CVN 73) is a nuclear-powered ship 1,092 feet long, displacing 97,000 tons and capable of 34.5 miles per hour. It carries up to 85 aircraft and is designed to provide an independent forward presence wherever needed.

3,000TH BOEING 737 ORDERED Airline companies buy airliners only after making the most exhaustive analysis of their merit and their ability to earn money. Boeing announced on August 6, 1992, that orders for the 737 had reached 3,000, the most for any jet airliner in history. It was just a start—orders are still pouring in.

DR. MAE C. JEMISON The stark, utilitarian efficiency of her surroundings cannot displace the joyous freedom Dr. Mae C. Jemison expresses as she floats free in the Spacelab. Dr. Jemison, who is fluent in Russian, Japanese, and Swahili, was the first African American woman in space. She flew on the Space Shuttle *Endeavor* in September 1992.

BOEING 747F FIRST FLIGHT On May 7, 1993, the Boeing 747F made its first flight, adding to the long list of 747 variations. The upturned winglets cut drag and are effectively an increase in wingspan. The 747 came into existence after Boeing's entry lost a military competition to Lockheed's C-5. Ironically, the winning C-5 lost hundreds of millions for Lockheed while the "losing" 747 made billions for Boeing.

LOCKHEED P-3 ORION A rising star, Lieutenant Commander Kathryn P. Hire graduated as a Naval Flight Officer in October 1982 and became the first woman in the Navy to be assigned to a combat unit. She flew her first mission as a crew member on a Lockheed P-3C Orion withVP-62 on May 22, 1993. She flew as an astronaut on the Space Shuttle *Columbia* in 1998, orbiting the earth 256 times as a member of the *Spacelab* team.

RAYTHEON ACQUIRES BRITISH AEROSPACE CORPORATE JETS

An aircraft heritage that reached back to the 1962 de Havilland D.H.125 was acquired by Raytheon on June 1, 1993, with the acquisition of British Aerospace Corporation's line of executive jets. Raytheon marketed the highly developed design.

1,000TH BOEING 747 DELIVERED

After a slow and somewhat rocky start, the Boeing 747 revolutionized the airliner industry with sales far beyond the most fervent expectations of Boeing management. The 1,000th 747 was rolled out in 1993 just 26 years after Boeing's Bill Allen and Pan American's Juan Trippe launched the program.

CITATION X BUSINESS JET

Arnold Palmer, one of the greatest golfers in history, is also an excellent pilot. On September 15, 1993, Cessna rolled out the new Citation X business jet for his approval. The Citation X can cruise at Mach .88 and has a range of 3,800 miles, giving it easy transcontinental and intercontinental capability.

FIRST OPERATIONAL NORTHROP GRUMMAN B-2 SPIRIT The first operational Northrop Grumman B-2 arrived at Whiteman Air Force Base station on December 17, 1993. The B-2 performed remarkably well in the 2001–2002 war against Afghanistan. The stealth bomber can deliver 16 precision-guided munitions to 16 separate targets in a single pass.

LOCKHEED SR-71 The Lockheed SR-71 Blackbird has what would be called a cult following under other circumstances. On March 9, 1993, it was announced that the Blackbird would come out of retirement to fly scientific flights for NASA, a decision that was wildly applauded. The simple fact is that the Blackbird can do things at speeds and altitudes that no other aircraft can do.

CHAPTER TEN

1994 to 2003:

Filled with Fear or Faith?

As the saying goes, the only certainty in life is that things will change. This has especially proven to be the case with politics. The world barely had time to digest the fact that Russia and the former member states of the Soviet Union no longer constituted the threat they once represented when trouble began to break out in smaller countries on a smaller scale. The first flash point was in Bosnia, where the first ever NATO combat missions attempted to forcibly solve the problems of ethnic strife. On one of these missions in February 1994, USAF F-16s shot down four Bosnian Super Galeb attack planes. There was also a definite sense of history during Operation Deliberate Force, when on June 30, 1995, the German Luftwaffe flew its first combat mission in 49 years with Panavia Tornados making reconnaissance flights from a base in Italy.

Lockheed Martin F-22 Raptor

Lockheed Joint Strike Fighter

This was low-level war, with no threat of atomic, chemical, or biological weapons evident, but it was dangerous nonetheless and required the full application of all the weapons of modern warfare, including the use of space-based systems, stealth aircraft, and precision-guided munitions.

Iraq continued to be a hot spot, refusing to permit U.N. weapons inspectors access and routinely firing on U.N. aircraft patrolling "no-fly" zones. On one instance in 1996, when Iraqi military movements seemed particularly threatening, two Boeing B-52s made a dramatic round-the-world flight in 47 hours, dropping 54 bombs on a target range near the Iraqi border en route. The message was understood, and the Iraqi military stopped its menacing actions.

There were still records to be broken, and the adventuresome continued to fly higher, faster, and farther than ever before. In 1994, Ron Bower made the fastest global circumnavigation in a helicopter, flying a Bell Long Ranger and completing the task in 24 days, 4 hours, and 6 minutes. A year later, a Boeing 777 made another record flight around the world, averaging 533 miles per hour and setting one great circle distance record of 12,455 miles. Balloonists also continued pushing the envelope, with Steve Fossett setting a balloon distance record of 14,235 miles in 1998, only to see the *Breitling*

Orbiter III finally achieve, in 1999, the first ever flight around the world in a balloon.

There was a similar variety in space records. The Space Shuttle *Discovery* rendezvoused with the troubled *Mir* Space Station, with Lieutenant Colonel Eileen Collins in command—the first woman to pilot an American spacecraft. On a subsequent flight, the Space Shuttle *Atlantis* would actually dock with *Mir*. The Russian cosmonaut, Dr. Valeri Polyakov, returned to Earth after making the longest space flight ever of more than 437 days. The 51-year-old American astronaut, Shannon Lucid, made her second trip into space and spent 181 days aboard *Mir*—surely enough for anyone, given the somewhat decrepit state into which the venerable space station had fallen. *Mir*'s situation did not improve a few months later when an unpiloted *Progress* supply craft collided with it, jeopardizing the lives of all aboard.

Much of the Space Shuttle work was directed toward the construction of the International Space Station (ISS); at one point, *Mir*, the Space Shuttle *Discovery*, and the ISS were linked, forming the greatest artificial mass ever put into orbit. Within two years, the ISS would be the scene of much activity including spectacular EVAs of up to five hours duration. The ISS would also serve as the destination for the first ever space tourists. In April

2001, Dennis Tito paid $20 million to join a Russian flight to the ISS. Mark Shuttleworth followed in June 2002, also paying $20 million for the privilege.

NASA continued with its deep space missions, sending the *Cassini-Hugens* space probe to explore Saturn and its largest moon, Titan. One of the greatest, showiest space events in history occurred when the *NEAR* orbiter was directed to land on the asteroid Eros and did so successfully. Another feat was the capture of photos of the Comet Borrelly nucleus by the *Deep Space I* satellite. And of course, the sense of going ever deeper into space, and ever backward in time, was heightened by the success of the Hubble Telescope, which was given a complete overhaul in space. The end of the century was marked with an increase in the degree of international cooperation, with, for example, the Echo-Star direct TV satellite being launched by a Chinese Long March rocket booster. There were dozens of other space successes including one that was technically brilliant but economically unsound: The Iridium company put up 66 satellites for a worldwide communication system, only to find that the ordinary cell phone had proliferated to such an extent that the system was virtually without value.

The wave of mergers went on, with Northrop acquiring Grumman to become Northrop Grumman on March 29, 1994. Grumman would close its aircraft manufacturing capability as Northrop Grumman embarked in a variety of new competitive arenas. Then Boeing acquired McDonnell Douglas. This time there was no hyphenated name. As McDonnell Douglas signs came down at St. Louis, Long Beach, and elsewhere, Boeing signs went up. One reason for the merger was that the McDonnell Douglas entry in the Joint Strike Fighter competition had lost out, essentially removing that venerable firm from the fighter business. Boeing and Lockheed Martin competed for the JSF $200 billion contract, the largest in history, and Lockheed Martin won with a highly capable aircraft that bore a strong resemblance to the F-22.

For the airplane fan, the problems of war and space did not matter as long as new and beautiful airplanes were developed. These included the Boe-

ing 777, Beriev Be 32K, Airbus A319, Tupolev Tu-214, Cirrus SR-20, Learjet 45, Lockheed Martin F-35, EMBRARER 145, Lockheed Martin C-130J, and Raytheon Beech T-6A Texan II.

But, as we all know, the world changed forever on September 11, 2001, when Arab terrorists used U.S. airliners to attack the World Trade Center and the Pentagon. The United States reacted, gathering a coalition and using pure air power in an attempt to destroy the previously impregnable strongholds of the Al Qaeda and overthrow the Taliban regime. The war on terrorism promises to be a long one, and new tactics will be brought to bear. But in the end, there will be advances in both air and space beyond our imagination.

Sadly, tragedy struck again on February 1, 2003, with the loss of the Space Shuttle *Columbia* and its seven crew members. The accident may well have placed the future of both the Space Shuttle Program and the International Space Station in jeopardy. Concern is being expressed as to whether the scientific return from the two programs justifies the risk involved. There may be pressure to evaluate the entire piloted space program to determine how to proceed. Some say that unpiloted spacecraft can perform substantially all of the current Space Shuttle and International Space Station missions, while others maintain that it is essential from an emotional and spiritual point of view to continue with piloted space flight.

Boeing 767

F-16 FALCON Designed from the start to counter a Soviet invasion of Europe, the air forces of the North Atlantic Treaty Organization (NATO) didn't engage in combat until February 28, 1994, when USAF General Dynamics F-16s shot down four Bosnian Serb Super Galeb attack planes.

NORTHROP ACQUIRES GRUMMAN The end of the Cold War brought about an immense reduction in defense spending, and major aircraft producers had to compete for an ever-smaller market. To stay competitive, there were a series of mergers, and on March 29, 1994, Northrop acquired the venerable Grumman Company for $2.17 billion. This symbolic photo shows the Northrop YB-49 Flying Wing, which first flew on October 21, 1947. The new firm terminated aircraft manufacture at Grumman.

T. KEITH GLENNAN The first head of the National Aeronautics and Space Administration (NASA), T. Keith Glennan died on April 11, 1995, at the age of 90. Under Dr. Glennan's leadership, NASA grew from 9,000 civil servants to 17,000 with a budget that increased from $300 million to $1 billion in just two and a half years.

FIRST FLIGHT OF BOEING 777 The first aircraft ever designed completely on a computer, the Boeing 777 made its first flight on June 12, 1994. The first 777 was an actual production aircraft. The years of prototyping and building test models is long gone, simply because it's too expensive and, with computer-aided design and manufacture, no longer necessary.

PREDATOR July 3, 1994, marked the first flight of the General Atomics Aeronautical System's Predator unpiloted combat vehicle. The day of the fighter ace seemed to be drawing to a close as unpiloted aerial combat vehicles gained popularity. The Predator operated in Kosovo and used a Hellfire missile to destroy an enemy vehicle in Afghanistan in October 2001. The 48-foot, 7-inch wingspan Predator flies at 80 to 140 miles per hour and can stay on station for 16 hours.

FLIGHT TIMELINE

January 25, 1994 The *Clementine* lunar orbiter is launched.

February 3–11, 1994 Sergei Krikolev becomes the first Russian crew member to fly aboard the Space Shuttle.

February 28, 1994 Two Air Force F-16s shoot down four Bosnian Serb aircraft in the first demonstration of NATO air combat.

March 29, 1994 Northrop acquires Grumman; the merger is effective May 18, 1994.

March 30, 1994 The Pilatus PC-12 gets Swiss certification.

June 12, 1994 The Boeing 777 makes its first flight.

September 13, 1994 The A300-600ST Super Transporter makes its first flight.

December 1994 Lockheed merges with Martin-Mariertta.

December 16, 1994 The Antonov AN-70 turboprop transport makes its first flight.

January 5, 1995 Ben Rich, of Lockheed "Skunk Works" fame, dies at the age of 69.

February 3–11, 1995 The Space Shuttle *Discovery* flies by *Mir* in preparation for a future docking mission.

February 18–21, 1995 Steve Fossett makes the first solo transpacific balloon flight from Seoul, South Korea to Leader, Saskatchewan, Canada, a distance of 5,430 miles.

TONY LEVIER Racing pilot Tony LeVier died on February 8, 1995, six days before his 82nd birthday. With no formal college education, LeVier used his incredible piloting skills to become a top test pilot with Lockheed, making the first flights in many famous aircraft, including the U-2. A voluble, outgoing personality, LeVier was able to hold his own even with such engineering giants as Kelly Johnson. In this 1944 photo, he stands next to a Lockheed P-38J.

AIRBUS A319 The latest version of the burgeoning Airbus family, the A319, rolled out on August 24, 1995. Airbus designs its aircraft so that crews are automatically checked out in all aircraft in the series. Typically, crews need to be checked out in individual models. From the original A300, Airbus has steadily expanded its market, doing what Douglas could not do—match Boeing's model lineup.

McDONNELL DOUGLAS SUPER HORNET The McDonnell Douglas (now Boeing) F/A-18E/F Super Hornet is shown taking off for the first time on November 29, 1995, with Fred Madenwald at the controls. The Super Hornet is a larger and more capable version of the earlier F/A-18 Hornet and has already entered combat in the war against terrorism.

LIEUTENANT COLONEL ROBERT JOHNSON With the passing of years, many of the World War II flying aces are making their last sortie. On December 27, 1995, Lieutenant Colonel Robert Johnson (left) died at the age of 78. Johnson had 28 confirmed victories in the European theater, flying 91 combat missions in a Republic P-47 Thunderbolt with the famous 56th Fighter Group. Johnson is shown here with his crew chief Staff Sergeant J. C. Penrod; his Thunderbolt was named *Penrod and Sam*.

FOKKER F50 AND F100 As the stress of competition grew stronger, smaller manufacturers like Fokker were slowly but surely pushed out of the market. The well-respected Fokker company went out of business on March 16, 1996. For economic reasons, Fokker probably tried to stretch its designs too far. The F27 was stretched to the F50 shown here; the F28 became the F100.

FLIGHT TIMELINE

March 31, 1995 The Cirrus SR-20 makes its first flight; it features a built-in parachute.

April 11, 1995 T. Keith Glennan, the first head of NASA, dies at the age of 90.

April 26, 1995 A MiG-29 sets an altitude record of 90,092 feet.

May 31, 1995 The FAA certifies its first aircraft from China, a Model Y-12 Harbin.

June 2, 1995 Captain Scott Grady is shot down and rescued in Bosnia.

June 30, 1995 The Luftwaffe conducts its first combat operation in nearly 50 years, in support of NATO forces in Bosnia.

August 11, 1995 The EMBRAER EMB-145 makes its first flight.

November 29, 1995 The McDonnell Douglas (Boeing) Super Hornet F/A-18E makes its first flight.

January 15, 1996 NASA astronaut Leroy Chiao becomes the 100th person to take a space walk when he departs the Space Shuttle *Endeavor*.

February 17, 1996 The U.S. *NEAR (Near Earth Asteroid Rendezvous) Shoemaker* craft launches to study the Eros asteroid. It will land on Eros in 2001.

February 29, 1996 European Space Agency astronaut Thomas Reiter returns after spending six months on *Mir*.

BOOMERANG Not the first asymmetric plane in history (the Blohm und Voss Bv 155 preceded it in 1938), Burt Rutan's all composite Boomerang, unveiled on June 17, 1996, is nonetheless an eye-catching design. From one angle it looks like a single-engine aircraft, from another a twin-engine, and from yet another a trimotor.

LOCKHEED MARTIN AND X-33 Space ventures are a risky gamble, as Lockheed Martin found out with its X-33 technology demonstrator. Dubbed VentureStar, the aircraft was to have been the forerunner of an orbital spacecraft that could take off and land conventionally. Unfortunately, technical problems ultimately forced cancellation of the contract Lockheed Martin had won on July 3, 1996.

SIR FRANK WHITTLE The English inventor of the jet engine, Sir Frank Whittle, died at his Maryland home at the age of 89 on August 9, 1996. A feisty, often acerbic man, Whittle fought long and hard for his jet engine against an indifferent British government.

TUPOLEV TU-144 SUPERSONIC TRANSPORT One of the most amazing comebacks in history was a product of the end of the Cold War. After spending 20 years in storage, the Tupolev Tu-144 took to the air again on November 29, 1996, from Zhukovsky airfield, outside of Moscow. The aircraft is going to be used for test work by NASA, some American manufacturers, and Tupolev. The first SST to fly, the Tu-144 was not economically viable at the time of its debut.

LOCKHEED MARTIN AND BOEING JSF Lockheed Martin (left) and Boeing were chosen to compete for the Joint Strike Fighter contract in November 1996. At stake was perhaps $200 to $400 billion dollars in aircraft production. Both aircraft proved to be excellent, but it was the Lockheed Martin entry that won, becoming the F-35. The aircraft will be built in three versions: conventional, naval, and short takeoff with vertical landing.

FLIGHT TIMELINE

March 16, 1996 Fokker goes out of business.

April 25, 1996 The Yak-130 two-seat trainer makes its first flight.

June 17, 1996 Burt Rutan unveils the asymmetric Boomerang.

June 24, 1996 Raytheon delivers the 5,000th Beech King Air business turboprop.

August 6, 1996 The Kawasaki OH-X helicopter makes its first flight.

August 9, 1996 Sir Frank Whittle, often considered the inventor of the modern jet engine, dies at age 89.

August 31, 1996 The two-seat version of the Eurofighter makes its first flight.

November 7, 1996 NASA launches the *Mars Global Surveyor* to orbit and map the Red Planet.

November 16, 1996 Russia's *Mars 96* probe is launched; the probe falls back to Earth.

November 16, 1996 Boeing and Lockheed Martin are chosen to build prototypes of the multiservice Joint Strike Fighter.

December 6, 1996 Rockwell Aerospace and Defense, formerly known as North American Aviation, is acquired by Boeing in a move announced on August 15, 1996.

December 15, 1996 Boeing makes plans to buy McDonnell Douglas.

MCDONNELL DOUGLAS X-36 First flown on May 17, 1997, the McDonnell Douglas (now Boeing) X-36 unpiloted aerial vehicle has no vertical or horizontal tails and was intended by the Phantom Works (now a Boeing research and development organization) to provide data for the development of future aircraft on a very low-cost basis.

STEVE FOSSETT The indomitable Steve Fossett set a hot-air balloon distance record of 10,363 miles on January 20, 1997. The 58-year-old investment millionaire later achieved his dream of a solo flight around the world—on his sixth attempt completed in July 2002. He covered 19,428 miles.

GULFSTREAM V Gulfstream always stays a bit ahead of the competition. The Gulfstream V made its first flight on November 28, 1995, in Savannah, Georgia. Capable of long-range flights as far as New York to Tokyo, the Gulfstream V was attractive to the USAF, which bought two as C-37As on May 5, 1997, to use for VIP travel.

DAMAGE TO MIR Russia, strapped for cash after the collapse of Communism and the Soviet Union, maintained the *Mir* space station long after it was prudent to do so. On June 25, 1997, Astronaut Mike Foale was shaken when the automated cargo ship *Progress* crashed into the space station during a practice docking. The damage was severe, but the crew was able to stop all the leaks and keep doing their duty.

MARS PATHFINDER The great appeal of the planet Mars, besides its stunning beauty and the eternal question as to whether or not life exists there, is that humans will someday in the not-too-distant future travel to the Red Planet. On July 4, 1997, NASA scored a great triumph when the Mars Pathfinder landed safely on Mars with its 22-pound rover buggy to gather data.

SUKHOI SU-37 The Sukhoi Su-37, which astounded the crowd at the Farnborough Air Show in 1996, took flight on September 25, 1997, further revealing the capabilities of this Thrust Vectored Control Fighter. Called a "fifth-generation maneuverability aircraft" by Sukhoi's General Designer Mikhail Simonov, the Su-37's remarkable maneuverability stems in part from the movement of its engine nozzles. Unfortunately for Russia, further development of the aircraft depends in large part on foreign funding.

BOEING RENAMES MD-95 TO 717 It was a sad sight to many McDonnell Douglas veterans when the signs at the plants in St. Louis, Long Beach, and elsewhere were changed to read "Boeing" after the Seattle-based firm acquired its longtime rival on August 1, 1997. A decision was made to retain the DC-9/MD-95 in production, but its name was changed to Boeing 717 on January 8, 1998.

FAIRCHILD DORNIER 328 The Fairchild Dornier 328J jet, aimed at the commuter jet market, made its first flight on January 28, 1998. The new aircraft was essentially this Fairchild Dornier 328 turboprop with jet engines installed. Only relatively slight modifications were made to the distinctive Dornier-style wing and to the landing gear. The airliner can carry 32–34 passengers at 460 miles per hour. The firm has fallen into financial difficulty, and the aircraft's future is questionable.

FLIGHT TIMELINE

October 15, 1997 The European Space Agency launches the *Huygens* probe, designed to research Saturn's Titan moon.

December 24, 1997 The *Asiasat 3* communications satellite is launched. The manufacturer, Hughes Global Services, will buy back the spacecraft from insurers when the craft fails to orbit properly. Renamed the HGS-1, the satellite performs two lunar flybys.

1998 The Bell/Boeing Model 609 civil tilt-rotor is offered for delivery in 2001, opening a new market.

January 8, 1998 Boeing renames the MD-95 airliner, acquired during the McDonnell Douglas merger, the Boeing 717; it is the last of the famed MD series.

February 28, 1998 The Northrop Grumman (formerly Teledyne Ryan) Global Hawk Unpiloted Aerial Vehicle (UAV) makes its first flight.

March 11, 1998 The first E-767 AWACS aircraft is delivered to the Japanese Air Self-Defense Force.

April 17, 1998 Bill Clem flies his home-built Autogiro to an altitude record of 24,463 feet.

April 21, 1998 Gary Osoba flies an ultralight glider for a record 315 miles.

May 30, 1998 Will Gadd sets a distance record of 179 miles per hour in a paraglider.

GLOBAL HAWK MAKES FIRST FLIGHT Pilots wince at the thought of unpiloted aerial vehicles taking their place, but the Northrop Grumman (formerly Teledyne Ryan) Global Hawk made a gigantic step forward when it made its first flight on February 28, 1998. The mission of the long-range, high-altitude Global Hawk is to supply responsive and sustained data from any enemy territory, day or night, regardless of weather, as need dictates.

HANS JOACHIM PABST VON OHAIN The inventor of the first jet engine to fly, Hans Pabst von Ohain, died at the age of 86 on March 13, 1998. His engine powered the Heinkel He 178, which made the world's first jet flight on August 27, 1939.

SPACE SHUTTLE AND MIR

History was made twice in this June 8, 1998, image. It depicts the ninth and last docking of a Space Shuttle (in this case the *Discovery*) and the Russian space station *Mir.* It also shows the greatest mass yet assembled in space, the *Mir-25* and the Space Shuttle *Discovery,* which totaled 548,231 pounds when joined.

PROTEUS Burt Rutan's designs may be unorthodox, but they are nonetheless attractive—even such strange-looking airplanes as the tandem-wing, twin-boom, twin-jet Proteus, built by Rutan's Scaled Composites company. The aircraft is modular and can have its dimensions changed to suit the mission, be it environmental sampling, reconnaissance, or participation in the X Prize, the contest for the first civilian flight into space. The Proteus made its first flight on July 26, 1998.

PIPER MALIBU MERIDIAN The venerable Piper Aircraft Company went through a long series of ups and downs before Charles M. Suma established the New Piper Aircraft, Inc., in Vero Beach, Florida. Suma is shown here with the prototype of the Piper Malibu Meridian, one of the hottest twin-engine executive aircraft available. The aircraft made its first flight on August 21, 1998.

LAST PANAVIA TORNADO DELIVERED A great pioneering effort in international cooperative aircraft manufacturing came to an end with the delivery of the last of 974 Panavia Tornados on September 28, 1998. This photo of the versatile fighter shows a Royal Air Force 617 Squadron (the Dam Buster squadron) being flown by Flight Lieutenant Jo Salter, the first female combat pilot in the Royal Air Force.

INTERNATIONAL SPACE STATION Astronauts Jerry Ross, left, and Jim Newman prepare to unfurl an antenna on the Russian-made International Space Station module *Zarya* on December 9, 1998. Operating in space inside the cumbersome, self-contained space suits is extremely taxing, and astronauts and cosmonauts all like to end the day's work by stripping out of the suit, washing up, and having a good meal.

FLIGHT TIMELINE

June 1, 1998 Per Lindstrand sets a hot-air balloon altitude record of 65,000 feet.

June 29, 1998 The Lockheed Martin Dark Star Unpiloted Aerial Vehicle (UAV) makes its first successful flight.

July 3, 1998 Japan's *Nozomi* Mars orbiter is launched.

July 4, 1998 The EMBRAER EJ-135 makes its first flight.

July 4, 1998 Ramy Yanetz flies a rigid-wing hang glider 251 miles for a new record.

July 15, 1998 The Raytheon T-6A Texan II makes its first flight.

July 26, 1998 More than 240 skydivers make the largest formation "free fall."

July 26, 1998 Flight tests begin for the Scaled Composites Proteus high-altitude aircraft.

August 21, 1998 The Piper Malibu Meridian makes its first flight.

September 1998 *Galileo* spots the sources of Jupiter's rings.

September 6, 1998 The Fuji Blimp sets a duration record for covering a television event: 14 hours and 9 minutes at the U.S. Open Tennis Tournament.

September 24, 1998 The Beriev Be 200 firefighting flying boat makes its first flight.

October 10, 1998 The F-22 goes supersonic for the first time.

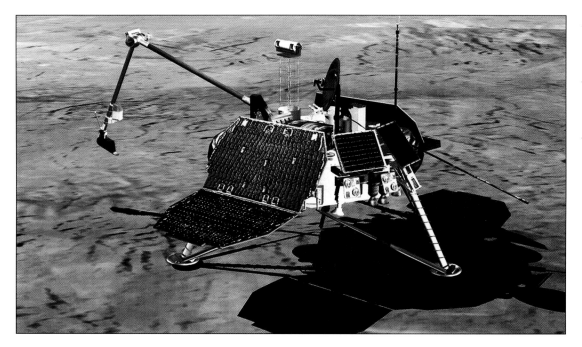

MARS POLAR LANDER This artist's conception shows the *Mars Polar Lander* using an articulated robot arm to collect soil samples. The 639-pound spacecraft was launched from Cape Canaveral, Florida, on a Boeing Delta II on January 3, 1999. Unfortunately, it disappeared into the Martian atmosphere on December 3, 1999, and was lost to NASA scientists. Since that time, the National Imagery and Mapping Agency (NIMA) claimed they located it, intact, on Mars.

SUKHOI SU-30 The first model of this aircraft flew as the T-10 on May 20, 1971. Continuous development led to the March 9, 1999, first flight of the Sukhoi Su-30. This photo shows a Su-30 in Chinese colors taking off at a Russian military base on August 9, 2000, for delivery to China. The arms trade with China is vital to Russia's economy and to China's developing technology.

BOEING 747 Despite its age, the Boeing 747 continues to set records. On March 15, 1999, Captain Jay Mallory set a Bangkok–Tokyo speed record of five hours and one minute, flying the United Airlines 747 at 575 miles per hour.

GLOBAL HAWK The Global Hawk made its first flight on February 28, 1998, from Edwards Air Force Base, California, and demonstrated its ability to provide high-altitude, long-range unpiloted reconnaissance. A Northrop Grumman RQ-4A crashed at Edwards on March 29, 1999. The accident cost the government $13,000,000—but did not kill a pilot. The Global Hawk had amassed 1,000 hours of combat time by June 15, 2002, and demonstrated its capability with a nonstop flight to Australia from California.

EUROCOPTER NH-90 The NH-90, which made its first flight on May 31, 1999, is a twin-engine multirole naval and tactical transport in the 18,000-pound class. The product of a NATO requirement, the helicopter was produced as a joint venture by France, Italy, Germany, and the Netherlands. The all-composite fuselage has a low radar signature, and the chopper uses fly-by-wire controls. The versatile aircraft can do search and rescue, medevac, special operations, electronic warfare, and many other missions.

FLIGHT TIMELINE

October 24, 1998 NASA launches the *Deep Space 1* to explore deep space, including asteroids and comets.

October 29, 1998 Space Shuttle *Discovery* launches with 77-year-old John Glenn, former astronaut and current senator, as part of its crew.

November 20, 1998 The first module for the International Space Station is launched by a Russian expendable rocket.

December 4–15, 1998 The Space Shuttle *Endeavor* delivers the second module (called Unity) to the International Space Station.

December 11, 1998 NASA launches the *Mars Climate Orbiter.*

December 22, 1998 The Spanish CASA C 295 transport makes its first flight.

December 23, 1998 Sikorsky and partners fly the first prototype of the S-92 Helibus.

January 3, 1999 NASA launches the *Mars Polar Lander* to land on and explore Mars. Contact will be lost as it descends toward the planet almost a year later.

January 24, 1999 The Ariane 42L puts the Galaxy XR satellite into orbit.

February 7, 1999 NASA launches the *Stardust.* It is expected to pass through an active comet in 2004 and take samples.

BOEING 737 Pilots call it "Fat Albert," but passengers and airlines love the hardworking, efficient Boeing 737. This 737-300 is shown at Rome's Ciampino Airport, at the initiation of a new company, Air One. The 737 has launched many a new airline, and by January 27, 2000, the Boeing 737 fleet had amassed 100 million flying hours, more than any jet in history.

BOEING 777 The Boeing 777 lifted off from Payne Field at Everett, Washington on June 12, 1994, on its first test flight, only to fly into head-on competition from Airbus Industrie. By January 2000, Airbus had more orders on record than Boeing: 476 versus 391. The stage was set for an international battle on a colossal scale.

AIRBUS A340-600 The Airbus Industrie A340-600, a four-engine aircraft that can carry up to 380 passengers, made its first flight from the Toulouse airport on April 23, 2001. Able to cruise for 8,637 miles, the A340 was a strong contender on the major international routes. Airbus stresses the flexibility of its aircraft, which have virtually identical cockpits, enabling pilots of one type to be checked out in another with no difficulty.

BOEING 737-900 The most startling thing about the Boeing 737 has been its capacity for growth. Shown here on July 23, 2002, the 737-900 approaches its gate at Ted Stevens International Airport in Anchorage, Alaska, the first customer for the new jet. The aircraft is 138 feet long and seats 172 passengers; the 1967 version, the 737-200, was 100 feet long and carried 130 passengers.

FLIGHT TIMELINE

March 1–21, 1999 Bertrand Piccard and Brian Jones make the first non-stop round-the-world balloon flight, covering 28,431 miles in the *Breitling Orbiter 3*.

March 27, 1999 Sea Launch conducts the first launch of a Zenit rocket from their floating platform.

May 25, 1999 The Airbus A319 Airbus Corporate Jet makes its first flight.

May 27, 1999 The Bombardier CRJ 700 debuts.

May 27–June 6, 1999 The Space Shuttle *Discovery* visits the International Space Station.

July 23–27, 1999 Eileen Collins is the first woman to command a Space Shuttle.

August 9, 1999 The Dornier E328 is certified.

December 3, 1999 Communication with the *Mars Polar Lander* is lost. The mission failure will be blamed mainly on software that did not translate English units to metric units.

January 2000 The USAF takes delivery of the YAL-1A airborne laser platform; it is a modified Boeing 747-400F.

January 2000 The BAE Hawk 127 makes its first flight.

January 7, 2000 For the first time Airbus records more orders than Boeing; in 1999 it was 476 for the Europeans versus 391 for the Americans.

CONCORDE CRASH The charmed life of the Anglo-French Concorde was marred on July 25, 2000, when an Air France aircraft crashed at Gonesse, outside of Paris. All 109 on board were killed, along with 5 people on the ground.

SECOND CRASH OF BELL/BOEING OSPREY The Marines desperately needed an aircraft with the capability of the Bell/Boeing MV-22 Osprey, because it combines the vertical lift and descent capability of a helicopter with an aircraft's speed. But the program was set back when the second Osprey crash occurred on April 9, 2000. Despite the loss, Marine support for the aircraft remains high.

BOEING JSF The Boeing Company doesn't lose many competitions, but its Joint Strike Fighter contender, shown here on its September 18, 2000, first flight, was narrowly defeated by the Lockheed Martin entry. The stakes were high, with forecasts of a 3,000 to 6,000 aircraft program over the years. The JSF is designed to be a multiservice, multirole aircraft.

RUSSIA LAUNCHES COSMOS 2372 SATELLITE VIA PROTON BOOSTER

On August 28, 2000, Russia launched the Cosmos 2372 military communications satellite via a Proton booster. This photo depicts the 19th launch of the Proton for the International Launch Services (ILS), carrying the *Sirius 3* spacecraft to a high inclination, highly elliptical orbit on December 1, 2000. ILS is a joint venture between Lockheed Martin Corporation of the United States and Khrunichev Space Center and RSA of Russia.

PREDATOR UCAV

Produced by General Atomics Aeronautical Systems, the unpiloted Predator made its first flight on February 2, 2001. It has since proven to be a remarkable reconnaissance aircraft and, when equipped with Hellfire missiles, an excellent attack plane. The Predator and its fellow UCAVs are revolutionizing warfare.

NEAR SPACECRAFT LANDS ON ASTEROID

NASA succeeded in making Buck Rogers seem tame on February 12, 2001, when it managed to land its *NEAR* spacecraft on asteroid Eros. The feat called for extraordinary sensitivity in maneuvering the spacecraft. Any error would have resulted in its total destruction. Yet the spacecraft landed successfully and sent back signals from the asteroid's surface. This photo was taken from a height of about 390 feet above the surface.

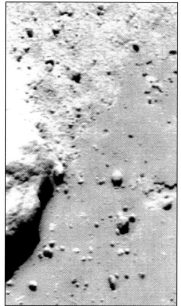

LOCKHEED MARTIN EP-3 ORION COLLIDES WITH CHINESE FIGHTER The Lockheed Orion had served in virtual obscurity from the time of its first flight on August 19, 1958, until an EP-3E ARIES II (Airborne Reconnaissance Integrated Electronic System II) aircraft collided with a Chinese F-8 fighter on April 1, 2001. Utterly brilliant flying enabled the Orion to land on a Hainan airfield, with all 24 of its crew members safe. A sizzling diplomatic incident ensued, but in time, the crew members were returned, and the aircraft was brought back—in pieces.

GLOBAL HAWK FLIES TO AUSTRALIA On April 23–24, 2001, the Northrop Grumman Global Hawk unpiloted aerial vehicle (UAV) made international aviation history when it completed the first nonstop flight across the Pacific Ocean by an autonomous aircraft, flying from Edwards Air Force Base to RAAF Base Edinburgh, South Australia, in 23 hours. The 116-foot wingspan aircraft provides real-time intelligence from high altitudes for long periods.

ALEXIS TUPOLEV Alexis Tupolev, son of Andrei, died on May 13, 2001, at the age of 76. Among his many designs were the Tupolev Tu-144 supersonic transport. Alexis lived and worked during an easier period than his more famous father but never achieved the same degree of prominence.

BOEING SONIC CRUISER

Boeing President and Chief Executive Officer Alan R. Mulally stands by a model of the Boeing Sonic Cruiser at the Paris Air Show on June 19, 2001. Designed to fly just under the speed of sound, faster than other nonsupersonic airliners, the Sonic Cruiser was an abrupt departure from past Boeing practice. The program was canceled in 2003.

AEROVIRONMENT SOLAR-POWERED HELIOS NASA's solar-electric, high-altitude flying wing, the *Helios*, lands at Dryden, Edwards Air Force Base, California, after a test flight. The 247-foot-wingspan, 1,640-pound aircraft is designed to fly at high altitudes (100,000 feet) for sustained periods. On July 14, 2001, operating from Hawaii, it achieved 76,271 feet, and on August 13–14, 2001, it achieved 96,500 feet.

FLIGHT TIMELINE

November 2, 2000 A joint United States–Russian crew takes up residence in the International Space Station.

December 19, 2000 Airbus formally launches the A380 mega transport to compete with Boeing's 747.

February 2, 2001 The RQ-1B Predator unpiloted aerial vehicle with a turboprop makes its first flight.

February 12, 2001 The *NEAR Shoemaker* probe lands on the asteroid Eros, taking pictures on the way down and transmitting data after it has landed.

February 20, 2001 The Russian SS-25 ICBM launches the Swedish *Odin* spacecraft.

February 21, 2001 The Bombardier CRJ900 makes its first flight.

March 14, 2001 The Boeing X-40A makes its first NASA research flight.

March 29, 2001 Boeing announces the Sonic Cruiser as its next airliner.

April 23, 2001 The Airbus Industrie A340-600 makes its first flight.

April 23–24, 2001 The Northrop Grumman Global Hawk makes a 23-hour flight to Australia.

April 28, 2001 American millionaire Dennis Tito becomes the first space tourist, paying $20 million to join a Russian flight to the International Space Station.

SEPTEMBER 11, 2001

September 11, 2001, marked not only a tremendous tragedy but a new era in aviation and warfare. A band of Muslim terrorists hijacked four aircraft, terrorized the passengers, and seized the controls. Three aircraft were used as weapons of mass destruction against the Twin Towers of the World Trade Center and the Pentagon. A fourth aircraft was also intended for a strike on Washington, D.C., but crashed when its valiant passengers rebelled.

All aircraft flights in the United States were immediately suspended, and for the first time, U.S. military jet fighters set up combat air patrols. Tighter airline security procedures have since been instituted across the United States.

The immediate aftermath of the attack on the World Trade Center in New York

The World Trade Center is ablaze after the September 11, 2001, attack

Aerial view of the World Trade Center disaster site

Beacons of light shine where the Twin Towers once stood

May 7, 2001 The Antonov An-225 *Mriya* super-heavy transport is test-flown. The aircraft had originally been built to support the Soviet Space Shuttle program; this is its first flight since December 21, 1988.

May 10, 2001 China launches the Long March 4B with two satellites onboard.

July–August 2001 Lockheed Martin and Boeing Joint Strike Fighter prototypes become the first practical supersonic fighters to demonstrate a vertical landing.

July 2, 2001 The Zeppelin NT begins making operating flights.

August 13–14, 2001 The solar-powered *Helios* sets an altitude record of 96,500 feet.

September 11, 2001 Terrorists hijack three U.S. passenger airliners and strike New York City's Twin Towers and the Pentagon. A fourth hijacked plane crashes in Pennsylvania.

October 2001 Unpiloted Predator aircraft launch weapons in combat in Afghanistan.

October 23, 2001 The *Mars Global Surveyor* enters precise Mars orbit.

October 26, 2001 The Lockheed Martin X-35 wins the Joint Strike Fighter competition.

December 1, 2001 TWA flies its last flight before being absorbed by American Airlines.

LOCKHEED MARTIN F-16CJ
A Lockheed Martin F-16CJ of the 79th Fighter Squadron, 20th Fighter Wing, is seen on Combat Air Patrol in support of Operation Noble Eagle, part of the homeland defense efforts after terrorists crashed airliners into the Pentagon and World Trade Center on September 11, 2001.

FIVE-HOUR EVA FOR COS-MONAUTS Russian Cosmonaut Mikhail Tyurin installs the International Space Station's new component during his first extra vehicular activity on October 8, 2001. It was the 100th space walk in the history of the Russian space program as well as the first space walk to take place outside the space station without a Space Shuttle present.

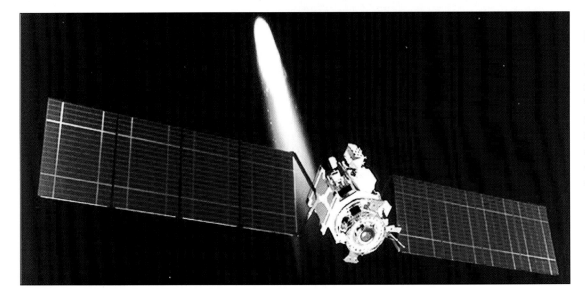

DEEP SPACE 1 AND COMET BORRELLY Launched in October 1998, the spacecraft *Deep Space 1* had already completed its planned mission when it was called upon to fly past the Comet Borrelly to learn more about the makeup of a comet. On September 22, 2001, it came within 1,400 miles of the comet, sending back a great deal of data, including black and white photos.

LOCKHEED MARTIN WINS JOINT STRIKE FIGHTER COMPETITION Lockheed Martin won potentially the most valuable fighter competition in history on October 26, 2001, besting Boeing's rival X-32 with its X-35. Now called the F-35, the aircraft will be produced in three versions: conventional takeoff, carrier takeoff, and STOL/VTOL. The contract is expected to garner from 4,000 to 8,000 aircraft sales over its life span. The stealthy multirole aircraft provides a robust air-to-ground capability.

T-50 GOLDEN EAGLE Every country wants the capability to design and build its own aircraft, and South Korea is no exception. This T-50, a supersonic jet trainer developed jointly by Korea Aerospace Industries Company and Lockheed Martin, made its debut on October 21, 2001. The T-50 outwardly resembles the Lockheed Martin F-16 but is only about 80 percent as large.

FLIGHT TIMELINE

January 21, 2002 The Gulfstream V offers a new Enhanced Vision System for low-visibility approaches.

January 28, 2002 Ryanair orders 100 Boeing 737-800 jets.

January 29, 2002 The Frontier Systems A160 Hummingbird rotor-craft UAV makes its first flight.

February 27, 2002 The Cessna Sovereign makes its first flight.

March 1–12, 2002 The crew of the Space Shuttle *Columbia* performs on-orbit service and repairs of the Hubble Space Telescope.

March 22, 2002 The first production Eurocopter Tiger is rolled out.

March 25, 2002 A Chinese Long March 2F launches an unpiloted Shenzhou III; China announces its intention to launch a human in 2003.

April 8, 2002 The USAF announces its intention to lease 100 new Boeing 767 tankers; Congress has other ideas.

April 26, 2002 Sukhoi wins the battle for a follow-on fighter in Russia.

April 26, 2002 The British consider using the X-45 as a means to develop UCAV.

May 22, 2002 The Boeing X-45A UCAV makes its first flight.

May 31, 2002 The Toyota single-engine four-seat aircraft makes its first flight.

J-STARS To aid intelligence gathering in the war in Afghanistan, the Northrop Grumman E-8 Joint Stars was deployed to assist in battle management and the command and control actions of air to ground forces. The aircraft is a modified Boeing 707, fitted with 18 operations and control stations. It is the ground-war counterpart to the AWACS and is highly regarded by commanders in the current wars in the Middle East.

CONCORDE RETURNS TO THE AIR On November 7, 2001, the Concorde returned to regular passenger service, 15 months after the tragic crash at Gonesse, outside of Paris. An intensive analysis had been made of the accident, and preventive measures were taken to prevent a repetition in the future.

SABENA GOES OUT OF BUSINESS The venerable and highly respected Sabena airline went out of business on November 7, 2001, reflecting the turbulent conditions that have made the airline business one of the most difficult in industry. The company had begun operations on May 23, 1923, and had a marvelous reputation.

CRASH OF AIRBUS A300 Just 1 minute and 45 seconds after takeoff, American Flight 586 crashed into the Rockaway Beach section of the Queens borough of New York City on November 12, 2001. Coming so soon after the September 11, 2001, tragedy, most people assumed this was a terrorist attack. However, the National Transportation and Safety Board investigation indicated the crash resulted from the improper operation of the rudder during a wake turbulence encounter.

BLU-82 BOMB The 15,000-pound BLU-82 bomb was originally used to clear helicopter landing areas in jungles. It was also used to create corridors in minefields. But its most effective use was against Taliban personnel in the Afghanistan campaign. The bomb is delivered by pushing it out the rear cargo doors of the USAF's Lockheed MC-130H Combat Talon aircraft.

FLIGHT TIMELINE

June 1, 2002 The prototype of the Aero Vodochody L159B Advanced jet trainer makes its first flight.

June 15, 2002 The Northrop Grumman RQ-4A Global Hawk completes its 1,000th combat flight hour in Operation Enduring Freedom.

June 19–July 3, 2002 Steve Fossett flies from Northam, West Australia, to Lake Yamma Yamma, Queensland, in 14 days and 19 hours. It is the first solo nonstop round-the-world balloon flight.

June 25, 2002 Lockheed Martin and Northrop Grumman win an $11 billion contract to upgrade Coast Guard forces.

June 26, 2002 The Royal Australian Air Force accepts its first Boeing BBJ (Boeing Business Jet).

July 1, 2002 The Pilatus PC-21 military trainer makes its first flight.

July 4, 2002 General Benjamin O. Davis, Jr., the Air Force's first black general, dies at Walter Reed Army Medical Center at age 89.

July 19, 2002 The Northrop Grumman X-47A Pegasus UAV completes initial low-speed taxi tests at China Lake, California.

July 20, 2002 Boeing F/A-18E/F Super Hornets are deployed to the USS *Abraham Lincoln*. It is the aircraft's first deployment.

B-1B IN AFGHANISTAN USAF bombers bear the brunt of the war in Afghanistan, and the Boeing B-1B Lancer is one of the most effective. Marred by controversy throughout its career, the B-1B has proven itself beyond any question in combat. It joins Northrop Grumman B-2s and Boeing B-52s in strikes against the Taliban.

RYANAIR BUYS 100 BOEING 737S Boeing's Executive Vice President of Sales, Toby Bright, right, and Michael O'Leary, chief executive of Ryanair, pose with a model of a Boeing 737-800 on January 28, 2002. Ryanair, Europe's lowest cost airline, just announced their order of 100 Boeing 737-800s.

BOEING CH-47 CHINOOK OVER NORTHROP GRUMMAN F-14 A Boeing Chinook CH-47 helicopter approaches the deck of the USS *Theodore Roosevelt* on December 15, 2001, in the Arabian Sea. A Northrop Grumman F-14 is in the foreground. The *Roosevelt's* aircraft participated in the bombing of the Tora Bora region in Afghanistan, in support of Operation Enduring Freedom. An improved Boeing CH-47F Chinook made its first flight on June 25, 2001.

HUBBLE TELESCOPE On March 11, 2002, the Hubble Space Telescope was shut down briefly so it could be repaired and refurbished. This is a September 1, 1999, photo of the incredible space triumph, which has furnished an incalculable amount of data, much of which remains to be analyzed.

FLIGHT TIMELINE

July 21, 2002 The Boeing YAL-1A Airborne Laser (ABL) makes its first flight.

July 27, 2002 A Ukrainian Sukhoi Su-27 fighter crashes into an air show crowd, killing 83 and injuring 200.

August 20, 2002 The Lockheed Martin Aero T-50 trainer makes its first flight.

August 26, 2002 Eclipse Aviation's six-seat friction-welded Eclipse 500 makes its first flight.

October 7, 2002 The USAF announces that direct-energy technology is ready to be used as weaponry.

October 20, 2002 An improved Soyuz TMA-1 spacecraft is launched to the International Space Station. Rock singer Lance Bass was scratched from the mission when he failed to come up with the price of the ticket: $20 million.

October 28, 2002 Boeing unveils its Bird of Prey (BOP) demonstrator aircraft, used to indicate what the next generation of stealth technology may be. The aircraft flew more than 40 hours.

November 4, 2002 NASA announces that the Space Infrared Telescope Facility (SIRTF), the last of the "four great observatories," will be launched in 2003.

November 4, 2002 The Defense Advanced Research Project Agency announces that its Wasp microair vehicle flew for 107 minutes.

EUROCOPTER TIGER The first production Eurocopter Tiger was rolled out March 22, 2002. It comes in several variations, including the following: the Tiger UHT multirole fire support helicopter with Trigat Fire and Forget missiles; the Tiger HAC antitank helicopter, and the Tiger HAP air-to-air combat and fire helicopter. The French/German-designed Tiger armed reconnaissance helicopter has been selected by Australia and will be built under license in Queensland.

USAF TO LEASE 767 TANKERS In a highly controversial decision, the USAF decided on April 8, 2002, to lease 100 new Boeing 767 tankers. Critics called it a boon to Boeing, but there is no question that the aging KC-135 tanker fleet needs replenishment with new aircraft. The tankers are the single most important aircraft type in the USAF inventory—without them the bombers, fighters, and cargo planes could not effectively engage in combat.

SUKHOI SU-27 The Russian aviation industry may be down, but it is not out, and it continues to produce outstanding fighters like this Sukhoi Su-27, pictured at the Langkawi International Maritime and Aerospace exhibition in Malaysia on December 6, 1995. Russia desperately needs to sell aircraft to help its balance of trade and offers its aircraft at rock-bottom prices. Buyers like the aircraft and the price but are cautious about service and parts follow-up.

BOEING X-45A UNPILOTED COMBAT AIR VEHICLE The Boeing X-45A UCAV is shown here at the time of its September 27, 2000, roll-out. The aircraft made its first flight on May 22, 2002, reaching a speed of 195 knots at 7,500 feet. On April 26, 2002, the British government indicated that it was interested in using the X-45 as a means of developing UCAVs in Great Britain. UCAVs are intended to supplement piloted fighters—but may someday replace them.

SPACE SHUTTLE COLUMBIA

The moment of greatest tension during a Space Shuttle mission is the launch. This January 16, 2003, successful launch of the orbiter *Columbia* took place at 9:39 A.M. CST in near-perfect weather The seven crew members on board included Ilan Ramon, the first ever Israeli astronaut.

Pictured here are the crew of the Space Shuttle *Columbia*. Left to right, front row: Rick D. Husband, Kalpana Chawla, William C. McCool; back row: David M. Brown, Laurel B. Clark, Michael P. Anderson, and Israeli astronaut Ilan Ramon. All seven perished in the tragic loss of the Columbia on February 1, 2003.

FLIGHT TIMELINE

November 11, 2002 The first EADS TBM 700 C2 single turboprop aircraft is delivered.

November 23–December 7, 2002 The Space Shuttle *Endeavor* brings the *Expedition 6* crew to the International Space Station.

December 9, 2002 Diamond Aircraft Twinstar makes its first flight.

December 9, 2002 United Airlines files for bankrupcy protection. It joins USAirways and several other U.S. airlines.

December 12, 2002 The *Galileo* spacecraft begins transmitting data from its flyby of Jupiter's tiny moon Amalthea, which took place on November 5.

December 14, 2002 Japan makes its fourth straight successful H-IIA medium-lift rocket, putting the second Advanced Earth Observing Satellite (Adeos-2) into a 500-mile polar orbit.

December 23, 2002 Iraq shoots down a U.S. Predator spy plane.

January 16, 2003 The Space Shuttle *Columbia* is launched. The crew includes: Rick D. Husband, William C. McCool, Michael P. Anderson, Kalpana Chawla, David M. Brown, Laurel B. Clark, and Ilan Ramon.

February 1, 2003 The Space Shuttle *Columbia* breaks up during reentry into the earth's atmosphere; all seven astronauts perish.

Index

Picture credits:

Front cover: **AP Wide World Photos** Airbus Industrie (bottom right); John Rossino/Lockheed Martin Corporation (bottom right center); **Photri, Inc.** (bottom left); NASA (top left); **SuperStock** (top center & top right); **Joseph H. Wherry Collection** (left center); **Wright State University Archives** (center).

Back cover: **AP Wide World Photos** (center); **Airbus Industrie** (bottom); **Peter M. Bowers Collection** (top).

Airbus Industrie: 383, 456; **AP Wide World Photos:** Endsheets, 16, 19, 26, 29, 37, 38, 69, 74, 76, 77, 78, 118, 120, 121, 134, 135, 138, 143, 150, 152–153, 156, 160, 161, 162, 164, 165, 166, 167, 168, 169, 172, 173, 174, 175, 176, 177, 182, 183, 184, 186, 187, 189, 193, 198, 202, 206, 208, 209, 213, 214, 216, 217, 218, 224, 227, 236, 237, 241, 243, 244, 247, 251, 261, 272, 284, 285, 286, 287, 288, 292, 293, 294, 295, 297, 298, 299, 300, 303, 304, 306, 308, 309, 310, 311, 312, 313, 314, 315, 316, 317, 319, 320, 321, 322, 323, 324, 325, 326, 327, 329, 331, 332, 333, 334, 336, 337, 339, 344, 345, 346, 347, 348, 350, 351, 352, 354, 355, 356, 357, 358, 360, 361, 362, 364, 365, 366, 367, 369, 372, 373, 374, 375, 376, 384, 386, 388, 390, 391, 392, 393, 394, 396, 398, 400, 402, 403, 406, 412, 415, 416, 418, 440, 454, 470, 472, 473, 475, 477, 478, 481, 482, 483, 484, 485, 487, 493, 494, 496, 497; Air France: 492; The Boeing Co.: 467, 484; Department of Defense: 481; Gulfstream Aerospace: 474; Lockheed Martin Corporation: 472; McDonnell Douglas Aerospace: NASA: 475, 478, 479, 480, 485, 487, 490, 497; U.S. Air Force: 490, 494; **John Batchelor:** 63; **Warren M. Bodie Collection:** Contents, 27, 28, 33, 41, 42, 43, 45, 49, 52, 86, 102–103, 104, 118, 127, 128, 131, 132, 135, 136, 138, 140, 142, 146, 147, 148, 149, 155, 156, 157, 158, 159, 161, 162, 163, 164, 165, 167, 170, 171, 174, 175, 176, 178, 179, 180, 181, 182, 183, 184, 185, 186, 188, 190, 199, 200, 201, 207, 210, 211, 212, 213, 215, 216, 218, 219, 222, 225, 227, 229, 231, 232, 236, 238, 240, 242, 244, 245, 246, 247, 249, 250, 252, 253, 255, 259, 260, 262, 263, 265, 266, 268, 270, 271, 274–275, 276, 281, 282, 292, 302, 307, 331, 333, 338, 344, 349, 353, 359, 370, 396, 456, 464–465, 470, 471; **The Boeing Co.:** 217, 216, 228, 301; **Peter M. Bowers Collection:** 24, 28, 44, 46–47, 50, 51, 52, 53, 54, 55, 56, 57, 58, 59, 60, 61, 62, 64, 65, 67, 68, 70, 71, 72, 73, 74, 75, 76, 77, 78, 79, 80, 81, 82, 83, 84, 85, 86, 87, 88, 89, 90, 91, 92, 93, 94, 95, 96, 97, 98, 99, 100, 101, 106, 107, 108, 109, 110, 111, 112, 113, 114, 115, 116, 117, 118, 119, 120, 121, 122, 123, 124, 125, 126, 128, 129, 130, 131, 132, 133, 134, 136, 137, 138, 139, 140, 141, 142, 143, 144, 145, 146, 147, 148, 150, 189, 191, 192, 193, 194, 195, 196, 197, 198, 199, 200, 201, 202, 203, 206, 219, 224, 225, 226, 228, 229, 230, 233, 234, 235, 236, 239, 240, 241, 242, 243, 244, 245, 246, 248, 250, 252, 254, 255, 256, 256, 257, 258, 260, 261, 264, 265, 266, 267, 268, 269, 270, 271, 272, 273, 278, 279, 280, 281, 282, 283, 284, 288, 290, 291, 293, 294, 295, 296, 299, 301, 302, 305, 307, 310, 317, 318, 323, 324, 325, 326, 327, 328, 329, 330, 332, 334, 335, 338, 339, 345, 346, 348, 349, 352, 353, 354, 356, 358, 359, 360, 361, 362, 363, 365, 368, 370, 371, 372, 373, 374, 375, 377, 378, 384, 385, 386, 387, 389, 390, 391, 392, 393, 394, 395, 397, 398, 400, 401, 402, 403, 404, 406, 408, 410, 411, 413, 414, 417, 418, 419, 420, 423, 426, 427, 429, 430, 431, 432, 436, 440, 442, 444, 454, 455, 457, 461, 468, 471, 480, 492; **Doyle Buehler Photography:** 220–221; © **CORBIS:** 7, 9, 110, 128, 204, 413, 421, 422, 438, 443, 444, 450, 452, 453, 474, 477, 491; AFP: 422, 435, 463, 486, 491, 496; Aero Graphics, Inc.: 412, 438, 452; Bettmann: Contents, 204, 205, 388, 396, 405, 407, 409, 410, 414, 430, 433, 434, 435, 436, 437, 449, 459, 468; John H. Clark: 457, 476; Bryn Colton/Assignments Photographers: 430, 448; Dean Conger: 460; Frederique Gosset: 441; George Hall: 392, 395, 399, 409, 416, 419, 420, 423, 428, 429, 430, 433, 439, 445, 451, 458, 459, 461, 462, 468, 476, 496; Hulton-Deutsch Collection: 210, 399, 401, 405, 409; Museum of Flight: 438, 446; Carl & Ann Purcell: 434; R.P.G.: 476; Roger Ressmeyer: 417, 446; Roger Ressmeyer/NASA: 450, 460; Reuters NewMedia Inc.: 434, 442, 443, 447, 448, 473, 480, 485, 486, 489, 490, 495; David Rubinger: 390, 411; Peter Russell/The Military Picture Library: 449, 479; Erik Schaffer/Ecoscene: 459; Denis Scott: 495; Mike Stewart: 474; Stocktrek: 428; James A. Sugar: 439, 453, 462, 472, 478; Sygma: 469, 486; John Van Hasselt: 469; Philip Wallick: 463; Ira Wyman: 442; Yogi, Inc.: 460; **Cradle of Aviation Museum:** 289; **Douglas/San Diego Aerospace Museum:** 106; **Eric Dumigan:** 194; **Experimental Aircraft Association:** 62, 67; **Hulton|Archive by Getty Images:** 14, 15, 16, 19, 20, 21, 22, 25, 27, 31, 32, 33, 34, 35, 36, 39, 40, 41, 42, 43, 44, 45, 50, 54, 57, 58, 100, 205, 206, 208, 209, 210, 211, 212, 256, 280, 300, 369, 371, 377, 378, 379, 388, 455; **Lt. Cmdr. Art Legare/U.S. Navy:** 340–341; **Lockheed Martin Corporation:** 105, 432; **McDonnell Douglas Corp.:** Contents, 151; Harry Gann: 9, 168; **NASA:** Foreword, 366, 380–381; **National Air and Space Museum, Smithsonian Institution:** Contents (Photo No. 79-15013, 97-15023, 97-15168, & 122253A.C), 13 (Photo No. 97-15031), 23 (Photo No. 91-17362), 29 (Photo No.4104A.C), 31 (Photo No. A52724), 40 (Photo No. A44401-C), 63 (Photo No.71-175-2), 66 (Photo No.122253.A.C), 73 (Photo No.85-16356), 93 (Photo No.A42039-C), 100 (Photo No.80-9275), 114 (Photo No.2269A.C), 129 (Photo No.122257A.C), 151 (Photo No.80-13000), 160 (Photo No.38361A.C), 187 (Photo No.A-28885A.C), 192 (Photo No.97-15023), 203 (Photo No.88-11321), 237 (Photo No.A38634E), 254 (Photo No.91-17354), 277, 290 (Photo No.97-15032), 387 (Photo No.97-15168); **National Archives:** 170; **Naval Historical Center:** 22, 37, 38, 48, 90, 215, 404; **©1994 North Wind Pictures:** 14, 15, 20, 27, 30; Illustration by W.H. Foster: 30; **Photri, Inc.:** 64, 68, 226, 262, 264, 278, 296, 305, 350, 360, 364, 436, 447, 466; Photri-Microstock: 223; **Saab-Scania:** Contents, 289; **SuperStock:** 15, 270, 488, 489; **United States Air Force Museum:** 154, 239, 319, 424–425; Courtesy National Air and Space Museum, Smithsonian Institution: 240; **U.S. Department of Defense:** Contents, 342, 343, 382, 441; **Joseph H. Wherry Collection:** 117, 127, 141, 149, 214, 238, 248; **Wright State University Archives:** Front matter, 8, 10–11, 12, 17, 18, 24, 25, 26.

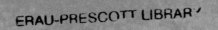